THE ART OF

DIGITAL MARKETING

THE ART OF

DIGITAL MARKETING

THE **DEFINITIVE GUIDE** TO CREATING STRATEGIC, TARGETED AND MEASURABLE ONLINE CAMPAIGNS

IAN DODSON

WILEY

Names: Dodson, Ian, author.
Title: The art of digital marketing : The Definitive Guide to Creating
   Strategic, Targeted, and Measurable Online Campaigns / Ian Dodson.
Description: 1 | Hoboken : Wiley, 2016. | Includes index.
Identifiers: LCCN 2016004206 (print) | LCCN 2016010091 (ebook) | ISBN
   9781119265702 (hardback) | ISBN 9781119265719 (ebk) | ISBN 9781119265726 (ebk)
Subjects: LCSH: Internet marketing. | Strategic planning. | BISAC: BUSINESS &
   ECONOMICS / Marketing / General.
Classification: LCC HF5415.1265 .D63 2016 (print) | LCC HF5415.1265 (ebook) |
   DDC 658.8/72–dc23
LC record available at http://lccn.loc.gov/2016004206

Printed in the United States of America.

V10010324_051619

Contents

Preface

The Digital Marketing Institute is the global certification standard in digital education for learners, educators, and the industry. Ours is the world's most widely taught digital marketing certification program, and there are more graduates certified by us than by any other industry body. Our mission is to establish a series of global professional standards to which both employers and professionals can subscribe. That is why we founded the Digital Standards Authority, an industry-based working group that defines and validates Digital Marketing Institute courses. The DSA validates our development of internationally recognized and respected standards that support digital marketing education by ensuring consistency in our industry-certified training.

Digital technology has transformed the way we live and work and has impacted every industry from retail to health care. Now more than ever, organizations and their employees face the challenge of developing and maintaining their business operations and customer engagement in a constantly evolving digital space. In a recent survey, only 37 percent of American employers said that they thought that recent college graduates are prepared to stay current on new technologies.[1] The increasing digital skills gap and consequent need for training is unmistakable, and something that we are dedicated to addressing.

Our goal is to empower professionals with the digital skills and knowledge needed to take control of their careers and maximize their potential. We achieve this through our courses, which are designed and developed by industry experts. This means that all of our course content is informed by industry best practices, current trends, and innovative insights that help our students cultivate a competitive edge within an in-demand industry.

The professional diploma in digital marketing, with which this textbook aligns, is our keystone certification. Composed of 10 modules, it provides an introduction to the key digital specialties: everything from mobile and social media marketing to SEO and analytics. We believe in equipping individuals with essential skills that endure, and knowledge that they can easily implement, regardless of their roles, size of their companies, or scope of their industries. We specialize in transferable, flexible learning, which is reflected in the Digital Marketing Institute's online study options. Our course

---

[1] Hart Research Associates, *Falling Short: College Learning and Career Success*, accessed December 17, 2015, https://www.aacu.org/sites/default/files/files/LEAP/2015employerstudentsurvey.pdf.

Digital Marketing
Digital Selling

Search Marketing
Social Media Marketing
Mobile Marketing
Digital Strategy & Planning

Digital Marketing

Digital Marketing

Figure 0.1   The Digital Marketing Institute's Certification Roadmap

content is available online 24 hours a day, 7 days a week, and students can access it whether they're at home on their laptops or on mobile devices on their way to work.

We want to make learning simple, accessible, and convenient. That's why we developed this textbook. It's an all-inclusive introductory guide that will teach you everything you need to know to kick start your digital marketing career. You can read it chronologically or prioritize the chapters that interest you most; like our courses, this book was created to allow you to study during your own time and at your own pace, and you can always refer back to it whenever you need to!

The Art of Digital Marketing has been designed to integrate with the professional diploma in digital marketing to produce a comprehensive learning experience. Each chapter relates to a module in the course and the book provides complete coverage of the course syllabus and contains only the most essential points of learning that will best prepare you to pass your exam and gain an internationally recognized and respected digital marketing certification.

Both the professional diploma in digital marketing and *The Art of Digital Marketing* are given their structure from the Digital Marketing Institute's iterative process, which focuses on monitoring, analyzing, and enhancing your digital marketing activities based on their results. That means with the help of this textbook (and by the end of the course, if you are taking it), you will be able to design, develop, and execute a fully optimized digital marketing strategy that incorporates all of the key digital channels.

The professional diploma in digital marketing is at the core of the Digital Marketing Institute's certification road map, which is shown in Figure 0.1.

This provides a framework with which our students can map their personal and professional development. Whether you choose a professional diploma in digital selling, decide to cap your studies with our masters in digital marketing, or simply use this text as an introductory guide, we're there to help you build and expand your career.

Chapter 1
An Introduction to Digital Marketing

Have you experimented with digital marketing driven by guilt, pressure, or an overeager boss? Have you found your efforts disjointed—frustrating—hit-or-miss? Given the sheer volume of information available on digital marketing, just finding where to start can be challenging. And even when you get started, how do you proceed in a way that ensures you are not wasting your time, effort, or budget?

This book provides you with a framework for applying your digital marketing skills in a structured and iterative fashion. You have now taken the first step towards digital marketing mastery, and pretty soon you will be able to use these skills to produce measureable results and ultimately, a return on investment. What more could you ask for?

What Makes This Book Different?

Not only is this book a fountain of knowledge, jam-packed with all the information you need to start your digital marketing journey, but our practical approach to learning will help you to grasp the key concepts and provide you with the skills required to excel in the digital industry.

Furthermore, this book follows a structured methodology underpinned by DMI's 3i principles. These principles are the framework required for effective digital marketing and they illustrate the need for a totally different approach to traditional marketing.

This methodology is described throughout the 10 chapters of this book, each of which covers one specific channel in the digital marketing repertoire. At the end of each chapter you will be given a specific action plan, and by working through these plans you can create a comprehensive, structured, and successful digital marketing strategy.

Start with the Customer and Work Backward

Successful digital campaigns share a range of characteristics, but campaigns that fail all have one thing in common: They don't acknowledge the empowered and informed consumer.

People Power

It is tempting to describe the evolution of the Internet in terms of names such as Facebook, Lycos, Google, eBay, PayPal, Amazon, Apple, Samsung, Netflix, and Yahoo!, as if the whole story of the web is the story of brands, companies, and technologies. The true evolution of the Internet is chronicled by the story of the empowered individual. You and I own the Internet, and the evolution of the Internet is our story.

The shift from Yahoo! to Google 10 years ago was not a result of Google's marketing—as users we made the leap because we gained more control over how we searched for information. The e-commerce site eBay allowed us to sell anything to anyone for any price at any time. Facebook allowed us to stay in touch with people all over the world whenever and however we like. All the great leaps forward in digital technologies have been characterized by one thing—they have given you and me more control over our lives.

The Internet is fundamentally different from all other communication channels because we can learn so much about our customers. We can identify their habits, their technologies, and their preferences. The freedom that the web offers has fundamentally altered the company/customer relationship, upending it and putting the empowered customer in the driver's seat.

With these advances in communication and web technology, the walls have fallen not only between a company and its customer but between fellow customers, who can publicly share their experiences—the good, the bad, and the ugly!

Market Research versus Market Reality

The primary challenge for any business, no matter how large or small, is quite simple—how to get its product or service into the hands of the customer.

How the company will achieve this is informed by market research, gut instinct, polls, surveys, and research about existing habits and activities. However, when conducting market research, especially surveys, we need to take one key factor into account—people lie!

The Internet enables us to learn from market reality by looking at what people actually do online. We can use social listening tools to research customers' activities and

Figure 1.1   Market Research versus Market Reality

preferences based on their online habits and to complement our market research, as shown in Figure 1.1. By accessing this market reality, our product is better targeted and our chances of a successful go-to-market strategy are greater.

Let's Make This Real!

Let's imagine that you run a crèche—a nursery school—in New York and you wish to create an online presence for your customers to locate you and engage with you—and with each other. It may be tempting to call this website Crecheworld.com.

However, a simple check using Google's Keyword Planner tool would show that in the past six months the number of unique searches for *crèche* in New York City was dwarfed by searches for *childcare* by a factor of 10! So you may think of your business as a crèche, but your customers call it childcare.

Even this early in the website planning process we have gone to the customers, looked at what they are actually doing, and changed our product appropriately. Market reality provides a sounder basis than market research for making crucial business decisions such as website naming.

Similar listening tools exist for all digital channels, and in each section of this book you will be introduced to the most effective tools for understanding your customers' actual online activities.

You may ask—does that mean that market research is redundant? Of course not. We have differentiated between these two activities in order to highlight the extent of the shift to consumer control. A smart approach is to combine the best of both of these activities into a single cohesive strategy, using one to validate and support the other.

What Are the 3i Principles?

The 3i Principles—Initiate, Iterate, and Integrate—form the foundation for all DMI Methodologies and are key to any successful marketing strategy.

Principle 1: Initiate

Our greatest challenge as marketers is shutting up! Digital truly is for dummies, in the sense that every question you may have about budget, resources, strategy, and channels is answered by the consumer—if only we would listen!

The initiate principle of digital marketing states that the customer is the starting and finishing point for all digital activities. The answer to all questions is "let the customer decide."

Many people are too quick to jump into managing digital channels. They set up blogs, websites, and social media profiles and start publishing nonspecific content about themselves, their companies, and their products. They fail to realize that digital channels are not broadcast channels in the traditional sense of the term.

In fact, they are interaction channels that facilitate a two-way conversation. By taking the time to find out what your customers are doing online, your digital activities will become radically more effective.

Your customers are speaking online. Are you listening?

Principle 2: Iterate

Within minutes of publishing an ad, we can see what the click-through rates, response rates, and conversion rates are. More importantly, the content or design of the ad can be changed a limitless number of times in response to user actions. This ability to publish, track response, and tweak accordingly is the greatest strength of the Internet and produces the second of our 3i principles—*iterate*.

This principle emphasizes the importance of tweaking a digital marketing campaign in response to user interaction. Each digital marketing channel is most effective when you apply an iterative process, and the more iterations of the campaign you apply, the more effective each becomes.

There are some key implications of this iterative process.

To begin with, the first published idea is not necessarily the best. The mythical advertising mogul who devises a killer campaign is a thing of the past. Why? Because your customers are better at describing what they want than any advertiser is. Remain open to what your customers are doing in their interactions with your campaign and be prepared to change it. Your campaign can, and will, improve over its lifetime.

Next, the length of the iteration depends on the channel. For example, if you send a weekly email newsletter you will review open rates and click-through rates within a day or two of sending your newsletter. You will then apply those insights to your next campaign in terms of what did and did not resonate with customers. So your iterative loop for your specific email marketing campaign will typically be a week long.

Principle 3: Integrate

Integration as a principle is crucial to effective digital marketing. It works at three levels:

1 *Integrate your efforts across digital channels.* Integration across digital channels is about using information gleaned through one channel to improve the effectiveness of another digital channel. It can be as simple as sharing information learned through search engine optimization with your email marketing team. Take our *crèche* versus *childcare* example: When including New York parents in an email marketing campaign for a crèche, using keywords like childcare will help to improve your open rates. Thus, sharing insights learned through one channel can drastically improve the effectiveness of another.
2 *Integrate your digital and traditional marketing efforts.* Integration of digital and traditional marketing involves using information gathered from your digital marketing efforts and integrating it into your traditional marketing strategy. For example, when writing the script for a radio ad you should use the same keywords that resonate with customers using search engines. Any opportunity to learn from your customers can be shared across all channels to improve the effectiveness of all of your communications and marketing campaigns.
3 *Integrate your reporting sources.* Companies who engage with digital marketing obtain an abundance of data about their customers. However, it is important to gather data in a way that allows you to make good business decisions. An integrated view of your customers is a good place to start. Luckily, a lot of the work can be done for you by using a tool such as Google Analytics. For example, this tool can provide you with detailed information on the source of the traffic coming to your website. What percentage of your site visitors come from email versus paid search advertising? Which visitors convert more quickly? Where should you be increasing your digital budget and where should you be reducing it? Making business decisions based on the true value of your digital marketing is a crucial step in implementing and justifying your digital marketing strategy.

So let's take the leap together! Let's discover what digital channels can do for us, and—more importantly—for our customers.

Chapter 2
Search Engine Optimization

An Introduction

Whoever controls the door to the Internet, controls the Internet. And now search engines have become the default entry point to the Internet. We start with a simple search by typing a few words into a search engine, often oblivious to exactly what happens behind the scenes. When we search in Google, for example, we are not actually searching the Internet; we are searching Google's index of the Internet, that is, the list of the sites that it has found online. So the challenge for effective search engine optimization (SEO) involves understanding how search engines work and how to play by their rules.

> Formal definition of SEO: The process of refining your website using both on-page and off-page practices so that it will be indexed and ranked successfully by search engines.
>
> Informal definition of SEO: Smell nice for Google!

Google is not a cheap date. You have to make some effort: take a shower, wash your hair, shave, and put on a spritz of aftershave and some deodorant. Optimizing a website so that it is found and indexed by search engines requires a considerable amount of grooming and this chapter will show you what to do and how to do it.

The Process

In this chapter you will explore the four key stages of the SEO process, as shown in Figure 2.1.

1 *Goals.* From the outset, it's important to be aware of the benefits of SEO. They will serve as key drivers as you navigate the development of your SEO strategy. You must decide upon and set up clear, realistic goals and targets for your SEO campaign. The benefits of

Figure 2.1   Four-Stage SEO Process

spending time developing goals far outweigh the risks of walking the plank blindfolded into the competitive world of search marketing. Just one error could result in a six-month search engine penalization—with SEO, ignorance certainly is not bliss!

2 *On-page optimization.* This deals with the granular, technical optimization of the various elements on your website. It involves ensuring search engines can easily read, understand, crawl through, and navigate the pages of your site to index it correctly.

3 *Off-page optimization.* This refers to techniques used to influence website position in organic search results that cannot be managed by on-page optimization of your site. It's a long-term, iterative process focused on gaining website authority, as determined by what other websites say about you. To put it simply, it's about building a digital footprint and earning online credibility.

4 *Analyze.* This stage is very much a cyclical process. You're now looking at the data coming back, analyzing it, and deciding upon the adjustments needed going forward. This will help you tweak your goals accordingly as you implement additional goals and changes.

Key Terms and Concepts

This chapter covers the key concepts and terminology used within the field of SEO that will equip you with the technical know-how, understanding, and insight to build and maintain an effective SEO strategy. Upon completion of this chapter you will:

• Understand the meaning of SEO.
• Understand organic search listings.
• Understand pay-per-click (PPC) listings.
• Understand the mechanics of SEO.
• Recognize and utilize the three main drivers of SEO.
• Understand on-page and off-page optimization.

Search engine optimization is the process of refining your website, using both on-page and off-page practices, so that it will be indexed and ranked successfully by search engines. With SEO, the best and most cost-effective way to increase your website traffic is to have a high position in organic search listings. Organic search listings refer to the websites that appear in search results based on their relevance to the search term the user has typed.

Search Engine Result Pages: Positioning

Have you ever tried searching for your fantastic new website, only to find it has been lost in the depths of cyberspace and is trailing behind hundreds of other sites? This all comes down to search engine results page (SERP) positioning! After reading this section you will know how to save your site from social Siberia by:

- Identifying and understanding the features of a SERP.
- Appreciating the importance of a SERP.
- Implementing your knowledge to achieve a high SERP listing.

A SERP is the web page that a search engine, such as Google or Yahoo!, returns that lists the results of a user's search. A SERP is divided into core sections. At the top you'll always find paid listings. As you can see in Figure 2.2, these are marked with yellow flags that clearly highlight these entries as ads.

But what about the listings that lie beneath the advertising? These are organic search results, or the listings that are featured on a SERP because of their relevance to the search terms that a user has entered into a search engine.

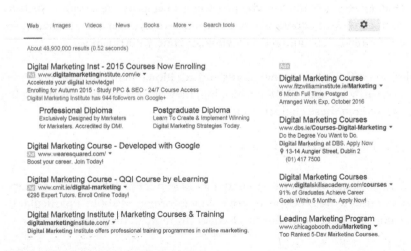

Figure 2.2   Google Search Engine Results Page

Source: Google and the Google logo are registered trademarks of Google Inc.; used with permission.

It's often said that the best place to hide a dead body is on the second page of search engine results, which is why it is essential to ensure your listing is as high as possible on the first SERP. Ninety-one percent of searchers will not click past the first results page, so it's time to adopt a competitive mind-set and strive to achieve a top-three organic listing. Your overall goal is to reach the number-one position!

Organic versus Paid Listings

Listings that are displayed on the first page of search engine results yield the highest search traffic—the higher the listing, the more clicks it will receive. Generally, paid listings will garner a 30 percent click-through rate (CTR), with organic listings making up the remaining 70 percent. While these statistics can vary depending on the market, generally this rule of thumb is widely applicable. It is important to note that as listing positions get lower, click-throughs drastically decrease. Approximately 67 percent of click-throughs on page one of a SERP occur in the first five results. A low listing will ultimately affect your overall conversion rate, so once again, it's important to strive for the top three positions.

Customers can seek information using a variety of different search practices, which is why focusing solely on text-based searches can hinder your SERP positioning and customer reach. Let's build on what we've just learned and take a look at the different ways you can optimize your SERP listings.

Location-Based Search

Search engines take into account the location of the person searching to deliver the most applicable search results. For example, with Google's My Business you can submit your business for display on a location-based search, so when John Smith searches for Italian restaurants in Tokyo, your chances of appearing in his SERP are increased. Be sure to complete all elements of the form by providing a category, description, pictures, videos, and so on to catch user attention. Google operates a five-star rating scheme, so customers should be encouraged to review and rate your business.

While listings with higher review scores and additional material, like those in Figure 2.3, won't necessarily increase SERP positioning, they most certainly will yield a higher CTR than those without these characteristics.

Knowledge Graph Listing

Google's Knowledge Graph tries to understand searchers' intent while anticipating their end goals. It tries to help people discover key information about a particular business that they may not have been able to discover through an organic listing.

For example, if a user searches for information on restaurants in New York City, Knowledge Graph will display both a variety of images at the top of the SERP and a

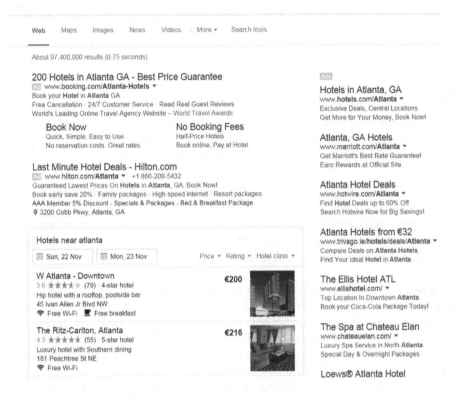

Figure 2.3   Location Based Search
Source: Google and the Google logo are registered trademarks of Google Inc.; used with permission.

panel on the right with a list of key information, a company description, reviews, related searches, and so on. It feeds on information from related websites, popular searches, Google local listings, and other sources.

Data Highlighter

Data Highlighter is a Google Search Console (GSC) tool that is very valuable when it comes to refining your SERP listing. With your mouse, you simply highlight the various data fields (title, description, image, etc.) on your page. This in turn allows Google to display your website data in new, more attractive ways both in SERPs and on the Knowledge Graph. While you cannot stipulate what data will display in a SERP, through Google Search Console, you can demote links to your site that decrease its chances of being listed.

Search Behavior

By now you should have a strong grasp of the key terminology, mechanics, and practices associated with SEO and SERP positioning. So, let's combine this knowledge and use it to understand more about our customers and to analyze their online search behavior. By the end of this section, you will:

- Know who the three key players in search marketing are and what their impact on your SEO strategy is.
- Understand search behavior and DMI's 5P Customer Search Insights Model.
- Know what key snippets of information can be obtained from each of the 5Ps.
- Be able to leverage the value of the 5Ps in your SEO strategy.
- Appreciate the importance of relevancy for customer acquisition.

What is online search behavior? Every time users search, they reveal a certain amount of information about themselves. When this information is gathered, it can be classified into different search behavior categories to analyze customer needs. From this categorization, you can develop an effective SEO content strategy. In search engine optimization there are three key players:

1 *The searcher.* The goal is to have people searching for *your* product or service. More specifically, you want searchers to look for the keywords you are using. You want to understand a person's every search behavior in order to target a searcher appropriately.
2 *The website owner.* Your goal as the website owner should be to align the optimization of your website with customer search behavior findings. The competitive intention here is to outrank, outperform, and outbid your competitors.
3 *The search engine.* Ultimately, your goal is to ensure search engines have indexed your website, so they can understand what your site is about. This is crucial. If a search engine can't understand your site, it won't display it.

Each of these players is viewed as a stepping-stone on the route to reaching and engaging with customers. You must successfully address each component to reach your end goal, whether that is a click-through to your site, a contact inquiry, a sale, or something else.

Understanding your customers is the cornerstone of every successful business, which is why search marketing is such an important medium for gathering customer insight. With every search, users leave small crumbs of personal information behind. So by using DMI's 5P Customer Search Insights Model, you get a greater understanding of customers than you ever imagined! Let's take a look at the 5Ps:

1 *Person.* Information about the searcher can include age, sex, religion, language, and socioeconomic group.
2 *Place.* You can discover the country or city a customer is in and whether the location is classified as urban or rural.
3 *Product.* You can learn which particular topic, interest, or subject area of a product searchers are researching and the need or the pain being addressed.
4 *Priority.* The search query provides an indication of customers' purchasing time frames; that is, how urgently they need the product or service and the window for engagement.
5 *Purchase.* Most importantly, you can find out how and where users want to buy and what stage they are at in the consumer purchase model.

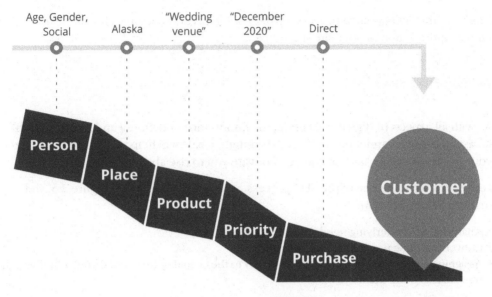

Figure 2.4   The 5P Model

To expand upon this, let's look at Figure 2.4 and apply the 5P model to the search query *Alaska romantic wedding venue December 2020*.

1 *Person.* Here, you could make an educated guess as to the age and gender of the user. But to be certain, this data can be obtained using an important tool you'll become very familiar with, known as Google Analytics (GA). GA gives highly detailed information (in this case demographic data), and can provide key person information.
2 *Place.* From the search query we can see the searcher's targeted place is Alaska. But by using GA you can also see where this person is located.
3 *Priority.* The priority is very much December 2020 and the searcher's purchasing time frame and urgency have also been identified.
4 *Product.* The product the user is looking for is a wedding venue.
5 *Purchase.* The purchase in this case is going to be direct. It's not something that the user will book online.

Ultimately, the key to all this can be summed up in one word: relevancy. The most relevant search results will always be displayed to users, so make sure to focus the three key players of SEO towards each of the 5Ps to ensure that your website is a strong contender against competitors.

Customer search behavior is something you must take into account in all aspects of online optimization. It should influence your decisions on every detail, from choosing keywords to creating content for your site. You need to understand who your customers are, what their online habits are, and how to solve their consumer pain in order to convert them from website visitors into loyal customers. With a better understanding of your customer's online habits and behaviors, let's now use this information to inform stage 1 of the SEO iterative process—what your goals and outcomes for the search engine optimization of your site should be.

Stage 1: Goals

As with all aspects of digital marketing, the importance of defining and setting tangible, measurable goals cannot be emphasized enough. Goals will help you create plans, direct your day-to-day tasks, and, of course, motivate you to rise above your competitors.

Let's start with stage one of the SEO process, which is highlighted in Figure 2.5. Get ready to be an expert in:

- Analyzing the underlying needs of your business
- Converting these needs into well-defined goals
- Assigning key performance indicators (KPIs) to these goals—to assess if you're on the right track to achieving them

Figure 2.5   Focus on the first stage in the SEO process

While addressing consumer pain is important, you can't forget to address your own. If you assess the needs of your business, it will create a beneficial ripple effect on the three key players of SEO: the searcher, the search engine, and you, the website owner. You need to identify the business pain, view this pain as a goal, create a strategy to achieve the goal, and assign KPIs to the strategy to monitor your progress in solving the pain. It's very much a cyclical process. Let's use the example of a sports footwear retailer:

Business pain: A decline in online orders
Goal: Conversions

Strategy: Increase website visitors through on-page optimization (keywords, blog, etc.)
KPIs: Sales, online inquiries

In this example, the searcher benefits through an enhanced user experience and relevant content, the search engine benefits through being able to easily understand and index your site, and you, the website owner, benefits through achieving your goals.

Goals vary depending on the nature of the business. Types of goals include engagement, visibility, and the most common goal, conversions. Every business is different in regards to what it classifies as a conversion. On one web page a user watching a video might be considered a conversion. On another it could be an online inquiry. After you've decided what your goals are, you can track your progress towards achieving your goals by creating KPIs. You can define and monitor goals and KPIs, then analyze this data to adjust your strategy using the GA reporting tool. We'll show you how to do this later.

Following are some examples of some typical goals and KPIs.

Types of Goals	Types of KPIs
• Engagement	• Organic traffic
• Conversions	• Visitor numbers
• Visibility	• Click-through rates
• Reputation	• Downloads
• Credibility and status	• Online inquiries
• Market leadership	• Sales
• Competitive advantage	• Website engagement and the like

Staying motivated in achieving your goals will be difficult if you're oblivious to the benefits from your efforts. The ultimate goal of SEO is to achieve that number-one ranking on SERPs for your website. But what are the benefits?

- *Increased organic CTRs.* Organic CTR is the percentage of clicks your website listing generates, based on the number of organic impressions served. Organic impressions are the number of times a page from your website displays in SERPs and is viewed by a user, not including paid listings. A number-one position will increase your organic CTR, which in turn reduces your advertising spend and ultimately leads to conversions.
- *Increased engagement.* You want users to engage with your brand at different stages of the buying process, visit your website, and stay there! Like a dog to a bone, a number-one ranking will lure searchers to your site. Increased engagement means users exploring and spending longer periods of time on your site.
- *Enhanced reputation.* Top listings yield both online and professional credibility, status, and reputation.
- *Market leadership and competitive advantage.* Outshining your competitors is vital, so strive for a number-one listing to avail yourself of this advantage.
- *Increased conversions.* Whatever you consider a conversion, this is what it's all about. They've clicked on to your site, spent time navigating it, and had a pleasant browsing experience. Great! But now it's about transforming these factors into conversions. A high search-engine listing will do this for you.

Take some time now to assess to the needs of your business, and from this devise your own goals and the corresponding KPIs. You should be referring back to your goals and updating them as you progress through each stage of the SEO process. Goal setting is another ongoing process that will continually change, depending on the successes or failures of the strategies you implement. Just keep reminding yourself of the benefits of your hard work and the results will speak for themselves.

Stage 2: On-Page Optimization

With your goals in place and their accompanying KPIs assigned, the time has come to move to the second stage of the SEO process: On-page optimization, which is highlighted in Figure 2.6. At the start of this chapter, we briefly discussed the mechanics of this process. Now we can explore it further.

Keyword Research

Keyword research is often the first step in this process. Keywords have a very strong impact on the other elements of on-page optimization, so the level of research you conduct will determine if your site is a zero or a hero in terms of search volume!

After just a little more reading you will:

- Understand the terms keyword, long-tail keyword, and keyword research.
- Know how to conduct both online and offline keyword research.

Figure 2.6   Focus on the second stage in the SEO process

- Be aware of the importance of keyword-rich content and the need for high-quality content.
- Be able to identify keyword research tools, the actions they perform, and the data they provide.

Key Terms

So, what exactly is a *keyword*? It's a significant word or phrase that relates to the content on your website. For example, if you're a freelance photographer, relevant keywords for your site could be *photographer* or *affordable wedding photographer*. Keywords are vital in ensuring your site displays in SERPs. They should be subtly incorporated into the content and meta data of your web pages in a way that reads naturally.

A *search term* is a commonly used phrase that users type into search engines to find you. Traditionally users typed in two to four words, but with ever-increasing digital literacy rates, much longer search terms are now being used. You must be able to know what customers are searching for and choose your keywords based on that. While generic search terms such as *hotels in Paris* will give tons of search results, they lack relevance.

Users now understand that the more specific their search terms, the more accurate and relevant their search results will be. This is where *long-tail keywords* come in. These are three- or four-word keyword phrases with low-volume search queries that are worth ranking highly. Why? Because searchers using long-tail keywords are usually closer to the point of purchase. Although long-tail keywords are quite specific, they have lower competition and bring much higher qualified traffic to your website.

Having covered the terminology, it's now time to do your homework and discover the keywords that people use when searching for information on the product or service you provide. This is known as *keyword research*. It means finding the search terms your customers most frequently use. There are two types of keyword research—online and offline. Typically, digital marketers will focus solely on online methods of keyword research, disregarding the abundance of excellent keywords that can be derived from offline research. But why should you bother with keyword research at all? Besides the fact that it will increase your ranking and impressions, it also helps search engines better recognize the intent behind users' search terms and bring them the most relevant results—which keeps all three key players happy.

Let's take a look at some key tools and practices that will assist you in your keyword research efforts.

Offline Keyword Research

Brainstorming. You really can't beat sitting down with your team to brainstorm keyword ideas. The best people to report on the common jargon being used in your industry are your colleagues. They are the people who interact with your customers, hearing and seeing the words and phrases they use when referring to your products and services. Something as simple as noting down common customer queries can be a huge bonus for keyword research. Using keywords composed of industry jargon can be tricky, so be very careful. Let's use the example of an IT solutions company. The standard, industry-accepted term for the service provided is *managed IT solutions*, and as such, the company will want to display in SERPs with this keyword. The problem here is that customers don't use this term, and search for *outsourced IT services* instead. The lesson here is that you should always select the keywords and search terms that your customers are actually using.

Marketing collateral. Open the office storeroom and gather your company's leaflets, brochures, posters, and the like. The content here can be particularly useful for generating low search volume keywords that are worth including. In addition, going one step further and sourcing competitor marketing material is an excellent competitor keyword research method.

Customer surveys. Qualitative research-based customer surveys are another method of establishing the phraseology and colloquial jargon your customer base is using.

Listening to customers. Substantial amounts of keyword data can be obtained by simply listening to your customers. Brief everyone in your company on the importance of listening to the words your customers are using. Collating these words into a list will save a lot of time and money when conducting your keyword research.

Online Keyword Research

In this stage of the process, generally we're talking about the use of key tools that allow you to perform filtered keyword research using the following criteria: custom date ranges, query volume, historical trends, levels of data, and related phrases by city or country. With such a wide variety of online keyword research tools available for free or for a fee, the web is your oyster! Researching and testing the countless tools available that work best for you is time well spent. To kick-start your efforts, the top four highly regarded research tools in the industry follow:

1 *Google Autocomplete.* This tool is probably the easiest online keyword research tool to use, and definitely the place to start. It's particularly good for long-tail keyword research; you simply begin typing into the Google search box. Once you start, you'll see that it will try to finish your sentence automatically, based on the most popular search terms entered. As you now know, Google scans your browser history to deliver the most relevant search results. If you're using Google Autocorrect for keyword research, make sure to clear your search history, cache, cookies, and temporary files—clear it all! That way it won't consider your previous searches when suggesting search terms, thus providing fresh data.

2 *Google AdWords Keyword Planner.* This is a tool built into the Google AdWords platform. Under the Tools section, you'll find Keyword Planner. The research and analytical functionalities are endless! After you've entered a particular keyword or search term and chosen the location you're targeting, click on Get Ideas. The Keyword Planner will return a report detailing the top listings containing that keyword or search term, plus other suggested keywords. In the listing you will notice two tabs, one for ad group ideas and another for keyword ideas. At this stage of the process focus on the latter. The ad group ideas tab concerns PPC ad campaigns and right now we're focusing on how to use this tool for organic optimization.

The listing will reveal copious amounts of information. For this SEO exercise, however, the only two data elements worth focusing on in Figure 2.7 are *search term* and *average*

Ad group ideas	Keyword ideas				Columns ▾		⬇ Download	Add all (801)
Search terms		Avg. monthly searches ?	Competition ?			Suggested bid ?	Ad impr. share ?	Add to plan
digital marketing courses		8,100	High			€7.43	6%	

Show rows: 30 ▾ 1 - 1 of 1 keywords |< < > >|

Keyword (by relevance)		Avg. monthly searches ?	Competition ?			Suggested bid ?	Ad impr. share ?	Add to plan
digital marketing course		8,100	High			€4.52	1%	
online digital marketing courses		880	High			€7.05	6%	
digital marketing courses online		590	High			€8.97	4%	
digital marketing course online		480	High			€4.95	1%	
free digital marketing courses		480	High			€3.07	4%	
digital marketing training courses		260	High			€8.13	2%	

Figure 2.7   Keyword Ideas in Google AdWords Keyword Planner
Source: Google and the Google logo are registered trademarks of Google Inc.; used with permission.

monthly searches. Start by looking at the search term and its corresponding search volume. Base your keyword selection on relatively high search volumes that are actually applicable. You want keywords with low enough competition so that you can get that all-important page-one listing. Again, don't disregard long-tail keywords. They use search terms with less competition and bring more relevant traffic to your website.

3 *Google Trends*. As with all aspects of digital marketing, popular keywords are ever changing, so it's important to keep informed and stay ahead of the curve. Google Trends is a great tool for analyzing the rise and fall of keyword trends. It's important to be aware of trending terminology and phrases so you're not targeting outdated keywords. This tool can also show how search terms are trending against each other and if there are any new trends you should be considering.

4 *SEMrush*. SEMrush is used widely by search marketers in the industry. It's an excellent tool for analyzing your competitors, the keywords they're targeting, and what type of estimated traffic volumes they're getting. Outperforming your competitors is one of your primary SEO goals, and to do that you need to assess their performance in comparison to your own.

Once you have chosen a solid list of keywords that allow you to rank highly in SERPs, it's time to incorporate those keywords into your website. Search engines encourage the use of keywords so they can display the most relevant websites on the first page of a user's search.

A Word of Warning

So by repeating a relevant keyword 50 times on one page, your website will rank number one, right? Wrong! Back in the day, search marketers thought it clever to try cheating search engine algorithms through a variety of disallowed keyword practices, such as keyword stuffing. This involved overuse of the top ranking keywords in their website content in order to rank highly. The Google gods are now smarter than ever and these kinds of forbidden SEO activities won't be tolerated. Websites found to be violating the rules will be severely penalized and could be removed from SERPs entirely. Nowadays, search marketers are wiser and times have changed. Keyword density, or how many times a keyword or phrase appears on a web page, is one aspect of SEO that is no longer important. Keywords should only be used to accompany high-quality, relevant content.

When the research is done and the optimum keywords have been selected, you must then decide where to place them. You should include your target keyword in the title tag, in the metadescription, and in the body copy of the web page (these mechanics will be covered in the next section).

Again, keywords should be used in combination with suitable content. When writing for your site, always focus on both the end user and the search engine. The content should be relevant, with keywords inserted into sentences naturally, so users don't realize they are reading SEO-optimized content. Most importantly, never compromise the quality of your content for keyword optimization. The penalties certainly aren't worth the risk.

The On-Page Optimization Process

By now, you should have carefully conducted your keyword research and chosen your optimal keywords based on this research. The next step is to incorporate these keywords into the on-page optimization of your site.

Your aim is to achieve a high first-page ranking and push your competitors into the barren wastelands of page two and beyond! Upon completion of this section, you will:

- Know the optimal content structure and hierarchy for on-page SEO.
- Recognize and appreciate the importance of each on-page mechanic.
- Learn how to conduct on-page optimization.
- Know about the key on-page SEO tools.
- Know how to create multiregional and multilingual versions of your website.

Style and Structure

With on-page optimization, the first thing you must be conscious of is the structure of your site. You should make sure there is a hierarchy among web pages and that the structure flows throughout your website, as shown in Figure 2.8. Think of it as a parent and child relationship. Every website should have a menu navigation bar, with the menu bar links acting as the parents. The subpages flowing from these parent pages are their children, and if these subpages have further subpages, they are *the children's* children.

The example here details the hierarchal structure of a typical e-commerce website. As you can see, the Women's page is a child of the Home page but also a parent of the Clothing, Shoes, and Accessories pages. Got that? The number of levels your site has depends on the nature of your business. If your content is buried too deep it can be

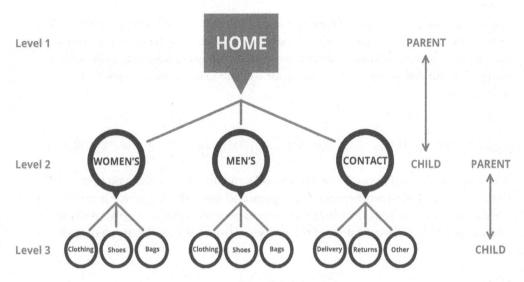

Figure 2.8   Typical Site Structure

difficult for both users and search engines to reach it, which is why ideally websites should have no more than three or four levels. Remember, always try to keep the three key players happy. A user-friendly site will be appreciated by the customer, which will please the search engine that will ultimately increase your ranking in SERPs.

Utilizing structure and breaking up your content using bullet points, headings, images, and the like is where a lot of websites fail. If you have a page-one listing but it looks difficult to read, your customers will bounce faster than you can say *keyword cannibalization*. Bouncing is the term used to describe the activity of users who enter a website, don't interact with it, and exit back out to the SERP or close the window entirely. Google considers bounce rates in determining your ranking, which is why website structure is so important. High bounce rates can lead to search engines viewing a particular website as a bad match for the search term used, and they could potentially demote your website as a result. Getting people onto the website is the first step, but keeping them there is the next. So create structure on your site and allow the customer to see a visually pleasing site that uses a variety of media.

Up-to-Date Content

Search engines and users are very similar, in that both favor websites with unique, relevant, and up-to-date content. Use yourself as an example: If you were searching for on-page optimization articles and the SERP returned listings from this year and five years ago, which link would you click first?

Maintaining up-to-date content isn't just about text on the page—photos, videos, slides, and images are all examples of different forms of media you can use to keep your content fresh and attractive to the reader. You still need text on the page for search engines to understand your content, but remember that you're writing primarily for your customers, to keep them on your site. Start analyzing user media habits. If, for example, you discover a high volume of activity associated with users watching videos, start thinking about embedding videos into your website to build an extra level of interaction.

Optimizing the Technical Mechanics of Your Page

When you've decided upon the hierarchy and structure of your site, you then need to optimize the technical mechanics of your page and insert the keywords into them. They are listed here in the order in which they would normally appear on your website so that you can get a better visualization of the process—from the top of your page to the bottom.

URLs

Insert your chosen keywords into the URLs of each web page on your site. This is an indicator that search engines look for. Making sure your URLs are optimized in this way is extremely important. That means eliminating the string of numbers and the &=%? symbols from the URLs and replacing them with easily readable keywords, to assist both your users and search engines. Hyphens or dashes are the only symbols that should be used as word separators. For years industry experts encouraged the use of underscores; however, Google has stated that this is not recommended, as underscores make it more difficult for algorithms to identify what the page is about.

Take these two URLs:

1 digitalmarketinginstitute.ie/courses/type/postgraduate-diploma-in-digital-marketing/
2 http://www.abcdefhgj.ie/index.php?option=com_content&view=article&id=13&Itemid=43

You can see which URL is *pretty* and descriptive and which fell out of the ugly tree. Your URLs need to be descriptive in order to inform your users what they're linking to. If the second link was emailed or shared on social media, users would have no idea where they're being taken or what the page is about. In the first URL, the link destination is clearly described, the hierarchy is visible, and the keywords are prominent and separated by dashes.

Page Names

"What's in a name? That which we call a rose, by any other name would smell as sweet." While Juliet may have been onto something here, she certainly wasn't referring to web pages. Keyword insertion here can be tricky, but you must name your web pages appropriately to ensure they're relevant to the page content. Page names act as labels that help us distinguish content and create meaning. They usually have one or two words, and for that reason it's not always possible to optimize them in terms of keywords. On the plus side, this is not totally necessary. Naming these pages with relevance is the solution here. As users and search engines go deeper into the website, pages should get more specific to the keywords you're targeting. Again, it's about creating a user-friendly and informative browsing experience.

Meta Tags

A web page is made up of hypertext markup language (HTML). Within the HTML are special tags, known as meta tags. Meta tags don't affect the web page layout, but rather provide important information about the page's content, which is used by search engines to index your site. By right-clicking on a page and selecting Source Code, you can see the HTML and meta tags of that particular page. Nowadays, higher rankings are given for relevance, user experience, and popularity than for meta tag optimization. In the industry, this topic is a bone of contention, and views on which meta tags carry higher importance vary greatly. Meta tags *are* an excellent additions to your SEO toolbox—just be careful not to waste your time on extraneous tags that add no SEO value and take up coding space! We've outlined the most important meta tags, which will assist your on-page optimization, below:

Title tag. Although technically not a meta tag, this tag will display the first part of your search engine results listing. Title tags help ensure your listings on SERPs say the right things about your business, contribute to click-through rates, and help search engines determine what the page is about. Have you ever noticed the name of a web page in the tab of your browser? That's the title tag. Most content management systems such as WordPress facilitate the creation of title tags. Again, think about your keywords for each page and incorporate this information into the title. When possible, *front load* your keyword—this means putting the keyword as close to the beginning of the title as possible. Search engines regard individuality highly, so be sure every page on your website has a unique title and remove any duplicate titles. Generally, titles should have between 50 and 60 characters in total. Google indexes the whole title regardless of character length, but the problem is that it also truncates titles that are too long—and this means part of the title is cut off. Not paying attention to your title's character count could result in the most important piece of information in your title being left out or shortened.

Description tag. While it may not contribute to your website ranking, this tag does make up the second part of your listing. Generally, you should aim for between 150 and 160 characters. Utilize your description tag as a sales pitch. Get your keyword in there, but also include a call to action, benefit, and unique selling point. That way you're telling people why they should visit your website, purchase from you, or make a query about your product or services. Snappy and informative description tags will engage your users and please the search engines.

Breadcrumb Navigation

This allows the user to return to previous sections on the website without having to use the main navigation bar to do so. As users go through each page, they leave a breadcrumb that is displayed on the top of each page—as shown in Figure 2.9—allowing them find their way home! So in the case of this particular page, you could return to the

Figure 2.9 Example of Breadcrumb Navigation

"Blog Posts" page very quickly by using breadcrumb navigation. It's something you should definitely consider. The name of your page is what will appear on your breadcrumb navigation graphic, so again, ensure page names are descriptive.

On-Page Headings

Your pages should be divided into headings to facilitate structure and guide both the users and search engines reading your content. Headings range from H1 to H6 and indicate the most important parts of your page's content and how the content is interconnected. Your primary heading should be an H1 heading; its subheading will be classified as H2; the subheading of H2 will be classified as H3, and so on and so forth. In Figure 2.10, "Professional Diploma in Digital Marketing" is the main heading, or H1, of this page. "Course Overview," the subheading of H1, is H2. By going into the source code of a website and searching for H1, you can see the headings of a web page. How many headings you want depends on how you wish to structure your content, although they usually don't go past H3. Try and get keywords into your H1s. From the users' perspective, when they click onto your page they will clearly see that this is the page they should be on. Search engines look at headings too, to get an indication about the page's content and what the keywords are.

First Paragraph

Under H1 lies your first paragraph, and ideally your chosen keywords should be within the first line of text. Users scan the first few words on every page, which determine whether or not they will bounce. So be smart with your first line and incorporate those keywords in a natural manner.

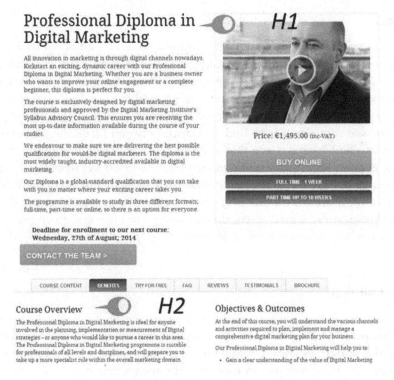

Figure 2.10   On-page Headings

Body of Text

The industry-accepted standard for word counts varies, but the recommendation for general web pages related to the product or service you provide is at least 300 words. Articles, white papers, and case studies should have 1,000 words minimum. Blogs, on the other hand, are a different story. With blogs, you should be aiming for between 1,500 and 2,500 words. Research has shown that articles containing 2,500 words garner higher rankings than articles with fewer words. With all these guidelines, you should always bear in mind that both search engines and users are seeking relevant, fresh content that is informative and provides solutions. Writing just for the purposes of reaching your word count is not advised. You also shouldn't write more content just to be able to insert a high number of keywords. Keyword density is now outdated and seen as SEO malpractice. Help the search engines to understand what your content is about by inserting keywords once or twice into the body of text and its heading, but primarily focus on delivering a solid piece of relevant writing. **Bolding** keywords in your web page content in the belief that doing so will increase ranking is a common misconception. Doing so is perceived by Google as keyword stuffing and is taken very seriously. Most importantly, for user experience, bolded keyword text looks unprofessional and does not read naturally. If you're using long-tail keywords, where possible try to keep the phrase together on the page.

Anchor Text

Interlinked content should be present throughout your site, allowing users and search engines to advance to the next page of your site with ease. This can be done with anchor text. Anchor text is a hyperlink shown as clickable text within your content. It's very important that *all* pages are accessible via a link somewhere on your site, so ensure your links are built into the content that navigates people through your site. Your goal is to find a balance between facilitating an excellent user experience and having a site that is optimized for search engines. Nowadays anchor text is more descriptive and contains your targeted keywords or phrases. For example, an alternative to the traditional *click here* anchor text could be *click here for more information on our professional diploma in digital marketing*. By being descriptive, users know where they're going, and the search engine is taking those keywords into account when it indexes the page and follows the link through.

Images and Alt Text

Alt text stands for alternative text, and it acts as an alternative to the image it describes. Its purpose is to describe the image both for users with accessibility difficulties and search engines. Users who are visually impaired might use software to help them read your website; in this case, the user won't necessarily be able to see the image on the screen. Providing alt text can allow these software programs to read aloud the descriptive alt text, creating a more positive user experience. Search engines also use alt text to determine what the image is about, which can improve your ranking and also helps with images being found in image SERPs. Be succinct and descriptive with your alt text; the maximum should be four to six words. When possible, insert keywords into the file names of your images (before you upload them), the alt text, and the image caption.

Social Sharing

Build your page to be easily shareable by your website visitors. This helps with building a digital footprint, by getting people talking about your brand on social media. More importantly, by providing easily shareable links you're bringing people back into your website. Search engines are taking social sharing into account too.

Site Map

The final element you must have on your site is an HTML site map. A site map is a page on a website that provides a map of the website's structure. The site map is in the form of text links to all the other pages on the site. It allows search engines to crawl through, index, and rank your website. Site maps should link to every page on the website and every page should link to it. You'll find they're normally linked in the footer of a website, and once created can be submitted for indexing through Google Search Console.

The Technical Aspects of SEO

Now that you know how to fully optimize the on-page elements of your website, let's venture deeper into the technical aspects of SEO that need your consideration, so you can prevent unforeseen issues down the line. Anybody who has worked on a late night essay or report knows how uncooperative technology can be sometimes—but fear not, soon you will:

- Understand the importance of browser compatibility and responsive websites.
- Be aware of structured data markup and schema markup language.
- Know how to fix and customize common technical page errors.
- Recognize the importance of secure websites to enhance user experience and site ranking.

Compatibility

When assessing the technical elements of your site, start by checking your website's cross-browser compatibility with Chrome, Internet Explorer, Safari, and Firefox. You can use Google Analytics to see the volume of traffic coming in from particular browsers. Browser compatibility is an essential element of a good user experience, so don't let your customers bounce over something as simple as this! There are tons of tools available to help with this; BrowserStack is the most highly regarded in the industry. Otherwise, compatibility can be achieved manually by installing these web browsers onto your computer.

Google's algorithm has shifted to include greater ranking emphasis on mobile friendliness. As such, responsive websites have become widely expected by users and search engines. Google is giving much greater SERP preference to websites that are compatible with mobile when users are searching on mobile. Generally speaking, search engines have a preference for *responsive websites*. These are websites designed to respond to the different sizes of screens that customers are using. Responsive sites contract and expand to the screen dimensions of the devices searchers are using—whether they are smartphones, tablets, or computer screens. Although responsive sites can sometimes inflict slower speed and loading times on your site, the pros far outweigh the cons.

An alternative to a responsive website would be a mobile-specific website, wherein you choose to build an entirely separate mobile website with its own unique URLs. These sites just include the vital pieces of information, content, and (most important!) call-to-action buttons. Search engines and users tend to favor responsive websites as they contain exactly what is displayed on the desktop version of the site and do not create the limitations on browsing for the user that mobile-specific sites do. Google's Mobile-Friendly Test, as shown in Figure 2.11, is a great tool that determines if your site is deemed mobile friendly by search engines. Type in your website's URL and the tool will tell you if your site is compatible. If not, it does give helpful indications as to why your site failed the test and provides tips on how to fix the problem.

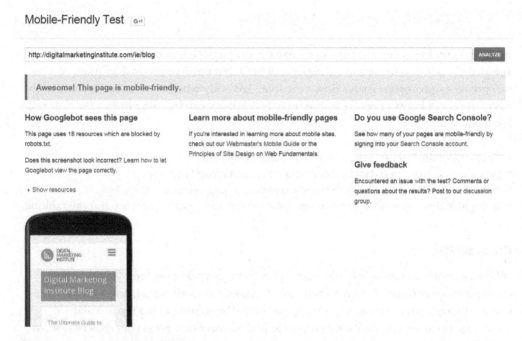

Figure 2.11   On-page headings
Source: Google and the Google logo are registered trademarks of Google Inc.; used with permission.

Structured Data Markup

Structured data markup is the next technical element of your site in need of optimization. It refers to the content on your site that is formatted in an easily readable way for search engines. *Schema markup language* is the result of a collaboration between Google, Bing, Yahoo!, and Yandex that allows you to easily implement structured data markup into your website to:

- Increase search result accuracy.
- Refine the way your listing appears in SERPs.
- Enhance the way information is displayed.

Basically, it enables you to better explain the content of your website to search engines. If, for example, you're writing a blog about bass, how is the search engine to know if you're referring to the guitar or the fish? Schema markup allows you explain these things to search engines. Have you ever seen a company's upcoming event or reviews displayed in SERPs? That's because the company has marked up their content, so that search engines will acknowledge these are listings of events and reviews and include them in search results and in the Knowledge Graph. In the next section, we'll cover the ultimate tool for schema markup, Google's Data Highlighter. Schema markup's influence lies in its ability to make your listings stand out from the crowd, increase your click-through rates, and help your customers discover more information.

Houston, We Have a Problem

When creating or redeveloping a website, changes can be made that inadvertently contribute to an interrupted user experience. Changing the URL of a page or removing it from your site entirely will leave users and search engines with something called a *404 error* page. This is an indication to users that they have clicked on a page that has been moved or no longer exists—otherwise known as a *broken link*. At all costs, try to avoid 404 errors on your site. Users and search engines severely resent 404s and the consequences of them vary from demoted rankings to lost conversions. Should your site ever deliver a 404 error, it's best practice to limit the damage to user experience by customizing your 404 page. Try to reduce user annoyance by making light of the situation, as the cartoon shown in Figure 2.12 does. Replace the standard 404 error text with something novel, such as "Oops, we've got a problem." Choose something that ties in with your brand's tone of voice and personality. You should also provide navigation link options to other areas of the site so as not to alienate customers and make them more likely to bounce.

A *301 redirect* is a permanent redirect from one URL to another, and is another method of limiting the negative impact that 404 errors create. Should you wish to change the URL of a page that has already been indexed, 301 redirects are the answer. You need to make sure that you're redirecting to the most relevant page on your website. Redirects can be carried out in two ways:

1 *Domain level*. Users type in www.example.com and the 301 redirects them to www .myexample.com.
2 *Individual URLs*. Users type in www.example.com/how-to-do-seo and the 301 redirects them to www.example.com/a-guide-to-seo.

The final technical element worth considering for your website is a secure certificate, known as an *SSL certificate*. These are small data files that you purchase and install on

404. That's an error.

The requested URL was not found on this server. That's all we know.

Figure 2.12   Customized 404 Error Page
Source: Google and the Google logo are registered trademarks of Google Inc.; used with permission.

your web server, creating secure connections between the web server and the browser. You can recognize websites with SSL certificates by looking at their URLs in the address bar of your browser; the URL begins with HTTPS and is accompanied by a padlock symbol. SSL certificates are the ultimate certification that the website is secure and are specifically recommended for websites that involve the exchange of sensitive, personal, and financial information. Although not a critical ranking factor, Google has stated that it considers HTTPS when determining ranking. Everything in SEO is about getting an edge over your competitors, so these are certainly worth considering.

Site Maps and Google Search Console

Now that we've looked at the technical elements of SEO, we're going to explore a tool that will greatly assist with your on-page optimization. Formerly known as Webmaster Tools, it has since been rebranded as Google Search Console (GSC). Probably one of the most underused tools that Google provides, it helps website owners see how Google crawls, understands, and indexes your site. Use it to help find the technical issues that may be hurting user experience, or worse, your ranking! This section will navigate you through the various elements and tools within GSC that you need to know in order to have a fully optimized website. So get ready to become a Google Search Console expert and also to:

- Know the various forms of site maps and their importance for SEO.
- Understand what is meant by robots.txt and canonicalization.
- Be aware of and know how to use the functions, reports, and tools within Google Search Console.

Sitemaps

You probably know that a sitemap is simply a list of every page on a website; that is, it provides a map of the site's structure. The majority of people will never use your sitemap, relying on breadcrumb and menu bar navigation instead. Regardless of this fact, search engines rely heavily on sitemaps to easily crawl your site and index it appropriately. Let's now take a look at the two types of sitemaps you can, and should, have on your site:

1 *HTML sitemap.* An HTML sitemap is the text version of a sitemap and shows text links to all the website's pages, as illustrated in Figure 2.13. They're easily readable by humans and excellent for internal linking, accessibility, and navigation purposes. When possible, always include every page of your site in the sitemap. For websites that provide a large variety of products it may not be feasible to list every product page in the sitemap. In this instance, a category and subcategory listing is okay, as shown in Figure 2.13. When search engines visit this page they will be able to easily access all the content on your site. Always remember search engines want to index your site, but it's your job to make sure they can actually find the pages!

2 *XML sitemap.* Figure 2.14 shows a sitemap written using extensible markup language (XML), which displays in a coding format. It follows the same rules as the HTML version of

Sitemap

Pages

- Extended Contact Us Success
- 10 week signup success
- Bootcamp signup success
- Careers at Digital Marketing Institute
- Class Network Error
- Class Network Notice
- Contact us course enquiry success!
- Contacts Us Extended
- Corporate contact form
- Corporate contact us success
- Corporate Training
- Corporate Training – Contact Success
- Course Enquiry
- Digital Marketing Institute Diagnostic Tool
- Digital Marketing Module Unlocked
- Digital Report Download Success

Figure 2.13   HTML Sitemap

XML Sitemap

Generated by **Yoast's WordPress SEO plugin**, this is an XML Sitemap, meant for consumption by search engines.

You can find more information about XML sitemaps on **sitemaps.org**.

This XML Sitemap Index file contains 14 sitemaps.

Sitemap	Last Modified
http://digitalmarketinginstitute.com/page-sitemap.xml	2015-11-13 10:55
http://digitalmarketinginstitute.com/news-sitemap.xml	2015-08-26 15:56
http://digitalmarketinginstitute.com/members-events-sitemap.xml	2013-11-18 12:15
http://digitalmarketinginstitute.com/testimonials-sitemap.xml	2014-09-28 22:44
http://digitalmarketinginstitute.com/education-partners-sitemap.xml	2015-11-10 12:48
http://digitalmarketinginstitute.com/course-sitemap.xml	2015-11-13 16:28
http://digitalmarketinginstitute.com/lecturers-sitemap.xml	2015-10-14 15:35
http://digitalmarketinginstitute.com/blog_post-sitemap1.xml	2011-07-29 04:04
http://digitalmarketinginstitute.com/blog_post-sitemap2.xml	2012-05-22 16:36
http://digitalmarketinginstitute.com/blog_post-sitemap3.xml	2014-06-10 13:14
http://digitalmarketinginstitute.com/blog_post-sitemap4.xml	2015-11-16 15:15
http://digitalmarketinginstitute.com/category-sitemap.xml	2015-11-16 15:15
http://digitalmarketinginstitute.com/post_tag-sitemap.xml	2015-11-16 15:15
http://digitalmarketinginstitute.com/topics-sitemap.xml	2015-10-14 15:35

Figure 2.14   XML Sitemap

a sitemap but is preferred by search engines, which find the language easier to understand. You need to submit your XML sitemap to Google Search Console, and in doing so, it allows Google to inform you of any major issues on your site.

Be extra vigilant with the creation of a sitemap; always check for minor mistakes, such as a missing homepage link. Common errors like this one happen oh so frequently, so ensure every page you want indexed is on that sitemap. There are a variety of free tools online that will generate whatever version of sitemap you require. The tools are normally automated, so that every time a page is added or removed the sitemap will automatically reflect these changes. Include your sitemap in your 404 error pages and in the footer of your site, and remember—while Google does rule the roost with search volume, don't ignore Bing. It generates a large volume of searches, so submit your sitemap there as well.

Robots: Helping You Hide

While it's great that sitemaps make indexing easier, what if there are certain pages you don't want to show up in SERPs? Robots.txt files are the solution. These are files or tags that allow you to dictate whether or not a page should be indexed by search engines. Take, for example, the login page for a website powered by WordPress. There is no benefit to user experience in having this page indexed, and furthermore, it could also pose a security risk. As such, the owner of this site can insert a robots.txt file into her site so this page will not display in SERPs. Robots.txt is also useful for advertisement landing pages that you may not want indexed for fear of content duplication that could incur penalties.

When your sitemaps have been created, the next step is to create a GSC account, register, and verify your website on it. This can be done in a variety of ways, including uploading an HTML file on your web server and adding a meta tag on your homepage. Once verified, Google will start pulling data into your GSC account. Crawl issues, indexing frequency, search terms, ranking, click-throughs, and penalization are all areas that will be analyzed and reported on. Within your GSC dashboard you'll find an area to submit your XML sitemap as well, so make sure you do this!

GSC Tool Reports

Out of the multitude of features of GSC, the tool reports are definitely one of its finest. For each tool it offers, extremely detailed information can be derived and compared in a variety of different ways. You can filter data by country, mobile versus desktop versus tablets, and so on. Let's take a look at some of the key tools and reports that will be beneficial to you:

The *crawl error report* is particularly useful for monitoring your website's technical performance. It provides information about the URLs that Google can't access—most commonly due to 404 errors. After reviewing and fixing your crawl errors, make sure they're removed by marking them as fixed. That way when you log in you'll know the errors shown are new and need action. Crawling errors are flagging issues that search engines are having with accessing your web pages, which could be hurting your ranking—so be sure to keep an eye on this report and always aim to have no errors displayed in it.

The *inbound links report* will be particularly useful during the off-page optimization of your site, but it's also very useful at the on-page optimization stage. This particular report will tell you which websites are linking to yours, how many links these websites are generating, and the most popular pages on your site that are being linked to. It will also tell you the anchor text being used to link to your site.

The *page speed report* is a great, addictive tool for awakening the competitive SEO beast within you! It works by grading your site on a scale of 0 to 100, taking various factors like server response time, compression files, and image size into account. The report will detail which fixes are absolutely necessary, which are worth considering, and the areas in which you don't have any problems. Aim for 85/100 and higher. Results displayed in green mean you're above the 85 mark, orange signifies you're below 85 (at approximately 60–70/100), while the red indicates you have big problems that need your attention. Studies have shown that for every one-second delay on your website, conversions can decrease by 7 percent! Users will not wait around for a page to load, so a strong focus on the areas that will improve your speed is vital.

The *HTML improvements tool* is an invaluable report for flagging issues with a website's meta data, such as meta tags that are too long, too short, duplicated, or missing. Most importantly, it also shows issues with *canonicalization*. This term applies to individual web pages that can be accessed from multiple URLs, causing duplicate content—search engines hate this! For example, if users of a clothing website could access a page for red shoes by visiting www.example.com/red-shoes, www.example.com/new/red-shoes, and www.example.com/ladies/shoes/red, the search engine will see these three pages containing the same content but be unable to decide which URL to display in SERPs. This causes a canonicalization error. Using canonical links, you can redirect two of these URLs to the one page you do want Google to index, thereby solving the problem and minimizing the risk of being penalized. Although there may still be multiple pages with duplicate content, canonical links help limit the Google gods' canonical anxiety!

Google's Data Highlighter is an easy alternative to using schema microdata markup. Built into GSC, it's a point-and-click tool that allows you to mark up the data yourself, to provide better SERP snippets. Data Highlighter is an easy way of telling Google about the structured data on your web pages and is especially useful for website owners who may not have microdata or coding experience. You can mark up a wide variety of things, such as events, articles, local businesses, and products. You can highlight things such as a product's name and its reviews, the imagery, the author and date of an article, and the contact details for a local business. Have you ever seen an upcoming event's time and location listed in a Google SERP? With Data Highlighter you can do this too, making your event easier for users to discover and allowing you stand out from competitors!

Stage 3: Off-Page Optimization

With the on-page element of your website covered, it's now time to move into stage 3 of the SEO process, as highlighted in Figure 2.15—off-page optimization.

In comparison to on-page SEO, off-page SEO requires an entirely different skill set. Here, you can leave the technicalities behind and focus on being opportunistic, proactive, and competitive. In other words, channel that inner hustler! The purpose of off-page SEO is to improve your website ranking, based on the amount and quality of links coming into your site. Get ready to embrace your inner extrovert and also to:

- Know the key off-page techniques you can apply to improve website ranking.
- Appreciate the various forms of links and be able to distinguish among them.
- Learn about content marketing and its influence on off-page optimization.
- Recognize the potential factors within link building that can cause problems and penalization.

Figure 2.15   Focus on the Third Stage in the SEO Process

Let's take a look at the four main off-page techniques you can use to maximize your site's SERP ranking.

Link Formats

The first thing you need to understand about links is that they have two elements:

1 *Link text* refers to the text that appears on the page.
2 The *link URL* is the destination to which that link text will take the user.

Figure 2.16   Internal Linking

Internal links define linking within your own website content from one page to another. Consider them a vital element of the SEO process. They help spiders crawl your website and reach pages they wouldn't necessarily find, build digital footprints, enhance user experience, and contribute to ranking. Take a look at Figure 2.16 for an example of internal linking from DMI.

The links all navigate internally to areas of the website itself, and the anchor text is descriptive—pleasing all three key players. Customers know exactly where they're going, search engines can use the link and anchor text to understand the page content, and you, the website owner, benefit from higher ranking.

An *inbound link* is one that comes from another website and directs a user to your website. It is considered a determining factor in your site's ranking. Search engines believe more in what others say about you than what you say about yourself, and they measure this through inbound links. Think of them as votes of confidence and popularity—the more a site has, the more authority and credibility it will gain. This makes their links more important and considered worthy of higher rankings in SERPs.

There are four different link formats you need to need to know about. Choose them wisely—your off-page SEO could be helped or hindered depending on the format you use.

1 *Uninformative link*. A link that says something like *click here* is an uninformative link. Don't be afraid to use these words in a link; they are, after all, a definitive call to action. Just try be more descriptive, so that both customers and search engines know where they're being linked to.
2 *URL link*. A link such as www.vidalsassoon.com is a URL link. Don't just link to the homepage, find the most relevant page and link to that.
3 *Topic link*. A link such as *hair care* is a topic link; it's a good way of linking to sites that contain the same subject matter as the page the user is on.
4 *Keyword link*. A link with keywords, such as *hair styling with Vidal Sassoon*, is a keyword link. This is an excellent way of inserting keywords into your anchor text for an SEO boost.

Link Building

Once a hailed off-page strategy contributing greatly towards ranking, its influence is dwindling. Search engines are beginning to focus more upon user experience than the quantity of quality, inbound links. Regardless of this fact, a solid link-building strategy will still positively affect your ranking, but this will be entirely dependent on your level of commitment and good judgment. Start developing a strategy by asking yourself some of the following questions:

- Am I going to ask bloggers for links, and if so, how will I do it?
- Am I going to create valuable, relevant content and wait for inbound links to come naturally?
- Will I create my own links and where will I do it?
- Will I reach out to my customers and ask them to link to my website?

While inbound links are great, there is somewhat of a quality caste system, with some given higher priority and status than others. It's important that you focus on building high-quality inbound links so that you don't waste your time gathering links that aren't influential and contribute nothing to your off-page SEO. Take a look at the following suggested techniques you can use to develop your own strategy:

Evergreen content. This is content that will be forever relevant and fresh. Obviously if you're writing about the latest industry fad, that won't be possible, but keeping it evergreen is something you should always aim for. Evergreen content is of an extremely high quality, well researched, and will be used as a resource by others. It naturally develops inbound links and helps your domain become authoritative.

Influential blogs or social media. Links from these sites carry great authority and are widely sought after. While creating original, quality, entertaining content will help you get links on these sites, remember that popular blogs get hundreds of link requests daily. Increase your chances of getting that link by making yourself known in the industry and befriending the influencers. By networking in discussion forums and relevant sites, blogs, and social media, you can build rapport with like-minded people in your industry, making your link request stand out from the rest. Why not consider guest blogging? This is when you create content for publication on someone else's blog, which includes inbound links back to your own site. As always, only include links when appropriate and beneficial to the user experience. It's a great way of creating a public perception that you are a thought leader, helps ranking, and increases website traffic.

Local links. If you're running a local business, links from other local and relevant businesses, organizations, charities, social events, and media organizations are imperative. If you're a photographer, you could ask for links from florists, wedding planners, and wedding fair organizers. Seek out those who have authority and standing in your industry. Be sure to get yourself on local listing sites such as Google My Business, TripAdvisor, and Yelp. They will let search engines know key information about your business, such as proximity to the searcher, which will determine your site's positioning in SERPs.

Authoritative websites. These are the crème de la crème. A link from an authoritative website is the golden nugget of off-page SEO, so find out who is authoritative within your industry and chase that link for all it's worth! Government websites are automatically high authority but normally have policies about not linking to third-party websites. Contact companies you've used before, offering a well-written testimonial to be featured on their pages. They'll benefit from the positive review and you'll get an inbound link!

However, be aware that linking can be either one-way or reciprocal. A one-way link is when somebody links to you, whereas a reciprocal link is when you link to each other. When linking, think about the pages that you're linking to. A common problem with link building occurs when someone decides to link to your site. He naturally links to a homepage without spending the time to find the most relevant page. You should always be building links into the core sections of your website, not just the homepage. Control the link as much as possible by doing the work for the website you're requesting the link from. Provide a keyword link containing the URL of the page you want linked to with the anchor text you want used. By linking to the most relevant page, the digital footprint from all your web pages will expand—ultimately increasing your overall domain authority.

As if link building wasn't challenging enough, you need to be aware of the following factors that may cause problems with your link building strategies:

Flash content. Flash is an older method of creating movement in a website. Should flash content contain links, search engines may not be able to see or read it. A flash link is a wasted link, so be sure to flag any inbound links like this to the website owners. It could be the difference between a page one and page two SERP listing.

Brokers or sellers. With e-capitalism comes opportunists—some good, some bad. Of the bad variety are link-building brokers or sellers. Approach these companies with strong caution! While we shouldn't generalize, outsourcing this process usually results in a one step forward, ten steps back scenario. Here, inbound links generated tend to come from extremely low-quality websites that are irrelevant to your content. You will find that a lot of link-building sellers operate *link farms*—a group of websites set up solely for linking to one another. Algorithms understand these SEO malpractices and penalize for low-quality links. A sudden surge of inbound links will trigger suspicion, and should you be found to have links that are not organically built, you will suffer the ranking consequences!

Broken links. Always check for and replace broken inbound links. A website's link to you from last year could now be broken, costing you valuable ranking and conversions. Remember, pages you have deleted that haven't been redirected will result in broken links. If you happen to stumble across the broken link of a competitor on a high-authority site, use this to your advantage. Make the website owner aware of the issue and provide her with another relevant link from your site!

Damaging links. Not all links are good, and those that aren't can affect your ranking. Websites that are considered spammy by search engines will consider inbound links from these sites as unnatural and could penalize you as a result. Luckily, a disavow tool within GSC allows you to submit a list of links you would like Google to ignore. Should you discover damaging links, this tool will help claw back some of the ranking you may have lost as a result.

Content Marketing

The next phase of your link building strategy is content marketing. This involves creating and sharing valuable, informative, and entertaining content with the aim of attracting customers onto your site—in order to drive sales and conversions. It's more about showing customers that you have an expertise and passion for what you do than trying to sell to them. Articles, case studies, white papers, infographics, and videos are among the popular media used—so start thinking about how you can inform, educate and solve problems for your customers. Having an article recognized and shared will help build credibility within your industry, increasing ranking and your domain authority. Aim to be an expert in your niche, so that people will immediately think of your site and link to it when that topic arises. For content marketing the same rules apply. Make sure to on-page optimize your content fully—with keywords, meta tags, headings, and so on.

Social Sharing

The fourth element of off-page optimization involves getting people to share your content across their social media networks—in other words, social sharing. You probably will have already seen social-sharing buttons while surfing the web. These are the small icons on social media platforms that allow users to easily share content from their own social media accounts.

Whenever possible, support every piece of content you create with social-sharing buttons. They facilitate free advertising for your site, increase your digital footprint, and generate brand awareness at the hands of your customers. You've put your blood, sweat, and tears into creating compelling content that entertains and informs the reader. What's the point in doing that if your customers can't share it? Conveniently placed Twitter, Facebook, and LinkedIn share buttons should be positioned throughout your site to allow customers to share your content quickly and easily across their networks. Algorithms are placing increasingly more emphasis on popularity as a ranking factor, to help them distinguish between quality content and poor content. As such, search engines are now taking social endorsements into account. As with inbound links, the more shares you get, the better! The ideal scenario is to have many individual sites linking to you, rather than having few websites generating lots of links.

Off-page SEO is not too dissimilar to networking. You need to mix in the right circles, be ready to jump at opportunities, and try to engage in conversation with that top dog before your competitor does. Ultimately you're trying to optimize your site to increase ranking, but also try aiming beyond that. Aim to become that top-dog authoritative site that people will spend countless hours chasing for links. It does involve working from the ground up, but the benefits are worth the effort!

Stage 4: Analyze

We've now reached the final stretch, and by this stage your website should be fully optimized, yielding lots of organic traffic with conversions to match! Remember in the first stage of the SEO process you set well-defined goals? Now is the time to analyze and review your performance against these goals so that when you start this process again, informed changes can be made to them. This is stage 4 of the process, as highlighted in Figure 2.17.

Prepare for a big dose of déjà vu and the skills to:

- Know the analytics tools that allow you track and measure search traffic.
- Be able to identify the KPIs of SEO and measure success against them.
- Use specific criteria to measure your website's performance.
- Be aware of the key features, tools, and reports in GA that help with SEO performance analysis.
- Understand the laws and guidelines associated with SEO.

Figure 2.17   Focus on the Fourth Stage in the SEO Process

At this stage you need to be aware of the volume of traffic coming into your site, where it's coming from, what the users are doing there, what keywords or content is bringing them in, and what pages are driving or expelling conversions. Luckily, there are tons of analytics tools to help answer all these questions—Moz and HubSpot are great, but Google Analytics is definitely the most highly regarded. It's free, has a huge variety of highly detailed data, and is easy to digest.

Before you can start using a tool like GA, take a look at the following criteria against which you'll need to measure your website's performance. Answer these questions and you'll be guiding yourself in the right direction towards improving your SEO efforts and understanding your customers:

- Can your website be found? How visible is it?
- What position are you in SERPs?

- Is your on-page technical SEO complete?
- Which sites rank above yours?
- How many web pages are indexed?
- Which traffic is coming in via general keywords and which via more targeted keywords?
- How many conversions come from each keyword?

Recording your performance is the only way of rating your own SEO activities, so compile all this data and create a report on your findings. In the early days of a new SEO project, analyze your activities weekly or biweekly. Once things start falling into place you can start looking at performance on a monthly basis. Don't become complacent—competitors are always lurking around the corner, waiting to pounce on your position.

Once you have compiled a detailed criteria report of your findings, you can then measure your SEO successes or failures, using these three KPIs:

1 *Position*. Where are you ranking in SERPs? This KPI is significant because it shows the effectiveness of the SEO measures you've applied to get good search positioning, based on relevant search terms. Your position can be gauged by using SEO tools like Google Search Console and Moz.
2 *Traffic*. What traffic is coming in, where is it coming from, and what content is being visited? This KPI measures the search volumes achieved for relevant terms and is the basis for calculating conversions. Use GA to review traffic source reports, visitor numbers, and the volume of traffic achieved based on the keywords selected.
3 *Conversion*. Is your organic SEO creating conversions? This is another important KPI because it relates the volume and relevance of your search traffic with some predefined objectives. Using GA, you can find conversion information to measure goals achieved, sales, leads, and inbound calls.

Within a typical dashboard page in GA, goal and event tracking are among the most important features. Ensure you have these enabled, as these are the tools that will allow you to see where the traffic is coming from and whether or not you're getting conversions. Events are distinguished by user engagements such as video views, document downloads, social shares, and the like. Goals are actions like newsletter sign-ups, web-form submissions, purchases, and so on.

An Ongoing Process

As with all aspects of SEO, analysis and review is an ongoing process. Dedication and commitment will bring you far—so by regularly carrying out these three easy tasks, you can boost your site's SEO performance ahead of your competitors:

1 Maintain a weekly or monthly calendar measuring your website performance against your baseline.
2 It's important to be able to associate peaks in traffic to certain marketing activities. In GA people forget to record other marketing, PR, or competitions they're doing offline.

Suddenly they see a spike in traffic, forgetting they've been carrying out other activities that are the reason for the spike.

3 Assess the impact of your SEO activities, spot any trends resulting from them, and identify any remedial action needed.

Customer retention is the key to conversion, so bounce rates should be minimized at all costs. If your GA dashboard shows a high bounce rate, don't panic—investigate! Find which pages, keywords, and traffic sources are causing the bounce rate and make the appropriate changes. With that said, a bounce isn't always a bad thing. A SERP will display the appropriate page for someone looking for your opening times. The user will visit it, check the information, and leave. This will be classified as a bounce, so spend time getting to know and understand your GA dashboard—if you don't, you could end up trying to fix something that isn't broken.

Law and Order: SEO

With cyberattacks and identity theft occurring every minute, data protection is something that has become widely expected by customers, search engines, and governing authorities. You need to be aware of the governing laws and regulations within your territory, not only to protect customers but also to protect your own website and reputation. Nobody will visit or buy from a site known to be unsafe.

Cookies are data files stored on users' browsers that track snippets of their online behavior. They're great for gaining a better insight into user habits and leveraging this data to enhance user experience. With SEO, you are legally obligated to notify users that your site uses cookies. Be forthright about it; users will appreciate the honesty. Plagiarism isn't just something you can get caught for in your schoolwork—it is a legal offense! Do your utmost to steer clear of any and all copyright issues. Make sure you have the licensing rights to borrow images, credit all content that's not your own, and where possible, create your own!

So, What Have You Learned in This Chapter?

That's it! We've come full circle in the SEO process—you can go back to the start of the chapter and begin the process all over again! Now with the knowledge, skills, and ability to fully optimize your site, go kick those competitors far into page two of SERPs. As you do, remember these tips:

- Use the DMI's 5P Customer Search Model to understand customer behavior and ensure your content is relevant.
- When it comes to selecting your keywords, the more research the better!
- Remember that search engines have a preference for responsive websites, so adapt your site accordingly.

- Customize your 404 error page to limit the damage to user experience—stand out from the crowd!
- Make connections with the right people to optimize your link-building strategy.

Finally, be aware that the rules of SEO change frequently—stay ahead of the curve and educate yourself by reading industry-leading articles and blogs.

Go to www.artofdmi.com to access the case study on SEO as additional support material for this chapter.

 **Exercises**

Exercise 1

You are a smartphone retail outlet selling to the U.S. market and want to research target search terms for your iPhone 7 accessories page.

Set up an account in Google AdWords.

- Under Tools, click Keyword Planner and Search for New Keywords.
- Select AdGroups Ideas.
- Type in five keywords or phrases; for example, iPhone 7 accessories, or something similar.
- Choose your target country and click Get Ideas.
- Visit the Keyword Ideas tab.
- Note how many average monthly searches have been completed for your chosen keywords or search terms.

Exercise 2

Go to a website that you visit regularly and access the source code of the page. (Right click on the page text and select View Source Code.) Complete a search in the source code by pressing Ctrl F.

- Does the web page include an H1?
- Is the H1 the main page headline?
- Does the H1 include a core message for the user?
- Is there any sign that the H1 is optimized for searching (are there any keywords included in it)?
- Is the site using the additional headings H2 through H6? Is it creating correct page and content structure?

Exercise 3

Using the same page as in the previous exercise, complete the following:

1 Search for the title. It should be placed near the top of the page (<title> title text </title>). This is the metatitle for the page.
   - Is the target keyword included in the title?
   - Is the title under 60 characters?
2 Search for the description. It should be placed near the top of the page (<meta-name="description" content="description text"/>). This is the metadescription for the page.
   - Is there a description visible?
   - Is the target keyword included?
   - Is it under 160 characters?

Exercise 4

Create a piece of search-optimized content for your website that will assist your customers during their research stage (to generate brand awareness). This content can take any form—for example, text, infographic, video, or audio—but must have a text element that can be optimized. Research your keywords and optimize all key on-page elements.

Exercise 5

Visit www.opensiteexplorer.org. Enter the URL for your website and click search. Note the domain authority and page authority. Now click Compare Link Metrics (on the left). Enter the URL for a competitor's website and scroll to the domain authority section.

- Who scores the best domain and page authority?
- Which site has the best quality links (check MozRank and MozTrust)?
- Which site has the most followed linking root domains?

 ## Action Plan: Search Engine Optimization

Digital Marketing Planning Scheme for Search Engine Optimization

Objectives

Positioning, engagement, conversions, competitive advantage

Action Items

- On page: Keyword research, content updates, metadata, UX
- Off page: Link baiting, cross-linking, directory listing, guest blogging, search engine submission

Frequency

- On page: Daily and weekly content updates with relevant keywords
- Off page: Weekly and monthly actions and review (outreach and inbound links)

Measurement Tools and KPIs

- Analytics, Webmaster Tools, Moz: Position, rank, click-through rate, visitors, conversions, website performance
- Diagnostics: Error 404 pages, blocked robots.txt, faulty backlinks

Spend

Media	Content	People	Systems
	x	x	

Chapter 3
Pay Per Click

An Introduction

Appearing in the number-one position of a SERP is no easy feat, but what if you were told that SEO was not the only way to achieve this mammoth accomplishment? Search marketing, in particular pay-per-click (PPC) advertising, is another lucrative option available to you. The difference between SEO and PPC, however, is in the name—you have got to *pay* for PPC!

Have you ever noticed those three listings at the top of a SERP with a yellow ad icon beside them, almost unfairly pushing down organic search listings? Those are the product of PPC-savvy digital marketers, reaping the benefits of high click-through rates (CTRs) by paying a little extra.

> Formal definition of PPC: The revenue model adopted by search engines whereby the advertiser pays only when a user clicks on an ad.
>
> Informal definition of PPC: A fairer playing field for big and small advertisers alike.

Process

Just like SEO, PPC has its own four-stage iterative process, which you can see in Figure 3.1. With this form of advertising every cent counts, and with the added element of expenditure you need to maintain an astute attention to detail so as to not spend your budget frivolously. Take a look at each of these four stages so you know exactly what is in store for you in this chapter!

1 *Set your goals.* Before beginning and investing in your PPC journey, you first need to learn about the benefits PPC can bring to your business. With this knowledge you can then define exactly what your goals will be and how to align KPIs with them.

Figure 3.1   Four-Stage PPC Process

2 *Set up your account.* In this stage you will be guided step-by-step through every element involved in setting up your very own Google AdWords account, from creating PPC campaigns to assigning budgets—you will learn it all!

3 *Manage your campaigns.* This stage details what happens after your campaigns have been launched and how best to manage them. The finer details of the AdWords interface will also be explored to help you discover the variety of options you can implement to yield a higher return on investment (ROI).

4 *Analyze your results.* The final stage in the PPC process is all about measuring your success through KPIs, tools, and reports. By using this data you will be able to better optimize your campaigns for the next iteration, while considering the relevant data protection and privacy issues associated with PPC.

Key Terms and Concepts

Not only will this chapter demonstrate how to implement and manage search advertising campaigns, it will ultimately equip you with the technical understanding and skills needed to become a master in building an effective PPC strategy! Your PPC apprenticeship starts here, and by the end of this chapter you will:

- Understand the key concepts, benefits, and goals associated with PPC advertising.
- Know how to create an AdWords account, assign access levels, and implement a coherent campaign architecture.
- Appreciate the importance of ad rank and quality score and how to calculate them.
- Be able to choose the optimal keywords for your ads, which can be delivered and scheduled in line with your bidding strategy.
- Learn the optimal way of crafting ad copy and landing pages for your campaigns and how to remarket to users.

- Configure your AdWords dashboard to suit your business.
- Segment data through a variety of reporting tools within the AdWords interface.
- Align your bidding strategies with KPIs.

Stage 1: Goals

As with SEO, the importance of defining and setting goals for paid search cannot be stressed enough. With a core grasp of the basics, let's delve deeper and begin stage 1 of PPC's own iterative process, which is highlighted in Figure 3.2. By the end of this section, you will have developed:

- An appreciation of the benefits PPC marketing can bring.
- An understanding of ad rank and quality score and how to calculate both.
- The ability to choose and set paid search campaign goals and KPIs.

Figure 3.2   Focus on the First Stage in the PPC Process

Goals: What's the Point?

Goal setting can be a laborious task, so before discussing how exactly this should be done, take a look at the key benefits of paid search to see why the effort is worthwhile!

- *Relevance*. Delivering answers to the multitude of questions searched for on a daily basis is not feasibly possible and fortunately isn't necessary either. The relationship between users, search engines, and marketers has taken a strange turn. People now view search engines as problem solvers, with we marketers acting as agony aunts who provide relevant solutions to their queries at the precise moment they ask. Paid search is all about relevancy—it allows us to reach the right people (those who are interested), find search queries related to our businesses, and look for ways to solve customer pain.

- *Timing*. Paid search lets us reach users at exactly the right time, which is essential. You need to be astute in understanding user search intentions and you also need to be able to match their search queries to specific times of the day. For example, matching a 24-hour locksmith with someone searching for *how do I fix a broken lock* at 9:00 P.M. would provide an excellent answer for that user while increasing conversion potential dramatically.
- *Self-qualifying users*. When a user enters search queries that ask questions such as *I need an answer*, *I have a problem*, or *I'm looking for a product* and your brand can answer those queries, then you have a qualified visitor. Traditionally, finding and targeting these customers was a tricky feat. With PPC, however, users can be brought directly to your site with minimal effort on your part.
- *Cost effectiveness*. Those of you who are frugal-minded marketers can take solace in knowing that your budget will be hit only when a user clicks your ad. Although a not-for-me verdict from users is not ideal, there is still a lot of benefit to this lost conversion. Even if users don't click the ad, it will still have increased brand awareness, and you didn't have to pay one cent for it. To maximize this frugality, be sure your ad actually delivers what it promises. Users are smart and will quickly exit your site if they discover you can't offer the service they require—meaning the money you paid for that click will be wasted.
- *Control*. Ultimately, the power to control every aspect of your ad campaign is the biggest benefit paid search can offer. You can make decisions such as:
  - How much to spend and bid
  - What you wish to show for the campaign
  - How often and at what times of the day your ad appears

The Not-So-Secret Formula

The Google AdWords ranking formula decides where your ad is displayed in a SERP. Your goal as an advertiser is to appear first—or at least within the top three ad results displayed at the top of the page. To do this, you really need to take a look at Figure 3.3

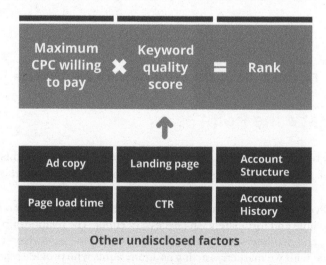

Figure 3.3   Google AdWords Ranking Formula

and understand the two key components of the ranking formula, which underpin everything to do with your campaign. So sit up, strap on your thinking cap, and start taking notes!

1 *Cost per click (CPC)*. Uncannily similar to an auction, you place a bid on the maximum amount of money you are willing to pay when someone clicks on your ad.
2 *Quality score*. With every keyword you create, a relevancy/quality score of 1 to 10 is assigned—1 being the highest. This score is then multiplied by your maximum cost-per-click bid to calculate your ranking—it's easy! Achieving a higher ranking will cost a lot less with higher quality scores because the two are multiplied together. Let's pretend 10 advertisers are bidding on the keyword *red shoes*. Every advertiser bidding in the auction is placed on a scale of 1 to 10, depending on how many ad positions are available on the page. Within a split second, the scores of each bidder are calculated and their ad ranking is determined.

There are also a number of other factors to consider that contribute towards your quality score, such as:

- *CTR*. An advertiser who historically has a CTR of 4 percent will be given a higher quality score than a competitor with a CTR of 2 percent. A high CTR indicates that the advertiser's campaigns are relevant to user search queries and the advertiser is rewarded as a result.
- *Landing page*. These are stand-alone webpages dedicated to specific products or services that you want your customers to focus on exclusively. Quality scores will also be bumped if users are brought to a relevant, fast-loading landing page that references the search queries they entered.
- *Ad copy*. Ads should contain the search term entered and direct users to a relevant landing page in order to achieve higher quality scores.
- *Account performance*. With Google, hard work never goes unnoticed. If your AdWords account and its campaigns have been performing well over a period of time, Google will view you as a very strong advertiser that works hard to provide relevant results to your consumers—and reward you as a result.

All this information is great, but what if you have never run an AdWords campaign before, and Google has no campaign history on which to base your quality score? In this case, it primarily comes down to the search query entered and the keywords you choose. Google will look at how that particular keyword has performed over time and on that basis assign a quality score. Ad copies and landing pages will still be considered, so don't forget about those!

How to Set Goals

Now that you've been enlightened about the powers that PPC possesses, take a look at these four steps for setting goals. The flowchart shown in Figure 3.4 comes from Avinash Kaushik, an analytics guru at Google. The process involves initially focusing on broad business objectives, assigning goals to each objective, and identifying the

Figure 3.4   Avinash Kaushik's DUMB Objectives

associated KPIs in order to convert the broad objectives into very specific campaign objectives.

1 *Define your business objectives.* If you haven't defined any business objectives, now is the time to decide what they are. They may entail generating more revenue, increasing brand awareness, or retaining existing customers. Once your objectives are defined, you need to map them onto a time frame: Are you trying to achieve a particular objective this month, this quarter, or this year?

2 *Develop goals.* Next you need to develop goals for each business objective. For example, if your business objective is to increase brand awareness, you may decide the corresponding goal is to increase traffic to your site.

3 *Identify your KPIs.* With your business objectives set and their corresponding goals assigned, you can then start identifying KPIs to track your success. Brochure downloads, CTRs, and unique visitors are examples of KPIs that could be used to measure your goal of increasing website traffic.

4 *Identify your targets.* The final step involves identifying targets. These are numerical values you have predetermined as indicators of success or failure. For example, by Q2 you want 250,000 visitors to your site.

When defining objectives, the dumber the better! In his blog "Occam's Razor," Avinash defines it as:

<u>D</u>oable
<u>U</u>nderstandable
<u>M</u>anageable
<u>B</u>eneficial

Don't fool yourself. Saying you want to increase revenue by $300,000 a month when you know you have only ever made $100,000 a month is not realistic. Set yourself achievable goals that contribute to the value of your business. If your goal is to drive online sales, don't strive to create more brand awareness if you hold the largest market share.

Business goals feed into KPIs, so hitting and exceeding your KPIs will eventually contribute to achieving your goals and ultimately contribute to the success of your business. The type of KPI used depends on the type of campaign, which can be broken down into the following three areas:

1 *Direct response.* These are essentially sales-focused campaigns. They require hard conversions such as a purchase, sale, or lead. The main KPIs you should be concerned with here are the conversion rate, cost per conversion, and efficiency in generating conversions.
2 *Branding and awareness campaigns.* From a branding point of view, the focus in these campaigns would veer towards prominence in SERPs and the CTR response to the campaign. Here the three key KPIs worth your attention would be your average position in SERPs, CTR, and CPC.
3 *Engagement campaigns.* The ancient mantra *quality over quantity* is demonstrated in its purest form in engagement campaigns. These campaigns are not about volume of traffic or quantity of conversions, but rather about driving user engagement with your brand and gaining quality traffic. When assessing CTRs for these campaigns look at the rate at which people are responding, user interest in your product or service, and the amount of time spent on the site.

Well-defined goals will help you to keep on track as we progress on to stage 2 of the PPC process. Make your goals as DUMB as possible and success won't be far behind!

Stage 2: Setup

Part One

The PPC wheels are now in motion, and having defined some tangible goals, the fun part can begin. Let's create some campaigns! As you can see in Figure 3.5, setup is the second stage of the process. With so many detailed yet vital elements required to complete the setup, we have divided this stage of the process in two parts. Upon completion of this section, your mastery of PPC setup will be half complete with a core knowledge of:

• Google AdWords account creation and access levels
• Campaign setup and architecture
• PPC targeting and location

Creating a Google AdWords Account

Google wants a fair playing field for everybody—both big advertisers and small, tech nerds and technophobes. Designed to please the masses, navigating the Google AdWords interface is easy and efficient, so let's set it up!

Figure 3.5   Focus on the Second Stage in the PPC Process

Do you have a Google account? Those of you with Gmail will have automatically been assigned one. If you don't have one, sign up for Gmail—it's the easiest way to get a Google account, which is required to create an AdWords account. The setup consists of four easy steps. Start by entering your email address and website URL. The next step throws you straight in the deep end by asking you to create a live campaign. At this stage you are not yet ready to create a campaign, so let's go through the steps and fill in the bare minimum. You can return to this step at a later stage.

As you can see from Figure 3.6, there are a series of fields you need to complete, so let's go through each of them:

- *Budget*. For this setup, enter a spend of $0.01—it will be unlikely to run. Budgets are always set at a daily level. Calculate daily budgets by dividing your monthly budget by 30.4.
- *Locations*. Choose the countries and regions you want to target here.
- *Networks*. For now, select Search Network. There are technically two and a half networks. The Search Network is used for Google Search and the Display Network is used for all of Google's partner websites, such as Gmail, YouTube, Blogger, and so on. The extra half a network comes from Google search partners, which you can opt in or out of. It is used to display in search engines powered by Google—Ask.com and eBay, for example. We will come back to these areas later in the chapter.
- *Keywords*. As it says on the tin, enter the keywords you created in Chapter 2. Otherwise, add in one sample keyword and come back to this section later.
- *Bid*. Enter $0.01 for the time being. This field is asking you to set your maximum bid. Budgets vary from business to business, but a recommended maximum bid of $1.50 will suffice. Google AdWords will let you know if your bid is too high or too low, allowing you to then adjust your maximum bid accordingly.

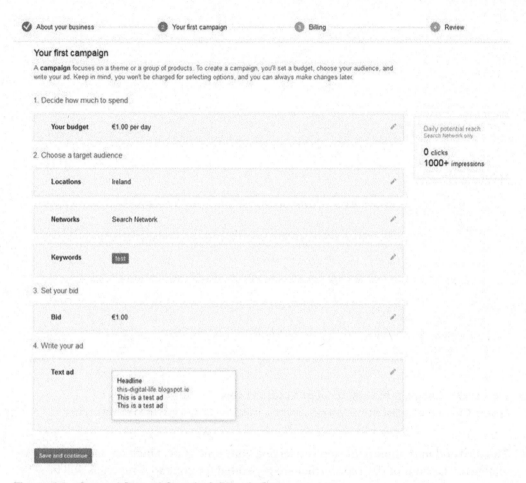

Figure 3.6   Second Step of Google AdWords Setup

Source: Google and the Google logo are registered trademarks of Google Inc.; used with permission.

- *Text ad*. Complete the ad copy according to the outlined character limits and restrictions—you can revisit this section again. We will cover it in greater detail later in the chapter.

Bills, Bills, Bills. When you are done, hit Save and Continue. The billing section comes next. You will have to enter in a payment method or your campaigns won't run. For tax and payment type purposes, be sure to select the country you are based in as your billing country. You then need to decide how you want to pay:

Automatic payments. This option works by automatically taking money out of your account when you reach a certain threshold, or after 30 days—whichever comes first. The benefit of this payment method lies in its ability to keep campaigns running if you forget or don't have the time to add money to your account. Just make sure you monitor your budget closely to avoid overspends.

Manual payments. If having total fiscal control floats your boat, this is the payment method for you. Here, you manually add your budget up front and Google will deduct from it every time somebody clicks on your ad. When the budget runs dry, your ads will stop.

Account Access level	Email-only	Read-only	Standard	Administrative	Managed - Standard	Managed - Read-only
Can receive notification emails and reports	✓	✓	✓	✓	✓	✓
Can sign in and run reports		✓	✓	✓	✓	✓
Can browse the Campaigns, Opportunities, and Tools tabs		✓	✓	✓	✓	✓
Can unlink manager accounts			✓	✓	✓	✓
Can view and edit any part of an account and its campaigns, including Billing			✓	✓	✓	
Can give account access, change access levels, and can cancel invitations from other users				✓		

Figure 3.7   Google AdWords Account Access Levels
Source: Google and the Google logo are registered trademarks of Google Inc.; used with permission.

The final and most important step is selecting your time zone. Once set, it can't be changed. The hour of day reports that are generated for your ad campaigns will be set according to the time zone you select, so be sure to pick the right one.

User Access. With your account set up, you may now decide to let some people in on the PPC action. To do this, you will need to assign different user access levels—of which there are four. Click the little gear icon on the top right-hand corner of the page and from there select Account Settings. Take a look at the table in Figure 3.7, which highlights all the features and limitations of each access level.

Campaign Architecture

Establishing a well-structured, consistent architecture at the very beginning of any campaign is of the utmost importance! Not doing so will make it agonizingly difficult to fix when you start adding more campaigns, ads, and keywords. Believe it or not, a poorly structured account can actually impact your quality score, which means for every click on your ad, you are paying more. Take a look at Figure 3.8, which shows how your AdWords account should be structured.

Top level. Campaigns appear at the top level and all budgeting is done here. You can configure language, target locations, and set your daily spend here too.

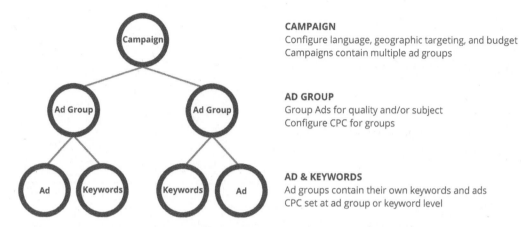

CAMPAIGN
Configure language, geographic targeting, and budget
Campaigns contain multiple ad groups

AD GROUP
Group Ads for quality and/or subject
Configure CPC for groups

AD & KEYWORDS
Ad groups contain their own keywords and ads
CPC set at ad group or keyword level

Figure 3.8   Google AdWords Account Structure Model

Middle level. Within each campaign you have ad groups. These house all the keywords and ads that you are going to target users with, and they should always be defined by a single theme. For example, you'd define one ad group for *red shoes* and another for *blue shoes*. *Bottom level.* The keywords within the ad group should specifically relate to the theme. For example, the *red shoes* ad group should have keywords like *new red shoes*, *cheap red shoes*, *red shoes online*, and so on. Use 10 to 20 keywords in an ad group.

Only one specific domain per ad group is permitted. This means if you have the domain www.example.com assigned to one ad group, you cannot also assign www.example.co .uk to the same ad group. You will have to create a separate ad group if you wish to do that. You can, however, have different landing pages from a domain within an ad group—for example, www.example.com/blog and www.example.com/choose.

Campaign Setup

Let's now take a look at how to create a campaign within the Google AdWords interface. As you can see from Figure 3.9, the tabs available are Home, Campaigns, Opportunities, Reports, and Tools. Click the red + Campaign button to open a drop-down menu that will provide you with a range of different options for creating campaigns. If you plan to ever run a Display campaign, make sure your Display and Search campaigns run independently of each other so that you can monitor the performance of each one separately. In this chapter, however, we are going to focus on the Search Network—so click that option.

You will then be brought to the campaign setup screen, as seen in Figure 3.10, where you should enter your campaign name. Campaigns and ad groups need to follow a very consistent naming convention in order to adhere to account structure best practices. For your own sanity, ignore the generic suggestions in Figure 3.10 and don't name them Campaign #1 and Ad Group #1. Make sure everything is named in a way that makes what you are looking for easy to find.

Figure 3.9   Specifying the Google AdWords Campaign Type

Source: Google and the Google logo are registered trademarks of Google Inc.; used with permission.

Next you need to choose whether you want your campaign to have Standard or All features. You can also choose to incorporate a CTA (call to action) button on the ad with options to call your business, download your app, and so on. For now, click on Standard. The next screen will ask you to choose between the Google Search and the Search Partners networks. If you don't have budget limitations and want to get as much visibility and CTR as possible, choose both. The recommendation is to start with both. You can then carry out a performance review later and decide which, if either, should be removed.

Targeting

Did you know you can choose the device you want to target? Your campaigns should be running in line with the types of devices you want to reach. In the targeting section you will notice you have been automatically opted in to target all devices. After a campaign

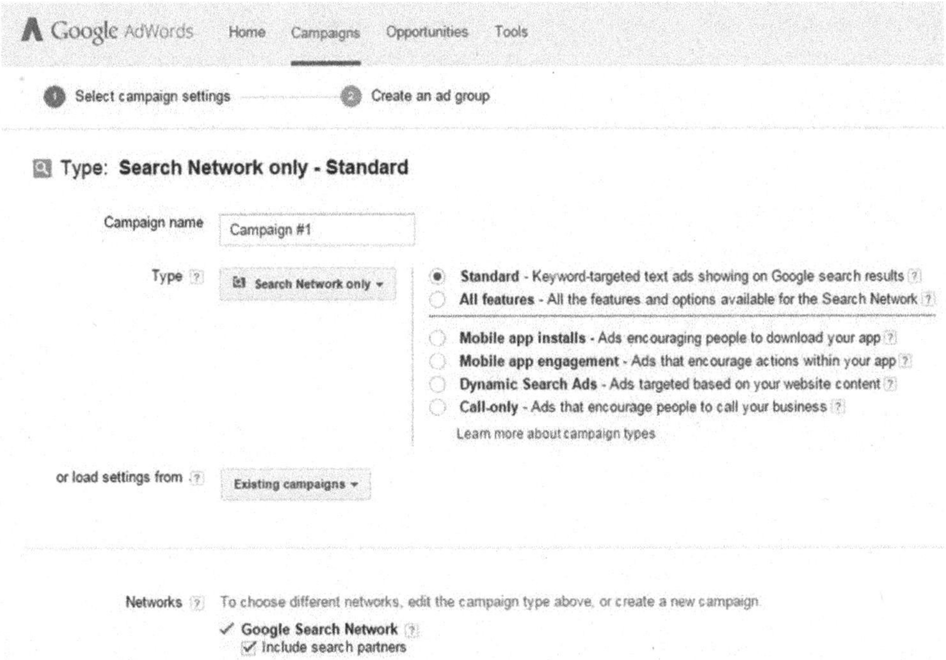

Figure 3.10   Google AdWords Campaign Setup

Source: Google and the Google logo are registered trademarks of Google Inc.; used with permission.

has been created, you can amend this and opt out of any specific devices you don't want to appear on. This could prove useful for those who have yet to optimize their websites for mobile, for example. You can't opt out from appearing on desktops or tablets. When starting off, try initially opting in to all devices; run a report on devices at a later stage to see how they perform.

Targeting by location is one of the best and most detailed features AdWords has to offer. It can be done in two ways:

1 *IP address targeting*. Selecting this option will direct Google to look at the IP address of users to see where they are based. So if you are targeting Boston, Massachusetts, then users with an IP address in that area will be served, whereas users in Phoenix, Arizona, will not.
2 *Query parsing*. This option directs Google to focus on what was typed in users' search queries. If they type a location into their search queries then the ad can also come up. For example, if the campaign is targeting Boston and a user based in Phoenix includes the word *Boston* in her search query, this will override the IP address targeting and show the user in Phoenix the ad.

As you can see in Figure 3.11, there are three options for you to target your campaigns by location:

1 *All countries and territories*. Really, there is no reason why anyone should ever target all countries and territories. If you want to target your campaigns globally, create separate

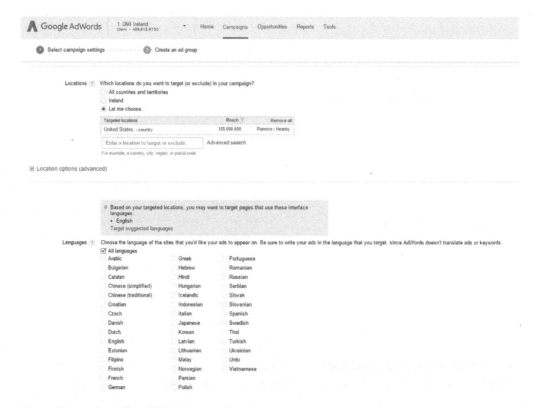

Figure 3.11   Google AdWords Campaign Setup
Source: Google and the Google logo are registered trademarks of Google Inc.; used with permission.

campaigns for each country. No one market is the same. Consumer behaviors, buying habits, product/service requirements, and device preferences vary greatly from country to country. For example, consumers in Africa are extremely mobile-savvy and prefer mobile over using a desktop. Bearing this in mind, mobile usage reports in Africa would be vastly different in comparison to the same report on UK consumers—meaning a one-for-all campaign would not fit. In summary, do not tick that box!

2 *Your country.* The next option will present you with the country you set your time zone to, in this example—The United States.

3 *Let me choose.* This is where it gets really detailed. Either enter the city or country you want to target or hit Advanced Search beside the text box. Here you will be presented with the following four target options:

i. *Search.* This is simply another method of entering your target city or country, as before.

ii. *Radius targeting.* Here you can type in a location and target a specific radius around it. If your business relies on foot traffic, this feature can be used to target customers within a certain radius of your business. Similarly, if you just have one store in one location and don't want to target an entire country, you can just target a radius around that particular store to acquire more qualified customers. The default is set to 20 miles, but that can be changed. Bear in mind that the location you enter in the search box will be seen as the central point of the radius. So when deciding on a central location, make sure your radius is covering land and not the sea, because for the most part our fishy friends don't have Internet access.

iii. *Location groups.* Here you can target multiple locations for a particular campaign. For example, you may want to target 20 miles around one region and 5 miles around another. Use this option to group these regions together into one super location group.

iv. *Bulk locations.* While it is not recommended, if you want to target multiple countries, use this option.

The final element within the targeting setup is to choose and customize your language. By default, the campaign will be set to target the language in which your account was set up. You can also target other languages, but be aware that the language you target might not be the language the user is searching in. For example, if a user searches in Arabic but his language on Google is set to English, you won't be targeting him. You should also be aware that when targeting other languages AdWords does not translate your ads. If you choose to target Arabic speakers and your ad is in English, these users will still see an ad in English.

Part one of the setup has now reached an end, but before you decompress it's time to go back, review, and edit the elements of your campaign that were glossed over. You need to be fully prepared for what part two has in store!

Part Two

By now, your account has been set up and your access levels, targeting, and location have all been defined. Without further ado, allow this section teach you how to get your AdWords account off the ground, so you can begin some seriously stellar PPC advertising by:

• Deciding upon the appropriate bid strategy for your business.
• Being aware of the various options to deliver and schedule your ads.
• Knowing how to use the optimal tools for keyword selection.
• Mastering the skill of choosing between keyword match types.

Bid Strategy

Let's kick off by choosing a bidding strategy. As you've just been introduced to the enticing world of Google AdWords, for now stick to either of the two options listed below. When you have become a true PPC Jedi, you can then begin to navigate the more advanced options.

1 *Manual bidding.* This option allows you to control all bidding and essentially works the same as the setting for your payment method. Even though it does give you more control, it also means you have to log in more often to manage your campaign.

2 *Automatic bidding.* Here, you are passing some of the control to Google—which is great for the busy executive but problematic for the control freak. A happy medium between these two lies in the ability to set a so-called ceiling bid. This is when you tell AdWords the maximum bid you are willing to pay without bidding more than that amount. It will then automatically adjust your bid—doing the work for you!

Which bid strategy are *you* going to use?

After this decision has been made, you need to set your default bid. Always bid between $1.50 and $2.00, because once you have gone through the campaign creation process, the system will tell you if you are below the minimum price it costs to display in the top three results of page 1, or at the very least, on page 1 itself.

Next up: setting your daily budget. You can figure this out by determining how much you are going to spend and dividing it by the number of days the ad will run. You should note that once your campaign goes live, AdWords can overspend on your daily budget by up to 20 percent. Similarly, there are days when it will spend a little less. Whatever the case may be, rest assured it will rarely spend more than 30 times your daily budget in a 30-day period. And if this situation does arise, Google will credit you the cost of the overage, meaning you get all those clicks for free! This is because search is based on demand, and so search volumes can vary greatly. As a result, daily budgets are never really set in stone.

Delivery

How quickly you want your ad to be served is dependent on the delivery method you select, and there are two options to choose from:

1 *Standard delivery.* If your budget is limited or has yet to be determined, this is the option for you, shown in the middle of Figure 3.12. It will space out how often your ads are displayed, giving you a fairly even delivery. For example, if in spreading your budget evenly Google estimates that it will only show your ad for approximately 40 to 50 percent of all searches pertaining to your product/service, it will only show your ad in every second search. When the time comes to optimize your campaigns, this option will give you a good idea of what times of the day your ad performs well. You should always set your delivery to standard and monitor performance; if you find that you are not hitting your daily budget, you can move onto the next option—accelerated delivery.
2 *Accelerated delivery.* If your budget is in any way limited, steer clear of this option! Here your ad will be displayed each and every time someone searches—in line with the ad rank formula, of course. So if your quality score and bid are good enough, your ad will display when someone searches. If your quality score and ad rank as a whole are too low, the ad will not display—even if it's set to accelerated delivery. There's no cheating in AdWords: Quality score and ad rank principles override everything! While this delivery method certainly gives you more bang for your buck, you should be cautious. If your ad is set to accelerated delivery and you have a limited budget, it could be drained entirely in just a few hours!

Ad Scheduling

You have already decided where and how often your ad is going to show, now let's determine when. Firstly, choose your start and end date. If you want the ad to run for the foreseeable future, simply leave the end date out, as shown in Figure 3.13. If your campaign is not starting for another few weeks, this feature is really useful because you

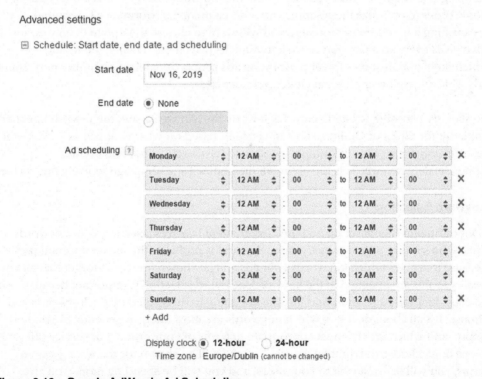

Figure 3.12   Google AdWords Delivery Method
Source: Google and the Google logo are registered trademarks of Google Inc.; used with permission.

Figure 3.13   Google AdWords Ad Scheduling
Source: Google and the Google logo are registered trademarks of Google Inc.; used with permission.

can leave the campaign enabled and it will automatically kick into gear when the start date arrives. If you have a fixed end date and your ad is concerning a time-sensitive offer, then you should set an end date for the campaign.

Ad scheduling is particularly useful for businesses with fixed opening hours that may only wish to show during the hours they're open. Or if your budget is very limited, and you know from previous campaigns that most sales occur at specific times, you can set your campaign to show during those hours.

Ad Rotation

When it comes to creating your campaign, you will see that the best practice for ad copy dictates that you have two to three ads per ad group. This setting determines how the ads that you create are rotated within that ad group. There are four options:

1 Optimize for clicks
2 Optimize for conversions
3 Rotate evenly
4 Rotate indefinitely

The default is to optimize for clicks, which shows the ad that is most likely to get the click. If you have a KPI for conversions, then this setting won't really suit your campaign. Instead, you may consider choosing the Optimize for Conversions option, but in order to optimize the rotation, previous campaign performance is required. If you are creating a brand-new campaign, you will want to choose the Rotate Evenly option. That gives every ad a fair chance to determine its placement. Finally, the Rotate Indefinitely option shows lower performing ads proportionately with higher performing ads. This one isn't really a great choice, so steer clear.

To start, try choosing Rotate Evenly. Let it rotate for two weeks and then switch to either Optimize for Clicks or Optimize for Conversions, based on what your KPI is. Never let it rotate evenly for 90 days, it's simply too long to have each ad rotating evenly. Approximately two weeks is the optimum time frame for a campaign to really find its feet.

Keyword Selection

Your campaign is now set up and the next element involves selecting your keywords. This is the starting point for every campaign and is probably the most important part, because it decides which keywords your ads will be shown for. Don't forget that all your quality scores are assigned to the keyword; keyword selection is important because your ad copy, landing page, bids, and the like are going to be defined by the keywords you choose. It's all about deciding which keywords are most likely to generate the highest return, and which are the most appropriate in terms of your product or service offering. If you don't choose the right keywords, your ad will be shown for the wrong search terms, you will be irrelevant to your users, and you will be spending money on an audience that is not going to convert.

Keyword Research Tools

PPC keyword research can be tough if you are not equipped with the tools for the task. Luckily, the two tools listed below will serve as your virtual hammer and chisel, allowing you to uncover the hidden keyword gems that lie within the digital landscape.

1 *Google Trends.* Google Trends allows you to see historical search trends for a particular keyword or category. While it does not give specific search volumes, it does give a nice overview of how popular particular search terms or categories have been over the years and is great for campaign research, planning, and insight.

   Probably one of the best reasons to use Google Trends is for competitive research. For example, by entering Samsung, HTC, and Apple, you can see which is the most popular brand just by looking at the peaks and troughs in the search terms. You can also identify if there are trends in the time of year when competitors are more or less popular than you. The great thing about Google Trends is it includes news stories when relevant. So if Google News has picked up a news story about Samsung and there's a peak in search volumes for Samsung as a result, it will add a little annotation informing you which news story caused that peak in search volumes.

   If you are unsure of the particular search term that you are looking for, click All Categories instead and take a look at a category (for example, food and beverages).

   You can break trends down by country too, as shown in Figure 3.14. This could prove particularly useful if you want to identify your competitors in other countries, and also if you want to see the level of interest in certain keywords versus the country you operate in.

   Spotting trends based on specific times of the year is incredibly useful and luckily Google Trends facilitates this, too. So, if you want to analyze trends during the holiday season over the last four years, you can change not only the date range but also the platform at which it is looking. Whether it's web, image search, or news search, Google Trends has you covered!

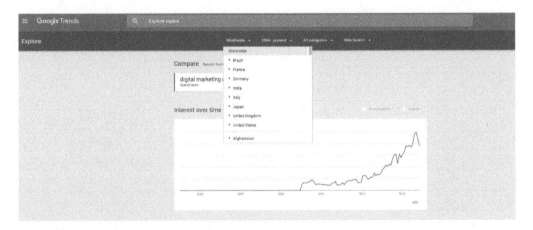

Figure 3.14   Google Trends by Country Option
Source: Google and the Google logo are registered trademarks of Google Inc.; used with permission.

2 *Keyword Planner.* This is an immediate to short-term tool, providing you with search volumes on specific keywords, over the past 12 months. Unlike Google Trends, it will suggest new keywords for you. It also has a traffic estimator which will tell you how much traffic you should get if you bid and spend a certain amount.

As you can see in Figure 3.15, the executive has typed in *digital marketing course* and *learn digital marketing* to see which keywords would be good to target for a campaign advertising digital marketing courses. After inserting your search term, you will find a list of keyword suggestions under the 'Keyword ideas' tab. Even though Keyword Planner will suggest ad groups for you, you should still use your best judgment in structuring those ad groups and follow the naming convention you created for your campaign. Keyword Planner also gives you suggestions for new keywords, a suggested bid, and the total search volume for the keyword—great for calculating how much it would cost you per click.

Keyword Planner also shows you the level of competition, or how many people are bidding on those keywords, by stating whether it is high, medium, or low. If the competition is high, the bid will be higher because there's a lot more advertisers vying for that top spot. Once you have reviewed all keywords you can then add them to a plan. When you have reviewed all the keywords within the ad group, you can then click Add All to Plan. Keyword Planner will then give you a very top-line estimate of how much you might spend per day, but Traffic Estimator will give you a much more detailed cost. After this you have a couple of options. You can either download all your keywords from the different ad groups into an Excel spreadsheet or you can advance on to Traffic Estimator.

Click the blue Review Forecast button on the bottom right to access Traffic Estimator. This tool is great for seeing the differences in traffic and impressions that you could get, based on daily budgets. Try playing around with the bids and budgets to see what levels would incur an increase in clicks. As you can see, it's a lovely interface! Not only does it tell you

Keyword (by relevance)	Avg. monthly searches	Competition	Suggested bid	Ad impr. share	Add to plan
digital marketing courses	8,100	High	€7.20	–	»
digital marketing training	1,900	High	€6.68	–	»
digital marketing training courses	260	High	€8.94	–	»
digital marketing courses online	590	High	€7.95	–	»
digital marketing certificate	880	High	€12.07	–	»
online digital marketing courses	1,000	High	€7.04	–	»
digital marketing degree	590	High	€35.18	–	»
digital marketing course online	590	High	€5.71	–	»
digital marketing	110,000	High	€4.35	–	»
digital marketing online course	590	High	€5.79	–	»

Figure 3.15   Google AdWords Keyword Planner Search
Source: Google and the Google logo are registered trademarks of Google Inc.; used with permission.

on average how many clicks you will get per day, but it also tells you what your total impressions, total daily costs, and average position will be. What can't it do?

Keyword Match Types

With your keywords well and truly chosen, you can now decide upon the match types that you are going to use. When bidding on a keyword, you need to choose a keyword match type that tells Google AdWords how precisely you want it to match your ad to the keyword searches.

You may remember that quality score is assigned to the keyword, but the quality score is defined based on the search query. Your keyword and search query are two very different things, and that's all down to the match type that you use. It defines what search queries and keywords will trigger your ad. While this may seem confusing at first, don't fret! Let's go through each of the five match types, using the example of a user searching for *cheap hotels in Seattle*, as in Figure 3.16, so you can have a solid understanding of what this is all about.

1 *Exact match*. This is the most specific match type, and in order for the ad to show for the keyword *cheap hotels in Seattle*, the user needs to write exactly that. You can choose Exact Match by typing two square brackets on either side of the keyword; for example, [*cheap hotels in Seattle*]. By doing so, it means the ad will only show when a user types in *cheap hotels in Seattle*. Nothing less, nothing more.
2 *Phrase match*. This match type is of the broader variety, in that you can capture a lot more social queries while remaining relatively targeted. It's chosen by typing inverted commas on either side of the keyword; for example, '*cheap hotels*.' The good thing about Phrase Match is that your ad will still show if the user types words before or after the keyword you've placed within the inverted commas. For example, if a user searches for *cheap hotels in Seattle*, the ad will still show, because the words *in Seattle* come after your keyword. Similarly, if the same user searches for *very cheap hotels*, the ad will still show because the word *very* came before your targeted keyword. If the user enters a word in between your Phrase Match keyword, such as *cheap Seattle hotels*, the ad will not show. There's no piggy in the middle with this match type!

Figure 3.16   Keyword Match Types

3 *Modified broad match.* When starting a new campaign, this is probably the best match type to choose. The targeting is broader, but you are able to define the words within a search query that the user types in. To choose this match type, type a plus sign in front of the words that the user must include in the search query for your ad to show; for example, *+hotels near +Seattle*. You may notice there are only plus signs in front of *hotels* and *Seattle*. This means that those words must be included in the user search query for your ad to appear. This also means the word *near*, which lies between those words, isn't set in stone. If the user types *in*, *at*, or *on* your ad will still show. When starting out, you need to be a little broad with your keywords so that you can identify which keywords work and which don't. Once you have done this, you can switch to Exact Match and make your targeting far stronger.

4 *Broad match.* Consider this match type as a giant fishing net trawling through a digital ocean, catching almost every search term regardless of relevance. This type could be recipe for disaster if your budget is limited, because it has the broadest reach. You can choose Broad Match by simply typing in the keyword with nothing before or after it. Your ad can show for misspellings, variations, and iterations of your keyword. For example, if your keyword is *umbrella*, your ad could show for *patio furniture* because umbrellas are mildly related to patio furniture. This is the point at which your quality score will start to suffer because you are not being relevant to the users you are targeting.

5 *Negative match.* Also known as negative keywords, this match type is a great way to prevent your ad from showing for certain search queries. For example, if a two-star hotel does not want to display in the search results for five-star hotels, it can use a Negative Match keyword to exclude search queries for *five-star hotels*. There are three Negative Match types: Negative Exact, Negative Broad, and Negative Phrase. In order to choose Negative Match, simply place a minus sign in front of the keyword. For example, -[*five star hotels*] is Negative Exact, '-*five star hotels*' is Negative Phrase, and -*five star hotels* is Negative Broad. Currently there is no negative variation for Modified Broad Match.

Got all that? Great! This concludes your PPC setup and with that, we can now progress to the next step of stage 2, the process behind the campaign.

Process

With your account and campaigns fully set up, now seems like the right time to take the next step within stage 2 (see Figure 3.5): exploring the processes behind the campaign and taking a look at how ad copy influences the success of all search marketing advertising. This section is a toughie, so your full attention is required in order to:

- Learn how to compose ad copy and the best practices, rules, and policies that govern it.
- Be able to use dynamic keyword insertion and ad extensions as part of your campaigns.
- Appreciate the best practices for designing a landing page.
- Align bidding strategies with your KPIs.
- Integrate remarketing into your search marketing strategy.

Ad Copy Composition

Let's kick off this section by learning how exactly to compose the ad copy that will be served to users. The folks over at Google AdWords are extremely strict with character

Digital Marketing Inst

Courses to Enhance Your Career.

Choose Online or Class Lectures.

www.digitalmarketinginstitute.com

Figure 3.17   DMI Google AdWords Ad
Source: Google and the Google logo are registered trademarks of Google Inc.; used with permission.

count for each line of your ad copy, so take note of these character limits, because you will need to stick to them! Ad titles or description lines with even one character over the limit will not be allowed, so you'll need to get creative!

Take a look at the ad shown in Figure 3.17. It is from the Digital Marketing Institute and shows adherence to these character count limits. Gold star for us! Ad titles (or headlines) have a 25-character limit, including spaces. The Display URL line is technically granted up to 255 characters; however, only 35 of those will be displayed. It's best practice to keep your Display URL line short and sweet. Use it to show users your website address; for example, www.example.com. You can then assign a different destination URL, which will navigate the user to the specific landing page the ad refers to; for example, www.example.com/sale. If you choose to do this, you must make sure the display URL and destination URL are on the same domain (in this example www.example.com). And finally, Description Lines 1 and 2 are allowed up to 35 characters each, including spaces.

Where do I start? When crafting your ad copy, start by thinking about what your customers would like to see if they entered a search term that triggers your ad. From here, you can then follow each of these best practices to create eye-catching advertisements that will have your user's hands twitching to click!

- *Make it unique.* Your ad should have a really compelling message with a unique selling point (USP) to suit. Give the user a reason to click your ad and something that differentiates you from your competitors. Try Googling the search term you want your ad to show for, then see what your competitors are saying in their ad copy to get ideas. For example, do you offer free delivery or have 24-hour customer service? If so, say it!
- *Flaunt your promotions and offers.* If there is a sense of urgency associated with your campaign, put it in the ad. Google has a really cool feature called Countdown Ads, which will count down, in real time, the number of days, hours, and minutes left until the offer expires. This is great way to encourage users to click through.
- *Include keywords.* Don't forget that keywords contribute to your quality score, so make sure you get them into your ad copy. Furthermore, your keyword will also be highlighted in bold if users enter it as part of their search terms. What better reason to put your keyword into ad copy than that?
- *Highlight a call to action.* Tell users what to do and also make it obvious what is expected of them once they click onto your site. Do you want them to find out more, purchase something, or sign up for your newsletter?

- *Match your ad to landing page.* What you say in your ad should relate exactly to the landing page users are brought to once they click your ad. In other words, don't advertise apples and bring the user to a page about oranges!

Stick to the Rules!

Besides the character-limit restrictions, you should also be aware of the following rules:

- There are restrictions on special characters (!?∗#), excessive punctuation, and capitalization.
- The word *click* is forbidden in ad copy. That means you cannot have a call to action saying *click here for more*.
- The use of trademark terms in ad copy is restricted without prior authorization from the trademark owner.
- You cannot mislead or misrepresent the service or product that you are offering.

Luckily, Google enforces these rules as you create the ad, meaning you will know instantly whether your ad adheres to them!

Creating the Ad

In your AdWords dashboard, click the Campaigns tab at the top, then select Ads underneath and click the big red + Ad button near the bottom of the screen. You will be presented with the screen shown in Figure 3.18.

You will be forced to choose an ad group before being able to submit your ad copy, so make sure you do so before completing this step. Simply fill in all the fields and you are ready to go!

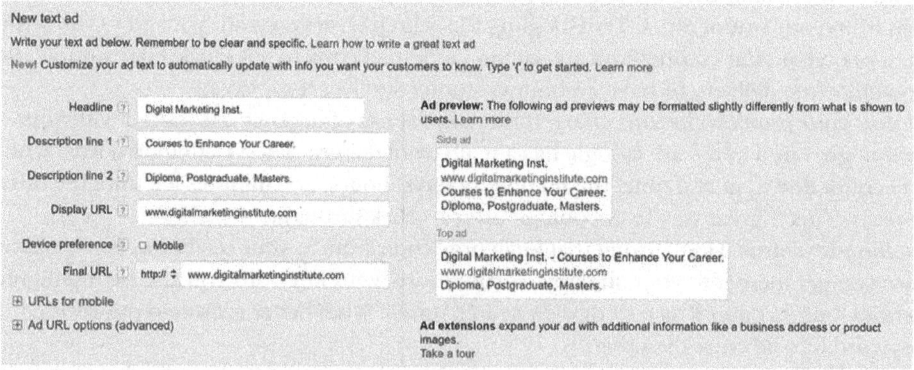

Figure 3.18   Creating your Google AdWords Ad
Source: Google and the Google logo are registered trademarks of Google Inc.; used with permission.

You should create two to three ads per ad group, using different ad copy for each. By doing this you can test different types of messaging and calls to action, and even different landing pages, to see which ones users prefer and which ones give the highest ROI. Even if you find that one ad that works incredibly well, never stop testing. Try new iterations of that one great ad and keep testing until you find one that performs even better!

Dynamic Keyword Insertion

This is a great technique for eye-catching ad copy. Dynamic keyword insertion puts *individual keywords from your ad group into your ad text.* The result is an extremely relevant ad to the user, and it saves you time you might spend creating multiple ads for each keyword that you are bidding on. *To use this feature you must use a special code in the following format:* {KeyWord:Chocolate}. As you can see, your brackets must be of the curly variety for the feature to work. Take a look at the example in Figure 3.19, which shows how it's done.

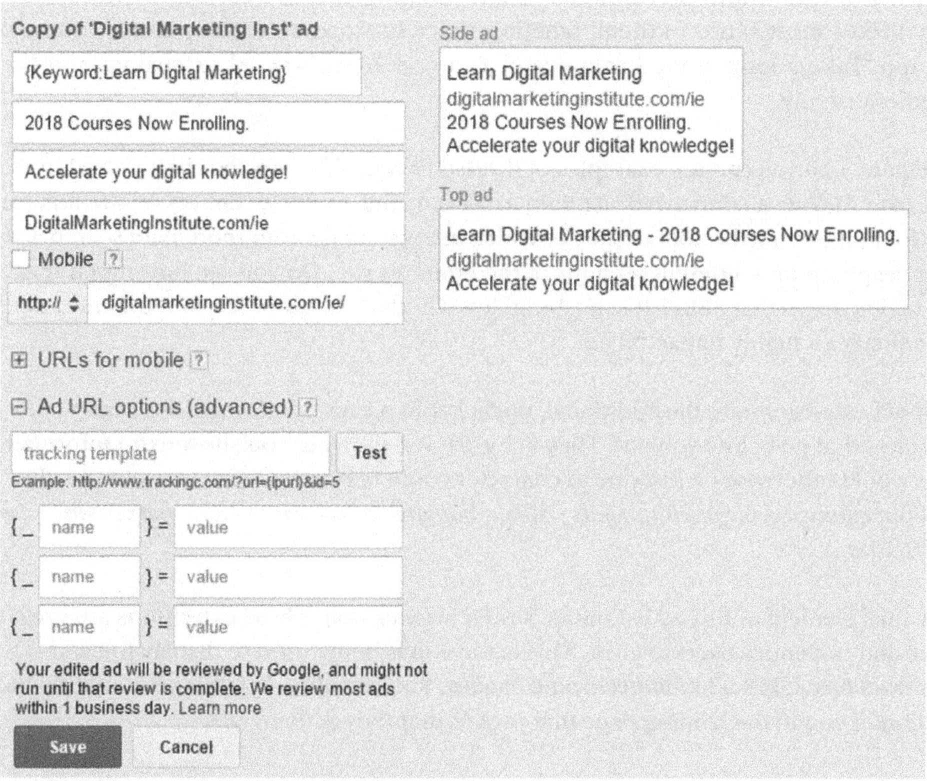

Figure 3.19   Dynamic Keyword Insertion
Source: Google and the Google logo are registered trademarks of Google Inc.; used with permission.

emirates.com - Emirates Airline
[Ad] www.**emirates**.com/ie ▾
Book your flight at Emirates.com. Check-in & select your seat online.
Spacious seats · 30kg+ baggage allowance · Gourmet cuisine · 140+ destinations
Destinations: Dubai, Perth, Bangkok, Hong Kong, Singapore
Emirates has 3,338,233 followers on Google+

Make a Booking Online
Book online, select your seat and
see what to expect on your flight

Say hello to free Wi-Fi
Stay connected in the sky with free
Wi-Fi on most of our A380 aircraft

Emirates Skywards
Frequent flyer? Make your travel
more rewarding. Join Skywards today

Services & Entertainment
Enjoy great meals & up to 2000
channels of premium entertainment.

Figure 3.20   Google AdWords Ad with Ad Extensions
Source: Google and the Google logo are registered trademarks of Google Inc.; used with permission.

Ad Extensions

Ad extensions take up more room on the search engine results page and also provide a richer, more relevant experience for the user. Extensions are great for enhancing your brand perception and encouraging users to convert in whatever way makes most sense to them, whether that's in-store, over the phone, online, or by app. Take a look at the examples in Figure 3.20 of how ad extensions can be used effectively.

In Figure 3.20 you can see examples of three different ad extensions being used by Emirates Airline: an enhanced site link, a call-out, and a review. Enhanced site links are the four links at the bottom of the ad, which are essentially four more paid search ads that deep-link into different sections of the Emirates site. Do you see how much space it's taking up on that SERP? It is pushing down both competitor ads and organic results, meaning it's a highly impactful ad.

Call-out extensions are the additional, unclickable pieces of information about your business that go below your ad. They are great for allowing you show extra information that would otherwise be lost due to character count restrictions. In this example, the call-out extension is *Spacious seats · 30kg+baggage allowance · Gourmet cuisine · 140+ destinations.*

The final element of this ad is Emirate's review extension. These extensions are great to have and can entice users to click. This extension is being used to display the text *Emirates has 3,338,233 followers on Google+.* You can also click this text, and the link will bring you to the landing page that proves that they actually do!

Check out Figure 3.21 for an example of a click-to-call extension being used by an AdWords management company. This extension allows users to call you directly from their cell phones by clicking the Call button.

Figure 3.21   Google AdWords Click-to-Call Extension
Source: Google and the Google logo are registered trademarks of Google Inc.; used with permission.

You can even drive customers to download your app directly to their cell phones through the app download extension shown in Figure 3.22. The best feature of this extension is that it is device responsive, meaning an iOS app will automatically download for iPhone users while Android will download for those using devices powered by that OS. Pretty nifty, right?

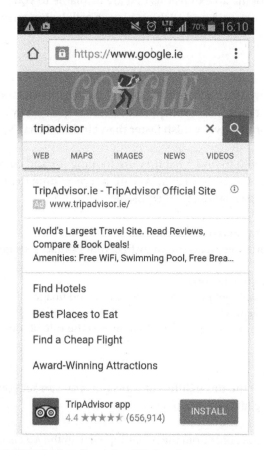

Figure 3.22   Google AdWords App Download Extension
Source: Google and the Google logo are registered trademarks of Google Inc.; used with permission.

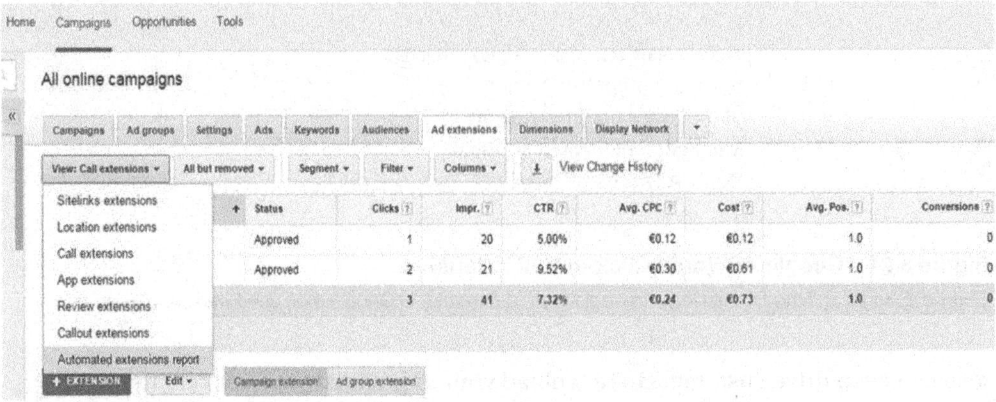

Figure 3.23   How to Create an Ad Extension within Google AdWords
Source: Google and the Google logo are registered trademarks of Google Inc.; used with permission.

These are only some of the ad extensions that are available to you. Create your own by going to the Ad Extensions tab and clicking View: Sitelinks Extensions, as shown in Figure 3.23.

Landing Pages

Did you know you have eight seconds to impress users who click on your landing page? If the content does not match the ad copy in the search query they searched for, you can bet your bottom dollar they will vanish faster than Lindsay Lohan's music career.

Users should be able both to find what they are looking for and convert within three clicks of entering your site. If they can't, you are not providing the ideal experience. Get your act together! The best landing pages should:

- Provide relevant, useful, and original content.
- Be transparent and promote trust—can they find your Contact Us page?
- Be easy to navigate.
- Fulfill the promise of your ad copy.
- Have a visible and prominent product or service title and image.
- Contain clear calls to action.
- Have minimal clicks to conversion—less than three is the rule of thumb!

Bidding

Let's now take a look at the three different ways that you can set your bids and get your campaigns performing at the optimal level:

1 Your first option is to set bids from the Ad Group view in the Ad Groups tab. As you can see in Figure 3.24, the ad groups appear on the left while their corresponding bids are listed on the right. These bids are set to the default maximum CPC, but they can be changed by hovering your mouse over the bid and clicking on the box.

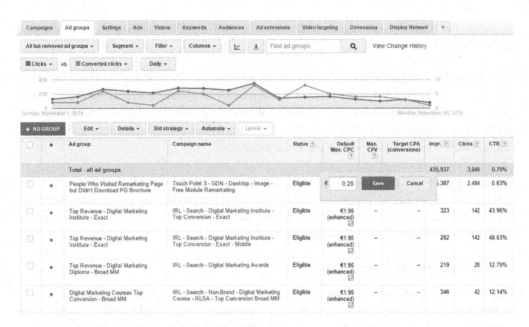

Figure 3.24   Setting Bids from Ad Group Overview
Source: Google and the Google logo are registered trademarks of Google Inc.; used with permission.

2 The second way to set your bid is by simply clicking into the ad group itself, from your ad group overview. You will then be brought to the screen shown in Figure 3.25. Simply click on Edit to change your default bid for that particular ad group.

3 The final method of setting your bids is at the keyword level. If you find that a specific keyword is outperforming or underperforming others, you can increase or decrease that bid by clicking the Keywords tab, hovering over the bid, and clicking on it.

It's important to note that keyword bids will override ad group level bids if they are higher. For example, let's pretend you have a bid of $1.75 on an ad group called Restaurants, but decide to change the bid on one keyword within the ad group to $2.00. If the following week you decide to reduce your ad group bid to $1.50, your keyword bid of $2.00 will override the ad group level bid and remain the same. If you want that

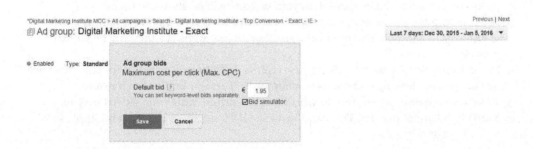

Figure 3.25   Setting Bids from Within an Ad Group
Source: Google and the Google logo are registered trademarks of Google Inc.; used with permission.

keyword bid to be the same as its ad group bid, you will have to change it manually using method 3 listed above.

Don't bid blind. When devising a bid budgeting strategy, it's vital that you bid based on priorities and KPIs. Applying a blanket bid across all ad groups and leaving them to run is bad practice and economically insane! Look at your performance in line with your KPIs and set your bids based on that. If your KPI is to drive sales, then increase bids on the keywords and ad groups that drive the most sales.

Analyzing your ad's average position should also be a key factor informing your bid strategy. If, for example, you want to increase conversions on a particular keyword but already have an average position of one, there is no point in increasing your bid because you cannot go higher than a number-one position!

Google Display Network (GDN)

GDN consists of websites that allow Google to place ads on its site through a platform called AdSense. When a user clicks an ad, the publisher and Google make money. Users can be targeted through standard text ads, image ads, and video ads. To check out your advertising options on GDN, click the Tools tab on your AdWords dashboard. It's a great way to place ads on websites that are relevant to what you are selling and that you know your target audience is visiting.

Remarketing

Remember that time you visited a website, only to see an ad exactly related to that page you were looking at a short while later? That's remarketing! If users have been to your site before, you can target them as they are browsing other websites and mobile apps, or even as they are searching on Google. Some call it cyberstalking, while others view it as a clever way of reaching consumers who have already visited your site. Take a look at the five different ways you can remarket to users:

1 *Standard remarketing.* As past visitors browse GDN websites and use GDN apps, your ads will be shown to them along the way.
2 *Dynamic remarketing.* As past visitors browse GDN websites and use GDN apps, ads with products and services they viewed on your website will be shown to them.
3 *Remarketing for mobile apps.* As people who have used your mobile app or mobile website use other mobile apps or browse other mobile websites, they will be shown your ads.
4 *Remarketing lists for search ads.* As past visitors do follow-up searches for what they need on Google after leaving your website, your ads will appear in the search results.
5 *Video remarketing.* When people who have interacted with your videos or your YouTube channel use YouTube and browse GDN videos, websites, and apps, they will see your ads.

Let's explain the benefit of remarketing by taking the example of three different users who have visited www.example.com.

If you are unable to obtain any information about them, how can you place a value on them? Take a look at these three scenarios and decide which two have the most value:

1 User 1 has visited the site before, navigated as far as the basket page, and then bounced.
2 User 2 has gone as far as entering their payment details before bouncing off.
3 User 3 bounced 30 seconds after reaching the About Us page.

Users 1 and 2 are the most valuable and likely to convert, just in case you are still scratching your head for the answer.

You can kick off your own remarketing campaign simply by inserting a piece of code between the <body></body> tags on every page of your site. Get your code from the Campaigns section of the AdWords dashboard. Select Shared Library from the menu on the left and click Audiences underneath it.

New AdWords account owners will be asked to set up remarketing; once you have completed the required fields, your code is ready to go! You can either export the code yourself, or if your skills don't stretch that far yet, email it directly to someone else, such as a web developer.

When your code has been inserted onto your site, you will see the Audiences section of your AdWords dashboard. You should pay particular attention to the Membership Duration section of this page, which indicates the amount of time users will be remarketed to before they are removed from the list. The default is set to 30 days, but it can stretch to as long as 180 days on the Search Network and 540 days on GDN. Your membership duration should be amended based on your knowledge of how long it takes users to convert. The List Size field will tell you how many users are on your remarketing list, divided by Search Network and GDN.

Be selective. Because every user and that user's online behavior is unique, you won't need to remarket to each person who has visited your site. For example, remarketing to a user who reached the basket page on your site should have a higher priority over remarketing to someone who has already purchased something. This is where custom audiences come in!

To create a custom remarketing list, click the red + Remarketing List button. Enter in a descriptive name for the list and then decide whether it is for a website or app. In the Who to Add to Your List field, you can select from a range of options for the users to be targeted. Better still, by clicking the +Rules button, you can remarket to anyone based on preset rules. Rules allow you to specify whom you target and to get quite specific with the message you serve. They are also great for excluding people who have already completed a valuable action on your site, such as a purchase. When you have set your membership duration based on how long you think it takes a user to convert, click Save.

Before you go creating ad copy worthy of a Pulitzer Prize, remarketing to the right people, and turning your bidding strategy into a cash cow, you need to know how to manage your campaign! Stick around—we are going to cover that in the next section.

Stage 3: Manage

If your friends are impressed by your newfound abilities from stages 1 and 2 of the PPC process, then what you learn from this next section will definitely bowl them over! Stage 3, highlighted in Figure 3.26, is about what happens after your campaign has launched and you are managing it effectively on an ongoing basis. Pretty soon, you will be able to tell your friends all about:

• The functions of each of the five main tabs within the AdWords interface.
• How to implement conversion tracking as part of your overall PPC strategy.
• The reports that can be pulled and where to find them.

Figure 3.26   Focus on the Third Stage in the PPC Process

Navigating the Interface

Once your campaign has been created, you will need to report on and analyze its performance—which can be done through the variety of tools AdWords has to offer. The tricky part, however, is choosing which tabs and sections of the interface are most relevant to you, because each business is unique. Fasten your seatbelt, this guided tour of the AdWords interface will help you decide and locate the tabs and sections your business needs.

These are the five main tabs that you will navigate through when you start to report.

The Home tab is great way of getting a quick snapshot of how your account is performing and telling you what the top changes have been over the last week.

The Reports tab is where you will click to get a more vibrant visual representation of how your campaigns are performing. You can pick and choose which data points you want displayed and display them in a table, a line chart, a bar chart, or a pie chart.

The Campaigns, Opportunities, and Tools tabs are much meatier, so let's look at them in more detail now.

1 Campaigns tab

All your campaign management will be run from this section and the screen shown in Figure 3.27 will also be the default screen when you log in. Let's now see what each of the sub tabs within the Campaigns section can do for you.

Ad groups, ads, keywords, and ad extensions. These tabs will show you the performance of these particular areas of your campaign for the date range you set. Set your date range by clicking the date range option in the top right corner of the screen. You can choose anywhere from the previous 7 days to the previous 30 days, and you can also define the date range by quarter or by half year.

Settings. If you want to modify the settings for all your campaigns at once, this is the tab for you! Here you can change the start and end dates of your campaigns and also edit the settings for your location, budgets, language, ad rotation, and ad scheduling!

Dimensions. Here you can really drill down into the performance of your campaigns and look at the times and days of the week when your ads are performing best. It also allows you to monitor which geographic locations are the top performers—perfect for reporting on campaigns that span several countries. Not only this, you can also see the best performing URLs, which could prove useful in seeing which landing pages are generating the most conversions! Finally, the Dimensions tab will let you identify the biggest changes in your CPC over the last week and where the changes have come from. Pretty cool, right?

Figure 3.27   Google AdWords Campaigns Tab
Source: Google and the Google logo are registered trademarks of Google Inc.; used with permission.

2 Opportunities tab

For beginners and seasoned professionals alike, the Opportunities tab gives very informative optimization tips and ideas—just like the ones shown in Figure 3.28.

These tips get very detailed, advising you on budget spends and how to achieve more clicks. They are all based on algorithm calculations, meaning they are a prediction of sorts

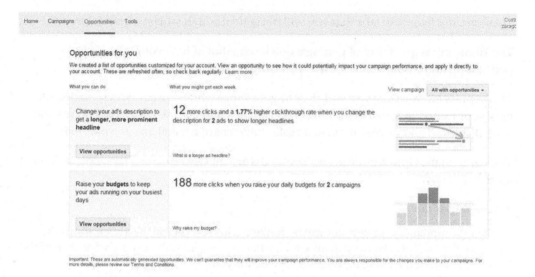

Figure 3.28   Google AdWords Opportunities Tab

Source: Google and the Google logo are registered trademarks of Google Inc.; used with permission.

and therefore subject to fluctuation. The best feature of the Opportunities tab is that the tips are updated in real time, meaning you could get totally different suggestions each week.

3 Tools tab

The Tools tab is where you will find the Keyword Planner, Display Planner, and most importantly, Conversion Tracking tools. The latter looks at the post-click success of your campaign, moving past search engine analysis and focusing on what users are doing when they enter your website. Ultimately, conversion tracking holds PPC accountable for the money it's spending, allowing you assess whether or not your investment is getting a return—even if that return is simply driving video views.

Don't be under the illusion that conversion tracking is only for businesses that seek online purchases or hard conversions, such as leads. It's for branding and awareness too! For example, if a user spending a certain amount of time on your site adds value to your business, then it's a conversion.

Conversion tracking can be done in two ways:

a. By placing a Google AdWords conversion tracking code on a page or element of your site that you use as an indicator of success for your business—for example, a thank-you page or a find-out-more button on your site.

b. By creating goals and transactions in Google Analytics (GA) and importing them into AdWords once the accounts are linked.

Which Tool Should I Choose?

The recommendation would be option 2 above, using GA. By creating the conversion in GA, you eliminate the need to create another one in Google AdWords. Even more importantly, option 2 is far more efficient for comparison purposes. If you create a Google AdWords conversion tracking code, that conversion is specific to AdWords and will only tell you how many conversions your AdWords campaign generated for that particular goal.

However, by importing a GA goal or transaction, it will allow you to see your PPC campaign performance in comparison to other channels. For example, you can see how many goals and transactions your PPC campaign generated in comparison to your organic search, display, or email campaigns.

The decision as to which option you choose is yours to make, so let's look at how both conversion-tracking techniques can be implemented!

Conversion tracking: Google AdWords style. If you do decide to ignore the recommendation (how dare you!) and go down the AdWords route, start by clicking the Tools tab and select Conversions from the drop-down menu. If you have not created conversion tracking before, you will need to click the red + Conversion button to begin. Regardless of which option you choose, you will still create all of your conversions here.

Next you need to select the source of the conversions you want to track, as shown in Figure 3.29. Usually you will be selecting the Website option, so let's just focus on that one for now.

Hit Select underneath the Website option and the process of creating a conversion tracking code will begin! You will need to complete each of the fields:

- *Name.* Choose one that is easily recognizable.
- *Value.* Assign a value only if you feel you need to.

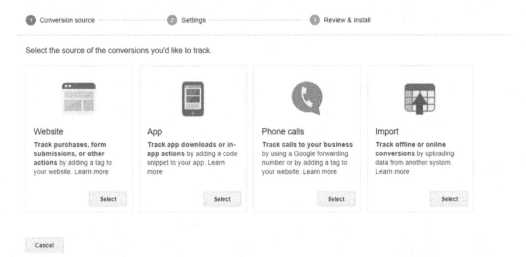

Figure 3.29   Google AdWords Conversion Tracking
Source: Google and the Google logo are registered trademarks of Google Inc.; used with permission.

- *Count.* Decide how you want AdWords to count your conversions. The Every option will count every single conversion from every visit. The Unique option will count only one conversion per user—ideal for lead generation.
- *Conversion window.* Here you choose how long you want the conversion to be counted. The default setting is 30 days.
- *Category.* Simply choose the category that best describes the conversion action.
- *Optimization.* Here you can opt in or out of including data from this conversion in the Conversions for Optimization section of the AdWords interface. Keep it ticked, it's good to have!

When you are done, hit Save and Continue to be brought to your very own conversion tracking code as shown in Figure 3.30. A momentous occasion for first timers—relish it. Just like that time you inserted a remarketing code onto your site, stick this one between the <body></body> tags of the appropriate webpage too. As soon as that page loads or the designated button is clicked, the conversion will be recorded for you.

Conversion tracking: GA style. Before importing goals or transactions, you need to tell GA to recognize when a click or conversion has come from a PPC campaign. To do this,

Figure 3.30   Conversion Tracking Code Generation
Source: Google and the Google logo are registered trademarks of Google Inc.; used with permission.

you must have both a GA and a Google AdWords account that are linked together. Don't worry, you will learn how to set up a GA account in Chapter 9! When it is set up, you can link the two accounts by clicking the cog symbol at the top right of the screen and selecting Account Settings.

When this is done, hit the Tools tab, select Conversions, and click GA from the menu on the left. If you have valid goals or transactions that have converted via Google AdWords in the last seven days, then you can import those goals and transactions by clicking the +Conversion button.

You are progressing quickly and your PPC mastery has almost come full circle. Let's now move onto the final stage of the iterative process to see how you can really analyze and report on your campaigns!

Stage 4: Analyze

Believe it or not, we are now at the final stage of the PPC process, as highlighted in Figure 3.31. This means only one thing—it's time to analyze and report on the successes (or failures) of your PPC campaigns! Pretty soon you will:

- Know how to use PPC reports to better optimize PPC campaigns.
- Appreciate the importance of segmenting data.
- Learn how to configure the columns within an AdWords interface.
- Recognize the main KPIs that indicate the performance of PPC campaigns.
- Understand how to link Google AdWords and GA.
- Be able to find your quality score.

Figure 3.31   Focus on the Fourth Stage in the PPC process

Key Performance Reports

With such an abundance of data available, how are you to know where to start your analysis? Try on these key performance reports for size:

Keyword Performance Report

A report that should be pulled biweekly, you can download it within the Campaigns tab. Click Keywords, select which metrics you want to compare, and hit the little downwards arrow button beside the search box. After choosing which format to download the report in, try downloading multiple reports and combining them into one super report. This way you can get a really detailed, handpicked report of your campaign's performance.

Ad Performance Report

Not only does this report allow you see the performance of each individual ad for the date range you set, but it also shows how your keyword groups are performing against each other—both of which are great for informing decisions on your bid strategy. You can download this in the same way as a keyword performance report; just make sure to set the data range at the top right corner of the screen first. Try pulling this report biweekly.

Campaign Performance Report

Great for a quick update, this one gives you a high-level overview of how the account is performing. Has it dipped in performance compared to last week or are there any trends you should be aware of? Download this report once a week to find out.

Dimensions Report

The reporting, insights, and level of data that a dimensions report provides is the cherry on the cake. Just like the other reports, click the download button and you can export all this data in whatever format you wish. When you have selected a view, take some time to explore the plethora of options available, all of which provide rich levels of data.

By selecting the time view, you can assess performance by day of the week, and this data is invaluable for mapping your customer's journey. To show how beneficial this report can be, let's use the example of a retail company. In terms of performance, it knows not every hour of the day is created equally. Sales lag during the middle of the night but Fridays are great because they tend to be paydays. The company also knows midday is usually good for desktop conversions because users are sitting at their desks, whereas more mobile conversions happen in the evening when users are relaxing at home. The retail company can use this data to track their customers' movements and customize how they are targeted.

Data Segmentation

If in-depth data soothes your soul, you could also try segmenting your reports. If, for example, you have multiple conversion types and want to see how your keywords perform against lead generation versus purchases, you may want to segment them by conversion type. Doing this will tell you the conversion type of each individual keyword.

You might also want to segment your reports by time of day, search term, or device. You can segment any of that data and add as many segments as you like. Just bear in mind that the more segments you add, the bigger the Excel file and the more data you will have to manipulate. Try just one to two segments per download, then you can start merging reports together.

Receiving Your Reports

Next you need to decide how you are going to receive the report. Within the Reports tab, click the little calendar icon and select who will be emailed the report. Here you can also schedule how frequently these reports are sent. Should you choose to save a report, you will need to give it an easily identifiable name, and when you have done that it will forever more be available to you within the Campaigns tab, from the Shared Library section of the menu on the left.

Columns—Supporting Your Reports

Columns are the most important and relevant way of generating richer insights when reporting, in any section of the interface. You can change them to alter the view or presentation of the data. To the left of the download button lies the option to change your columns. To add or remove a column, click the Columns option and select Modify Columns. You will then be able to drag, drop, and rearrange columns to your heart's content, as shown in Figure 3.32.

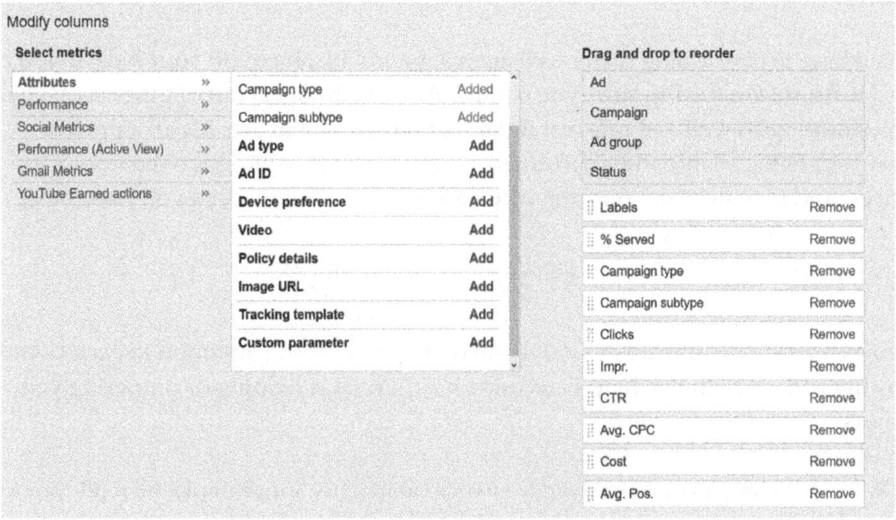

Figure 3.32   Column Modification within Google AdWords
Source: Google and the Google logo are registered trademarks of Google Inc.; used with permission.

The types of columns that are presented depends on the view and tab that you are in, but generally you will always be able to select attributes, performance, social, Gmail, and YouTube metrics. If you have GA and Google AdWords linked, you will also be able to see all of your GA metrics.

How to Link AdWords and Google Analytics

Without a doubt, GA is the best tool for analyzing the performance of any campaign. GA setup will be covered in greater detail in Chapter 9, but you should know how to use it in the context of PPC too. As you now know, in order to import goals and transactions from GA into AdWords, both platforms need to be linked—so let's do that now. For this to work, you need to have the same email address registered to both accounts. You must also have the same admin access in AdWords as in GA. To start, click the Tools tab in AdWords, select Google Analytics, and your GA account will automatically be presented to you. All that's left to do now is select the view that you want to link and hit save. Easy!

KPIs

With a clearer understanding of the reports that can be pulled from AdWords, let's now look at the KPIs you should be reviewing and optimizing on a continual basis in the context of your PPC campaigns. You should make sure to develop achievable KPIs that will contribute to the overall success of your business. For example, if your goal is to generate more revenue then don't focus on engagement metrics. Instead, focus on hard-conversion metrics, sales metrics, and ROI.

If something is performing really well against your KPIs, increase your bids, if you can afford to do so. On the flip side, you should also take budgets out of other areas that are not performing so well and reinvest them into the areas that are. It's all a process—define your KPIs, analyze the performance against those KPIs, make the necessary changes, and reanalyze the performance based on the changes that you have made.

Is Google AdWords Working for Me?

When measuring the impact of Google AdWords, pay strong attention to each of the following KPIs, which will help determine if AdWords is helping or hindering your business.

- *CTR.* This KPI measures the relevancy of your campaigns; for example, how relevant your ads and landing pages are to the keyword the user has searched for.
- *Conversion rate.* Use this KPI to measure the success of your campaigns and whether they are contributing to the overall success of your business.

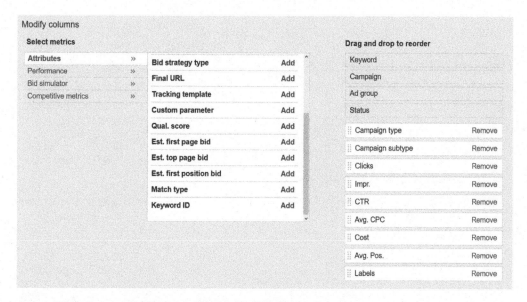

Figure 3.33   How to Add the Quality Score Column
Source: Google and the Google logo are registered trademarks of Google Inc.; used with permission.

- *Average CPC.* Need to measure the efficiency of your campaigns? This is the KPI for you. It considers your quality score and whether or not you are getting the most value per click.
- *Quality score.* Probably one of the most important KPIs, this one will essentially affect your CPC and have a knock-on effect on conversions. To find out what your score is, select the Campaigns tab at the top of the page, click the Keywords tab, hit Columns, and then select Modify Columns. Click the Attributes option and from there you can add the quality-score column onto your dashboard, as shown in Figure 3.33.

Alternatively, you can view your quality score by hovering over the little speech bubble underneath the Status column within the Keywords tab, as shown in Figure 3.34. This will give a breakdown and ranking of your quality score.

With a rock-solid understanding of how to report and analyze the success of your AdWords campaigns, let's complete this PPC process by looking at the laws and guidelines you need to abide by.

Laws and Guidelines

We have now reached the final stop aboard this PPC train, and before it turns around to begin the journey all over again—why not jump off and explore the terrain of laws and guidelines? Key attractions include:

- The cookie policies and data protection guidelines that must be adhered to
- The PPI policy and Digital Millennium Copyright Act
- The importance of abiding by trademark rules and regulations

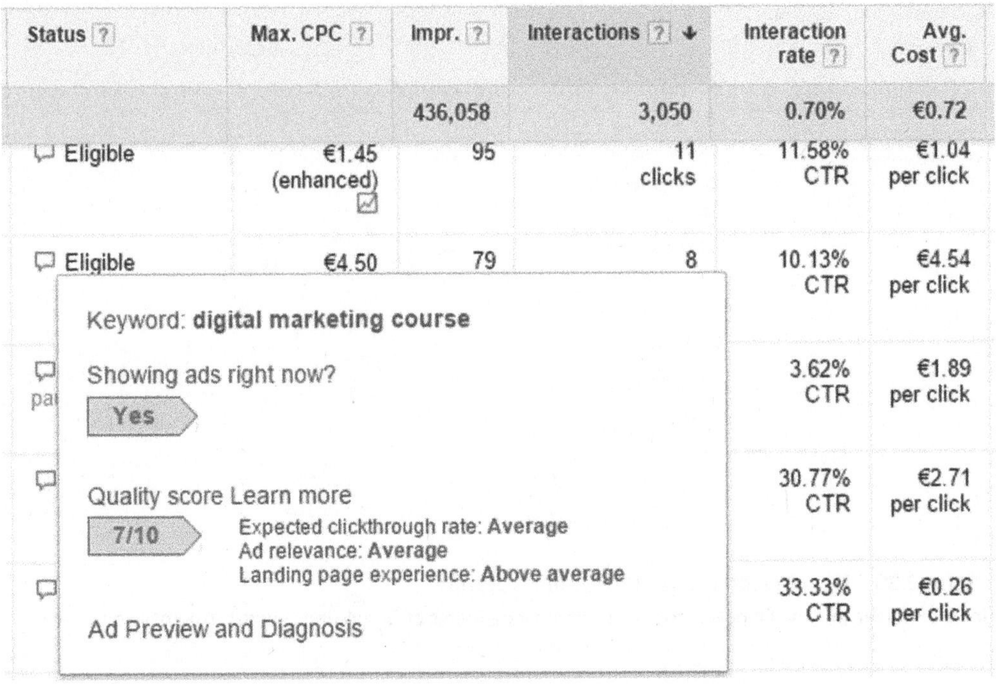

Status ?	Max. CPC ?	Impr. ?	Interactions ? ↓	Interaction rate ?	Avg. Cost ?
		436,058	3,050	0.70%	€0.72
⌑ Eligible	€1.45 (enhanced) ☑	95	11 clicks	11.58% CTR	€1.04 per click
⌑ Eligible	€4.50	79	8	10.13% CTR	€4.54 per click
⌑ pai				3.62% CTR	€1.89 per click
⌑				30.77% CTR	€2.71 per click
⌑				33.33% CTR	€0.26 per click

Keyword: **digital marketing course**

Showing ads right now?

> **Yes**

Quality score Learn more

> 7/10   Expected clickthrough rate: Average
Ad relevance: Average
Landing page experience: Above average

Ad Preview and Diagnosis

Figure 3.34   Quality Score View within Keywords Tab
Source: Google and the Google logo are registered trademarks of Google Inc.; used with permission.

Data Protection

One of the most important areas surrounding search marketing is data protection. It is your job to ensure that any data collected is used fairly and lawfully, and for limited, specifically stated purposes. Remember all those times you saw a website's cookie policy when you first clicked in? Every website must do this to be in line with cookie legislation directives. These directives state that you must always be upfront and clear with your users about what you intend to use their data for. This use should be in line with their data protection rights, and their data should be kept safe and secure and never transferred outside the country you are using it in without adequate protection.

Privacy

When running your PPC campaigns, make sure that you do not collect any personal information about users, such as their names and addresses. This is related to the Personally Identifiable Information (PII) policy, which Google quite strictly enforces.

Copyright

The Digital Millennium Copyright Act provides a process for a copyright owner to give notification to an online service provider concerning copyright infringement. Google AdWords' trademark policy is based upon this act. It stipulates that trademarks within ad copy cannot be used unless the trademark owner has sent Google the necessary form granting permission to the advertiser. If you are found to be in breach of this rule, you could face stiff penalties.

So, What Have You Learned in This Chapter?

From starting off with well-defined goals to setting up your AdWords account, navigating the interface, and developing bid strategies in line with your KPIs, you are now PPC royalty—but before you go here are a few more jewels for your crown:

- Set achievable, well-defined, DUMB goals!
- Save time and tears by carefully structuring your AdWords account at the very beginning of your campaign.
- Choose the devices you want (or don't want) to target carefully.
- Ensure your landing page fulfills the promise of your wonderful ad copy!
- Get savvy—always set your bids according to your KPIs, past performance, and your ad's average position.

Go to www.artofdmi.com to access the case study on PPC as additional support material for this chapter.

 **Exercises**

Exercise 1

Using your Google AdWords account, create a new campaign by following the steps below:

1 Choose your campaign name and networks.
2 Configure your language and location targeting.
3 Set your daily budget and maximum bid.
4 Define your ad rotation and delivery options.
5 Set a start and end date.
6 Decide on your ad scheduling preferences.

Exercise 2

Smith-Wyer is a credit insurance company based in New York City, offering bonding, guarantees, and collection services. Their business is declining and they've hired you to run a Google AdWords campaign advertising their services.

Using the Google Keyword Planner, identify at least 20 appropriate target keywords that deliver on the above brief. Look at query volumes and suggested bids to estimate competition for your keywords of choice and structure them into sensible ad groups with a similar theme.

Exercise 3

Change your daily budget for your campaign using the two methods below:

1 Within campaign settings
2 From the campaigns tab

Exercise 4

Link a Google AdWords and GA account, ensuring you have met the following prerequisites:

1 The email address is the same on both Google AdWords and GA.
2 The email address has an administrative access level on Google AdWords.
3 The email address has an edit or higher access level on GA.

Exercise 5

In Google AdWords, create a Google AdWords remarketing code within the Audiences section of the shared library. Set the membership duration to 30 days.

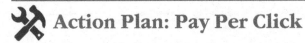

Action Plan: Pay Per Click

Digital Marketing Planning Scheme for PPC

Objectives

Conversions, leads, sales, traffic, visibility, brand awareness

Action Items and Frequency

• Keyword research: Quarterly
• Targeting: Monthly
• Scheduling: Weekly
• Bidding and budgeting: Weekly/monthly
• Tracking and reporting: Daily/weekly

Measurement Tools and KPIs

AdWords: Conversions, click-assisted conversions, clicks, CTR, impressions, search impression share

Spend

Media	Content	People	Systems
x		x	x

Chapter 4
Digital Display Advertising

An Introduction

You know those ads that follow you around the Internet? The ones that somehow know exactly what you have been searching for? Your computer is not psychic—you are simply experiencing remarketing, one of the tools of digital display advertising (DDA).

As a digital marketer, you can create online ads just as you would for an offline campaign. These online ads (or display banners) contain copy, logos, images, maps, and video—anything that will hook users as they browse. Then you can call on certain publishers to pick the most relevant websites, social media channels, and devices for your ads to appear on.

You learned in Chapter 2 that SEO is all about driving traffic to your site. Just as you should optimize your site so that it shows higher in search results, you should also optimize the *ads* that direct users to it—by including a hyperlinked call to action, for example. Makes sense, right?

DEFINITION

Formal definition of DDA: A form of digital marketing that uses display ads appearing on web pages as a means of communicating relevant commercial messages to a specific audience based on their profiles.

Informal definition of DDA: Your onscreen pickup line!

Process

In the opening sections of this chapter you will be provided with an overview of the DDA industry, the key terminology involved, and the benefits and challenges that face

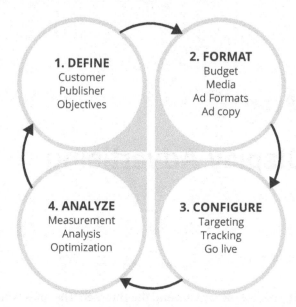

Figure 4.1   Four-Stage DDA process

display advertisers. Then we will cover in detail the four key stages of the DDA iterative process, as shown in Figure 4.1:

1 *Define.* This stage starts by helping you to identify and segment your customers based on demographics like age, location, and interests. You will learn how to find the right publisher for your ads and how to set display campaign objectives in line with your overall goals.
2 *Format.* This stage will introduce a range of creative ad formats, among which you can choose the most appropriate, according to your target audience and budget. Once you have looked at formats, you will learn about the media channels available to you and how you can create compelling ad copy across these channels.
3 *Configure.* You can maximize your campaign's potential by using targeting tools like Google Display Planner and assigning KPIs to help you track your campaign on an ongoing basis. Once you go live, you can't hide from the eyes of the public—so it is best to iron out any bumps early on.
4 *Analyze.* The final stage is when you measure the success of your campaign using analytics. Then you can enhance and optimize your ads as necessary before getting ready to relaunch.

Key Terms and Concepts

It is this chapter's aim to equip you with the knowledge and confidence you need to launch your own display campaign. When you have completed this chapter you will be able to:

• Recognize the importance of DDA on a global level and be aware of its benefits and challenges.

- Know how to select the most appropriate audience for your ads and the websites on which they appear.
- Appreciate the various creative ad formats available and how you can optimize the space you buy.
- Understand different targeting, tracking, and measuring tools that help you to analyze your campaign.
- Be familiar with the mechanics of display advertising, its associated terminology, and the laws to which it must adhere.

Display Advertising: An Industry Overview

Before you dive into the mechanics of display ads, let's take a step back and look at the big picture and the process we saw in Figure 4.1. This section will first focus on the DDA industry from a global perspective, then explore the mechanics behind DDA and some of the benefits and challenges it presents.

It cannot be denied that DDA is a pretty awesome branding tool. Even though it may not generate revenue in the same way as an email marketing campaign, it can influence a user's future buying behavior. By the end of this section, you will understand that as a digital marketer, you should:

- Allocate your budget across different media.
- Be aware of online consumption and of social media usage in particular.
- Appreciate the importance of mobile in display advertising.

Ad Spend: Offline and Online

The amount you spend on advertising varies across a range of media. For instance, the global spend for TV, outdoor, and online advertising increased in 2013, whereas formats such as radio and newspapers suffered.

However, advertisers are still willing to fork out for TV, even though viewers can easily fast-forward past ads or change channels. Less is spent on newspapers and magazines, which are losing out to display advertising—many publishers now sell advertising space in the physical newspaper and offer display banners as part of the deal.

The biggest spending success story has been online—that includes display, email, Google AdWords, mobile, and social. Traditional advertising spend in the United States has leveled out, whereas online spend is growing rapidly. And this trend will not go out of fashion anytime soon.

Unlike the one-way nature of traditional advertising, digital can engage users in a dialog and be used to communicate with them in a more fluid way. Still, as a digital marketer you need to be smart in terms of what media you use and not kick offline formats entirely to the curb. Outdoor ads can drive potential customers online—where you can engage them with display, social, and email. Offline and online formats are inextricably linked, so you should utilize both when developing your marketing strategy. And since there is nothing worse than seeing an ad offline and going online to find that the promotion has ended, you must keep a consistent message across both formats.

The Move to Online

So how has this love affair with online come about? Think about it. With increased accessibility, there are more and more users online. In fact . . .

- Of households with children, 98 percent have a device for online access—for households with no children, it's 76 percent.
- While on our smartphones, 87 percent of us multitask on other media.
- On average, adults have access to four devices for online access at home.

That means more people are using email, more people are logging on to social media, and more people are researching online before buying offline. More people are buying online too, thanks to the surge in popularity of online payment systems such as PayPal. Businesses are investing in Google AdWords, SEO, and organic search to connect with these multiscreening users where it matters most.

When people do go online, Google is their favorite place to visit. The runners-up in our popularity contest are Facebook, Twitter, and YouTube; further down, Amazon and Wikipedia get a nod of approval.

American users access social media sites at least once a day, so it comes as no surprise that these platforms are among the most popular sites.

Facebook is the social site used most often—and its vast network combined with comprehensive targeting and budget tools make it an advertiser's playground. Twitter and LinkedIn have a smaller reach but they can still be pretty effective.

Different social advertising platforms (and how we can target our audience within them) will be further explored in the "Display Ads on Social Media" section.

Going Mobile

Whether we are waiting for the train, prolonging our lunch breaks, or relaxing at home, we are glued to our mobiles most of the time. There are now more mobile devices in the United States than there are people, and marketers need to recognize and exploit this opportunity by advertising on mobile technologies.

Advertisers should target mobile users that search for local information with geographically relevant, mobile-optimized ads. Once they have finished searching on their phones, one in two of them will go on to buy through their phones, too.

So what is in the pipeline for the display industry? There are lots of opportunities from technologies such as retargeting, remarketing, and real-time bidding. Advertisers should also focus on producing ads for mobile devices, creating richer ad formats and incorporating snappy videos into their ads that users will want to watch.

Technology and Mechanics

Having provided an overview of the display industry and the direction in which it is headed, let's focus on the nuts and bolts of the DDA process.

Soon you will be able to hold your own in a DDA conversation at your next digital dinner party, as you will:

- Be familiar with essential DDA terminology.
- Know the stakeholders in display advertising.
- Understand the mechanics and the technology involved.

Display Ads: Key Terms

Ad click	Occurs when a user clicks after seeing an ad.
Ad impression	The number of times an ad is seen (not necessarily interacted with or clicked on).
Ad unique user	A user who sees an ad from a given device for the first time.
Click	The number of clicks on a hyperlink.
Cookie	A text file or Internet tag that a website places on a user's hard drive to remember data about that user, such as search history.
HTML	Hypertext markup language is the set of commands—or code—used by web browsers to interpret and display page content to users; it is the language that people use to build websites.
Keyword	The term or phrase that triggers your ad to appear and target potential customers. For example, if you own a bakery, you might use *fresh cookies* as a keyword in AdWords—it then triggers Google algorithms to match that phrase.
Page impression	The number of times that a user views a certain page within a website.
Rich media	Interactive media (including text, graphics, animation, video, and audio) used to promote products and services on digital computer-based systems.
Visit	The number of times that a user visits a website—each new visit occurs when there is at least 30 minutes between requests for new content.

How Display Advertising Works

Now that you know how to talk the talk, let's walk you through the display process. The key stakeholders involved are detailed below and in Figure 4.2.

Figure 4.2   Key stakeholders in DDA

1 *Create ad*. It starts when advertisers create the ad, choosing a format in line with your budget. For example, if you want to advertise on *The New York Times* website, you need to bear in mind that this will cost more due to the heavy traffic on that site.

Next, you design the ad with an engaging call to action and a balance between text and imagery. When the ad is ready, you can choose your publisher—by working with agencies or by using a Google tool called DoubleClick, which allows you to search for suitable publishers. The Google Display Network is probably the most well-known publisher. It includes the full suite of Google products and its partners (e.g., YouTube).

2 *Publish ad*. Once you have identified your publisher and adhered to its format specifications, the publisher places your ad on sites based on your target audience and budget. So say you want your ad to be across 10 of the most prolific websites and targeted at people who have browsed for shoes in the past week—there will be a cost for that. In addition to choosing the sites on which you want your ad to show, you can also decide the time of day and across what platforms or devices that it should appear.

An agency can also play a part in this stage of the process; advertising houses such as Ogilvy and W+K match your ads with the people you want to reach and can often help you with design, too.

3 *Serve ad*. Websites are crucial stakeholders in the DDA process, as they enable users to see your ads. There are millions of websites across the GDN and beyond, including The *New York Times*, Facebook, and LinkedIn—the sites on which you want your ads to appear. These websites host your ad through their advertising banner spaces. Ad impressions occur due to any of the following variables:
• Your ad matches the end user's search.
• You hold a *tenancy agreement*, an arrangement in which you occupy a particular space and your ad appears there irrespective of the user's search history.
• You end up bidding against an advertiser who is paying the same amount for the same timing—in this case, your ad rotates with theirs, like a carousel.

4 *Click ad*. Ultimately, consumers are what make the display advertising world work. They see your ad and you want them to take action as a result (like buy, subscribe, or just fall in love with you). That is why so much is spent on advertising. It's also why every message you send should allow the user to take this action. But even though you want consumers

to convert in some way, you should remember that display advertising is not really about revenue generation; it's primarily used as a branding tool. So even though CTRs may be low, your ads are still having an impact. Those users are smitten.

5 *Track ad.* Once users interact with the ad, the responsibility is on you to monitor the ad on an ongoing basis. If you have space on a publisher's website for a month, you should continually refine your ads for the best results. If your call to action is weak, you should change it. If your ad is underperforming, you should pimp it up. Whatever it takes!

Display Technology

DDA depends on some pretty slick technology to make it all run smoothly. For example, you can use *real-time bidding*—an auction process that matches you with ad impressions and with end users as a result (the publisher acts as a medium). Basically, it allows the most relevant person to see your ad.

Mobile has fast become the starlet of DDA, and everyone wants to please her. So you no longer create display ads for PCs; instead you target them to appear on smaller-screened laptops and mobile devices. And since most websites are now mobile-responsive, your ads will be displayed in the best possible light, whatever device the user is on.

Benefits and Challenges of Display

Now that you understand what drives display advertising, the key people behind the wheel, and a little more about the journey, let's explore the benefits and challenges that you may face down the DDA road.

Benefits

Influence. Some forms of traditional media simply raise awareness, but research has shown that DDA actually influences buying behavior. It lets us reach a mass audience with a message that sticks.

Targeting. Targeting tools provide advertisers with a better ROI, less waste, and more focus. With tools such as AdChoices on the GDN, you know that your ads are reaching a specific audience.

Control. You can control where your ad will appear, who will see it, and how they can interact with it. Ultimately you want your ads to generate clicks. Failing that, you root for interactions, or for conversions between online and offline responses.

Integration. Create matches made in heaven by integrating display and social media with TV, radio, and print. But always remember to maintain a consistent message across all channels.

Segmentation. You need to create ads that satisfy different needs and wants. Segmentation allows you to cozy up to your different customer groups and get to know their behavior through how they interact with your ads, what makes them tick, and what makes them click.

Challenges

Banner blindness. With the average user being served more than 1,700 banner ads per month, you can appreciate why he might dismiss your ads.

Low click-through rates. CTRs on display ads can be as low as 0.1 percent. One in a thousand may not seem like much, but if you apply it to one billion users on Facebook, it becomes a pretty big target audience. Also, that one in a thousand could have a branding impact on another 990 people—through sharing the ad across her own network.

Stage 1: Define

We can't start planning creative ad formats or designing clever calls to action until we understand the people we are targeting and how best to target them. Stage 1 of the iterative process—define, as highlighted in Figure 4.3—will turn you into a display ninja in no time, adept at:

- Understanding how display advertising works.
- Knowing your audience and finding publishers to help you connect with it.
- Setting SMART campaign objectives that work within your budget.

Finding the Audience

From the outset of your display campaign, you should ask yourself who the people in your target audience are—their gender, age, location, and likes and dislikes. You can then segment this audience (which is far more humane than it sounds)!

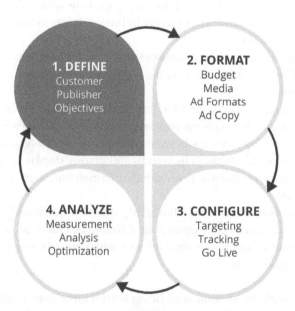

Figure 4.3 Focus on the First Stage in the DDA Process

Figure 4.4   Debbie Digital Customer Persona

Users leave a trail online; for instance, as they browse sites or engage with email marketing. Their clicks tell you who they are, where they live, and what their interests are. You may not know how they take their coffee just yet, but you *do* know that they are interested in your brand. And so you should avoid scaring them away with too many calls to action; a few details now will be enough to engage them later. Patience, grasshopper.

If a user decides to register for updates, great—this implies their intent to buy. You can also collect data from the registration form and use it to shape, augment, and tailor your digital marketing strategy. For instance, you can create personas, personalities, and preferences, such as Debbie in Figure 4.4.

Debbie can be segmented according to her age, marital status, her hobbies, and the fact that she earns a steady income. Once you have developed her persona, it becomes easier to predict her personality, her preferences, and her buying behavior. Then you can meet her needs and requirements with your marketing strategy. Thanks, Debbie!

Researching Publishers

Now that you have defined your target audience, you need to match this audience with the most appropriate publisher for your ads.

MSN Homepage Rich Media: 300x250 Expanding

Creative Acceptance Policy
All creative must meet the requirements of the MSA Creative Acceptance Policy

Ad Specification Details

Ad Type / Ad Size	Initial Size	Download File Size (GIF/JPG)	Max Initial Download File Size	Full Expanded Size	Max Weight Secondary (Polite) Download	Max Weight Progressive Download (Video/ Streaming Only)	Audio Specifications/ Limit	Animation/ Looping Limit	Alt Text Limit
Rectangle 300x250	300W X 250H	20k	40k	970W X 450H	175k	1.5mb	Allowed on user click only	Allowed ; Duration: 15 sec	65 char

Note(s):
- If Flash is not installed, or minimum bandwidth requirement met, the static back-up image will be displayed in the 300x250 area.
- 15 seconds of total animation allowed on page load.
- Unit must be click to expand and click to close

Figure 4.5   MSN Ad Specification
Source: MSN.

Back to the user's trail. Say a user searches for *adventure holidays*. Now that you know what he is interested in, you can show your ads on the most relevant sites. Ultimately, you are looking for a publisher that facilitates targeting based on segments like demographics, location, and interests. You should ask potential publishers for testimonials and KPIs, plus examples of work they have done across PCs, mobile devices, and social media. Google offers a range of tools to help you choose the best publisher for your display advertising—for example, the AdWords Display Planner.

Once you have found a publisher, you need to follow certain ad specifications and formats (like size and download speed) to make it a happy relationship. The example in Figure 4.5 is a 300 x 250 expanding ad. In this case the advertiser needed to satisfy certain criteria before MSN would publish it.

Setting Objectives

As a digital marketer, you can use display to help you:

- *Build your branding.* Building on the success of your existing brand.
- *Raise awareness.* Utilizing online advertising in addition to offline to introduce a new product.
- *Engage customers.* Offering people new ways to interact with your brand.
- *Encourage direct response.* Gathering data when users fill out forms, enter competitions, or request quotes.

- *Connect on social media.* Enabling your followers to act as brand advocates as they engage in customer-to-customer (C2C) advertising.
- *Generate leads.* Creating subsequent email marketing campaigns as a targeted form of revenue generation.
- *Increase conversions/sales.* Driving sales later in the campaign process when your display branding tool is combined with other digital marketing elements.

So how can you achieve these goals? You can start with some SMART objectives . . .

Specific. Create a numeric goal; for instance, to achieve 100 sales by June 17.
Measured. Put systems in place to accurately track your progress towards this goal.
Actionable. Take certain actions to influence the outcome.
Realistic. Set achievable goals—for instance, there is no point in shooting yourself in the foot by aiming for a 50 percent CTR with your display ads.
Timed. You have a deadline by which you want to achieve your goals.

Stage 2: Format

You have now got the lowdown on target audiences, publishers, and how best to set your objectives and feel ready to start advertising online. But what formats should your ads appear in? Good question..

Time for stage 2 of the iterative process, as highlighted in Figure 4.6. Let's starting by diving into the creative space to help you:

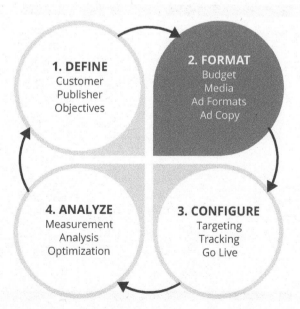

Figure 4.6   Focus on the Second Stage in the DDA Process

- Understand the different dimensions available.
- Know how to maximize ad space.
- Realize the benefits of advertising on social media.

Ad Formats

Just like how you were taught in kindergarten that boys and girls come in all shapes and sizes, so do ad formats. And in order to best utilize DDA, you need to be aware of each one.

Types of Display Ads

The most commonly used ad formats are listed next and are also shown in Figure 4.7.

- *Leaderboards* are generally at the top of the page, and because they are the first messages that people see, often perform best.
- *Mid-placement units* or *MPUs* are expandable, dynamic ads in the middle of the page. They can move up or down, are often animated, and see higher CTRs than most other formats.
- *Skyscrapers* and *wide skyscrapers* are the areas to the left and right of the homepage.
- *Islands* are small and niche areas that hold static ads. And no man is one either.

Roadblocks, takeovers, and in-tandem ads. A roadblock is a combination of two or more ads for the same campaign, on the same page, with the same message.

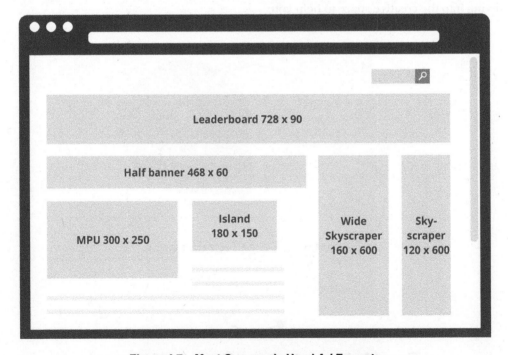

Figure 4.7   Most Commonly Used Ad Formats

Figure 4.8   Roadblock Ad Format
Source: TheJournal.ie.

In the roadblock shown in Figure 4.8, there are ads for the product within the leaderboard banner, the MPU, and both skyscrapers. All of the ads share the same key message but the design has been changed for each ad—with a variation in color within the MPU. This is also an example of a *homepage takeover* (*HPTO*). Everywhere you look on the screen, you see content related to the product. Bear in mind, this option is pretty expensive. Roadblocks are often used in affiliation programs between advertisers; for example, if Newstalk radio station (seen in Figure 4.8) were to team up with a coffee chain.

The ads in Figures 4.9 and 4.10 are examples of *in-tandem ads*: two or more ads on the same page that interact. Some of these ads may be animated, as shown by the couple in Figures 4.9 and 4.10, but ultimately they are designed to work in parallel, so that one carries one message, the other carries a similar one, and they work in tandem. Aptly named, don't you think?

Creative Ad Formats

Now that you know what ad spaces look like, how can you optimize them? Well, you can start by getting creative with the following ad formats:

Animated. These ads typically consist of three slides on a carousel. Looking back at the animated leaderboard in Figures 4.9 and 4.10, the first view of the ad in Figure 4.9 asks, "What can you get for €1?," the next shown in Figure 4.10 starts with "Sky Sports for €1," and the next might simply be "Switch to UPC." Three is the magic number here—any more frames will confuse the end user.

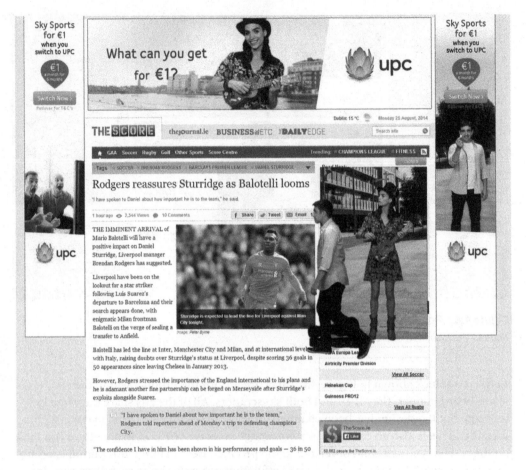

Figure 4.9 First Frame of an Animated Leaderboard
Source: TheJournal.ie.

Static. These strong and simple ads are often used by powerful, blue-chip companies that only need to say, for example: "Internet Explorer 10. Download here." This message will carry a lot of weight within a very small area.

HPTO. As you now know, this is an ad display in which most of a publisher's webpage is replaced with advertising content. Even if it has no effect on users' buying behavior there and then, they will remember it the next time they browse.

Floating. The floaters temporarily interrupt navigation—so if users move their cursors over a display ad, a floating ad comes up. They might tempt people to start interacting with your ads in new ways, but make sure that you do not disrupt the user's experience so much as to have a negative influence on your brand.

Expandable ads. These dynamic ads differ from the floating kind in that people choose to click and expand them, rather than the ad appearing out of nowhere. You can use expandable ads to encourage interaction with your brand even if the user does not click through. You have the option to include videos, competitions, email subscription forms, social media buttons, and a link back to your website. Usually you will not be charged extra for taking over this space because you will have stuck to the publisher's specifications—you have just been clever with optimizing the space provided.

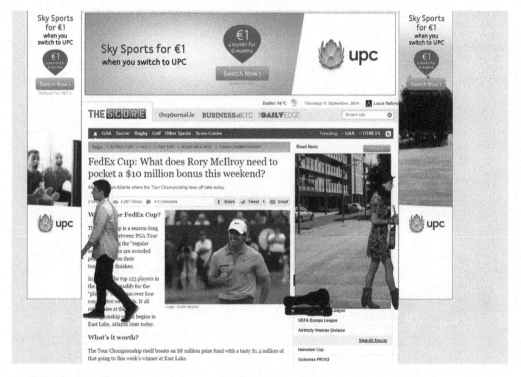

Figure 4.10   Second Frame of an Animated Leaderboard
Source: The Journal.ie.

Rich media. These ads enable video streaming and are pretty effective—because as mentioned earlier, one in two users will interact with videos in display ads. If you can get airtime of up to 30 seconds with your audience you will have earned some serious display advertising kudos.

Filmstrips. Filmstrips consist of five different segments (maybe three of which contain video); the user can explore all segments by scrolling, hovering, or clicking on the creative. They provide a content-rich experience, and since they do not interrupt the homepage, people can interact with them whenever they want. Filmstrips offer advertisers a powerful branding canvas, because even if people do not watch your videos you are promoting your brand the entire time.

Display Ads on Social Media

Advertising on social media is becoming increasingly popular thanks to the size of the audience available. Let's start by looking at YouTube and the types of formats it offers in Figure 4.11.

All of these ads come at a different cost. They generate a different number of impressions and clicks and have different implications for your brand.

YouTube ads allow users to skip them after 5 or 10 seconds, and the ads are targeted in line with the user's browsing history.

Ad format	Placement	Platform	Specs
Display ads 	Appears to the right of the feature video and above the video suggestions list. For larger players, this ad may appear below the player.	Desktop	300x250 and 300x60
Overlay ads 	Semi-transparent overlay ads that appear on the lower 20 percent portion of your video.	Desktop	480x70 (Flash) or text
Skippable video ads 	Skippable video ads allow viewers to skip ads after 5 seconds, if they choose. Inserted before, during, or after the main video.	Desktop, mobile devices, TV, and game consoles	Plays in video player.
Nonskippable video ads and long, nonskippable video ads 	Nonskippable video ads must be watched before your video can be viewed. Long nonskippable video ads may be up to 30 seconds long. These ads can appear before, during, or after the main video.	Desktop and mobile devices	Plays in video player. 15 or 20 seconds in length, depending on regional standards. Long, nonskippable ads can be up to 30 seconds in length.
Sponsored cards 	Sponsored cards display content that may be relevant to your video, such as products featured in the video. Viewers will see a teaser for the card for a few seconds. They can also click the icon in the top right corner of the video to browse the cards.	Desktop and mobile devices	Card sizes vary

Figure 4.11   YouTube Ad Formats
Source: Google and the Google logo are registered trademarks of Google Inc.; used with permission.

Facebook is a powerful advertising tool because you can see what your audience likes, shares, and comments on. So any ad that users see on the right-hand side of a Facebook stream is targeted specifically at them. You can segment your audience according to demographic, location, interests, behaviors, connections, and so on.

Facebook ads will vary depending on where you want your ad to appear and the results you are after. Your ads can appear within the news feed (on desktop or mobile) or down the right-hand side. You can decide on the type of ad you will use depending on your objective. For example, you can use photo, video, or text for page post-engagement and links for website conversions.

Advertising on Twitter can help you to reach users on mobile devices, since 65 percent of Twitter's ad revenue is from mobile tablets or smartphones. Ads appear as what are called *promoted tweets*—so if users search for Starbucks, promoted tweets from Starbucks will appear in their feeds.

Twitter uses similar targeting as Facebook (location, interests, followers, etc.) to ensure that promoted tweets are directed to the most relevant users. Your ad can be discovered by the audience of your choice, and you only pay when people follow your account, retweet your message, or take action as a result of your ad.

Social ads within LinkedIn are also extremely targeted, but in a slightly different way, as shown in Figure 4.12.

In LinkedIn you do not really target by demographics or interests. Instead you target by job title—sales manager, marketing director, and so on. You can also target people by company or by group; for example, a group within the MBA Association. You can even

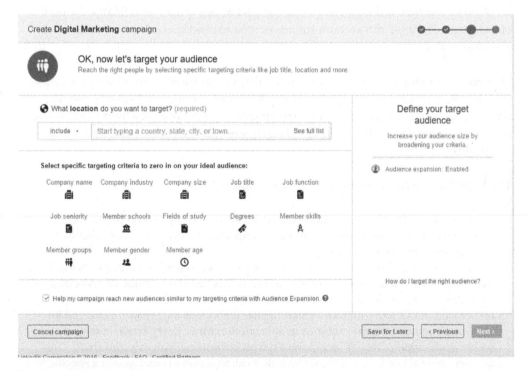

Figure 4.12   LinkedIn Ad Targeting
Source: LinkedIn.

see how big your target audience is and how many people can potentially see your ads (shown on the right-hand side of the figure). This is a whole different ballgame from guessing how many people might see your billboard. And it can be very effective, too— in fact, 60 percent of LinkedIn users have clicked on ads on the site.

Pinterest and Instagram have smaller subscriber bases, but they still offer a great way of engaging users with imagery. With Instagram, you can take advantage of Facebook's insights, too.

So now you have covered the type of ads available, how advertisers can capitalize on them, and the social platforms that you can use. Feel free to choose the best mix of formats to suit your own company's objectives and budget.

Allocating Budgets

Now it's time to talk money!

To plan your campaign spend, you need to consider the following factors: your target audience (how much it will take to reach them), the publisher's price points (whether you can afford the big ones or if you should go local), location (because websites in prolific areas such as New York City will cost more), competition (whether you will be involved in real-time bidding, competing for advertising space), and finally, the cost of the creative (taking into account rounds of amends and special formats like expanding ads).

Integrated campaigns require a variety of media, so you should spread your budget strategically across the spectrum. For example, Coca Cola utilizes display, print, TV, outdoor, and experiential advertising (which means giving people a brand-enhancing experience, even if they do not engage directly with your product) in its advertising campaigns.

The costs that you need to take into consideration include:

- *Cost per mille (CPM):* This is the most common way to be charged; you pay for every thousand times that your ad appears in a page impression—irrespective of whether the end user engages with it or even sees it.
- *Cost per click (CPC):* You are charged when a user clicks your ad. With display's low CTRs this structure will not drain your budget, and since it is based on unique IP addresses your competitors cannot rack up costs with clicks either.
- *Cost per lead (CPL):* Say you have a smart banner that opens out—you are charged for displaying it and also if a user submits its subscription form. Every action costs you.
- *Cost per acquisition (CPA):* If you spend $100 on advertising, you can convert 10 customers at a CPA of $10. You could include a call to action to email you at a specific address—then you can work out from the number of emails the cost you incurred to acquire those customers.

- *Tenancy/sponsorship:* You have exclusive ownership of a position for a set period of time. You are charged a fixed amount, irrespective of factors such as CPM.

Marketers use a set formula to calculate costs:

$$\frac{\#\ \text{ad impressions} \times \text{CPM}}{1,000}$$

So 1 million page impressions at $5 CPM will cost $5,000.

Let's try out a couple of quick exercises using this formula . . .

- How much would it cost to buy 200,000 page impressions on CNBC at $5 CPM?
- You have $6,000 to spend and want to run a campaign on CNN.com. If they work off a CPM rate of $4, how many impressions will you get for your budget?
- You want to run a display campaign on a blind site that charges $1.60 CPM. How many page impressions will a budget of $3,000 get you?

Did you get through those okay? This formula is an important one to remember because it allows you to work out the cost of your advertising—which in turn can help you to shape your display campaigns.

Media and Format Options

Now that you know the costs involved in digital display media and how to calculate these costs, where do you go to buy? Well, there are a few options:

- You can go *direct*; for example, by advertising directly on CNN.
- You can use *value networks* like the GDN. They make it easier for you to allocate your budget and place your ads.
- You can seek the expertise of digital ad agencies. Since going direct or even using value networks can quickly drain the budget of novices, these guys can help you to get your money's worth. AdRoll is a popular one at the moment—they specialize in retargeting.

Google owns 33 percent of all online advertising revenue and can offer advertisers a range of digital media formats. These include:

- *Search*. Text ads shown on Google above or to the right of search results.
- *Mobile*. Text ads on Google mobile search results. Text and display ads served on the GDN.
- *GDN text*. Text ads shown on the Google Display Network, which consists of millions of websites that allow ads on their sites.
- *GDN display*. Display ads served on the GDN.
- YouTube. Video or display ads on YouTube.

Ad Copy

When creating your ads, you should include:

- A clear call to action (CTA).
- A strong design that fits that particular ad format.
- Copy that is in keeping with the publisher, the target audience, and your keyword research.
- Your brand displayed prominently.
- Direct, concise, and urgent language.

Once you have all these elements in place, you need to check if your ads are working.

Split testing may just become your new favorite hobby—it saves you time by publishing multiple versions of an ad campaign and monitoring the best-performing version. You should use whichever campaign delivers the best ROI going forward, carrying elements of that campaign over to your creative iterative process. Usually split testing will offer a higher ROI because you have done your research, your content is more targeted, and a user will be more likely to interact/ convert.

There are six parts of a display ad that you should always split test:

1 Content
2 Offer
3 Pricing
4 Creative
5 Call to action
6 Banner size

Figure 4.13   A/B Testing

So if you want to test calls to action, one test could supply a phone number as a call to action, while another could be a button that the user can click to learn more.

The display ads in Figure 4.13 contain very subtle differences. The call to action (for example, "Learn More") and the copy may be the same, but the creative is different. You could run both on the same day for the same audience and whichever performs better is the one you would choose going forward. This is called A/B testing. Advertisers can add more tests if they have the resources and reporting capabilities—for instance, Google uses as many as 10 tests (A/B/C/D/E, etc.) with some of their own products.

Stage 3: Configure

By now you will be familiar with stages 1 and 2 of our iterative process. Right?! So let's move on to stage 3—which has been highlighted in Figure 4.14.

In this section you will learn how to capitalize on each stage of your integrated marketing campaign, so you can link online and offline activities with a consistent and effective message that engages customers. Before long, you'll be a display ninja, adept at:

- Targeting well-written ads to appear on the most appropriate media.
- Tracking and measuring your ads before optimizing them for better results.
- Scheduling your communications effectively so they have maximum impact.

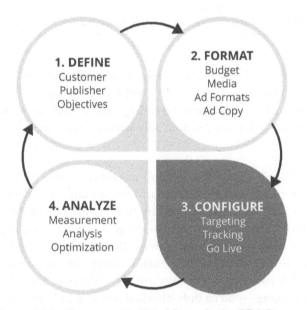

Figure 4.14   Focus on the Third Stage in the DDA Process

Targeting

Now that you know what your ads will look like and how to make sure the best-performing ones are picked, you need to make them appear at the right time, in the right place, to the right people. Because ads are no longer generic—they are incredibly targeted. So when you see an ad on LinkedIn, that ad is aimed specifically at you. It is relevant to your browsing history, your searches, and your patterns of behavior. It may remind you of Big Brother's all-seeing eye, but that is how the process works!

See some of the ways below that you can target customers using the GDN.

Targeting option	How it works
Contextual (automatic placements)	Google evaluates all the keywords in a Display ad group and places your ads on websites that match this theme.
Managed placements	You select the specific sites where you want your ads to run.
Topics	Targets your ad to websites that include content about topics you select.
Interest categories	Targets your ads to users with specific interests based on websites they visit.
Remarketing	Shows ads to people who previously visited your site.
Auto-optimization (DCO)	Google automatically optimizes both targeting and bidding to find additional conversions. Also known as Display Campaign Optimizer.
Inferred demographics	Targets your ads to users based on gender and age.

The first form of targeting described here is contextual targeting: Using relevant terms and keywords to try to find ads that will match the advertiser to the end user. Advertisers can also apply behavioral targeting, which is (you've guessed it!) based on people's behavior—what they search for, what cookies they leave on websites, and so on.

Remarketing is a Google tool that takes full advantage of the GDN. For example, when users visit Booking.com they drop an Internet tag on that site even after they leave. Those users may then be followed by holiday-related ads. You can show ads to people who have already visited your website, browsed your products, searched for you via mobile, and watched your videos. Before these users got distracted, they expressed an interest in what you have to offer—so you need to catch them and hook them with your ads when they are most likely to buy. And you are not charged for this tracking—you're only charged when a unique user clicks through or sees the ad.

Retargeting uses the same idea but it drills right down into a user's buying behavior and is thus far more specific. It is also used by publishers other than Google. Retargeting focuses on the people that have almost bought and tries to close that sale. In short, it converts window shoppers into buyers.

When using these targeting options, you should avoid discouraging potential customers by stalking them with your ads. Instead, you should apply ad frequency capping—in which you limit the number of times that your ad shows to a unique user within a given period of time.

Tracking

Your ads are live, the right people are seeing them, and you've got that warm and fuzzy feeling. However, you still need to track your campaigns and monitor your ROI to make sure that your little gems are working as hard as they can.

The way in which an ad's impact is measured has evolved. You no longer have to use the blunt instrument of a CTR, because after all, there is more to business than clicks! Advertisers also take the following metrics into account:

- *Interaction rate*. The number of times that a user interacts with an ad divided by its impressions. At 2.48 percent on average, interaction rates are much higher than CTRs and are more in line with a PPC or a Google AdWords campaign.
- *Video completion/conversion rate*. The number of times that a user converts and watches a full video, such as a 30-second video that plays to the end. Since 50 percent of users would prefer to watch embedded videos instead of clicking a display ad, advertisers should get that camera rolling.
- *Expansion time*. The average time that an ad is viewed in an expanded state. Display ads are becoming more playful and less static. If users choose not to click on the ad, they can expand it to watch video streams and interact with its embedded material, such as games and competitions.
- *Average display time*. The average time that a rich media ad is displayed to a user. It should be quite short—so if an ad has video, ideally it will be displayed for fewer than 30 seconds.

You should apply all the relevant metrics you can to suit your business objectives. In this way, you can overcome the challenges of display advertising and start to see more of its benefits. Remember to take advantage of the variety of reporting sources available to you, including:

- *Publishers/agencies*. They can use analytics to tell you about your performance.
- *Sales*. You can check if they have increased since the campaign started.
- *Ad networks*. Large media outlets like the GDN.
- *Analytics*. Those internally and those reported by Google (Google Analytics, AdSense, and DoubleClick).
- *Offline reports*. Since online and offline are linked, any increase in performance offline (purchases, phone calls, coupon redemption, etc.) can indicate the level of success of online activities.

Going Live

Throughout the campaign, you should use a systematic process for your communications and decide how frequently you want to send them. You can set a clear time frame or schedule so that you can see clearly what ads are running, where they will appear, when they will appear and any follow-ups needed, who the target market is, and the cost involved.

Stage 4: Analyze

Not to sound like a broken record but remember—successful digital display advertising is an iterative process. It involves tracking and optimizing all aspects of the campaign, allowing you to maximize effectiveness and ROI and helping you to achieve your business goals. And that is why the analysis process within stage 4 (highlighted in Figure 4.15) is so important.

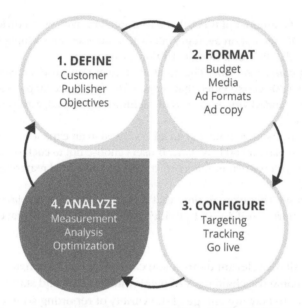

Figure 4.15   Focus on the Fourth Stage in the DDA Process

Measure

You need to continually measure your message and your creatives with publishers to create a culture of testing. This is made easier if you first set out KPIs such as:

- Click-through rates
- Interactivity rates
- Expansion rates
- Bounce rates
- Page views
- Average time on page
- Direct traffic sources
- Conversions

Another method of analyzing success is measuring your ROI. A wise man once said, "Show me the money," and as a marketer, you want to see that your hard work has paid off—literally. So how do you calculate your ROI? Check out the example below . . .

> Say you want to convert 15 new customers.
>
> Your budget is $1,750 for the media and you have a design budget of $650.
>
> Your media budget gets you 150,000 ad impressions with an estimated CTR of 2 percent (although it will usually be a lot lower).
>
> The website that hosts your ad gets 3,000 unique visitors and you are aiming for a 10 percent conversion rate (again, normally this is lower). This results in 300 inquiries. Your publisher tells you that 20 percent of these will be quality leads, so you get 60 sales leads.
>
> And since your publisher also tells you that usually one in four sales leads results in a conversion, that is 60/4 = 15 new customers.
>
> Now you have met your business objective, but you also want to check your ROI. So if each new customer buys a product worth $100, your ROI is 15 × 100 = $1,500.

Boom! You have officially been shown the money.

In addition to hard metrics such as conversions (which are the ultimate goal), you can use soft metrics such as:

- *Page or ad impressions* to determine whether your campaign is delivering; if you have a million ad impressions but nothing has happened, something is fundamentally wrong.
- *CTRs* to measure which creative is most engaging.
- *Unique users and impressions* to assess your reach and coverage.

Analytics can be a little confusing—but there are great tools out there, such as Google Analytics, that can clear things up. It offers real-life tracking capabilities so that you can trace every cent you spend and you can customize it with your own digital marketing activities. For instance, Figure 4.16 shows an example of paid search, organic search, and display.

Within the Analytics dashboard you can create your own goals and objectives. You can also tailor how you want your reports to look, how specific you want them to be, and whether you want to use funnel visualization to identify the different data sources feeding them, as illustrated by Figure 4.17. This gives you end-to-end visibility of the users that engage with your ad before converting.

Your own funnel visualization process might be different. You might want it to run from left to right instead of from top to bottom. And that is the beauty of Google Analytics—you can augment and customize your analytics in whatever way you like.

Now that you have covered the measurement and analysis within stage 4, you can optimize your ads for even better results. This in turn brings you back to the start of the

Figure 4.16 Conversions Per Channel Grouping in Google Analytics
Source: Google and the Google logo are registered trademarks of Google Inc.; used with permission.

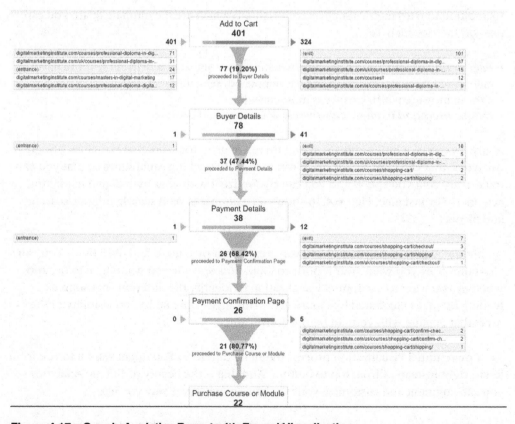

Figure 4.17 Google Analytics Report with Funnel Visualization
Source: Google and the Google logo are registered trademarks of Google Inc.; used with permission.

iterative process, during which you can prepare to launch your new and improved display campaign.

Laws and Guidelines

Right now your head is probably swimming with all the ins and outs of the display campaign process. And you probably want us to stop talking so you can start advertising, right? Easy, tiger—first there are a few legal considerations you should know about.

Laws and guidelines will differ across all locations, and some may be more stringent than others. But still, when it comes to display advertising there are some universal restrictions (the most obvious example of which relates to alcohol). Wherever you live, you need to be aware of that particular region's laws and guidelines.

Maintaining Privacy

Within the arena of display advertising, one major consideration is privacy, and advertisers need to adhere to privacy policies at all times. For instance, most websites now include strict cookie policies, and it is mandatory for digital marketers to display these policies. If you are going to join the game of Internet tag you need to be transparent in your actions. Within the privacy arena lies the whole area of data protection, too. You must follow whatever legislation applies to your area in terms of storing, using, and destroying the information you have gathered through your marketing activities.

Creative Copyright

"Borrowing" creatives from Google Images to use in your ads is an absolute no-no. Instead, advertisers can source images from libraries such as iStock or Shutterstock, which allow you to buy a copyright for promotional purposes. In some cases you can contact the photographer or artist and request copyright through them— sometimes you will pay, sometimes you might catch a lucky break. But you should never assume that just because something is free for download that there will be no repercussions.

Accessibility

Who are you allowing to see your ads? And are you adhering to the privacy laws of those that are accessing them? All over the world, there are advertising standards bureaus in place to protect not only the consumer but also the advertiser. In the United States, for example, you should consult the American Advertising Federation (AAF) if you plan on advertising transnationally or globally. They will tell you what you can and cannot do.

Having covered the legal bit—that concludes this chapter on digital display advertising.

So, What Have You Learned in This Chapter?

Here are some final pearls of wisdom:

- *Keep things simple.* With your message, with your creatives—clear, succinct ads are more likely to grab attention.
- *Use your publishers.* They have the expertise and insights that can make a huge difference to your campaigns.
- *Try out tools.* Use AdWords Planner, DoubleClick, and other Google tools to help you plan, manage, and optimize your display campaigns.
- *Be smart.* Set SMART objectives in line with your online and offline targets.
- *Think laterally.* Do not just focus on CTRs, which are a pretty blunt measurement of success. Use the other KPIs that have been covered, like ad impressions and interaction rates, to get a sense of how your ads are doing.
- *Know your audience.* Once you have created segments, you can build personas, predict behavior, and meet preferences.
- *Stay on track.* Measure your campaigns on an ongoing, iterative basis—linking to analytics and testing for success whenever possible.
- *Get creative.* At the end of the day, after all the planning and testing and analyzing, you want customers to like your ad. And it is the creative ones that will help you stand out.

Now go forth and put yourself on display!

Go to www.artofdmi.com to access the case study on DDA as additional support material for this chapter.

 **Exercises**

Exercise 1

Think about your own business, or take as an example a business that you are interested in. List all of the potential primary and secondary target audience types there might be for that brand and add interests for each. Write down what their interests might tell you about their online habits.

Exercise 2

You have been given a budget of €25K to run a display advertising campaign. You have been told to advertise on PC, mobile, and tablets. After some research, you realize the majority of your target audience uses Android smartphones. Devise a budget plan and apportion budget to each of the above elements accordingly.

Exercise 3

You are now working with a smaller budget of €5K—€10K for your display advertising campaign. The likes of a HPTO are not feasible at this stage. What are the alternative options and strategies you can undertake for display advertising?

Exercise 4

It is Q1 of a new year and you have been rewarded with a sizable digital marketing budget. Display advertising is top of your agenda. Using SMART principles, set out five objectives that you want to achieve for the quarter and year. Outline a plan for how you will go about achieving each objective.

Exercise 5

Develop a social media display advertising campaign aimed at the following audience:

- Females 24–35 years old.
- Working professionals.
- People looking to get married.
- People who live primarily in the capital city of your country.
- People who have an interest in sports.

 ## Action Plan: Digital Display Advertising

Digital Marketing Planning Scheme for DDA

Objectives

Reach, frequency, awareness, brand uplift, influence, conversion, click

Action Items and Frequency

- Budgeting: Per campaign
- Media purchase: Per campaign
- Creative: Per campaign
- Targeting: Weekly
- Tracking: Daily
- Optimization: Weekly

Measurement Tools and KPIs

- Ad-serving software: Impressions served, flight management, CTR
- Social-listening software: Brand mentions
- Web analytics: Campaign clicks, brand search increases, conversions

Spend

Media	Content	People	Systems
x	x	x	

Chapter 5
Email Marketing

An Introduction

In a constantly evolving digital landscape, tools and platforms come and go. Email, however, has remained a steadfast and dependable channel with 3.2 billion email accounts worldwide. That's three times more than the number of Facebook and Twitter accounts combined, and if optimized correctly, an email marketing campaign can be all-powerful, driving better returns on investment and higher levels of engagement. The fact that you can dispense with printing flyers, save trees, and be an email marketing pro? Well, those are just added bonuses!

Definition

Like many of the specialties within digital marketing, the key to a powerful email marketing strategy is structure.

Formal definition of email marketing: A structured, systematic process that is one of the most successful channels for delivering highly relevant marketing communications to targeted subscribers.

Informal definition of email marketing: Instant inbox gratification!

Process

So what makes email marketing so valuable, besides its ability to establish brand visibility in the eyes that matter most (those of your customers, just in case you weren't sure!)? Like every other digital marketing specialty, the success of email is based upon a rigorous, consistent process. The Digital Marketing Institute's 3i principles underpin a general methodology that incorporates every field of digital marketing, and email is no exception.

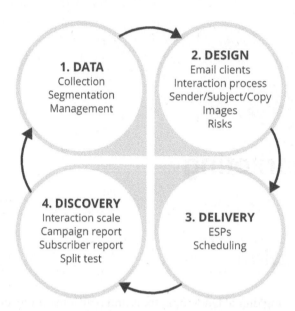

Figure 5.1   Four-Stage Email Marketing Process

Initiate. Start with the customer and work towards a fully optimized email marketing campaign. Who are your target subscribers? What kind of email content will best suit their preferences and needs?

Iterate. Measure and analyze the performance of your email marketing campaign. Are your target subscribers opening your emails and engaging with them? Are they ignoring them? You can use this information to learn from your mistakes, repeat your successes, and continually improve the execution of your campaign.

Integrate. Incorporate your email marketing campaign into your overall digital marketing and offline marketing efforts.

Before we start exploring email marketing in deeper detail, take a look at Figure 5.1 and the list that follows for the four vital steps that comprise an effective email marketing process:

1 *Data.* The first step in any email marketing campaign should always be the creation of a subscriber list. This is a compilation of email contacts who have consented to receive your communications (they've opted in). You can create as many lists as you need in order to segment your subscribers so that you can target them with relevant, personalized content that they will actually care about.

2 *Design.* This step involves deciding which content you should include in your email and the design principles you must follow, to ensure that your email ends up in a subscriber's inbox, ready to engage and excite them.

3 *Delivery.* This step is all about the delivery of your marketing emails. You will learn how they are managed through an email service provider (ESP), which facilitates everything from email style and layout to scheduling. Step 3 covers what happens to an email after it has been sent and delivered. You will learn how to utilize testing to decide what your

email should look like and when you should send it to guarantee the best possible open rates.

4 *Discovery*. Analysis and reporting are fundamental when revising and refining your digital practices. Leveraging analytics tools will allow you to track every cent spent on your email marketing and let you track open rates, total opens, and unique opens. You will be able to track ROI through CTRs, unsubscribes, and bounce rates. Analytics tools are a gateway to highly detailed, clinical data that will enable you to tailor your email marketing strategy, taking into account both your successes and failures.

Key Terms and Concepts

Even if you haven't carried out any email marketing activities (yet!), it's very likely that you will feel quite comfortable with the concept of email. Most users will have more than one email account, be it business or personal, and are familiar with a variety of email clients—from Gmail to Yahoo! Mail. It has already been mentioned that email marketing is highly structured and process-driven, which means everything you need to know will be easy to learn and simple to implement. It's just about following the process! By the end of this chapter, you will feel confident in your ability to:

- Understand and harness the direct influence of email marketing on a global basis.
- Collect and collate subscriber data so you can maximize your audience targeting.
- Craft a compelling and contagious (in a good way) marketing email, from subject line to imagery and text formatting.
- Optimize the delivery of your emails by avoiding spam filters, embracing split testing, and scheduling efficiently.
- Describe and replicate the anatomy of an effective email marketing campaign.
- Identify the email marketing metrics that matter and incorporate them into your reporting.

Stage 1: Data—Email Marketing Process

Before you learn more about the details of acquiring data and subscriber management, you first need to know about spam and its intrinsic relationship to the data you use as part of an email marketing campaign. This is part of stage 1 of the process shown in Figure 5.2 and it will involve being aware of:

- The formal definition of spam: What it is and what it entails for you as a marketer.
- Examples of what email subscribers perceive as spam and the criteria on which they base their decisions.
- Methods to avoid triggering spam filters and escaping the damning judgment: spam!

Spam, Spammity Spam

Just like the questionably colored, unidentifiable precooked meat in a can, the receipt of unsolicited email communications can be gross! Unsolicited email means

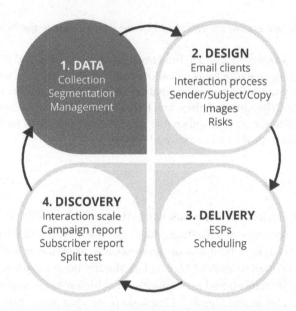

Figure 5.2   Focus on the First Stage in the Email Marketing Process

that a user didn't ask, or opt in, to receive the email. Spam can also apply to bulk email, a term that applies to the same unsolicited email being sent out to hundreds of thousands of users who have not opted in to receive it. This is a practice that can result in *blacklisting*, which means that the sender is added to a list of naughty email senders that email clients can block and keep away from their users' inboxes. Blacklisting, in essence, means the death of an email marketing campaign and can be incredibly damaging to a brand as well.

Examples of Spam

Spam is insidious. At first a spam email can look entirely inoffensive; say, a simple inquiry about whether or not you are interested in eye drops manufactured in China. The difference lies in whether or not you have expressed a previous interest in buying eye drops. Did you fill in a contact form on a website? Did you give your email address to someone because you had the intention of buying eye drops? Did you opt in? A bulk email example of spam could include a newsletter on the topic of fly fishing that you have never subscribed to, which is only a good thing (not to mention a massive coincidence) if you happen to like fly fishing.

Spam Really Is in the Eye of the Beholder

What email subscribers consider to be spam really boils down to personal preference. Recipients can audit the contents of their inbox, which include your marketing email, and can choose to send your message to their junk mail folders based on a range of criteria. One of the main reasons your email could be marked as spam is because a subscriber is unfamiliar with you, your business, or your brand. Sometimes users forget that they have opted in to receive marketing messages: They could have subscribed to too many sites' email lists, or they could have subscribed too long ago to remember what they subscribed to. Another key reason has to do with relevancy: They could have opted in initially, but if they view the content of follow-up emails as irrelevant or unrelated to the reason they opted in, they're more likely to regard them as spam.

Often these are factors over which an email marketer has limited control. But there are a number of actions that you can take to make sure you are abiding by the best practices to limit the likelihood of being considered a spammer.

Five Ways to Avoid the Damning Judgment: Spam!

Avoid Spam Filters

Email clients are designed with an incredible focus on protecting their users from disruptive, annoying spam, and one of the methods used is built-in spam filters, which audit email messages based on a number of factors. Sometimes email marketing messages can fall victim to spam filters even if the recipient has opted in, so it's important to be aware of the criteria these filters use to make their judgments and avoid them when crafting your email messages.

Image and text imbalance. Using too many images can cause an imbalance that can trigger spam filters. Avoid creating or using designs that simply have text overlaid on an image, as a spam filter will only detect the image and not the text built into it.
Too much formatting. This includes the use of excessive capitals and capitalization, bold text, and irregular font sizes.
Attachments. Try not to use attachments; include all necessary information within the body of the email, as attachments can trigger spam filters. You should also use your email to direct traffic to your website, or social media, or somewhere where you can generate a higher ROI, as this method serves as a much more valuable call to action than asking the recipient to download and read an attachment.
Obscene terms. This doesn't refer to profane or scandalous language (although that's not recommended either) but the use of incentivizing terms like *sales offers*, *crazy deals*, *free money*, or anything else that might sound suspicious to a spam filter.

Save Subscriber Lists from Spam

Did you know that you are only allowed to send a marketing email to individuals who have been active subscribers in the 12 months prior to that email? Whether or not they have been active may seem like a hard thing to quantify, but essentially it means that if an individual has opened, clicked, or engaged with an email in any way within this 12-month window they can be counted as valid subscriptions. Marketers may also send an email if they have obtained an individual's contact details—during the course of a sale, for example—over the past 12 months and have told him the purpose of gathering his contact details.

But what does that mean? A good example would be if you visited Amazon.com, bought a Kindle, filled in a contact form, and were signed up for an email newsletter as a result. Up until very recently the box that signed you up for that email newsletter would have been automatically checked as part of the contact form. Now you have to make a conscious decision to tick that box yourself, so that you can demonstrate you know exactly what you are signing up for besides purchasing the Kindle.

If a sale is being made over the phone instead, you can tell customers, "I'll need your email address to send you a receipt, but could I also send you our newsletter to keep you updated on our latest products?" If they say okay, then you can classify them as subscriptions!

If you have a subscriber list and you aren't sure if individuals have subscribed or been active over the last 12 months, then never assume that they are happy to receive emails from you. Target them with an opt-in email to be certain and make sure the option to unsubscribe exists on every email you send, to avoid any potential uncertainty.

Stay Relevant to Stop Spam

As a marketer, you can only send an email if its message relates to similar products and services that the recipient has previously shown an interest in. This is very important because if you are part of a company that sells kitchenware, such as plates and cups, it means you can target your subscribers with emails for textiles (such as napkins and placemats) that they can use in a kitchen. However, you can't start trying to sell them cars all of a sudden (which would, quite frankly, be a bit of a bizarre product range anyway).

The key is to never mix your marketing messages: Everyone likes to know where they stand! Ensure that your emails are clear and consistent, avoid anything that could cause confusion, steer clear of too many calls to action, and keep things simple for the recipient.

Don't Conceal Your Identity

Leave that to comic book superheroes and vigilantes and remember: Marketers cannot send an email if the identity of the sender has been disguised or obscured. This means when you are carrying out an email marketing campaign, recipients need to be able to identify the email sender, so even if you are just emailing to thank them for signing up to your newsletter, you need to remind recipients who is emailing them and why.

Transparency is key, and it also extends to providing an email address at which you, the sender, may be contacted. Using a valid email address rather than a so-called noreply is important for two reasons. Firstly, it shows a subscriber that the sender is tangible and reputable, and not a robot that can't be contacted sending out spam. Secondly, it provides a subscriber with an email address to which they can send an opt-out request.

As a marketer, you always need to be aware of the need for your email messages to have a human context, not only so you can stay relevant and relate to your subscribers, but also so you don't have to worry about being blacklisted or triggering a spam filter.

Don't Buy or Share Lists

If you are a business that sells office supplies and you are targeted by an individual offering to sell you the email addresses of every law firm in the country, keep in mind that while that individual may have the right to use those subscriptions, you do not. So regardless of how tempting it is, never buy subscriber lists, because it could land you in a lot of trouble. Similarly, you should not share lists either. Why would you share a subscriber list with someone when you have invested a lot of time and effort into nurturing that database? If in doubt, always think about whether or not you are being transparent with the recipients of any marketing email: Will they know who is contacting them and how the sender got their contact details?

Subscriber Management

Before starting any email marketing campaign, the first area that you should focus on is subscriber management. This is the first stage in the iterative process for email, and it is primarily concerned with data. To put it in almost offensively simple terms: Without email addresses you cannot conduct an email marketing campaign! This means you need to know:

- How to acquire subscribers and mine for data to heighten customer insight.
- How to segment that data to target subscribers efficiently and maximize open rates.
- How to update and maintain your subscriber lists on a regular basis for effective campaign targeting.

Data Collection

When you first engage with an ESP, it will ask you to import your subscriber list, which is a database of email addresses to which you can send your marketing emails. There are a variety of methods that you can implement to gain the consent of your target audience to market to them via email: This is also known as gaining the opt-in of your subscribers. Obviously, the more subscribers you win, the better, but it is imperative that they are of a high quality. For example, would you rather acquire 10,000 subscribers who have a 0 percent interaction rate with your emails, or would you prefer 1,000 individuals who open your emails and click through to your website to browse your products or services? Let's work on the assumption that you chose the latter option (and we hope you did!), because it's important to remember that the end goal is not to mindlessly accumulate masses of email addresses. It's about building a list of subscribers who are likely to engage with your email marketing messages.

To safeguard the quality of your subscriber list, you need to pay close attention to the methods through which you collect subscriber data.

Offline Methods for Data Collection
- *Printed materials.* These can include business cards, leaflets, flyers, and packaging. You can also think of innovative ways to integrate offline with online methods; for example, by using QR codes on printed materials that will take users to an online sign-up form on their smartphones.
- *Events.* You can collect email addresses at offline events such as trade shows, exhibitions, and conferences and import them into your subscriber list.
- *Customer touchpoints.* If you are serving customers in a brick-and-mortar store, this is a perfect opportunity to ask for their email addresses so that you can send them email updates on your products. Similarly, if you have a telesales or customer service department in your company you could create a KPI measuring those teams to reward the individuals who acquire the most email addresses.

Online Methods for Data Collection
- *Website sign-up forms.* These are a simple, nonintrusive way to collect email addresses. They can be attached to a particular call to action, such as signing up for a newsletter, and can be featured on any page of a website. It's best to have this contact form on secondary and tertiary pages as well as on the homepage, as it's likely that subscriptions will increase as users browse deeper into your website and become more interested in and familiar with your brand. You should also include contact forms on key landing pages including the Contact Us and About Us pages of your website. If users are visiting these pages they are looking for information and will be more inclined to sign up for a newsletter or receive useful emails.
- *Social media.* You can use social media platforms such as Facebook, Twitter, and LinkedIn to promote offers that require users to submit their email addresses. You can also run competitions on social media to acquire email addresses; for example, entering the first 100 people that subscribe on a particular date into a drawing to win an iPad (you can adapt the terms of the competition to suit your business).
- *Customer touchpoints.* As with offline customer interactions, there are opportunities for you to acquire email addresses at various stages in the online customer journey. You could include pop-up windows in the online buying process and encourage online customer service reps to ask for email addresses via social media or instant chat.

The Anatomy of an Effective Web Sign-Up Form

Easy to Find

It has already been mentioned that web sign-up or contact forms such as the one shown in Figure 5.3 should be on every page of your website to increase the likelihood of capturing email addresses. Less than 10 percent of sign-ups are captured on the homepage, so make sure all your webpages feature a sign-up form that's easy to identify and see.

Figure 5.3   DMI Web Sign-Up Form

Nonintrusive

Incorporate a sign-up form that doesn't interfere with users' browsing experience. A giant pop-up that takes over the entire webpage and demands their contact details probably won't perform as well as a small sign-up form that sits neatly on the page and doesn't interrupt the user's activity.

Seek Only Relevant Information

If you use a sign-up form with countless fields and try to ask your subscribers for too much information, there's a greater chance that they will abandon filling in the form altogether. Streamline the action that your subscribers need to take: Ask for relevant information only, and keep the form short and simple to make it as easy as possible to complete.

Data Collection Example: Okabashi

Okabashi is a company that sells shoes, primarily flip-flops, around the summer season. It decided to use a lead generation tool to maximize the number of email addresses it was capturing.

When end users came onto the homepage and started exploring the website further, a pop-up appeared that allowed them to fill in their contact details if they chose to (see Figure 5.4). As with any effective sign-up form, this pop-up was nonintrusive (as a pop-up, users could click to exit it immediately) and appeared when a user had drilled down into the website and indicated an interest in the brand.

Figure 5.4 Okabashi Web-Sign Up Form
Source: Screenshot reproduced with permission of Okabashi.

For every 100 unique visitors to Okabashi's homepage, the automatic sign-up form generated 3 unique email sign-ups. After a user had browsed through a further five pages, the sign-up form popped up again (as shown in Figure 5.5), and 9 out of every 100 unique visitors filled out the form.

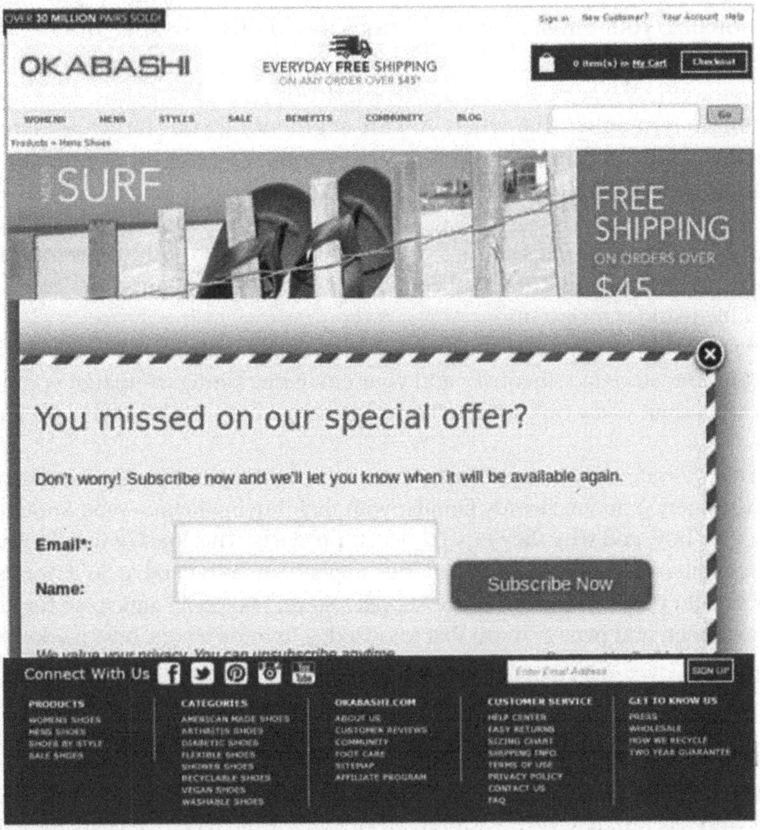

Figure 5.5   Successive Okabashi Web Sign-Up Form
Source: Screenshot reproduced with permission of Okabashi.

Okabashi serves as the perfect example of the success you can achieve by utilizing a web sign-up form that is *easy to find, nonintrusive, and seeking only relevant information*.

Data Segmentation

After you have accumulated your subscriber data, it is essential that you know how to optimize your use of that data: The true value lies not in the data itself, but in what you do with it. Marketers achieve optimization through a process known as *segmentation*, which is the act of dividing your subscriber list into segments and defining those segments in accordance with your subscribers' attributes, likes, dislikes, and requirements. Think of it as a Venn diagram.

A Venn diagram, like segmentation, allows you to create distinct sets, or segments, of data based on both different and shared characteristics. Simply put, segmentation allows you to personalize your email communications based on these specific characteristics of your target audience.

It's important to remember that when you are segmenting your target audience you should create clearly identifiable segments, or groups of subscribers with similar defining features. These features could include:

- *Demographics.* Demographics refers to the gender, education, culture, or age of your subscribers; in other words, the email content you target a teenage audience with might not be applicable to older recipients.
- *Geography.* Equally important is the location of your subscribers. If you are the owner of a brick-and-mortar store in Vancouver and your email marketing campaign is centered on an in-store promotion, you won't want to target users on your email list who are based in England.
- *History.* Don't forget to harness the history you have built up among those subscribers who are also customers. You are already familiar with their buying habits—you know when they buy, how they buy, and why they buy particular products. This kind of insight is invaluable because you can use it to anticipate what they might want to buy next! So if, for example, a customer bought paper from your office supplies store, you could anticipate future purchases such as ink, toner, and pens and use that knowledge to inform your next marketing email to them.
- *Relationship.* Your relationship with your subscribers matters. It is something incredibly valuable. Something profound. If nurtured and cared for properly, it can result in those three little words that make a marketer's insides flutter: return on investment. Let's put it into context. Would it make more sense to send an email announcing price increases to someone who has purchased consistently from you for the past five years, or to have that be the first communication you send to a brand new acquisition? Navigate your relationship with consideration and tact, and you will be able to use it to your email marketing advantage.
- *Customer lifecycle.* You will have a subscriber list of individuals who are all at very different stages in the customer life cycle. Whether they have yet to make a purchase or are dormant customers who haven't purchased in years, this information can provide you with an understanding of how you should be communicating with them. In the case of the dormant customer segment, for example, you could use a target campaign filled with special offers and incentives to re-engage that segment.
- *Dynamic segmentation.* Closely related to the idea of tailoring marketing emails based on buying history and the customer life cycle, is the concept of *dynamic segmentation*. This type of segmentation is based on information gathered throughout the customer life cycle.

An Average Customer Life Cycle

1 A customer subscribes to your newsletter after purchasing online. She has already purchased something, which is great, but what can you do to foster that all-important sense of customer loyalty and encourage her to purchase again?

2 A couple of months later you target her with an email, which she clicks on. She also clicks through the links within the email, which takes her back to your website, demonstrating a continued interest in the brand.

3 After that, she visits your website and demonstrates her current interests by browsing different product pages, indicating a probability that she will buy again.

4 A few months after that she highlights the quality of her engagement by sharing your product on Facebook, demonstrating her customer advocacy and growing your brand for you.

5 A little while after that, she likes and shares your updates on Facebook, positioning herself as a brand ambassador and boosting your reach into communities and networks that you might never have had access to before.

Insights can be drawn from every one of these interactions. Unlike a traditional, or static, subscriber list, dynamic lists evolve as these different actions are taken. Link activity in particular helps to provide details on how subscribers interact with your email in terms of what and how often they click, and this informs the development of a dynamic subscriber list. Dynamic lists are especially useful for interacting with customers, allowing you to automatically include new customers on email newsletters and exclude old ones, and for building lists based on the particular interests of your subscribers, allowing you to ensure that you are marketing to them as efficiently and effectively as possible.

Dynamic Segmentation Example: Digital Marketing Institute

Figure 5.6 illustrates a Digital Marketing Institute email marketing campaign announcing the launch of the masters in digital marketing.

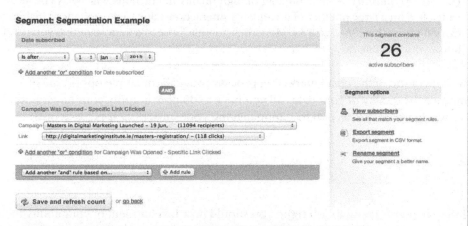

Figure 5.6   Dynamic Segmentation by "Specific Link Clicked" Criteria
Source: Screenshot reproduced with permission of Campaign Monitor.

You can see how many subscribers are contained within the particular segment shown and what actions they took. In this instance, that action was clicking a link that took recipients to a registration page for the masters course on the Digital Marketing Institute website. Being able to capture these subscribers and their specific activities, and use that information in future email marketing campaigns, is the single most advantageous aspect of dynamic segmentation.

Data Management

Even after you have accumulated and segmented your data, and used the results to the benefit of your email marketing campaigns, the story doesn't end there; there's life in the old data yet!

You should look to enrich and refine your data all the time, in keeping with the established email marketing principle of quality over quantity. The final part of step 1 of this iterative email process is assuring the quality of your subscriber database by maintaining it regularly.

- *Clean old data regularly.* So how do you know if your data is old? If you send out an email to 1,000 subscribers and it has a bounce rate of 1 percent, you will know that your email wasn't delivered to 10 of your subscribers and that their email addresses need to be cleaned. This could involve checking for spelling mistakes or checking to see if the subscriber has changed jobs (if it's a work email address). If you have any additional contact details for those subscribers, all you have to do is call them and ask for their most up-to-date email addresses.
- *Apply segmentation consistently.* You should view segmentation as an ongoing activity, and an essential element of data management, as you can update and refine your subscriber lists based on your subscribers' behavior and clicks.
- *Quality not quantity.* A small number of high-quality interactions will always be more valuable than a large number of low-quality interactions, due to the enhanced insights you can gain from these interactions. More than anything else, it's important that you really know your customers.

Every iteration of the email marketing process provides an ample opportunity to improve the quality of your data. All you have to do now is apply your newfound knowledge from this section to start managing your subscriber lists like a pro!

Stage 2: Design and Content

If this chapter is doing its job right, you should now be confident of your ability to acquire email addresses, segment your subscriber lists, and manage your data. Once you know whom you're going to target your email marketing campaign to, the next fundamental stage of the iterative process is design, which is highlighted in Figure 5.7.

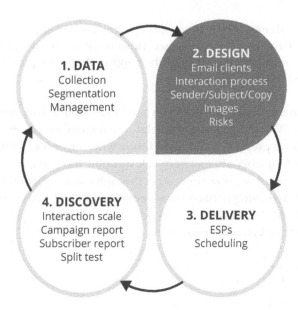

Figure 5.7   Focus on the Second Stage in the Email Marketing Process

Ultimately, your main goal at this stage is to encourage interaction: to invite as many users as possible to open your email and engage with it. You can achieve this through a combination of optimized content and appealing design. In order to master the design phase of your email marketing process you will need to:

- Identify and understand the email clients on which you can host your emails.
- Understand what content you should incorporate into your email.
- Know when it is appropriate to incorporate images and attachments.
- Appreciate the potential risks that accompany any email marketing campaign.

Email Interaction Process

Depending on the consumption channel, be it a website, a social media platform, or an email, users apply personal preferences to the messages they expect to receive and how they expect to receive them. This means that marketers have a responsibility to approach the sending of communications with a certain propriety. You can segment these consumption channels into different communication zones, which should help you to distinguish how you should conduct yourself—think of it as online finishing school!

A website is a public zone. Anyone can access it and so there's a lack of personalization, which creates distance between the website and the user, making it more difficult to target individuals.
A social network is a social zone. Users are part of a community, which facilitates communication between the marketer and the target audience; there's a closer connection to users but not all of them subscribe to receiving marketing messages.

An email is a personal zone. An email account is a user's personal asset and the closest link that a marketer can have to its target audience. However, because it's a private space marketers have to remember to be tactful in their approach and not present themselves and their message in an invasive or disruptive way.

The closer you move to users, the more you need to accommodate their preferences. It's just good manners! With this in mind, it's helpful to remember that users often carry out a simple prioritization exercise within their inbox when engaging with emails. Imagine you have come back to work after a two-week vacation and you have a terrifying 500 unread emails in your inbox; how do you get through them? What do you do? You would start by distinguishing between work emails, personal emails, and general emails. Then you could break those emails down into varying levels of importance by taking into account the following criteria:

- Sender familiarity
- Time of day
- Location
- Work priorities
- Personal priorities

When scanning a full inbox, most users will start by looking to see who sent a message, so familiarity with the sender is always an incredibly important factor. Then they might look at the subject line to gain an understanding of what the email is about. Finally, they would look at the message preview to acquire slightly more insight into the message before choosing whether or not to commit to opening the email.

Within some geographies there can sometimes be cultural and gender biases with regard to the displayed sender name, so it's imperative that you really know your target audiences and take advantage of your knowledge of their preferences so that you use the most appropriate sender name.

You should always personalize the sender name, too. Grounding your email in a human, personal context is the best method of guaranteeing engagement. Try not to use reply addresses such as sales@ or info@; personalization is a simple, effective method to improve open rates.

Email Open Rates: A Risky Business?

Even if subscribers have opted in to receiving your marketing messages, there are still risks that accompany marketing directly to their personal communication zones—their inboxes. Some things to watch out for are:

- *Relevance of the message.* You have to ensure that your email is meaningful to the recipients. If it doesn't interest, engage, or entertain them, they are likely to unsubscribe. Be sure to use segmentation to ensure your emails are as relevant to their audience as possible.

- *Frequency of sending.* Although appropriate frequency with respect to sending emails will vary based on your industry and business, be sure not to saturate subscriber inboxes, as this could infuriate users. A good rule of thumb is to start by sending no more than two emails a week, perhaps on Tuesdays and Thursdays when open rates are traditionally higher. From there you can define how often you should be targeting users.
- *Interruption factor.* If you are going to interrupt subscribers during traditional work hours on a weekday, you need to be certain that you are not interrupting them with an email that has no relevance to them.

(Email) Client Confidential

An email client, also known as a mail user agent (MUA), is a computer program that allows users access and manage their email. So, what email clients are recipients using? Common examples include Outlook, Hotmail, Yahoo!, and Gmail; some are very much work-oriented and some are more likely to be adopted for personal use.

Take, for example, Microsoft's Outlook email client. There's a task pane on the left with various folders, and the inbox with the sender name, subject line, and a short summary of the email copy. There's also a preview of the email on the right that displays commands such as Reply, Reply All, and Forward, as well as the email copy itself. The line between the email summary and overall preview can be adjusted, and that truncated view is important to bear in mind when you are crafting subject lines; keep them concise and direct.

Don't forget that when you are designing an email, you are not just designing it for its display on an email client; you should design it for the device on which it will be viewed as well, be it a smartphone, tablet, laptop, or desktop. Leave no screen unturned! Back in 2010 a lot of the MUA market share was owned by Outlook, which was the email client of choice for over half of all users. Five years later the data is dramatically different, as the Apple iPhone now dominates email-client market share with 26 percent and the Apple iPad is the third most popular email client. Outlook is now fourth. This means that, with the rising prevalence of smartphones and tablets, you have to foster a culture of testing to ensure that your marketing emails display on both various email clients and various mobile devices.

Compelling Email Copy

There is no more important method for increasing open rates than email copy that really interests and engages its reader. Here the subject line is key; it's your email's value statement, its pickup line. You have a small handful of words with which to seal the deal and secure an open (no pressure!), so the first two or three words are crucial. Make sure that your subject line is relevant to the recipient, rather than you, the sender. If you are targeting a segment that is engaging strongly with you and your brand, perhaps you could go for a slightly harder sell and incorporate keywords such as *10 percent off* or *buy one get one free*. If you are targeting a new list, you might want to be a little more subtle. Subject lines are industry-dependent too, so what you might use in the travel industry (pricing discounts, for example) might not work as well if you are targeting the education sector.

To accommodate all of these little permutations, testing is essential. If you use an ESP such as MailChimp, you can split test your subject lines with a small subset of recipients to see which keywords work best before sending out your emails to the rest of your recipients. For example, if you have an email database of 1,000 and you want to ascertain that you are sending the best possible email to them, you can take 100 recipients out of that 1,000, split them into groups A and B, and test open rates based on different subject lines to see which variation will give you the best ROI.

If sender and subject line are all-important elements to improve open rates, then the email copy itself is essential to guaranteeing engagement. So, what are the key features of email copy that affect engagement?

- *Relevance*. As with the subject line, you must make sure that your email is composed of relevant messaging that is targeted at a specific audience. You need to know what your segments want and don't want; harness that knowledge to the advantage of your email marketing campaign.
- *Calls to action*. Include clear and specific calls to action that take advantage of relevant messaging and generate click-throughs that meet your overall objectives, be they social sharing or a visit to a product page.
- *Personalization*. After you have gotten to know your email list and have accumulated a little more data, you can start using personalization to generate more email engagement.
- *Structure*. A well-structured email is essential for ease of consumption. Use clear headings to introduce new paragraphs and bullet points to break up information, and make the message easily digestible. Try bold text to highlight key points where appropriate, and include a balance of text and appropriate imagery. You can also include hyperlinks that link to additional information rather than generating a text-heavy email or using attachments.

The Anatomy of a Poorly Designed Email

- Far too text-heavy
- Includes an attachment
- No paragraphs or headings
- No calls to action

The Anatomy of a Well-Designed Email

- Headings and paragraphs that break up the text and let the reader scan the copy
- A concise, direct subject line
- A succinct call to action and social-sharing buttons
- A balance of text and imagery

See Figure 5.8 for an example of a paragon of good design.

Figure 5.8   A Well Designed Email from Cook Smarts

Source: Screenshot reproduced with permission of Cook Smarts.

Imagery Is Everything

Although there is nothing more engaging than a beautiful image, maintaining a balance of text and imagery in your email copy is paramount to that email's success. Images should support, rather than contain, your email's message. Always make sure that the key points and calls to action you want to convey to a recipient are in the text. A lot of email clients don't automatically display images, so users have to right click to download the pictures; if the main CTA in your email is included in an image there is no guarantee that that they will have bothered to download that image. Besides maintaining this balance, another element you should consider in your emails is alternative text. When uploading images into your email, there is a field for alternative text that you can fill in. This means that if your email is delivered with the images turned off, the alternative text will still display and the image's message be conveyed. So if you have an image that reads *50 percent off your next ski holiday* and the image is turned off, the alternative text will still display (as in Figure 5.9), and rather than instantly deleting the email, a recipient might still engage with the offer.

When Mobile and Email Combine

According to Radicati's mobile statistics report 2014-2018, by the end of 2018, worldwide mobile email users are expected to total over 2.2 billion. By that time 80 percent of email users are expected to access their email accounts via mobile devices, so it is very apparent that the unity of mobile and email is on an increasingly steep path, and that mobile is becoming the number-one device for email opens. But what does this mean for you? Essentially, you need to achieve mobile integration for your email marketing campaign and design emails that are optimized equally for viewing on tablets and desktops. If you use an ESP such as MailChimp, you can use a mobile template to simulate how your email will be rendered on this device. What you are trying to achieve through optimizing your campaign for mobile is increased engagement, regardless of screen size.

At every stage of the email design process, think about how the email will look on all devices. PC screens are often approximately 23 inches, while tablets are 10 inches and mobiles screens average 7 inches. If you have a very text-heavy message that you created with desktop users in mind, look at it on a mobile device. See how long it takes to read, and how much you have to scroll, pinch, and zoom. You can then reduce the amount of text and increase your use of imagery. If you have used five calls to action in a desktop-friendly email, limit that to two for a mobile, knowing that it's that little bit more cumbersome to click through on a mobile device.

Through testing, it's possible to ensure deliverability across a broad range of email clients and devices. ESPs allow you to view an email in browsers such as Internet Explorer, Firefox, and Google Chrome. Don't forget to see how your email looks on mobile, and check spam-filter results. It is valuable insights such as these that will

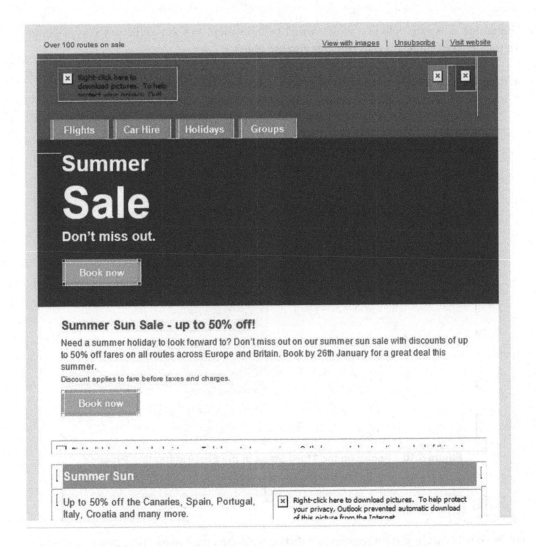

Figure 5.9   Email with Images Turned Off Displaying Alternative Text

enable you to develop an email that gets delivered, opened, and read—the golden egg in any email marketing campaign!

Stage 3: Delivery

We are moving into the next step in our process, as shown in Figure 5.10. You have a consummately segmented subscriber list. An impeccably designed email that is optimized for every email client and mobile device imaginable. You are poised to send what could be the greatest marketing email ever created. Now all you need is to guarantee is its safe delivery, which won't be a problem as soon as the key components of the delivery stage are covered and you are able to:

- Recognize the key characteristics of email service providers.
- Identify when subscribers are most likely to open emails.
- Personalize the design of an email and when it is sent to accommodate subscriber preferences.

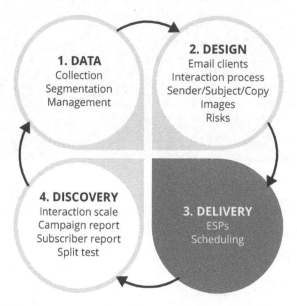

Figure 5.10   Focus on the Third Stage in the Email Marketing Process

ESPs

ESPs have been a constant touchpoint throughout the email marketing process. If you are brand new to email marketing, join a few different services to identify the ESP that best suits your requirements. A lot of ESPs offer a free subscription, so it won't cost you anything to test their features and make an informed decision. Other notable benefits to using an ESP include:

- *Security benefits.* With an ESP, you don't have to worry about constantly updating your email software, as the provider will take a proactive and reactive approach to updating its own software, which will dramatically reduce the risk of a security breach. Sending your emails through an ESP also means you are sending them through an already approved server, which assure delivery success.
- *Easy to access.* Most ESPs can be accessed anytime, anywhere. As long as you have an Internet connection, you will have the flexibility to send an email campaign whenever you need to.
- *Attractive templates.* If you don't have an in-house graphic designer and can't afford to outsource design work, ESPs provide you with a variety of professionally predesigned templates that you can customize to suit your aesthetic preferences.

- *Insights*. ESPs offer enhanced reporting features that allow you to both test and measure the success of your email marketing campaigns, so you can refine them every time.

Let Me Check My Schedule

When it comes the success of your email marketing campaign, like most things in life, timing is everything. What you really need to know is this: When are people most likely to open my email?

The recommended time frame is between the hours of 5:00 A.M. and 9:00 P.M. Why not the Dolly Parton-popularized 9 to 5? Because if you target your subscribers between the hours of 9:00 A.M. and 5:00 P.M., you are completely neglecting the evening, a time that people catch up with their emails after a busy day in the office. Whether they are on their commute home, relaxing before dinner, or reading before bed, the evening can be a prime time for scheduling if you want to increase those open rates!

For B2B (business-to-business) marketing, the optimum times to send are Tuesday through Thursday between 10:00 A.M. and 12:00 P.M. and after lunch between 2:00 P.M. and 4:00 P.M. The rationale behind these time frames is simple. Think about when you are most likely to check your emails (the ones that don't pertain to work and require your immediate attention!). On Mondays you are trying to acclimate to being back at work after the weekend. On Fridays you are probably trying to get through work in anticipation of the weekend. Early mornings are a difficult time to gain anyone's attention (especially precaffeine) and any time after 4:00 is just too close to the end of the working day.

For B2C (business-to-consumer) marketing, on the other hand, optimal send times vary dramatically across industries but will be more in line with evening open rates, because a lot of people cannot access their personal emails during the day. But if open rates vary across industries and locations, what should you do to acquire those opens? Test it. If you are targeting segments of 100 people and you find out that 10 are opening at a certain time and 90 are opening at another time, then you can use the behavior of that 90 percent to shape your subsequent campaigns.

Stage 4: Discovery

Now the only step standing between you and supreme email marketing success is the reporting and analysis step, highlighted in Figure 5.11. Being able to evaluate your email marketing activity from design to delivery is critical to iterating its success. You can use reporting to identify and address both issues and opportunities in your email marketing process, and crown yourself an analytics wizard when you know how to:

- Recognize key reporting features in ESPs.
- Identify KPIs for email marketing.
- Understand and measure key email marketing metrics.

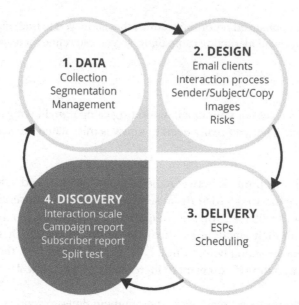

Figure 5.11   Focus on the Fourth Stage in the Email Marketing Process

Reporting and Analysis

In order to measure the effectiveness of email marketing, you first need to define your goals. Why are you creating this marketing email? What are you trying to achieve? These questions might seem like those related to an existential crisis, but the reality is this: If you want to know the data you need to report on, you need to choose the email marketing metrics that best align with your goals. Common email marketing metrics include:

Open rate. The percentage of recipients who have opened or viewed your email.
Total opens. The total number of times recipients have opened your email (this includes recipients who have opened it more than once).
Unique opens. The total number of opens from original, or unique, subscribers. If you target 1,000 people, you can only have 1,000 unique opens.
Click to open rate. The number of unique clicks divided by the number of unique opens expressed as a percentage.

Why are open metrics important KPIs? They provide information on the quality of your subscriber list, the relevance of your message content, and the effectiveness of your subject line. In short—if you have excited and engaged your subscribers, they *will* have opened your email!

Click-through rate. The percentage of subscribers that opened your email and clicked on a link within that email.
Unique clicks. The total number of unique users who clicked on a link.

Total clicks. The total number of clicks from users (including those eager beavers who clicked more than once!).

Why are click metrics important KPIs? They measure and validate the relevance of the message content as well as the quality of the segmentation and targeting. For example, if a link to a blog post on a certain topic did particularly well, you could use that insight to help determine what kind of content your subscribers are most interested in!

Unsubscribes. The total number of subscribers who have opted out, or unsubscribed, and no longer want to receive your emails. This metric is usually a good indicator of whether you're targeting the right audience.

Bounce rate. The percentage of emails that could not be delivered to subscribers and were sent back to your ESP.

Hard bounces. Messages that are permanently rejected due to an invalid email address or because the recipient's server has blocked your server.

Soft bounces. Messages that are temporarily rejected because the recipient's inbox is full, the server isn't working, or the email exceeds the size limit set by the recipient or ESP.

Although it's easy to get carried away by high open rates and low bounces, don't forget that it's the quality of interactions rather than the quantity that matters when you are measuring your email marketing success. This ties in with the value of setting goals against which you can measure your campaigns. Are your emails driving traffic to your website? Are they generating conversions? Are they achieving what you want them to?

Portrait of an Email Marketing Campaign

So now that you know about the email marketing metrics that matter, how can you access them on your ESP? Figure 5.12 outlines the performance of a July newsletter that was sent to over 17,000 unique subscribers across 55 lists (just in case the importance of segmentation hasn't been emphasized enough!).

The graph shows data for a 24-hour period, so you can see that the majority of unique opens happened in the first hour. The average email will have a life cycle of approximately 36 hours, dependent on industry. This means it's important that the biggest uplift in interactions happens within the first few hours after delivery.

On this graph we can also see that there were 2,934 unique opens, but 4,804 *total* opens, which indicates that some subscribers were opening the email more than once. That provides an open rate of 16.76 percent, which is around the global industry average (between 16 and 20 percent). The 219 bounces mean that the email addresses provided either don't exist, contain misspellings or another anomaly. In relation to the overall subscriber list, 219 bounces is an incredibly low figure, equating to a 1.24 percent bounce rate. Similarly, only 0.3 percent unsubscribed, a very small number that can be removed from your next campaign, and only one marked the email as spam! Not a bad return on a subscriber list of over 17,000.

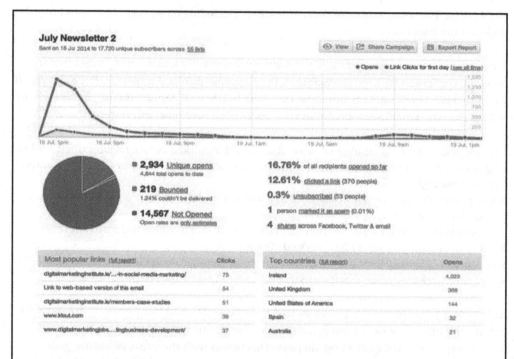

Figure 5.12   Newsletter Performance Report within an ESP
Source: Screenshot reproduced with permission of Campaign Monitor.

The share of recipients who opened the email and clicked a link was 12.61 percent —that's 370 people who can be categorized as hot leads. You emailed them, they interacted with the content, and they clicked through. Remember, the quality of interactions should be your real target focus, not the quantity!

Having said that, a huge number of subscribers have not yet opened the email. The more time zones your subscriber list covers, the longer it might take for recipients to open an email. With a little bit of luck, the not-opened figure might drop a little bit and the open rate could increase to 20 percent, which would be incredibly positive, as the click rate is so high.

So what are subscribers clicking on?

In Figure 5.13, we can see a dashboard overview of all link activity, which is particularly useful when it comes to thinking about what content you should include in your email. The most popular link clicked on within this particular email was to a product page advertising a diploma in social media marketing. With this kind of insight you can decide to further target these subscribers, either with a follow up email or phone call about the social media diploma. Whatever the case may be, it's important to include a clear, concise call to action.

As most of us play out the tiniest details of our lives on social media, it should come as no surprise that social shares and forwards are integral to discovering what content your subscribers are consuming and what they want.

Link Activity & Overlay
July Newsletter 2 - Sent last Wednesday at 2:36 pm

371	**people clicked** Giving you a **12.62%** click rate.	**616**	**total clicks** Made by 371 people
1.66	**clicks per person** Average of all those who clicked.	**2,568**	**didn't click** That's 87.38% of all those who opened.

Link (URL)	Unique	Total
digitalmarketinginstitute.ie/courses/t...nal-diploma-in-social-media-marketing/	**65** (who)	75
Link to web-based version of this email	**48** (who)	54
digitalmarketinginstitute.ie/members-case-studies	**43** (who)	51
www.klout.com	**36** (who)	38
www.digitalmarketingjobs.ie/marketingbusiness-development/	**29** (who)	37

Figure 5.13   Link Activity Overview within an ESP
Source: Screenshot reproduced with permission of Campaign Monitor.

As we can see in Figure 5.14, a total of four people shared the July newsletter, with two mentions on Twitter, one Facebook like, and one forward of the email itself. With social sharing, you can extend your reach and get access to previously unreachable audiences. Even a small number of shares can have a positive, extensive knock-on effect.

This email marketing campaign has enjoyed clicks, social shares, and opens and it's still only been 24 hours since delivery. Thankfully, in the email marketing landscape you have the benefit of being able to split test to improve your chances of success! It has been mentioned before, but it's important to emphasize the power of split testing. No matter how big or small your email list, take a small segment of them and split them into A and B categories. Test two different versions of your email on each, and run with whichever performs the best! Elements that you can target for split testing include:

- *Sender name.* Will you test a female name against a male name? Or perhaps a company name against an individual?
- *Subject line.* Will you highlight one particular article in your newsletter? Or maybe focus on a percentage discount for one of your products?

Split testing is the best way to guarantee relevant and targeted content to audience segments, and ultimately, better engagement with them.

Split testing can reveal a significant level of difference between alternative email marketing campaigns and greatly improve email marketing success.

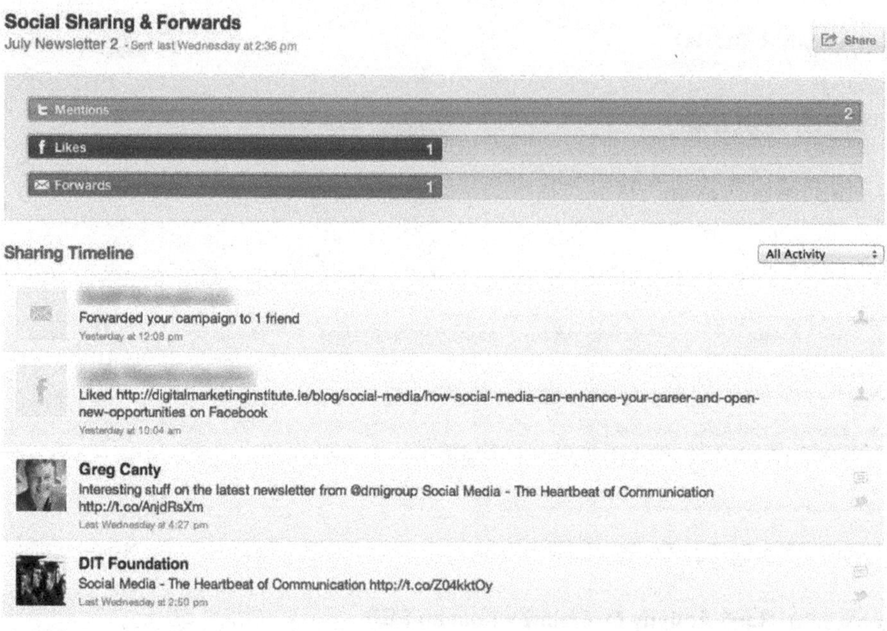

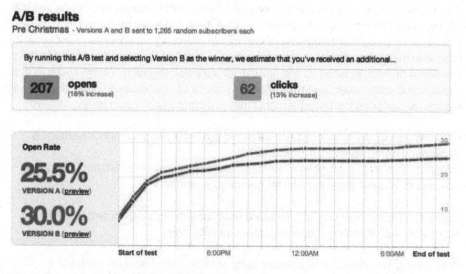

Social Sharing & Forwards
July Newsletter 2 - Sent last Wednesday at 2:36 pm   [↗ Share]

Mentions   2
f Likes   1
✉ Forwards   1

Sharing Timeline   [All Activity ⬍]

✉ Forwarded your campaign to 1 friend
Yesterday at 12:08 pm

f Liked http://digitalmarketinginstitute.ie/blog/social-media/how-social-media-can-enhance-your-career-and-open-new-opportunities on Facebook
Yesterday at 10:04 am

Greg Canty
Interesting stuff on the latest newsletter from @dmigroup Social Media - The Heartbeat of Communication
http://t.co/AnjdRlsXm
Last Wednesday at 4:27 pm

DIT Foundation
Social Media - The Heartbeat of Communication http://t.co/Z04kktOy
Last Wednesday at 2:50 pm

Figure 5.14   Social Sharing and Forwards within an ESP
Source: Screenshot reproduced with permission of Campaign Monitor.

Figure 5.15 shows A and B results for an email that was part of a pre-Christmas campaign. One audience segment was targeted with one promotion, another segment was targeted with another. Using split tests, version B was crowned the winner, as the ESP can estimate the additional number of opens and clicks an email can yield.

A/B results
Pre Christmas - Versions A and B sent to 1,265 random subscribers each

By running this A/B test and selecting Version B as the winner, we estimate that you've received an additional...

207 opens (18% increase)   **62** clicks (13% increase)

Open Rate
25.5% VERSION A (preview)
30.0% VERSION B (preview)

Start of test   6:00PM   12:00AM   6:00AM   End of test

Figure 5.15   Split Testing Report within an ESP
Source: Screenshot reproduced with permission of Campaign Monitor.

Laws and Guidelines

Now that you have come full circle and explored every key component of an effective email marketing process, the only thing standing between you and email marketing mastery is a firm understanding of the laws and guidelines that govern it.

These laws and guidelines are strict in some locations and not so strict in others. Regardless, you need to be aware that there *are* laws, guidelines, and conventions that pertain to email marketing in your region, and issues to consider, particularly regarding data protection. Data protection laws inform what is considered spam; remember that spam is in the eye of the beholder, and the definition will differ greatly across geographies.

It's important to be aware of local privacy regulations too; common characteristics of electronic privacy regulations include:

- Providing the option to opt out of marketing emails.
- Telling subscribers why their information has been collected.
- Ensuring that marketing emails are only about relevant products and services and using email addresses only for the purpose for which they were originally collected.
- Remembering that opt-ins are only valid for 12 months.

Key governing bodies that you can consult include the Information Commissioner's Office for the United Kingdom and the Federal Trade Commission for the United States. The FTC is responsible for enforcing the CAN-SPAM Act of 2003, which sets the national standard for the sending of commercial and marketing emails and requests compliance in a number of areas, from sending behavior to content.

So, What Have You Learned in This Chapter?

Enough to safeguard your status as an email marketing superstar! If in doubt, take comfort in the fact that you are already utilizing email *every single day*. This means you are already cognizant of your subscribers and their email experience, whether you know it or not! And just in case you need a reminder of how to ensure that experience is the best possible:

- Keep it clean—make sure your subscriber data is up to date and segmented on a regular basis.
- Delight and excite—engage your target audience through the creation of captivating content and use personalization!
- Avoid the spam can—be mindful of your use of formatting, language, attachments, and imagery.
- Remember that your ESP is the most important weapon in your arsenal—it can help you with everything from design to scheduling.

- Test, test, test . . . Split test content! Test engagement! Analytics are everything; if there's something you can measure, do it, and enhance your email's effectiveness!

Go to www.artofdmi.com to access the case study on email marketing as additional support material for this chapter.

 # Exercise

Exercise 1

Set up a free account on an ESP. Import your contacts and begin to build your email databases. Rate your end users in terms of open rates, interaction, and CTRs.

Exercise 2

Create an email marketing campaign using split testing. Send your email to a select number of email addresses. From here test subject lines, content, and sender details. Using this information, decide which split is performing better and why.

Exercise 3

You have a database of 1,000 subscribers that you inherited from your predecessor. You conduct an email marketing campaign and not only is the bounce rate 50 percent, but many more unsubscribe also. Take the steps necessary to clean your data.

Exercise 4

You have 1,000 B2B customers and 1,000 B2C customers. You need to schedule the best time to email them on the ESP.

What time are you going to target your audiences?

How will you carry out your scheduling?

Exercise 5

Your email list is performing quite well but you need to segment your audience based on their link interactivity. How will you do this with your current database and what does this mean for your list?

Action Plan: Email Marketing

Digital Marketing Planning Scheme for Email Marketing

Objectives

Penetration, interaction, advocacy, conversion, inform

Action Items and Frequency

- Data collection: Update daily
- Cleaning: Monthly
- Segmentation: Ongoing and per campaign
- Newsletter creation: Dependent on publication schedule
- Trigger emails: Dependent on publication schedule and data collection
- Tracking and monitoring: Weekly/monthly

Measurement Tools and KPIs

- Email marketing system: List size, open rate, CTR, unsubscribe rate, bounce rate
- Analytics: Conversions, sessions, new versus returning users, comparing emails, demographics, on-site behavior, devices
- Combination: List growth versus website visitors, site semographics versus list demographics, forecasting

Spend

Media	Content	People	Systems
	x	x	x

Chapter 6
Social Media Marketing (Part 1)

An Introduction

Find me on Facebook. Follow me on Twitter. Check out my blog. Ten years ago these phrases meant nothing, yet now they are part of everyday speak. More and more people are connecting through social media—to stay in touch with friends, to date, or to interact with brands and businesses. Which is great news for digital marketers like you.

This is no time to be a wallflower. Because in order to survive and thrive, you will need to be active on the main platforms, competing in an online popularity contest with other companies.

Welcome to social media marketing (SMM).

Formal definition of SMM: A form of Internet marketing utilizing social networking sites as marketing tools, thereby gaining traffic, brand exposure, and interaction with customers through social media.

Informal definition of SMM: Flirting with your biggest fans!

Process

This chapter begins with an overview of the SMM landscape before exploring the goals it can help you achieve and the channels you can use. In Chapter 7 you will see how to implement and analyze your social media campaigns.

The four stages within the iterative process are shown in Figure 6.1; the first two are described here:

1 *Goals.* The chapter kicks off by explaining social media formats and how you can choose the best ones to achieve your objectives. You will also learn how to form an effective SMM

Figure 6.1   Four-Stage SMM Process

strategy by setting goals—because even though social media is reactive, your strategy still needs to be built slowly so that it can improve gradually over time. A bit of foresight now will work wonders down the line!

2 *Channels*. This stage will cover the different channels in which social marketing likes to swim—including the usual suspects, such as Facebook, LinkedIn, Twitter, Google+, YouTube, and blogs. It will help you to identify which of these channels will increase customer reach and show you how to improve your profiles as they grow.

As SMM is such a big topic, stages 3 and 4 will be covered in the next chapter to avoid an information overload!

Key Terms and Concepts

Social media marketing is an amazing way for businesses to keep solid relationships with existing customers and to woo new ones. This chapter will help you to play Cupid by:

- Understanding the concepts and mechanics of social media and how you can use them to your advantage.
- Discovering how to set up engaging Facebook and Twitter business profiles.

- Creating a professional LinkedIn profile and participating in LinkedIn groups to expand your network.
- Running effective Google+, YouTube, and blogging accounts.

Social media gives you the power to direct your business's online life. Whether that life is long and happy depends on what channel you post to and how you manage your profiles—in short, how you maximize your social media marketing.

This chapter will help you become a social media butterfly and starts with an overview of the world in which you can fly.

Stage 1: Goals

In order to meet your social media goals, you need to understand the game first. This is the first step of the process and is highlighted in Figure 6.2. This section will act as a pre-match pep talk, equipping you with everything you need to help you:

- Distinguish between earned, owned, and paid media. ✓
- Recognize the most common forms of social media.
- Grasp what makes social media marketing effective and the implications for businesses.
- Identify different SMM goals and explain how to set your own.

Figure 6.2   Focus on the First Stage in the SMM Process

Media Types: Earned, Owned, and Paid

Before getting into how you can promote yourself on social media, let's look at the options that are available. You can choose to post content through the following media types:

- *Earned media* is free publicity, generated by fans and customers in response to content they like (your kudos for making them happy).
- *Owned media* includes communications that a brand creates and controls via its own platform (you blow your own trumpet).
- *Paid media* is any paid activity that drives traffic to owned media properties (you pay up for the shout out).

Whatever option you choose, remember that there will be hidden costs involved. An engaging profile requires great copy, multimedia assets like photos and videos (which you may want to take yourself), and a solid strategy. And since there is no point having the world's greatest profile if no one knows you exist, you will have to fork out for some kind of advertising to reach socially tuned-in audiences.

Finding and training the right staff, compiling digital assets, and advertising your business takes time and money—so bear that in mind when setting out your short- and long-term goals.

Forms of Social Media

Social media comes in all shapes and sizes. Facebook and Twitter are two of the big boys but blogging platforms such as WordPress, review sites such as TripAdvisor, and Podcast platforms such as PodOmatic can also be classified as social media channels. And let us not forget YouTube, Vimeo, Flickr, and Instagram, which have surged in popularity thanks to people's love of capturing moments and sharing them with friends.

Whatever the format, remember that social media never sleeps. Smartphones have completely revolutionized how people connect with one another—so businesses can now reach consumers on the move, 24 hours a day. Managing this can be a full-time job in itself, but one that can reap unlimited rewards.

Stakeholders of SMM

The three key players within social media are users, advertisers, and social platforms. And they have quite an interdependent relationship—users want to have a place to engage and can do so on social platforms. These in turn need to be paid for, since server space and staff do not come for free! The advertiser covers these costs and also uses the platform to reach users. The relationship is shown in Figure 6.3.

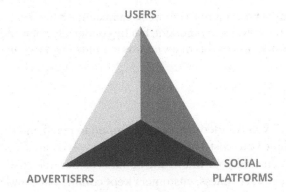

Figure 6.3   The Three Key Players within Social Media

The way in which users interact with websites has changed considerably. Initially they visited sites and little else happened. Then so-called transactional experiences appeared and users were able to buy online. The likes of eBay introduced a dialogue between users and advertisers for the first time and marked the beginning of the interactive process.

Today this dialogue has expanded into a full-blown conversation between users and advertisers around the world. The continual communication has allowed users to tell businesses what they want (through user-generated content) and for businesses to stand out from the crowd with original and engaging profiles.

Trying It On for Size

Social media marketing may not be for everyone. Before jumping headfirst into the social media rabbit hole, consider whether SMM will fit your business, and if so, which channel (or channels) you should use.

Here are the main considerations you should take into account:

- *Target market*. Does your ideal audience use social media? If the answer is hell, no! then there is no point in wasting time and money.
- *Public reach*. Social media blurs the lines between personal and public content. Users can rate and slate your business very quickly and visibly, so just make sure you have nothing to be ashamed of. Your reputation and credibility are in their hands. Also, since you have greater access to a user's interests and behaviors, you need to be careful about how you use this data.
- *Instant communication*. When social media strategies are put in place, communicating in a traditional way becomes a thing of the past. Your interactions with consumers are no longer monitored, controlled, or carefully managed, as the process is much faster. This does give your brand a more human, approachable feel but it also means slip-ups can happen easily. So be careful if your content manager is in a bad mood!

- *Ongoing nature.* Social media is not a six-week campaign—it has a calendar with no endpoint. That can be quite a scary thought, but by continually adjusting goals and tweaking objectives, the process becomes far less intimidating. Deep breaths.

Going for Gold

Once upon a time . . . you decided whom you wanted to reach and thought of a great way to tell those people you exist—social media. Next you created a profile so amazing that users started to consider your brand and some even became customers. You made the transaction process so seamless, customers kept coming back and told all their friends. And you all lived happily ever after!

For a fairytale ending like this you will need to get some specific goals in place. These may include:

- *Business goals* like lead generation, sales, and cost reduction.
- *Customer service goals* like consumer satisfaction and the chance of referrals/repeat business.
- *Product goals*, such as research, design, and enhancement.
- *Communication goals* to build your brand personality and reputation (with an effective crisis management strategy in place).
- *Marketing goals*, such as branding, awareness, and engagement.

Once you have set out your goals, you can explore the best channels to help you achieve them. The next section will cover these different channels in detail and how you can use them to enhance your business online.

Stage 2: Channels

Having touched on the various forms of SMM, whether it is right for your business, and the goals it can help you achieve, let's move on to stage 2 of the iterative process, which is highlighted in Figure 6.4 —channels. Starting with a close look at Facebook, you will learn how to:

- Understand the differences between personal profiles and business Facebook pages.
- Effectively create and promote a well-maintained Facebook page.
- Generate engagement with compelling posts and use insights to see what works best.

Facebook

The Facebook platform has exploded over the past 10 years as a social and marketing tool for millions of people around the world. With 1.4 billion active users—of whom 1.25 billion log on via mobile—the opportunity for digital marketers is huge. Users can

Figure 6.4   Focus on the Second Stage in the SMM Process

be reached 24 hours a day, seven days a week. Facebook is one of the best platforms with which to engage people.

You are probably already familiar with personal profiles, where friend requests are made and accepted or declined. This is a pretty time consuming (and often heartbreaking) way of trying to connect with your audience. Users can ignore your requests, so you do not have the instant connectivity you crave. Also, personal profiles are not optimized for search engines (i.e., they do not show up in Google searches). This is great for individual users who want their privacy protected, but not so great for brands trying to grow their online presence.

Instead, most brands create a business page from a personal account. These pages:

- Can have unlimited likes or connections, and take just one click of the Like button for a Facebook user to connect.
- Are optimized for search engines (because the open settings place the page in the public realm).
- Include a large amount of analytics, such as the ages, genders, and locations of an audience and how often it interacts with certain posts. You can also track your page's performance and the posts on it—that is, how many people the page reaches and whether it is engaging users.

With business pages, it is easier to tweak content to better suit your audience—which is why smart brands go for them over personal profiles.

Facebook uses an algorithm called EdgeRank to organize a business page's content. It looks at friends (or "liked" organizations) on the page to feed the most relevant content for each user into one continuous stream. This stream is called News Feed—and it is the most important piece of real estate you can get your eager mitts on.

You may be under the assumption that page "likes" mean nothing. If so, you have been sadly misinformed! Since EdgeRank promotes posts that have been published and liked by friends over other types of content, each "like" means your posts have a greater chance of connecting with the people you want.

However, not everyone who has connected with you will see each post you publish on her News Feed. So how can you become more visible to your followers? Good question. Read on to find out . . .

Creating Your Business Page

Start by considering your identity. Ask yourself:

- Am I a local business or a place?
- Am I a brand or a product?
- Am I an artist, a band, or a public figure?

Your answers will help you pick the most relevant option available. Next, you need to make your page scream, "Look at me!"—in the most professional way possible, of course.

Some key points to bear in mind when creating your page:

- Include your business details. There is no point in having a million friends if none of them know how to contact you.
- Upload an eye-catching cover photo in addition to a suitable profile picture. Remember, your profile picture will appear beside your business name, so choose one that represents you well—poorly lit selfies will not cut it.
- Keep the tone and style of your brand consistent throughout the page.
- Update your page with entertaining and informative content regularly to keep users engaged. Even though people may "like" your page, getting them to come back and interact with it is a whole different story. The updates that fans see in their News Feed should make them want to take a closer look.
- Add your page to your Facebook favorites—it will be easier to find once you log in and you will also be notified whenever users interact with your page, meaning you will have more opportunities to connect with them.
- Make sure you have at least two administrators to manage your page effectively. This minimizes the risk of the page going down or being hacked—forgotten passwords will be less of a worry, too.

Making Your Page Engaging

As marketers, it is massively important to only post engaging content on Facebook, always bearing in mind that impact is key. Your customers do not want to hear what you had for breakfast (unless of course, it is related to your business!).

In order for your post to gain traction, it must be relevant, interesting, and easily understood. Convoluted and complicated posts will not encourage people to "like" or share what you have to say. And those buttons are what can help you grow your fan base from hundreds to thousands and beyond.

You can optimize each post by asking whether the user will:

- Find it interesting or funny.
- Click on the post to find out more.
- Share it with their friends.

If you think your post will not have any of the above effects, it probably needs work.

In theory, Facebook offers unlimited space for posts; however according to research carried out by Jeff Bullas, Facebook posts with no more than 40 characters receive 86 percent more engagement than posts with a higher character count. While writing a long paragraph is easier, and whittling down descriptions to 40 characters or fewer means having to get more inventive, the statistics don't lie. As with all online content, the golden rule is to keep it short and simple. Use a conversational tone and try to evoke a response with your posts—in this way you can encourage two-way interactions with users.

Some tips to bear in mind:

- *Paint a picture*. Emotive imagery is a great way of catching people's attention.
- *Try, try again*. Okay, so you may not get it right first time . . . or the second . . . or even the third! But keep going. Change one or two things at a time until you find a style that works.
- *Quality, not quantity*. Avoid publishing hundreds of dull and dreary posts every week. Instead scale back on the number and only post content when it serves a purpose.
- *Stay positive*. No one likes a Negative Nancy! Use an upbeat tone and make your page a place where people will feel good about themselves.
- *Make them laugh*. Throw in a little humor where possible—a witty status or a funny picture can go a very long way.
- *Get the camera rolling*. Video has emerged as the new power tool in the world of Facebook. Clips play automatically in News Feeds, which immediately hooks people in. Engaging videos get shared by personal and business pages alike, with the potential to reach a massive global audience.
- *Stay balanced*. Even though the aim of your content will most likely be to drive revenue, you will risk losing users' interest if you constantly go for the hard sell. Instead, sweeten

them up and earn their trust by sharing content that interests them, even if it does not directly relate to your business. An effective page means striking a balance between viral content and business-led posts. So by all means, include your deals and offers to drive revenue, but mix it up with entertaining, educational, and engaging content to encourage interaction.

Using Analytics

You could be posting the cleverest content in the world, but without knowing how to analyze it, it becomes as useful as a waterproof teabag.

Studying a post's reach can reveal lots of interesting data about its activity, such as:

- Did it go to 15,000 people or just 1,000?
- How many of your fans did it reach? When are these fans online?
- Is the post's success due to paid reach or organic reach?

By the way, organic reach is how well your posts perform by themselves, without paying for any advertising, while paid reach is boosted advertising for your posts. Sponsored posts will reach audiences that currently aren't fans as well as your own followers, so when a post is performing well, you might want to pay for boosting its reach. This will increase the likelihood of your post being seen on Facebook, while generating more likes for your page.

Analytics can help you when you're writing your content and when you're deciding on the best time of day to post it for maximum traction. You can learn which topics are hot to adjust future content accordingly. Also, since there is no such thing as bad press, you can even use negative feedback (if fans hide your posts, report them as spam, or are prompted to unlike your page) to learn from your mistakes. We all make them, after all.

About Social Plug-Ins

Not only can you connect with your audience on the Facebook platform, you can also use social plug-ins to encourage these connections to share their experiences across the web. The plug-ins appear on different websites but the information in them comes directly from Facebook.

For example:

- The Like button allows users share pages and content from your website back to their Facebook profile in one click.
- The Send button allows users send content privately from your site to their friends.
- Embedded Posts allow you easily insert public posts on your site.
- The embedded video player lets you add Facebook videos to your site.
- The page plug-in lets you embed components from your Facebook page right into your website.

- The comments plug-in allows users comment on your website's content using their own Facebook accounts.
- The Follow button allows users subscribe to the public updates of other users or companies on Facebook.

Facebook Features

You can encourage likes, shares, and comments on your Facebook page and beyond by offering your fans incentives.

A popular way of doing this is to run a contest in which you ask your fans and their friends to "like" a post and comment on it, before entering them into a contest to win a prize. The prize can be anything, from a weekend away to a novelty hat. Usually it is something pretty awesome, so the post and your page get a lot of traction. It should also be relevant to your industry, so if you are a dog walker, offering an iPad might be a bit of a stretch. .

There are some considerations around running contests on Facebook:

- Facebook does not want to be liable for any of your terms and conditions. So make sure that you utilize its tools for the right reasons and that your competitions are fair.
- Stick to "like" and "comment" as your calls to action, meaning you ask people to "like" your page and to comment on the competition post. Newly enforced company-page policies now state that you cannot ask fans to share a contest post with their friends. If in breach of this rule, your contest could be cancelled and you may even risk having your page be suspended. Best to behave yourself and stay inside the lines.
- Manage the contest carefully, making it interesting, shareable, and engaging for your audience. Users are bombarded with a lot of salesy messages. How can you make yours stand out? Here are a few tips:
  - Offer a prize that users will actually want.
  - Include an eye-catching image and snappy copy, with a very clear call to action.
  - Promote your contest daily until your deadline.
  - Consider boosting your post to increase your reach.

Another way to attract fans on Facebook is through utilizing its Offers and Events features.

Creating an offer is done through a status update by clicking the Offer/Event+ button. Start by giving it a title, which can only contain 25 characters. Then describe your particular offer in 90 characters or fewer and make sure to include a call to action.

If your offer is an online purchase, use an online redemption link. Facebook will then email the individual user who claims your offer. Users can redeem in-store offers by simply walking into your store with a printout of the e-mail, or a saved version on their phone. Simple!

Figure 6.5   Facebook Event Page
Source: Screenshot reproduced with permission of Facebook.

Events are a great way of increasing brand awareness and they can be easily customized. Take for example an event page for a Kodaline concert in Figure 6.5, which has a huge cover image of the band attached to the event.

Since users share events with friends and connections, all of the imagery gets passed along too—which means great advertising for your company.

You can apply what you have learned from creating an effective Facebook page (how to maximize its reach with engaging content and how to analyze your results) to other social media channels, which will be covered in the upcoming sections. Stay tuned . . . .

Twitter

Introducing Twitter, another key player in the world of social media, which quickly grabs a hold of users' attention and encourages them to share and engage with content.

Soon you will be able to hold your own in the chirping world of Twitter, once you know how to:

- Set up a Twitter business account.
- Recognize the best ways of interacting with other users.
- Effectively promote your Twitter profile, utilizing features like social plug-ins and lists.

A Bird's-Eye View

Although Twitter's logo is a cute little blue bird, the platform is an information-sharing powerhouse and packs a powerful punch in terms of microblogging and connecting with other users.

Like Facebook, Twitter is a mobile platform that is constantly connected. It has over 280 million active users around the world—80 percent of whom are logging on via their smartphones. Not too shabby for a little bird, right?

The average number of followers per user is 208, and with over 500 million tweets sent every day, the platform is buzzing with activity all the time.

Creating Your Account

Private accounts mean that a user's tweets are protected from Google and other users are unable to retweet them. So as a business seeking promotion and publicity, you definitely want to go for the public option.

A few more things to bear in mind when getting set up:

- Your user name is limited to 15 characters, with no spaces, hyphens, or any other characters allowed.
- Your About Me section must be under 160 characters. So feel free to show off, but keep it short 'n' sweet.
- You must include a profile image and a background picture. As with Facebook, make sure your snaps are of a good quality and relevant to your company.
- Register your account as quickly as you can. The early Twitter bird catches the worm, after all!

When creating your Twitter handle (the name that appears alongside your account), let there be no confusion. It would be such a waste to go to all the trouble of setting up an amazing account, only to have people forget the name because your handle is too complicated.

Your handle should be:

- Relevant
- Short
- Registered early
- Unique
- Memorable
- On-brand

For example, take Manchester United's handle—@ManUtd. It does exactly what is says on the tin—it is just a shortened version of the account name itself. Loyal fans and glory supporters alike will easily remember that one.

Ready, Set, Tweet!

Once you have registered an account that looks great and has a memorable handle, you can start tweeting. Tweets are short messages of 140 characters or fewer. Take a look at the famous example in Figure 6.6.

See how a picture really can paint a thousand words? It had over 3 million retweets and is a perfect example of how powerful social media content can be. The tweet shown in Figure 6.7, from the popular marketing blog Mashable, includes a lot of content—call-to-action buttons, pictures, and key information—but it is well organized and easy to digest. Watch and learn.

Twitter can be a very serious forum but it can also help your brand to let loose a little and have some fun. If in doubt about what to tweet, think back to what works best for Facebook and then do the same on Twitter. Your content should be short, snappy, and very visual. Track Social believe the ideal Twitter character count is between 70 and 100 characters. According to Salesforce's 'Strategies for Effective Tweeting', posts with a smaller number of characters than 100 have a 17 percent higher engagement rate than those that do not. If a post seems weak, do not publish just for the sake of it. Hold back and revisit it at a later time—maybe then inspiration will come and you can tweak it to make it stronger. If in doubt, leave it out!

Figure 6.6   World-Famous Tweet by Comedian Ellen DeGeneres
Source: Twitter.

Figure 6.7   Effective Tweet from Mashable
Source: Twitter.

More often than not, a link to something else will be contained in a tweet and this will count towards the character limit. A handy way to sidestep this is to make use of space-saving tools such as Goo.gl or Bitly, better known as URL shorteners.

For example, this could be the link you want to tweet:

http://www.example.com/blog/page/category/year/month/day/article/id=1A2B3C

Bit of a mouthful, right? By entering it into Bitly it gets condensed to something like this:

http://bit.ly/8FapX

That's more like it! Every character is precious in a tweet, so if a link of 20 characters can be included instead of one with 87 characters, you have more room for a catchy line of copy.

Figure 6.8   Twitter Card
Source: Twitter.

Like Facebook posts, tweets are published from users' accounts and appear chronologically on a News Feed. Ads are also contained within this stream and are called promoted tweets.

This is where marketers can shine as the tweets they sponsor appear directly into the user's stream.

Twitter cards, such as the one shown in Figure 6.8, are large, interactive pieces of media within the News Feed. The message must still be 140 characters or fewer but it can also include:

- An image.
- A headline.
- A CTA button, which in this case is "read more."

Users can retweet and favorite this piece of content in the same way as ordinary tweets, so it will seem organic and does not immediately stand out as paid content.

Another great innovation from Twitter is adopting a carousel-style method for displaying ads within the feed, as seen in Figure 6.9.

These ads are similar to Twitter cards, but they run alongside one another. They are a really effective way of displaying multiple paid content posts without breaking away from the News Feed.

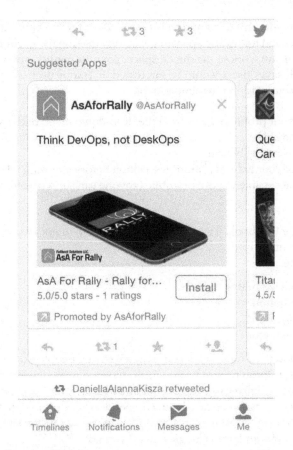

Figure 6.9   Twitter Carousel Ad
Source: Twitter.

Remember, there is no point in having a witty and pretty account if no one knows it exists—especially if you have paid for certain tweets! When promoting your profile, seize every opportunity possible. You can publicize it:

- At events
- In newsletters
- On television and radio
- In social ads
- In your email signature
- On webinars/talks/slides
- On business cards and posters
- During any offline conversations

Key Features

Twitter has a few great tools to help you stay ahead of the social media game:

Twitter lists. This handy feature allows you to segment audiences and organize followers within a pool of Twitter accounts.

For example, you might want to compile a list of speakers for an event. Attendees can then access the public list and follow the speakers, instantly making the event more interactive and connected. Or if you work in the digital space, your list might consist of the top companies that tech-savvy users would be interested in. Happy users = loyal followers! You can create a Twitter List in four simple steps:

1 Click Lists from your profile page or from the drop-down menu under your profile pic on the top right-hand side.
2 Click the Create New List button.
3 Enter the name of your list and a short description before choosing whether you want it to be private (only accessible to you) or public (anyone can subscribe to it).
4 Click Save List.

Social plug-ins. Like Facebook, Twitter uses lots of these to tempt visitors into sharing content from different websites.
The plug-ins include:

- The Share a Link button.
- The Follow button.
- The Hashtag button.
- The Mention button.

Once they have found their way onto a company's website, people can tweet directly and share content through Twitter.
Advanced search. Many businesses use this feature to search for businesses they wish to follow. By doing so they can keep an eye on competition, stay up-to-date with industry standards, and become involved in relevant conversations. It is pretty simple to use—just type *Twitter advanced search* into Google and off you go!
Geolocation services. These allow users to selectively add locations, such as cities and neighborhoods, to their tweets. It is a cool way of informing followers where in the world you are tweeting from and means you can share more than just a link or status update.
Multimedia elements. Images and video can also be added to tweets—and it gets better. Video can now be recorded within Twitter itself! Just grab your phone, hit record, and get ready for your close-up.

To Tweet or Not to Tweet . . .

Just as with Facebook, posting regularly to a Twitter account may not suit every business. However, it does have some key advantages:

- It enables one-to-one conversations to take place like never before.
- It is a very public forum that may be quick to tear down individuals and businesses but is even quicker to build them up.
- The all-powerful hashtag (which groups tweets into one collective space) has been responsible for bringing attention to the world's greatest travesties and its biggest accomplishments. It gives you instant access to the global stage—if you like that kind of thing.

Even if you are a total Twitter newbie, we recommend that you at least give it a try. Because soon enough, you are bound to discover just how rewarding a little blue bird can be.

LinkedIn

Now that you have a clear understanding of how Facebook and Twitter operate, let's move on to LinkedIn. It is a platform whose aim is to "connect the world's professionals and enable them to be more productive and successful."

This section will equip you with all the know-how you need to:

- Create an engaging LinkedIn profile.
- Use the platform effectively by participating in groups and engaging with other companies' pages.
- Advertise job vacancies and career opportunities in your organization.

About LinkedIn

Believe it or not, LinkedIn is a year older than Facebook—it was born back in 2003. And it has grown quite a bit over the past 13 years, with 347 million active users and two new sign-ups every second. The platform has a massive reach, across more than 200 countries and territories.

So who uses LinkedIn? Well lots of people, really—more than 3 million companies have LinkedIn company pages and 94 percent of recruiters use it to vet prospective employees and their résumés. Although it is in essence a social networking platform, it has a more professional, industry-focused approach than the likes of Facebook or Twitter.

Creating Your Profile

You can boost your company's credibility by encouraging all employees to set up a professional LinkedIn profile. It humanizes your brand, and by showing off the individual skilled workers involved in its day-to-day running, it helps people to get to know you better.

When creating your own profile, you need to fill in sections about your work history, education, and relevant education to give people a taste of who you are. The next step is to write a LinkedIn summary, which will appear above all of the other sections and is what most people will see first. This is the area where users can really sell themselves, and to do that effectively, sentences should be SMART, as shown in Figure 6.10.

Try to avoid the use of fluffy language, such as "I'm a great leader." Instead say, "I'm a great team leader. I have led a team of 15 people who have risen in the ranks and achieved sales uplift of over 20 percent." Such a specific and measurable statement will be far more attractive to prospective employers and clients alike.

Rich links, images, presentations, and even videos can be contained within every LinkedIn profile. Each section can be linked back to a reference or can include an image

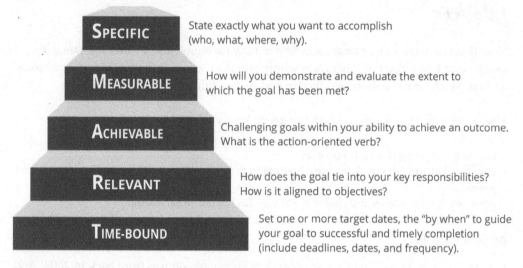

Figure 6.10   SMART Criteria
Source: The SMART acronym was first coined by George T. Doran and was inspired by Peter F. Drucker's *The Practice of Management*, published in 1954.

or video. These make profiles come alive, and if managed effectively, can really help you to stand out from the crowd.

With LinkedIn, there is no place to hide—your skills, that is. They are displayed prominently in your profile once you, your friends, and your colleagues add them. And since it is only polite to pay it forward, you can endorse your connections in return. Simply go to their profiles, see which skills you want to endorse, and then click (you guessed it) Endorse. No rocket science required.

Another way you can boost credibility is by including personal recommendations. The rule of thumb when it comes to LinkedIn recommendations is that both users must be connected. One will send a recommendation to another through the platform, which will automatically be added to their LinkedIn profile after it has been approved.

When building your profile, take the time to utilize your connections—because the more skills endorsed and testimonials received, the juicier your profile will be. Also, make sure to update skills and endorsements as you increase your connections so you are seen in the most professional light possible.

Building Your Network

LinkedIn can be a very lonely place if you are not engaging and connecting with others. Take the leap and approach as many people as possible, including:

- Email contacts
- Alumni

- Colleagues
- Friends
- Family

This is no time to play coy. You should follow as many contacts and influencers within your marketplace as you can. There are leaders across a whole range of industries on LinkedIn, including Richard Branson and Barack Obama, who both write for the site regularly.

By following specific companies and publications such as *Business Insider*, you will be notified in your LinkedIn stream whenever they post new content—that way you can stay up-to-date and not miss anything important.

You can chase all the people you like, but how do you let other people to find you? Connectivity plays a massive role within LinkedIn communities and so you need to put yourself out there. Having a vanity URL makes it easier for people to find you. Here is what the link to your profile might look like without a vanity URL:

LinkedIn.com/pub/doug-digital/234123ABCDEF

Not exactly snappy, is it?

To get a vanity URL, click underneath your profile picture and your public URL will appear. You can then shorten it to something like this:

LinkedIn.com/in/Doug-Digital

Much better!

Just like Facebook and Twitter, LinkedIn places social plug-ins on various websites so that users can easily share content when outside the platform. To get started, go to developer.linkedin.com/plugins.

Groups and Pages

LinkedIn groups are probably the most social aspect of the platform, as they are where most discussions take place.

By participating in these groups, you can maintain an active discussion with peers and colleagues, as seen in Figure 6.11 —you may even be seen as an industry thought leader.

Company pages are similar to Facebook business pages; while LinkedIn profile pages represent individuals, its company pages allow fans to connect with brands.

So what does it take to start a company page? First of all, more than five people within your company must have a LinkedIn profile that states that they work for you. You can then use your company's email address to apply for a LinkedIn company page.

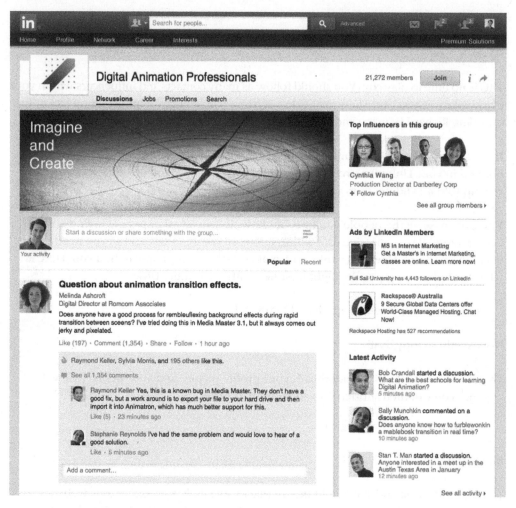

Figure 6.11   LinkedIn Group Discussions Tab
Source: LinkedIn.

Next, it is time to populate your page with as much relevant detail as possible, such as:

- Your location
- Your URL
- How many employees you have
- The main industry your company is in
- The year it was founded
- Whether it is a privately held or public liability company

Finally, add your logo and branding to the page. It is a really visual way for people to see what your company is about. An example of a LinkedIn company page is shown in Figure 6.12.

Figure 6.12   LinkedIn Company Page Home Tab
Source: LinkedIn.

Company pages can also contain videos, images, employee testimonials, and employer information—all of which play a part in selling your business as a great place to work! Subpages of company pages are called *showcase pages*. They are designed to grow a specific community around a particular product or division of a business.

Another type of LinkedIn page that offers branding opportunities is the career page, seen as a tab in Figure 6.12.

When recruiting your own staff it is useful to have a LinkedIn career page, as you can showcase your personality, highlight available jobs, and include some of your employees (plus their testimonials, if you like). However, if you do not have a LinkedIn recruiter account, this option is pretty expensive (around $6,000 per person every year).

Is LinkedIn Right for You?

Most likely, yes. LinkedIn lets you showcase your strengths while connecting with like-minded business owners and industry leaders outside of your everyday life. There is always more we can learn—and LinkedIn is a great place to do it.

Both personal and company pages can be brilliant marketing tools for your business, as long as they are managed in an effective and engaging manner. As with all of the channels that this chapter has discussed, you get out of it what you put in!

Google+

You now know how to utilize some of the biggest social media networks to help grow both your online presence and your business. Keep focused on stage 2 of the process, it's important to master!

Next up is an introduction to a platform managed by one of the biggest Internet companies in the world—Google. You will gain a key understanding of Google+ so that you can:

- Know what Circles are and how you can use them to connect with other users.
- Understand the benefits that Hangouts can have for your business.
- Create an engaging Google+ business page and track its results.

About Google+

Google+ is a social networking service with 1 billion registered users and 540 active monthly users. It combines lots of Google's products, including YouTube, Gmail, Blogger, Maps, Android, and Google My Business. If you have a Gmail account, you already have a Google+ account, which may come as a surprise to you!

Your account can be as public or as private as you want. You can choose to display or hide your email, add or remove your phone number, and even limit who can see certain posts and photos.

Google Circles

These are groups of people that users share content with or follow.

There are family circles, a close-friends circle, a colleagues circle, and a news and updates circle (to name just a few). As you can see in Figure 6.13, these groups can be edited and shared easily by just dragging and dropping them to your chosen locations.

Within these circles, users can segment shared posts—so if someone wants to keep a photo of a family vacation private among family members, they can share the photo on Google+ but only let those in their family circle to view it. Google+ offers a really targeted way of sharing content you care about with only certain people, as opposed to sharing it with the entire planet.

In this way, it is a lot less public than Twitter or Facebook, which may or may not appeal to you. However, just like those guys, Google+ allows users to use social plug-ins to share content in a more public way. These plug-ins are imported into a website, and

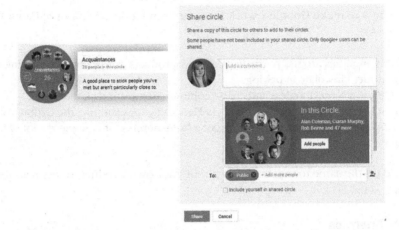

Figure 6.13　Google Circles
Source: Google and the Google logo are registered trademarks of Google Inc.; used with permission.

people can +1 your content (which is Google lingo for "like"). When using Google Plus, your first sentence must be a very gripping teaser, which means it should be 60 characters or fewer.

Google Hangouts

One of the best features in Google+ is its Hangouts feature. This is similar to live video conferencing or Skype but it brings in Google Chat. There is also Hangouts on Air, meaning live Google Chat can be hosted and then broadcast on YouTube—great if you want to share an instructional video about your product.

Many brands have done this already. Rovio (the brand behind *Angry Birds*) did a live Hangout with all of their developers to show how they built the game and the different tools and characters that are involved. People were able to ask questions through Twitter or Google+, which were then answered live online as people watched via YouTube.

That is about as interactive as it gets, right? Letting your customers ask live questions and having them answered by relevant people in real time, all online, all through Google+.

Getting Started

You can create a Google+ page for your business by going to https://business.google.com/create

Remember, you will need a Gmail account first—visit www.google.com to sign up for one. You can then create circles and build communities by connecting through your email and with other people on Google+.

If unsure how to make Google+ work for your brand, take a leaf out of Cadbury's book. They use it to:

- Create communities around particular Cadbury products, for example, by giving tips on using Cadbury chocolate in baking.
- Promote new ads on Google+ and create communities around all the hype.
- Broadcast live product demonstrations via Hangouts; for example, the Cadbury Creme Egg Bake hangout with Eric Lanlard, which got a huge number of views and a lot of traction on YouTube.

You could do the same to create a buzz about your own product, or even about an upcoming event.

Google+ Analytics

Google+ is connected to everything else in the world of Google, so you can instantly see the origin of all your social traffic.

On Google Analytics you can see social reports for your website, which means you can measure how Google+ has contributed to social sharing and conversations. This is a really cool tool that is completely unique to Google+.

That is the lowdown on Google+. Although maybe less known or used than other channels, it is a simple yet effective and highly visual marketing tool with a massive global reach. It is not one to be ignored.

Across all of these social media channels, the importance of video has remained consistent. Video offers brands a new way of connecting with followers. Coming up, you will see how you can maximize your reach on the big daddy of video platforms—YouTube.

YouTube

Video has more power than any other form of media when it comes to engaging users. In the video-sharing world, the YouTube platform remains king.

Discover what it means to say "lights, camera, action" to your business and get ready to:

- Understand how YouTube works and what some of its key features are.
- Effectively set up and promote your own channel.
- Know the types of video you can use and how to promote them across the web.

About YouTube

The following stats from YouTube are truly mind boggling:

- YouTube now has more than a billion unique users every single month.
- YouTube now claims over 400 hours of content uploaded every single minute.

- The number of hours people spend watching videos (aka watch time) on YouTube is up 60 percent y/y.
- More video is uploaded to YouTube in one month than the three major U.S. television networks have created in *60* years!
- YouTube is localized in 74 countries, across 61 languages.

So if you were thinking that YouTube was just a bunch of cat videos, think again!

Setting Up Your Channel

If you already have a Google account, you automatically have access to a YouTube account—you just need to link the two. YouTube channels should look clear and uncomplicated, and cover photos act as great branding for your channel in the same way they do for other social media platforms.

Once you have set up an account, you can access features and buttons such as Like, Subscribe, Watch Later, and Watch History.

There are a wide variety of features within YouTube, all making it possible to interact with different communities across the site and to hear what they are saying about brands, competition, and the industry in general. These include:

- *Comments.* You have the option to have a comments section enabled for every video uploaded onto YouTube. People can also give a video a thumbs-up or a thumbs-down, which was unique to YouTube for a long time, as the only site that let users *not* like content online. Be aware that the Thumbs Down button leaves your brand vulnerable and could negatively affect your business.
- *Subscribe button.* This can be placed directly into a YouTube video and is a great way of encouraging engagement.

Types of Video

Screen recordings are pretty popular with brands. These are captured by using low-cost tools such as Camtasia Studio or ScreenFlow, and such recordings are perfect for product demonstrations.

A webinar is another great way for businesses to interact with audiences. It might be a 20-minute video showcasing a product or a snappy piece with five useful tips and tricks. There are lots of webinar tools out there. So get creating, get recording, and get broadcasting live to your subscribers. You can then store your webinar on your YouTube channel for people to watch later.

If you prefer to stream your content live, you can use Hangouts On Air (introduced in the previous section). After YouTube users have watched it live it is automatically recorded and uploaded to YouTube for people to watch after the event. The most popular types of video on YouTube are computer screen recording, webinars, live video, and recorded video.

Creating and Sharing Content

YouTube content can be created in many different ways. You can bring in the big guns by using professional tools like Final Cut and PowerDirector. However, these require skill, training, and resources (particularly time and money)—and even though the outcome is high-quality videos that look really professional, these videos only make up a small portion of content on YouTube.

If you are just starting out and do not have a very generous fairy godmother or access to high-quality recording equipment, you will probably want to consider other options—for instance, flash tools like Animoto to compile images, videos, and music. And of course, you can always film videos from your trusty phone; in fact, a smartphone video is the most popular format on YouTube.

Mobile journalism (mojo) is the new buzzword when it comes to creating content. Long gone are the days of shaky handheld videos (unless that is the style you want!).

A smartphone lens is probably just as good as that of some professional cameras. Also, free editing tools (such as iMovie on the iPhone or YouTube Editor) can be used to edit footage quickly and easily. Making the most out of these free tools when starting out is a great way of keeping costs to a minimum. There are lots of mobile video, audio recording, and editing tools available for both iPhone and Android—simply find out which one works best for you.

Once your content is live, there are a couple of ways it can be shared from YouTube to other social platforms. Users can click the Share button when watching your video, and that will produce a direct link. Alternatively, they can click the Embed button to generate a piece of HTML code, which can then be imported into a website, as can be seen in Figure 6.14. The YouTube video will sit live on the webpage and visitors can play it without having to leave the site.

Keep your eyes and ears open to see if anyone is vlogging (video blogging) about your business—then you can share their videos, too. Simply type your product or service into YouTube Search to see if you have made it into the grapevine. As with all social media channels, you should embrace every opportunity you can to share the fact that people are talking about you!

Making It Work for You

The world of video sharing can seem pretty overwhelming to those who have never dabbled in it before—so here are a few pearls of wisdom to remember:

- Promote your business channel to your customers by embedding videos across your website. Show them you are tech and media savvy.
- Subscribe to relevant YouTube channels. It is a good way of keeping tabs on the competition.

Figure 6.14   How to Embed a YouTube Video
Source: Screenshot reproduced with permission of YouTube.

- Post regular and engaging video updates. Three-year old content will not cut it.
- Share product demonstrations, including helpful hints and tips. Because sharing is caring.

Now that you know how to create profiles and channels across the major social media platforms, let's take a look at the world of blogging.

Blogs

There are millions of web logs (blogs) online right now that cover a wide range of subjects—from travel to baking to the glamorous world of stain removal, this is an integral channel of stage 2.

Whatever your business, you can benefit greatly by creating a blog. This section will help you get started by:

- Recognizing that blogs provide strong SEO benefits and give credibility to your business.
- Understanding best blogging practices.
- Seeing how blogs can be shared on social media platforms to increase awareness.

Blogs in Brief

A blog is a piece of content hosted and shared on a website. It should be updated regularly to include the latest news, trends, and events. Blogs give businesses credibility, as well as a voice in the market, and well-written blogs will keep visitors coming to a website even when other content or offers have not changed.

The most popular blogging platform is WordPress—it is used around the world and is known for its safety, ease of use, and customizable options. Another platform that has really caught on is Tumblr. This microblogging platform and social networking website allows users to post text, photos, quotes, links, music, and videos—all from their browsers.

Best Practices

There are many different styles of blogging—some people prefer one that is chatty and informal, others one that is downright nuts. Blogging is a very open and creative form of social media, however, certain guidelines should be followed to ensure your content is engaging and professional:

- Your posts should be anywhere from 1,000 to 2,500 words long. The actual length will be dependent on topic and audience, but any fewer than 1,000 may fall short of Google's algorithm and reduce your chances of showing up in the first pages of search results.
- Include at least one to two images per post to make the post eye-catching.
- Ask open questions at the end of each post to encourage engagement.
- Pack a punch—your content should be easy to consume and organized with the help of lists, bullet points, and headers.
- Keep a conversational tone and avoid industry jargon at all costs.
- Include links within your posts: *Back linking* to a particular resource is a great way of adding credibility to your blog.
- Be consistent and make sure your content is strong, all of the time. Once you build momentum, keep going—post regularly and don't leave weeks between posts.
- Add relevant tags and keywords to your posts to optimize them for search engines. If your posts are about mobile marketing, make sure to add some tags around mobile!

For inspiration, check out the popular blogging website BuzzFeed. Most of its articles utilize listicles, which are lists that grab your attention right away. The headlines of these lists might be "37 ways to embarrass your dog" or "15 epic cat fails." Given headlines like these, people expect really funny and engaging content—and they get it too, making BuzzFeed one of the most visited websites out there.

Business/Community Blogging

This is a really effective way of ensuring that your business stays on top of the industry. You can contribute to a community that is interested in a particular topic, allowing you to become a source of great content for people in that industry. In other words, you can show off.

Once you have started blogging, you can gain traction by asking for your blog to be hosted by another, more popular blog that is relevant to your audience. In doing this, you can showcase your blogging skills and get off the ground more quickly than if you were to fly solo.

Promoting Your Blog

Blogging is a powerful way of keeping your brand in front of existing connections, but it also helps you to reach new audiences around the world. You should spread the word about your blog on YouTube, LinkedIn, Facebook, Twitter, Instagram and Google+, making use of these wonderfully connected social media platforms that have been discussed in the previous sections.

All of this cross-platform sharing will increase your blog's visibility online, which in turn will increase marketability. And digital marketers love a bit of marketability. Remember to add your blog's RSS feed to your Twitter, Facebook, and LinkedIn accounts. Doing so means that every time you post a new blog and hit Publish, the new entry will automatically filter out to these sites—you can choose to write your own description too.

Just as with all the channels covered so far, social plug-ins are a handy way of encouraging people to share your content across the web when users are not on your site. The WordPress plug-in Disqus, which enables people to promote their blogs on their LinkedIn, Facebook, and Twitter profiles, is a powerful tool when it comes to spreading the word about new posts.

Does blogging require time? Yes. Does it require effort? Definitely. But it is also a great way for companies to get their message out into the public sphere and to connect with a new audience. It's a channel that needs dedication and patience to build up, but it is certainly something worth doing.

So, What Have You Learned in This Chapter?

By now you will have a pretty good idea of how you can use social media to your company's advantage. Here are some final tips to help you on your way:

- Vary all of your content by keeping it funny, engaging, and informative.
- Be quick to respond to users' queries and interactions.
- Be professional, but know that letting your hair down once in a while is allowed and even encouraged!
- Remember that hard work always pays off. Responsive and effective social media platforms will really grow your business if you put the time in.

Now that you have emerged from your cocoon and become a social media butterfly, get ready to spring into action. Start setting up those company profiles today!

Go to www.artofdmi.com to access the case study on SMM as additional support material for this chapter.

Exercises

Exercise 1

You are a four-star boutique hotel located in a suburb of Chicago. Your main target market is couples (aged 30 to 45) and small weddings (up to 70 guests). Weddings are a new venture for your business.

Using the business above:

1 Set up your social media goals under the following categories:
   - Customer service goals
   - Product goals
   - Communication goals
   - Marketing goals
2 List the social media channels you will use to market the business.

Note: When deciding what channels to use, consider the target market (gender, age, location) and the type of products and services you are offering.

Exercise 2

Log into Facebook and set up a business page for the hotel in exercise 1. Complete the following:

- Fill in About Us details.
- Add a profile picture.
- Set up a preferred audience page.

Exercise 3

Using the business page created above, choose five competitor pages and add them to Pages to Watch in your Facebook page Insights.

Record:

- Which page is at the top of the list?
- What posts worked well for them?

- What are the images/video used?
- What are the engagement levels?

What can you learn from this information?

Exercise 4

Log into Twitter and open Twitter Analytics.

- How many tweet impressions have you received over the past 28 days?
- How many mentions and tweets linked to you in the past 28 days?
- What is the top tweet for the current month?
- Who has been most engaged with you?
- Are the correct people connected with you and are your followers based on interests, location, and gender?

Exercise 5

You briefly met a potential client at a networking event but only managed to get his first name (Conor) and his job title (Product Specialist). You would like to connect with him by carrying out an advanced search for him on LinkedIn.

- Take note of additional search areas that are available in premium accounts.
- Refine your search until you have located this person.
- Draft a personalized connection request (it can be completed by visiting Conor's profile and clicking Connect).

> NOTE: The action plan for social media marketing can be found at the end of Chapter 7.

Chapter 7
Social Media Marketing (Part 2)

An Introduction

From a customer's point of view, social media is an awesome way to connect with people she already knows—and to connect with people or businesses she *wants* to know. As a digital marketer, you need to use this curiosity to drive your business without approaching customers in an obtrusive way. While social media is a playground where people can flit between discussions and encounter great deals and offers on their own terms, your job is to deliver content that your target audience wants to receive, which will be of great benefit to them—and even better benefit to you.

Implementing an effective social media strategy for your business is imperative to the success of a social media campaign, and the only way to build and sustain relationships with customers is to listen to them.

Process

Chapter 6 gave you the lowdown on the first two stages of the SMM iterative process, as shown in Figure 7.1. This chapter will keep the wheel spinning so that you will have complete knowledge of the third and fourth stages:

3. *Implementation*. Being engaged with your customers on social media platforms such as Facebook, Twitter, and LinkedIn will keep customers interested, but don't just be the best friend—be the mentor who will know what your audience wants in advance, by planning and scheduling content. In this stage you will learn how to set appropriate goals for your chosen social media platforms and to create and manage your campaigns in line with your budget and proposed timeline.
4. *Analysis*. While some friendships come to a natural end, your social media campaign never stops turning. But as a true friendship blossoms with understanding and trust, your campaign cannot succeed without constant analysis. This stage guides you through the analysis and measurement services that each major platform offers, in order to track the effectiveness of your social media campaigns.

Figure 7.1   Four-Stage SMM Process

Key Terms and Concepts

This chapter will teach you to understand why implementing social media strategies will better equip you to reach achievable goals, and how you will benefit from the analysis tools that each social media platform offers. Upon completion of SMM part 2, you will:

- Master the intricacies of each social media platforms' analysis features.
- Be adept at scheduling appropriate content for each social media platform.
- Learn how to set suitable goals for your chosen social media platform.
- Create and manage your social media campaigns to budget and schedule.
- Be aware of privacy and data protection issues associated with SMM.

If Facebook, Twitter, LinkedIn, and all of the other social media platforms were in high school, each would be a member of a completely different clique. Your role as a digital marketer is to be a social butterfly who understands what drives each network, why it works, and how to keep the members of each network engaged.

Stage 3: Implementation

You have learned the basic elements of SMM, now let's put them into use. The implementation stage—stage 3 of the iterative process—is highlighted in Figure 7.2 and is when you tailor your campaign around how you fit in the market.

In this section you will learn:

- How to understand where your position is in the market.
- The different ways to listen to your audience.
- That careful consideration must be given to your campaign.

Figure 7.2   Focus on the Third Stage in the SMM Process

Soccer is the number-one sport in the world because of one thing: goals. Once a world-class striker shoots that ball to the back of the net, it's a victory. A soccer game without any goals is a game not worth watching; likewise, in the sport of digital marketing, the more goals the better.

We identified business and marketing goals for social media in the previous chapter, and we looked at the social media channels that most businesses use. So now it's time to channel your inner digital marketing striker: Use social media platforms to your advantage, listen to your audience, and score some phenomenal campaign goals!

Understanding Your Fit

A soccer player does not play a game wearing a kit that is two sizes too small. When preparing an SMM plan, you need to take some time to consider where you fit in the market.

- *Where does your audience hang out?* Knowing what social media channels are consistent with your audience is very important. Is it one particular channel, such as Facebook, or is it a mixture of various platforms?

- *What tone and style of conversation should you use?* While a light, fun tone would suit a teenage audience, it would not be appropriate for corporate engagement.
- *Who will speak on behalf of your organization?* Deciding who will take the reins and be the company's mouthpiece is not a decision to be made lightly, as responsibility and accountability for image management will lie with that person.
- *What is the key demographic for your product and how can you reach it?* All of the *W* questions have to be asked: Who are the people in it? What do they do? What do they like? What is their age group? Where do they live?
- *How will you respond to negative feedback or comments?* Social media communication should engage your audience, and while the aim is always to please the customer, from time to time you might get a negative reaction. If this happens, don't get downhearted; negative feedback can be a key learning tool. That said, you will have to deal with it. The most effective solution is to respond publicly and take the conversation offline as quickly as possible to discuss any issues one-to-one with the customer.

Resources

A soccer team is made up of 11 players, but if all of those players are strikers, who will defend the goal? You may have awesome ideas for your social media strategy, but you need to evaluate what resources you have in order to make sure that every aspect of your strategy will be covered.

People and Skills

The people assigned to the SMM strategy need to be made accountable for shaping, developing, and driving the strategy. When initiating your strategy, figure out whether current team members possess the abilities to see your plan through, or whether training, up-skilling, or hiring new staff members is necessary.

In the same way that not all soccer players are strikers, SMM team members play different positions. You will need people who can take on management duties, people who can engage with customers on a one-to-one basis, people to take control of IT, and people to oversee finances.

Budget

An SMM strategy is a cyclical process and budget is certainly something that needs to be reviewed frequently. Checking analytics is essential; if you find that the initial projection for your budget is too high or too low, action will have to be taken.

Listening

Launching your SMM strategy can be nerve-racking. In fact, it's quite like the start of a new relationship. When you initiate your strategy, remember this: Be a good first date.

A good date is one who listens. Listening to your customers is really important, because you can learn so much from them. The factors to be aware of when listening are:

- What channels to use.
- What tone and style to adopt.
- Whether you are getting different kinds of responses from different demographics.
- Who are the influencers of your target audience and can you leverage them?

By listening to your audience, you find out a lot about your competitors too—there is no hiding on social media! Check out how your target audience reacts and engages with your competitors' social media strategies and learn from their successes (and failures).

Influencers

There's a reason why the town mayor holds public forums: A good mayor wants to keep all of his or her townsfolk happy—and wants to stay in power. When you identify key influencers and listen to them, they can help you, and in return you can give them the product they want.

Engage with Happy Customers

Customers who have had a positive experience with your brand already like your brand. When they talk about you positively, look after them. Like what they say, comment on positive feedback, and when possible, reward them.

Engage with Unhappy Customers

While it's easy to just ignore complaints on social media, don't! If you solve an unhappy customer's problem and win his favor, there is great potential for that customer to become a big advocate of your brand.

Find and Engage with New Customers

Identify potential customers who have complained about a competitor or service and approach them with a solution to their issues.

The reason you listen is to find out what exactly the customer wants—then you can figure out exactly what to deliver. There are two main ways of listening: Being reactive or being proactive.

Being Reactive

Twitter user Alexa Burrows sent a seemingly random tweet lamenting the end of her holiday and jokingly asked airline company JetBlue for a welcome home parade. JetBlue's SMM team was listening and had the exceedingly clever idea to arrange a welcome home party. How's that for service? When you reply directly to social media

Figure 7.3   An Example of Reactive Tweeting from JetBlue
Source: Twitter.

users who tag you in posts, you build audience trust. So by addressing and solving their problems, you open the door to gaining loyal customers.

Being Proactive

Being proactive means working with foresight. During your search for new customers, look for ways to convince them that you have the best service. WestJet, another airline, started an incredible campaign offline. They set up a stall at a boarding gate and asked passengers waiting for their flight what they would like for Christmas. When they landed, wrapped gifts appeared on the luggage carousel—all of the presents that the passengers had wished for. To see the campaign for yourself, type WestJet Christmas Miracle into YouTube (don't forget your hankie!).

Luckily for WestJet, they have the resources (not to mention the finances) to arrange such an effective proactive listening ploy, but even if your budget does not stretch to campaigns like this, you can certainly take inspiration from it.

Tools

In the same way that you can Google any question and find the answer in a matter of milliseconds, one of the great beauties of the digital world is that there are a number of tools you can employ to help you listen to your audience and find out what they are saying about you. Topsy, Klout, Mention, and Google Alerts are some of the best listening tools on the market.

Content Planning

You should let your date do the talking over that first cup of coffee. By listening to their likes and dislikes, you'll have all the information needed to really woo them the next time you meet! The same goes for paying attention to people in your audience: By really listening to them you can gain a lot of important insights, such as what they think of your product and what needs improvement. This, in turn, will help you figure out what type of content to post on your social media platforms. And once you have that figured out, you can begin to formulate your content plan following each of these four stages:

1 *Plan it out.* As you learned in SMM part 1, scheduling is very important. Create a formal schedule and stick to it as closely as you can. Carefully consider how often you can post on each social media platform and always track each post.
2 *Integrate.* Your social media plan does not stand apart from your overall marketing campaign—it has to be linked to every other aspect of the campaign.
3 *Manage.* Use tools, such as Hootsuite, SocialOomph, and Sendible, to schedule social media posts and updates. Using tools like these will also allow you to monitor the level of engagement each post attracts and how many posts is enough (or too much).
4 *Adapt.* Sometimes you spill red wine all over your mother-in-law's white dress and sometimes you forget to schedule a tweet—but hey, these things happen. In unforeseen circumstances, you need to be prepared to take ownership of the problem, assess your situation, and come up with a way to rectify the missed opportunity.

When creating your content plan, keep these questions in mind:

- What is the purpose of my social media activity?
- Who exactly do I want to "like" my page?
- What content will my audience find valuable?
- Should I create a content calendar?
- How often should I post?

And most importantly:

- What content will my audience engage with?

B2B versus B2C Content

In the context of social media content, think people-to-people rather than business-to-business. Don't aim your content at a faceless company, when in reality you are dealing directly with a person.

In the same vein, think of the market as a community and deliver content that will interest and engage its members. Short and snappy video testimonials are fantastic forms of content. Nontypical success stories work really well for this type of application. For example, instead of posting a video based on a young, privileged Harvard grad making millions of dollars, use an 80-year-old grandmother instead!

Infographics are also a powerful method of compressing a lot of information into one post—information that you know will both interest the people in your audience and (hopefully) encourage them to share. Take note of the following factors when planning your content for each business approach:

B2B	B2C
B2B? Think P2P	Product or service updates
Community	Community
Education	Photos
Industry updates	Entertainment
Testimonials	Customer stories
Short videos	Events
Infographics	Offers or deals
Customer POV	Short videos
	Infographics
	Customer POV

Content Scheduling

The best way to prepare your content is to break it down into a schedule. Take the chart in Figure 7.4 as an example.

There are a number of considerations for scheduling content. Think about which network(s) to post to, what tone of voice works best for each, and what time of day is best to reach your target audience. Don't 'content burst'—it is better practice to stagger your updates so as not to overwhelm your customers with a flurry of posts.

Platform Specificity

There is no monogamy in SMM! You have got to know and love each platform—and then each of them will love you back. Different platforms have different needs and restrictions. Twitter posts have a limit of 140 characters, Instagram is most effective when using multiple hashtags, and certain times of the day are better for posting certain types of content. Take a quick look at Figure 7.5, which shows a post map for Facebook and Twitter and lays out the best times to publish certain types of content.

Days/Weeks	1	2	3	4	5	6	7	8
Blog posting								
Campaign								
Products								
Offers/deals								
Events								
Behind-the-scenes view								
Thought leadership								
Local interest								
Industry-relevant								
Testimonials								
Shared from elsewhere								

Figure 7.4   Facebook and Twitter Post Scheduling Chart

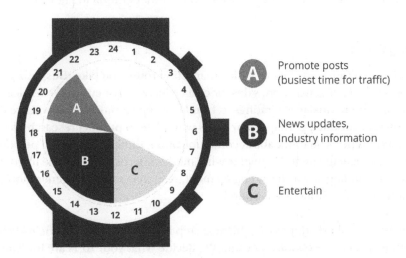

Figure 7.5   Best Times to Publish by Content

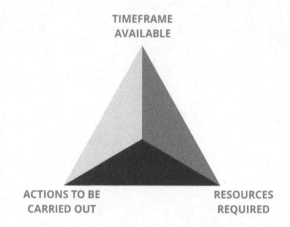

TIMEFRAME
AVAILABLE

ACTIONS TO BE
CARRIED OUT

RESOURCES
REQUIRED

Figure 7.6   Factors Affecting an SMM Action Plan

Post scheduling of course, is not a cut-and-dry process, so it's always a good idea to use your scheduling tool to review what times and types of posts work best for your audience on each network.

Action Plan

In order for any SMM campaign to be successful, you must acknowledge the constraints that your business has in relation to the time frame available: Don't set a deadline unless you know you can deliver. Examine the resources you have at your disposal—for example, certain parts of the plan may require particular skill sets; do you have a staff member who can perform those tasks? You can think about the actions required to implement the plan once you have considered the other criteria in Figure 7.6.

Marketing Goals

Your goals will differ according to which marketing route you take. Business goals should be set for lead generation, sales, or cost reduction. For customer service, your goals may be about satisfaction ratings, referrals, or repeat business. If you are thinking in terms of your product, perhaps your goals will relate to product research, design, or enhancement. When you think about communication, think about brand personality and reputation management. No matter what marketing road you decide to go down, always keep branding, awareness, engagement, response rate, lead generation, and conversion in the forefront of your mind.

Once you set your marketing goals, the next step is to choose the specific KPIs for each goal. With respect to Facebook, for example, decide what your KPIs are for lead generation—and do the same for Twitter, LinkedIn, and the like.

Social KPIs will be determined by engagement and advertising. For example, with respect to engagement indicators you may look at elements such as reach and follows;

for advertising indicators, impressions and clicks may prove the most important. Take a look at the comprehensive list of engagement and advertising KPIs below.

Engagement indicators	Advertising indicators
Reach	Impressions
Follows	Clicks
Trending	CPC
Likes, shares, comments	Conversions
RT (retweet), favorites, replies	Conversions
Direct messages	Registrations
Click-through on posts	RSVPs
Competition entries	App installs
Offer redemptions	Conversions

Quality Scale of Interaction

Just as a date laughing at your jokes doesn't guarantee a goodbye kiss, for social media, there's a big difference between somebody liking a Facebook post and getting her involved in the conversation. As shown in Figure 7.7, the Like feature on Facebook is the lowest level of interaction after actually viewing the post, and even though the feature is not on all social media platforms, it's still a good way to gauge the quality scale of interaction.

The ultimate goal of posting something on social media is that your audience will see it, engage with it, and spread the word. Each channel is unique and each has different qualities that you need to understand. As we continue through the chapter, let's examine each one in more detail.

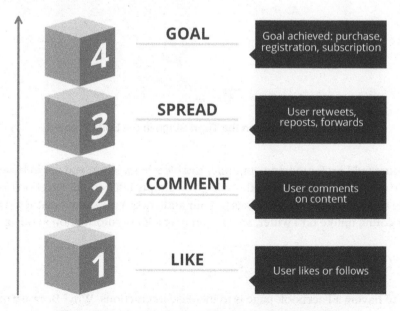

Figure 7.7   Quality Scale of Social Media Interaction

Facebook Strategy and Advertising

If social media platforms were high school stereotypes, Facebook would be the homecoming queen.

With over 1 billion users, Facebook rules the social media roost. But Facebook is more than just a pretty face; it is an extremely effective advertising tool and one of the channels used for stage 3 of our process, highlighted in Figure 7.8. This section will burrow deep down to the core of Facebook advertising and at the conclusion you will:

- Be familiar with all of the different types of ads you can run from Facebook.
- Learn the skills required to segment and target different audiences.
- Understand the mechanics of creating a successful Facebook ad.

Figure 7.8   Focus on the Third Stage in the SMM Process

Even if you would prefer to hang out under the bleachers, when you are in business you have to be in with the in-crowd—otherwise, you simply fall behind. Facebook is an incredible tool for delivering messages to your audience: You are not restricted in character count, unlike on Twitter, so you can post a lot of information in one go.

Facebook Page Strategy

The goal of having a Facebook page is to increase interactions. Why? Because the more interactions your Facebook page has, the cheaper your ads will be. When Facebook can actually see the type of people that are interacting and engaging with your posts, they don't have to target the right kind of people on your behalf.

Increasing Your Engagement Level

So how can you grow your Facebook profile to attract more customers?

Post consistently and regularly. Schedule your posts for when the majority of your audience is online.
Use a calendar to plan ahead. Planning your posts ensures they're in line with your marketing communication goals.
Target your posts. Segment your audience into demographic groups and adjust your messaging according. Your posts will only be shown to those fans who match a specific targeting criteria.
Use imagery and videos. Facebook audiences love images, and with the autoplay feature, more videos are now being consumed on Facebook than YouTube.

How to Post Consistently and Regularly

Take a look at Figure 7.9. There is so much that you can do with one small text box— add images, show a video, create an offer, and even show emotion.

By clicking the little arrow beside the blue post button, you can schedule posts to guarantee that a steady stream of content is being published. Be sure to dedicate some time to organize scheduling, and return at another time to respond to any interactions.

Select Your Audience Carefully

The really cool thing about Facebook is being able to direct your posts to a very specific demographic. If you wanted to let the cheerleaders know there was a big game coming up, you would not announce it to the entire school! The same goes for selecting an

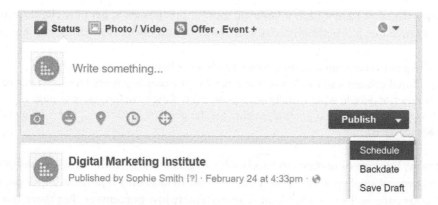

Figure 7.9   Facebook Posting Facility
Source: Screenshot reproduced with permission of Facebook.

audience on Facebook. If you are promoting a product geared towards women in their 30s, you can select that demographic specifically.

You can be very precise about whom you choose to view a particular post. You can narrow it right down to:

- Gender
- Relationship status
- Educational status
- Age
- Location
- Language
- Interests

Say, for example, your business is related to wellness and you are releasing a product related to men's health. By specifically aiming the post advertising the product to your male customers, you go straight to the target audience.

Have a Heart!

When posting, use the features that allow you to add emotions and verbs to describe how you are feeling. Facebook has added this option for a reason: People respond to emotion and they appreciate a personal touch. Staying with the personal theme, it is a good idea to publish behind-the-scenes photographs of your company. It helps customers relate to the company on a deeper level.

This option shows just how incredible Facebook is as a digital marketing tool. Companies do not have to be faceless institutions anymore: Letting customers in on the people behind the company brings them closer to the brand.

When the Price Is Right

While it's true that Facebook is a fantastic tool for businesses to get new clients and generate revenue, it is getting harder to reach your audience for a number of reasons.

- Users began to complain that their News Feeds were becoming clogged up with promotional content and Facebook listened. Over the past few years Facebook has reduced the number of people who actually see a post, even if they are fans of your page.
- Facebook did not just change its algorithm for the good of its users—it saw a financial benefit for itself.

Right now, because of updates to Facebook's EdgeRank algorithm, ordinary users will see less promotional content on their news feeds. In fact, only 8 percent of people who "like" your page will see a post. That is an extremely low percentage, but there is a solution—adapt and pay. To get any significant impact out of Facebook, you need to spend money with Facebook.

Boosting Your Post

There are many different ways to advertise on Facebook, but let's start with boosting—the mechanism that allows you to sell without selling.

Boosting a post is the easiest form of Facebook advertising and it's an extremely useful one to use during an important promotion. It is a good way to introduce yourself to Facebook Ads and to learn how it works.

The process is simple; follow these three steps:

1 Click the Boost Post button under the text box.
2 Choose which audience you want to target.
3 Choose how much you want to spend and how many days you want to boost the post for.

It's worth being strategic about which posts you boost. View your post history to see the types of posts people interact with, how many people view video posts, and which type of posts get the most shares. Popular posts that haven't been boosted give a good indication of how well that type of post would do if it were to be boosted. When you are starting out and familiarizing yourself with Facebook advertising, boost at least once a week. This will let Facebook know that you are a spender rather than someone who uses the platform for free.

Facebook Ads

Boosting may be the easiest way to bring attention to your Facebook page, but there are multiple other advertising routes to take and all of them serve a specific purpose. The ad in Figure 7.10 is designed to encourage people to click through to the website. Pay attention to the word *Sponsored* in the top left-hand corner. This word appears on every Facebook ad so that people will know that the post has been paid for. The ad in Figure 7.11 is a video ad—see that little play button on the image? This is a good way to provide your target audience with educational content—ideas that they can share.

The ad in Figure 7.12 is an ad with a Use App button (bottom right) that encourages people to install an app. Figure 7.13 is an example of an event ad—which is an interesting ad type, as it lives online but gives you the chance to meet your customers in person. And finally, Figure 7.14 illustrates another type of ad—the offer. This is a popular type of ad, as it provides something useful to the customer and it enables you to collect useful information, such as email addresses.

Ads Manager

The Ads Manager function allows you to set up any type of ad you choose. Before you can use it, however, you need to create the ad, so that you can register your credit card details. There will come a stage when you may have multiple ads running at the same

 **Jasper's Market**
Sponsored ·

It's fig season! Not sure what to do with figs? Here's a great dessert recipe to share.

Fig Tart with Almonds

The simplicity of this tart perfectly accents ripe figs. If you don't have enough time to make a handmade crust, pick up one of Jasper's pre-made pie crusts.

WWW.JASPERS-MARKET.COM

Figure 7.10   Clicks to Website Facebook Desktop Ad
Source: Screenshot reproduced with permission of Facebook.

time—and here is where Power Editor comes in. Power Editor is the most convenient place for managing your ads, allowing you to manage all ads in one place and to make changes very easily. Be aware, however, that Power Editor can only be used with the Google Chrome browser.

Audience Insights

Audience Insights helps you to define the size of your target market and to target ads more specifically to your audience. Narrow down your audience by choosing from a range of options, including interests and behaviors, age, gender, location, work information, relationship status, and family. Check out the Behaviors feature of Audience Insights, which allows you to specifically choose people who have already spent money on Facebook. It also allows you to segregate higher-than-average spends on Facebook—pretty nifty, right?

 **Jasper's Market**
Sponsored · 🌐

👍 **Like Page**

Stop by Jasper's and take a look at our latest shipment of fresh produce!

Like   Comment   ➤ **Share**

Figure 7.11   Video Views Facebook Desktop Ad
Source: Screenshot reproduced with permission of Facebook.

Suggested App

 **Jasper's Market**
Sponsored · 🌐

Use our app and get delicious recipes for Jasper's Market's latest produce. It's fun, easy, and most of all, free!

Jasper's Market
Business

Use App

Figure 7.12   App Installs Facebook Desktop Ad
Source: Screenshot reproduced with permission of Facebook.

Figure 7.13   Event Response Facebook Desktop Ad
Source: Screenshot reproduced with permission of Facebook.

Figure 7.14   Offer Claims Facebook Desktop Ad
Source: Screenshot reproduced with permission of Facebook.

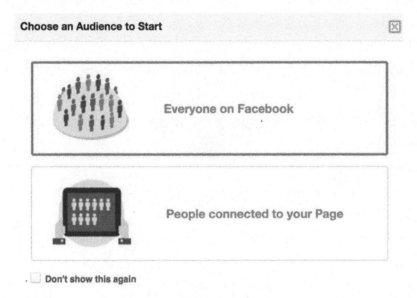

Figure 7.15   Choose your Audience for Facebook Insights
Source: Screenshot reproduced with permission of Facebook.

The first step is to choose your audience, as shown in Figure 7.15.

Next, define your audience attributes. You will see from your demographics what kind of people are already on your page. In Figure 7.16 you can see that 49 percent of users are female and that 25 percent of those women are in the 25-to-34 age cohort.

Then if you want to get really specific, you need to target your audience according to lifestyle. For example, if you are in the business of pensions, you might want to target the Raisin' Grandkids lifestyle group, as seen in Figure 7.17.

Objectives

When you first create an ad, Facebook will display a list of objectives for you to choose from, as illustrated in Figure 7.18.

Choosing which objective is best differs from business to business. If your sole objective is to increase the number of clients you have, compare various types of ads to discover which are giving you the maximum ROI. The best way to do that is to use Power Editor, which allows you to monitor multiple types of ads all at once and compare the ROIs of each. When you have discovered the best way to make more than you are spending, you'll know which objective is best for you.

Audience

After you have decided on your objective, the next step is deciding whom to target. Once you choose the specifics—age, location, gender, education level, and interests— take note of the speedometer on the right.

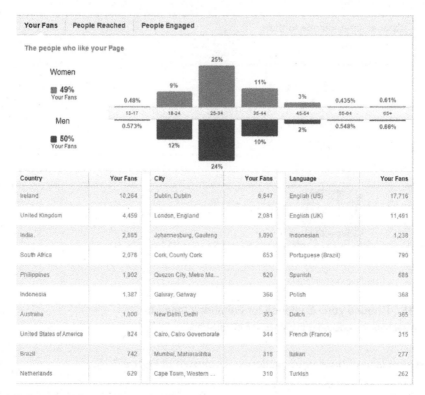

Figure 7.16   Facebook User Demographics
Source: Screenshot reproduced with permission of Facebook.

Lifestyle
US demographic and interest data based on purchase behavior, brand affinity and other activities. Source: Personicx

Lifestyle	Selected Audience		Compare ▾
Savvy Singles	4%		+0%
Country Single	0.8%		+0%
Rural Parents	2%		+0%
Established Elite	5%		+0%
Hard Chargers	1%		+0%
Shooting Stars	2%		+0%
Raisin' GrandKids	3%		+0%
Suburban Seniors	1%		+0%
Summit Estates	5%		+0%
Metro Mix	0.8%		+0%

See All

26% of audience matched

Figure 7.17   Facebook Insights Lifestyle Report
Source: Screenshot reproduced with permission of Facebook.

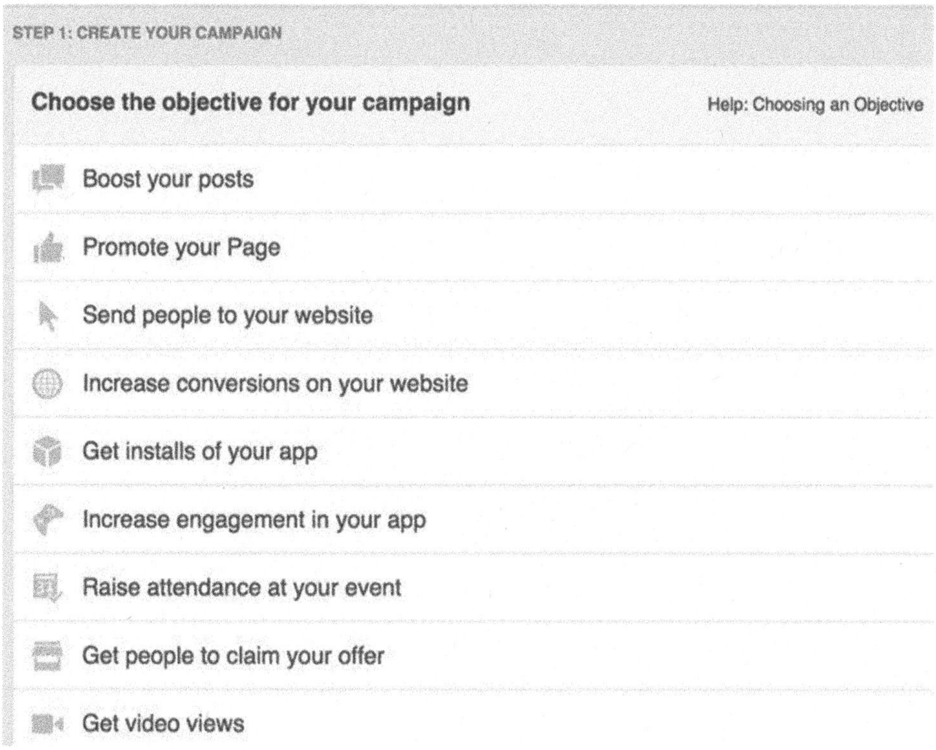

STEP 1: CREATE YOUR CAMPAIGN

Choose the objective for your campaign   Help: Choosing an Objective

- Boost your posts
- Promote your Page
- Send people to your website
- Increase conversions on your website
- Get installs of your app
- Increase engagement in your app
- Raise attendance at your event
- Get people to claim your offer
- Get video views

Figure 7.18   Choosing an Objective for a Facebook Ad
Source: Screenshot reproduced with permission of Facebook.

Make sure that the pin is smack bang in the middle of the speedometer, as in Figure 7.19—if it is too far to the right, your reach will be too broad; too far to the left and your reach will be too specific. The aim is to have an evenly defined audience. You will have to test different things to center the pin, such as changing the level of education or adding more interests to make sure that pin is hitting the 12 o'clock mark.

Advanced Training

Facebook's custom targeting function allows you to reach a highly specific audience. The catch is, you must have an email database. By uploading email addresses from your database, Facebook will be able to run an ad campaign that will appear right in front of those people. Not only that, Facebook gives you the option of displaying your ad to those who match the likes and interests of those on your email list, and this can be done whether they "like" your page or not.

Another fantastic feature is the Facebook pixel, which remarkets to people who may have visited your website because of a Facebook ad but who did not fulfill your call to action (CTA). Installing the pixel will assist in bringing visitors back to your website and in finding new customers who fit your target audience specifications. Always perform

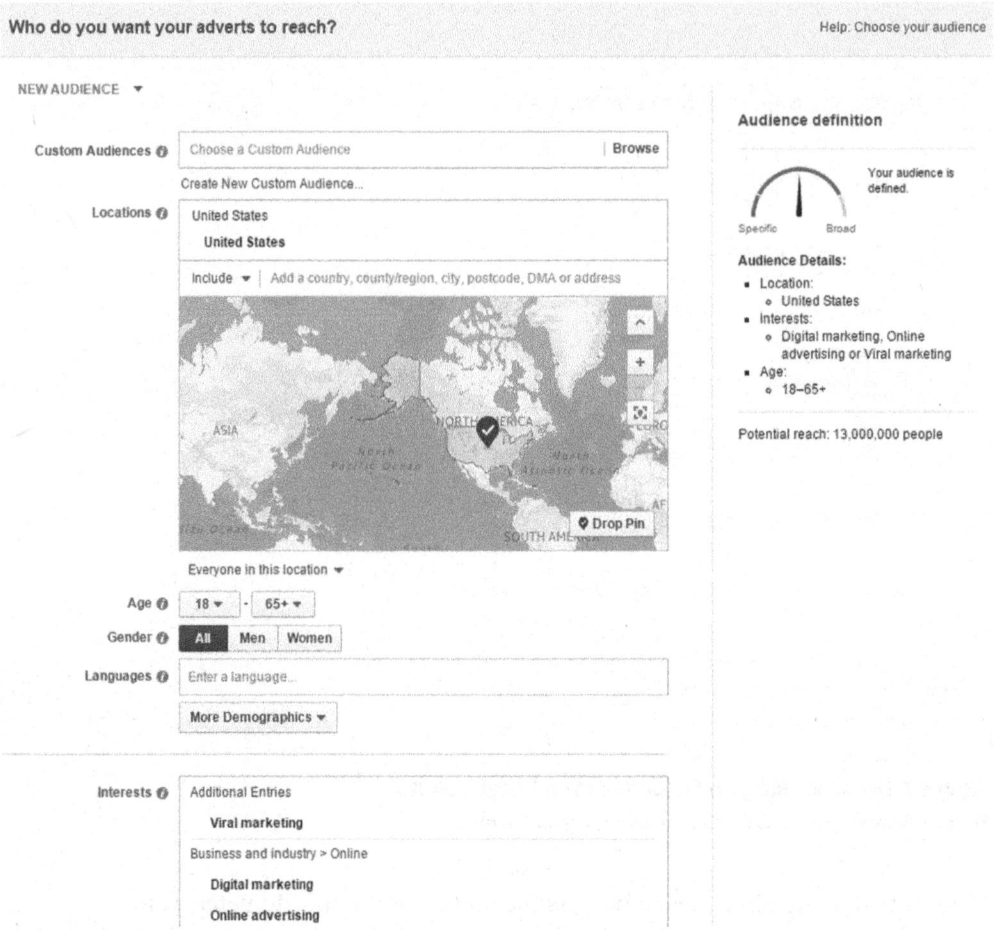

Figure 7.19   Facebook Speedometer Ad Targeting Gauge
Source: Screenshot reproduced with permission of Facebook.

split testing with your ads to work out which one is getting a better response. Run at least two ads at the same time and use a combination of multiple images and various CTA buttons to do comparisons so you can see what is and is not working.

Writing the Ad

Once you have locked down the type of ad you wish to create and the audience you wish to target, it's time to write your ad. Writing your ad follows the same rules as any type of advertising—an eye-catching headline and compelling text—but there are limits. The headline can be up to 25 characters and the text up to 90 characters. If you are stuck for ideas, "like" the pages of your competitors. By doing so, their ads will appear in your right column and on your cell phone. Pay attention to threads that are being run often because they are most likely to be performing well, meaning the copy is well written and engaging.

Budget Setting

To define your ad, decide on the daily budget and the maximum budget per interaction, page "like," and link click. From this, set a schedule to determine how long the campaign is going to last. Before running a campaign over a long period of time, test it by running it for a week to see what works. Edit, modify, and improve it until you are sure it is primed and ready to go.

Reports and Insights

The Reports and Insights function not only details your results, but also tracks how well your ad performed. You can set a schedule in Facebook to receive reports with your ad results via email at a specific time so that you never forget to monitor ad performance.

Places

If your business is a physical location, register it on Facebook Places so that your customers can check in. Each check-in is marked as a visit on your Facebook page, and users can tag photos, status updates, videos, and so on from your location.

Facebook Groups

Aside from advertising, Facebook Groups is the only other element of Facebook where you can generate an income from your client base, as ads are not yet limited. Better still, it's free!

Groups can be closed (users must submit a request to join), secret (users can only be invited to join), or public (open to everyone who wishes to join). Facebook groups are useful for a number of reasons: You can develop a network of like-minded users, collaborate with industry peers, or just be part of a community that is linked to your business and listen to what is going on. Try joining a number of groups to figure out what is driving discussion and then create your own based on your findings.

Apps

The benefit of adding apps to your Facebook page is essentially to make it a mirror for your website. An example of a useful app is an HTML tab. This can be used for a menu if you run a restaurant or a price list for a service such as a hair salon. It is also possible to set tabs for webinars, for selling products, for an opt-in page (where people can sign up for free gifts), or a Contact Us form.

In general, you can do anything that you can do on your webpage on your Facebook page by using third-party apps. To name three examples, you can host a YouTube channel using Probist or Cueler, run contests using Woobox, or host a webpage within your page using Thunderpenny.

A business that does not possess a Facebook page is at a huge disadvantage. A business that does not use the advertising mechanics of its Facebook page should not be in business! Social media advertising may be a relatively new format, but it is extremely important. Facebook is the top dog at the moment, but that does not mean that it should be the only one. As long as there are social media platforms, there are opportunities to promote your business. Let's move on to the next section and see what LinkedIn can do for you.

LinkedIn Advertising

If Facebook is Social Media High School's queen bee, LinkedIn is that whiz kid who made a million dollars before she even graduated.

LinkedIn is different from other social media platforms because the audience it attracts is already a specific target: the workforce.

The average user on LinkedIn earns over $100,000, making it the most important social media platform for the corporate world. Why *wouldn't* you advertise on this platform?

In this section we will navigate through the ways you can use LinkedIn to promote your business, and by the end of it you will:

- Be adept at joining and creating groups.
- Know the best practices to ensure strong engagement within groups.
- Understand the best ways to search for a job on LinkedIn and to find your next hire.
- Master the mechanics of creating the various types of advertisements on LinkedIn.

If you have a business that thrives on industry discussion, you cannot neglect LinkedIn. While it may not be as fun as Facebook or Twitter, it is extremely useful for making vital connections with other leaders in your industry. Having a presence on LinkedIn not only proves you are serious in and about your industry, but also could attract the next bright spark to join your team.

LinkedIn Groups

LinkedIn groups are very similar to Facebook groups: You can join those that already exist or you can create your own. There are two types of LinkedIn groups: *private* (you submit a request to join or are invited to join) and *public* (anyone can join). The discussions that take place in LinkedIn groups are led by those in the industry, and the best discussions are those that really engage the group. Some groups allow you to post promotions or to run advertisements for jobs when you are hiring. And when you master the art of engaging discussion, you can post these promotions seamlessly in your group.

Leader of the Pack

By participating in group discussions regularly and delivering quality input, you grow your position as a top contributor. This high level of engagement in discussions is the best—and fastest—way to grow your number of connections on LinkedIn.

So how can you connect with group colleagues who have similar interests? LinkedIn Connect. To connect with like-minded LinkedIn users, simply type in the keywords for the type of group you are interested in, and when the list appears it will show which groups you belong to and which of your contacts also belong. Then just join a discussion, become known in the group, and work your digital marketing magic.

Creating a group is also simple. Just navigate to the Create a Group button, as shown at the bottom of Figure 7.20. When you click on it, name the group, decide on the group type (public or private), give a summary of what the group is about, and insert a link to your website.

Group Access

Depending on whether you want an exclusive, invitation-only group or one that will accept anyone who is interested, set the group to either public or private. You can also

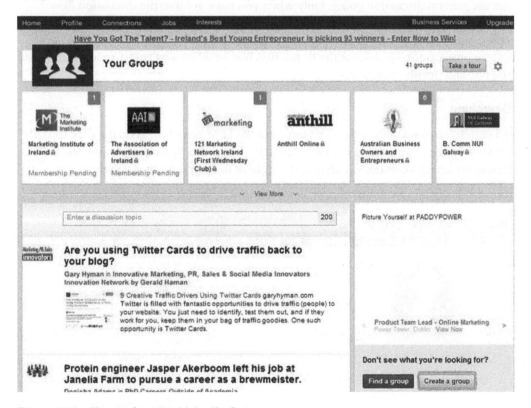

Figure 7.20　How to Create a LinkedIn Group
Source: LinkedIn.

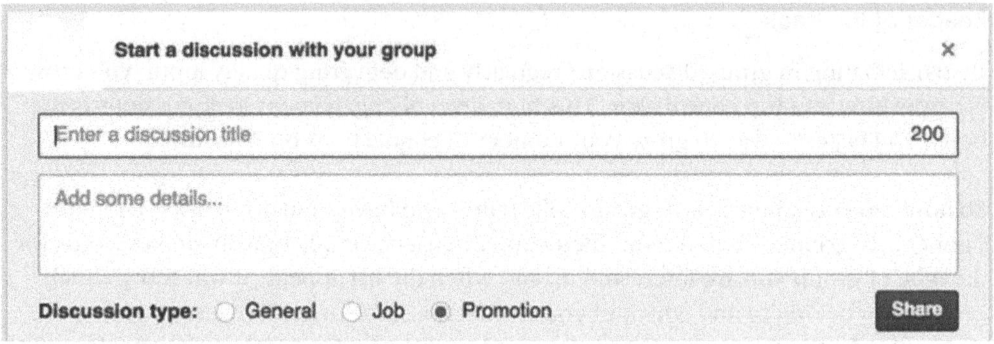

Start a discussion with your group ✕

Enter a discussion title 200

Add some details...

Discussion type: ◯ General ◯ Job ⦿ Promotion **Share**

Figure 7.21 Start a LinkedIn Discussion and Choose Discussion Type
Source: LinkedIn.

set membership policies and you can preapprove members by email address or email domain.

Promote

When you are starting out in a LinkedIn group, get involved, learn the ins and outs, and get the general discussion going. Only when you have got into the discussion flow should you promote your post. Again, it's very easy to do. At the bottom of the Start a Discussion box shown in Figure 7.21, you can choose the type of discussion (general, job, or promotion)—just select the Promotion button when you wish to promote! Create the title and details around that.

Searching

To search for companies, jobs, or groups, use the large search field on the very top of a LinkedIn page, illustrated in Figure 7.22. To look specifically for people, use the advanced search function, which is to the right of the magnifying glass icon.

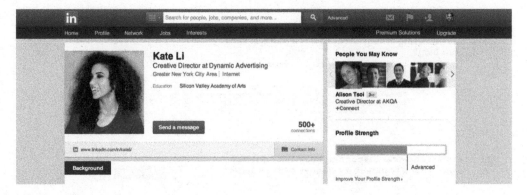

Figure 7.22 LinkedIn Search Field and Advanced Search Function
Source: LinkedIn.

Best-Practice Tips for Searching for People on LinkedIn

The beauty of LinkedIn is that you can really hit the bull's-eye when searching for people. The way to do this is to use quotation marks to get specific results about a specific type of person. For example, if you are looking for a social media manager, search for *"social media manager."* Type *or* between terms if you are looking for multiple synonyms for skills or job titles.

Take a look at Figure 7.23 to see exactly how it works. As you can see in the Title text box, the title social media manager is enclosed in quotation marks with the word *OR* written after it (after that is something like *"community manager"* or *"digital marketing manager,"* also enclosed in quotation marks).

You can also exclude classes of people from a job search. If you don't want trainees, for example, just type the word *"not."* That way you can filter results and come up with only the kind of people that you are looking for.

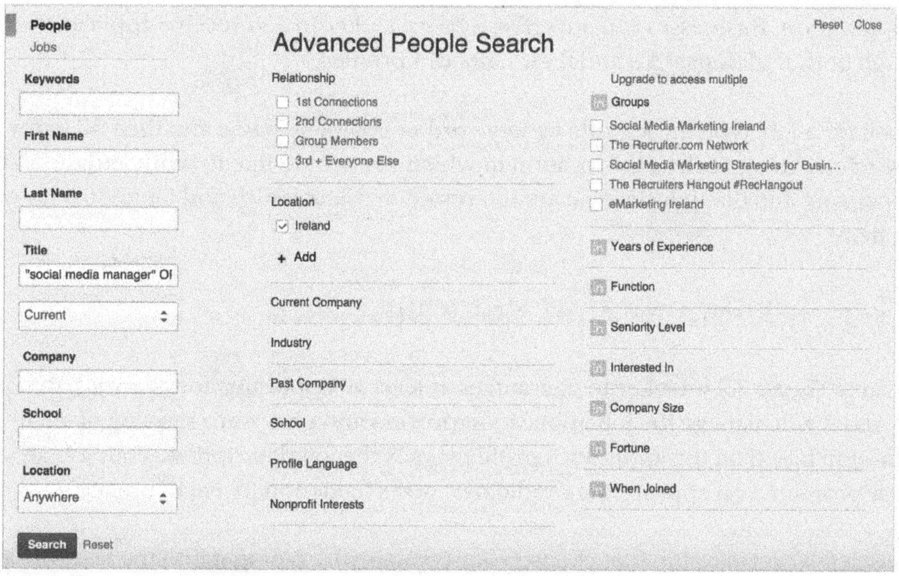

Figure 7.23   Strategies for LinkedIn Advanced Search
Source: LinkedIn.

LinkedIn Premium

A LinkedIn premium account has extra features for business professionals. For one, you have access to more profiles when you search (you can only see up to 100 profiles on a free account). In addition, you can see who has viewed your profile insights over the past 90 days, save important profiles, and add notes to profiles using the profile organizer.

There are even higher levels above LinkedIn Premium: With the LinkedIn Recruiter and LinkedIn Sales Navigator options, you can see the full profiles of anybody on the LinkedIn network, regardless of whether they're a connection.

Using LinkedIn to Search for a Job

One of the main purposes of LinkedIn is to search for and apply for jobs. Based on a user's profile, LinkedIn will suggest the most appropriate jobs to each member and will alert members about new, relevant jobs by email. If you have a LinkedIn premium account, your application can be flagged as a featured applicant, so that you will stand out. Premium members can also get insights about job roles before they even submit a job application. Businesses can advertise jobs on LinkedIn and receive applications through both traditional CVs and their LinkedIn profiles.

To look for a job, type the job title by keyword or company name and then fill in the rest of the information, such as the location in which you would like to work and the size of the company and the industry you are interested in. Click Finish and LinkedIn can work from there.

Using LinkedIn to Find Your Next Hire

As seen in Figure 7.24, LinkedIn guarantees at least 10 applicants for every job that you post, and it will manage the job application process and give you a ranking of each application based on the applicant's profile versus the job description. Your job ad will also be promoted on appropriate candidates' news feeds and by email update.

To post a job on LinkedIn, first choose your company by typing it into the text box and selecting it from the list. Next, choose a job title so that LinkedIn can better match your job with potential applicants. Write your job description and details and choose whether you prefer to receive applications directly via email or at your company's career site.

LinkedIn Advertising

LinkedIn ads enable you to target LinkedIn members based on a number of demographic criteria: location, age, gender, company, education, industry, job title, and even a specific job function.

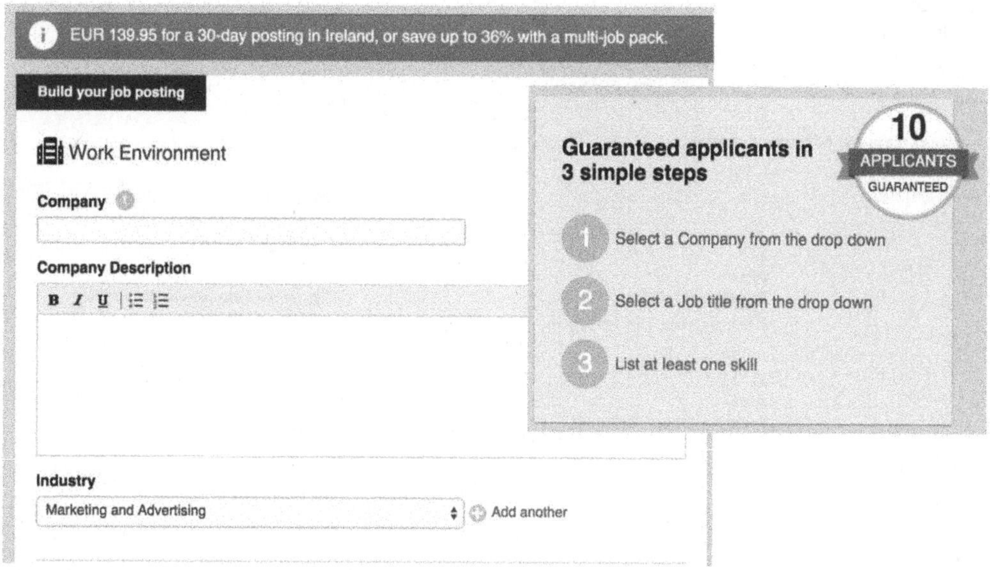

Figure 7.24   Posting a Job on LinkedIn
Source: LinkedIn.

When deciding on the cost of the ad, you are given two options to bid for your ads: cost per click (CPC) or cost per thousand impressions (CPM). Before you gain experience, be careful when choosing which option you want. Many people think that choosing to pay for CPM is the better option because it looks cheaper; however, bear in mind that an impression is defined as every time the ad is *shown*. So, even if you choose to pay $2 per 1000 impressions, the same person might see the ad multiple times—in which case many of these impressions will not result in any action being taken. Until you get really good at your ads use CPC, because at least then you know that you are getting clicks. CPM becomes much more valuable when you know how to write an ad that gets people to click. When deciding on a suggested bid range, go to the higher end of the scale. Why? Because LinkedIn then knows you are serious. The Suggest Bid Range field helps you to choose a number based on competing bids from other advertisers. By bidding a higher number, not only will you outbid everybody else, you will get preferential treatment from LinkedIn—and you still won't actually pay the highest price.

Sponsored Content

LinkedIn supports multiple advertising formats, including sponsored updates on your company's LinkedIn page, which is similar to Facebook boosted posts, so rather than creating an ad, you may sponsor content instead. Simply choose which piece of content you wish to promote and the audience you would like to target, as shown in Figure 7.25. Decide on how much you would like to pay per campaign, check out, pay up, and your ad is ready to go!

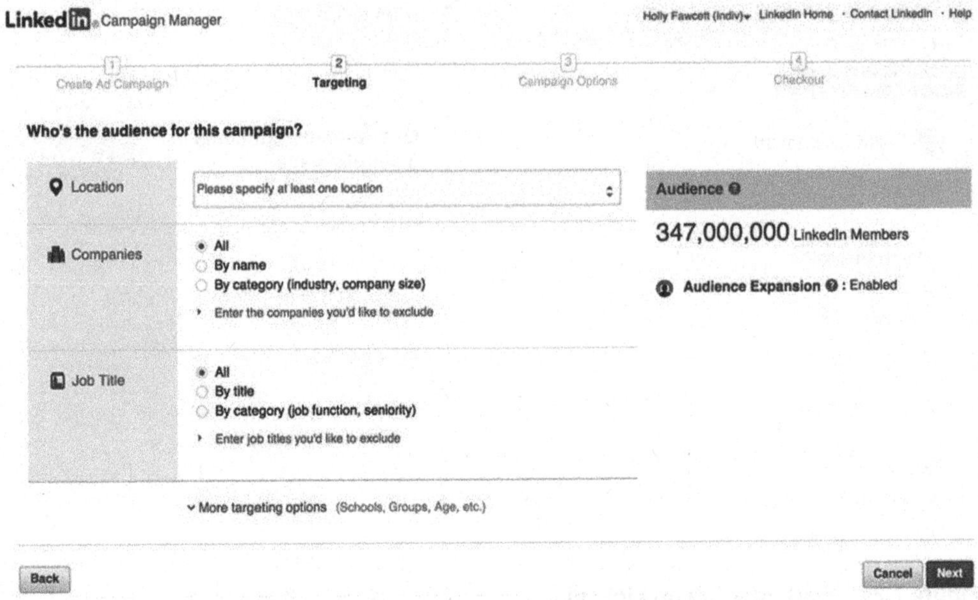

Figure 7.25   Sponsoring Content on LinkedIn
Source: LinkedIn.

Best Practices for a Strong Ad

Your ad will have a lot of competition—so how do you make it stand out from the crowd? Ensure that your headlines, copy, and images are as clear and attractive as they can be. Look to your main competition for ideas: Draw inspiration from the pictures they use, and the titles and text that they write.

Headline. Choose a strong, catchy title.
Copy. Split test your ad to target different demographics and determine which ad works best. Always include a CTA and let people know *exactly* what they need to do. By telling your audience to do something specific, you immediately get a higher turnaround rate of people taking that action.
Image. Choose an image that means something to your audience: a person, or an example of your product, for instance. You only have 50 pixels squared, so try to make it stand out.

Sponsored InMail Campaigns

LinkedIn gives you the opportunity to send direct emails, or InMails, to whomever you want—even if they are not your connections. This can be very powerful, especially if you want to target a particular audience in a localized market. Within the InMail, there will be a clickable icon that gives the email recipient the opportunity to follow through on a CTA, which always improves conversion rates. You should note that sponsored InMail campaigns are not available through the normal self-service advertising platform, to avail yourself of the service you need to contact LinkedIn's marketing solutions area.

LinkedIn KPIs

Choose specific indicators for each of your marketing communication goals: For advertising indicators, use the number of impressions, number of clicks, CPC, click-through rate (CTR), and number of leads or contacts gained. Keep a close eye on your CPM and CPC. Your personal LinkedIn account provides information on profile engagement and connections. Growth of the company page and the number of followers is something you can also monitor, along with the company page engagement with posts.

Advertising Indicators	Account Indicators
Impressions	Your Personal LinkedIn Account
Clicks	Company Page Growth in Followers
Cost-Per-Click (CPC)	Company Page Engagement with Posts
Click-Through-Rate (CTR)	Leads (contacts)

While Facebook may be the top dog when it comes to SMM, LinkedIn is the smart dog. There are no disadvantages to advertising on this platform; when done right it can make your business stand out amongst your peers and potential hires, which can only be a good thing.

Twitter

If Twitter were in high school it would not be part of any clique. With its strict character limitations, Twitter is the smart wisecracker who can deliver a witty one-liner. It is not as popular as Facebook, but still, almost everyone wants to hang out with it. Just because businesses aren't riding on its coattails as with LinkedIn, Twitter is definitely something that is worth your while to spend time, resources, and money on.

This section will tunnel through how advertising on Twitter is of benefit to your business, and when we reach the light at the end, you will:

- Be an expert at creating all three different types of Twitter ads.
- Know how to analyze the activity dashboard and measure what works best for you.
- Be able to choose the best type of tweet to promote.

Twitter Advertising

There are three main promotions you can do on Twitter: Promote a trend relating to your business or event, promote your account to get more followers, and promote a tweet to get engagements or a specific CTA.

Figure 7.26   LinkedIn Promoted Trend
Source: Twitter.

Take a look at Figure 7.26: It shows a promoted trend with the hashtag #ILoveCoffee. It is obvious that it is promoted due to the yellow arrow icon. Figure 7.27 suggests a certain Twitter account to follow. Figure 7.28 is an example of a promoted tweet, which advertises a language school. It is quite easy to promote a trend or account, but promoted tweets and Twitter cards take a little more effort. So let's take a closer look.

The promoted tweet in Figure 7.28 has a large image and a clearly defined link to the website, but no CTA; the tweet itself would have appeared on the tweet stream of members of the target audience. For this type of Twitter ad, the advertiser is charged by Twitter on a cost-per-engagement basis, so if Twitter users interact with this sponsored tweet—by favoriting, replying, or retweeting, the promoter pays.

Creating the Ad

The first thing you are asked to do when creating an ad is to decide on a name for your campaign. Next, choose to either compose a tweet, as shown in Figure 7.29, or select a

Figure 7.27   Users Twitter Recommends that You Follow
Source: Twitter.

Figure 7.28   Promoted Tweet for a Language School
Source: Twitter.

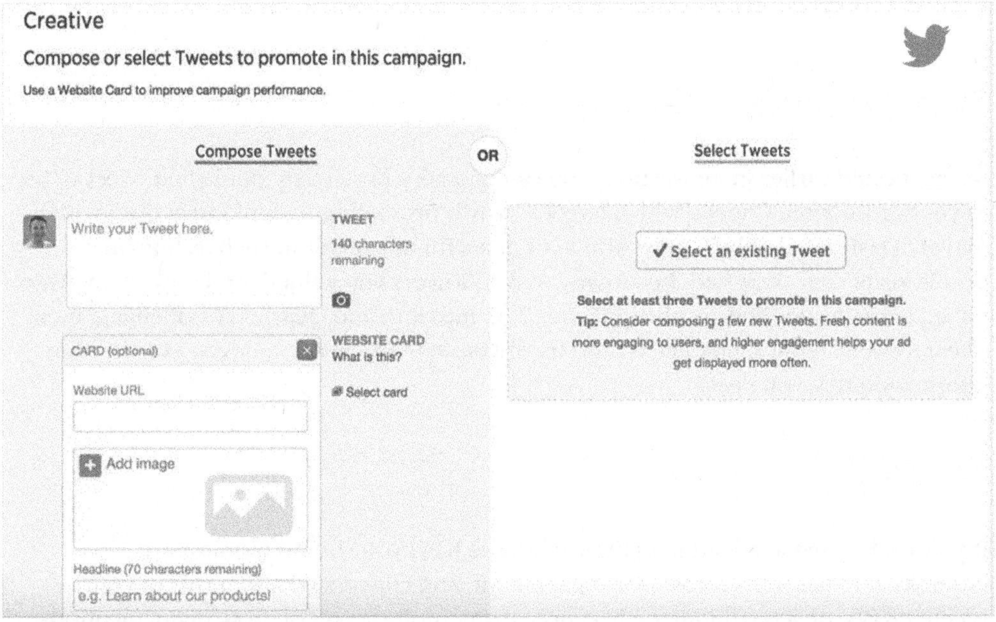

Figure 7.29   Creating a Twitter Ad
Source: Twitter.

tweet that you have already written (usually one that has received the most organic engagements).

Next, select the location and after that select additional targeting criteria: keywords, followers, interests, tailored audiences, and TV targeting. Given the in-the-moment nature of Twitter, TV targeting is very interesting. It allows you to specifically target a TV program on a particular night, on a particular channel, and to run your ad only during that time. Anybody who is discussing or engaging with that TV program will therefore see that tweet in their streams.

Creating a Twitter Card

The most popular form of promoted tweet is the Twitter card, which features a CTA to encourage app installs, websites visits, lead generation, and so forth. This is the best way to collect email addresses, grow followers, or increase engagement with a particular tweet.

Creating a Twitter card is a really straightforward process, as illustrated by Figure 7.30. Insert your website URL, add an image (800 × 320 pixels), type in your headline, and choose from the variety of CTAs, such as read more, shop now, view now, visit now, book now, learn more, play now, bet now, donate, apply, quote, or book.

Get ideas for how to do Twitter cards well by observing Twitter cards that appear in your own stream. They are such a snappy way of getting attention, and as they are not yet being overused, they are seriously effective ways to advertise your brand.

Tweet Activity Dashboard

As mentioned earlier in the section, you can choose a previously published tweet to use as your promotion. Choose which tweet is worth promoting by looking at the Twitter Activity Dashboard, which gives you a lot of useful information, such as how many profile visits your page had, how many new followers you gained, and how many tweets linked back to you. The graphs in Figure 7.31 measure and clearly lay out engagement rate, retweets, replies, link clicks, and favorites, so that you can analyze exactly what information that you need.

Twitter KPIs

If you are looking at advertising indicators, the KPIs you should monitor are impressions, clicks, CPC, cost per engagement, and conversions. In terms of your account KPIs, observe things such as how many replies you got, how many mentions,

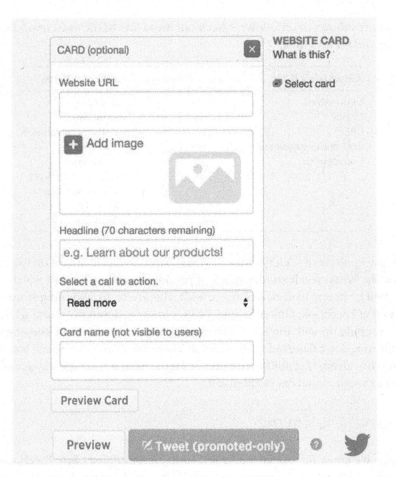

Figure 7.30   Creating a Twitter Ad
Source: Twitter.

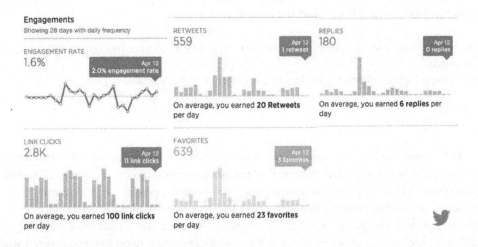

Figure 7.31   Twitter Activity Dashboard
Source: Twitter.

and how many follows or unfollows. Check out these lists of the most important KPIs for advertising and for accounts:

Advertising KPIs	Account KPIs
Impressions	Replies
Clicks	Mentions
CPC	Follows/unfollows
Cost per engagement	Tweets
Conversions	Retweets
	Clicks on a Tweet
	Direct message
	Favorites
	Trending

Twitter is the epitome of society today. It is fast paced, it has its finger on the pulse, and it bores easily. When you learn the knack of producing snappy Twitter ads that your audience will be happy to click or engage with, you are on to a winning strategy. We have looked at Facebook, LinkedIn, and Twitter in some depth now, and while it may seem like keeping up with the Kardashians is more manageable than keeping up with these platforms, don't flake out on us just yet! There are even more social media platforms with advertising abilities that could be of major advantage to you. Let's carry on to the next section and check them out.

Additional Platforms

At this stage we know that social media is a veritable *Breakfast Club*. Facebook is the most popular, LinkedIn is the smart one, and Twitter is the class clown. It doesn't stop there, however; there are many more platforms out there, all with distinct identities that you may use to your digital marketing advantage. Let's wander down the path of social media discovery and at the end of it, you will:

- Be familiar with the advertising mechanisms offered by YouTube, Instagram, Pinterest, and Snapchat.
- Understand which platforms best suit your industry and audience.

YouTube

YouTube needs no introduction—along with Facebook it is one Internet success story that everyone has heard of. If Facebook is the homecoming queen, YouTube is its date at the prom! As the way we consume information evolves, people are becoming accustomed to using video rather than text—so if you are not already on the video bandwagon, you should be. YouTube is owned by Google and it uses the Google AdWords platform, so in order to use it successfully, you will need to be registered with Google and comfortable with Google AdWords.

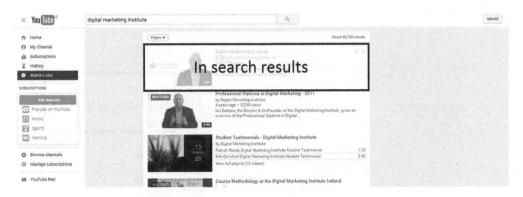

Figure 7.32   In Search YouTube Ad
Source: YouTube.

There are three main types of ads available: those that appear in search results, those that appear before videos, and those that appear alongside videos. Take a look at these images to get an idea of where the ads would be placed.

Option 1: In Search Results

Note the highlighted videos in Figure 7.32. These are ads that appear first because an advertiser has paid for them to appear before organic search results.

Option 2: Before Videos (Rolling Ad)

This type of ad is shown in Figure 7.33 and plays before a chosen video, particularly if that video has a high number of views. There will normally be a countdown of five seconds before the viewer can stop the rolling ad.

Figure 7.33   Before Video YouTube Ad
Source: YouTube.

Figure 7.34   Beside Video YouTube Ad
Source: YouTube.

Option 3: Beside Videos

As shown in Figure 7.34, rather than having your ad play before a video, you can place it on the right-hand side of the video.

Each ad has its own benefits but the only way to figure out which method works best for you and what will bring the best ROI is to test and test again!

Pinterest

Pinterest is an image-driven social networking site with over 72 million active users—and growing. In fact, it is the fastest-growing social network platform. It has a female-dominated user base, so although the male user base is growing, it is definitely worth considering if your audience is primarily female. Interestingly, 80 percent of Pinterest usage takes place via cell phone. It is also a popular platform amongst people in their 40s and over, because unlike Facebook it is more about sharing ideas than revealing personal information. In this way it is very good for driving targeted traffic. If that isn't enough, this reason might convince you to adopt Pinterest into your social media campaign—out of all the other social media sites that are being used, Pinterest has the highest ratio of buyers.

Let's think of Pinterest as the homecoming queen's best friend—the nice, organized one who decorated the gym for the prom. Pinterest is a hobby and ideas platform, which can certainly be used to business advantage. In fact, there is a conversion function on Pinterest to turn a regular Pinterest account into a business account. (If you don't already have an account, you can go straight to setting up a business account.)

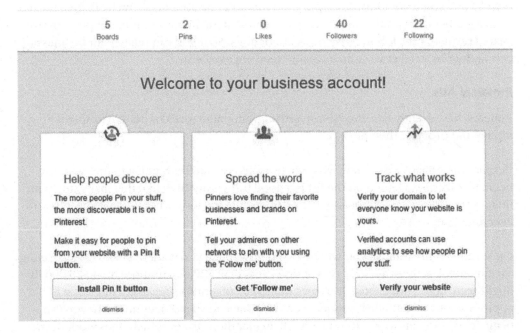

Figure 7.35   Pinterest Business Account Set-Up
Source: Screenshot reproduced with permission of Pinterest.

Pinterest Analytics

A Pinterest business account's analytics page displays the average daily impressions, average viewers, and average monthly views. It also gives a breakdown of each pin you put up: How many impressions it got, the number of re-pins, the number of people who clicked, and how many people liked it.

Signing Up for a Pinterest Business Account

This process, which is shown in Figure 7.35, starts on the left-hand side of the page, in the Help People Discover box, with the Install Pin It button (when an image has a Pin It option, anyone can pin that image to a board on their Pinterest accounts). Next, it asks you to Spread the Word by installing the Follow Me button. Then you need to verify your website to Track What Works so you can start to track how many clicks you are getting directly from Pinterest users. To do this, you will receive a piece of code to insert into your website.

So you have got the pins but where to pin them? On a board of course! One of the nice things about Pinterest is that it harks back to the good old days of pinning a postcard or shopping list to a corkboard in your kitchen. With Pinterest, however, you don't have to place your bathroom conversion ideas with your inspirations for wedding dresses —you can create a variety of different boards based around different topics. As far as your business account in concerned, keep it simple to begin with—but set up at least three boards, one about your business, one about humor, one about your niche in general and what's going on in your business. Keep in mind that the highest number of posts that are shared relate to cats, followed by posts about dogs. So if you can relate your business to cats or dogs in a clever way, do it! Guaranteed engagement.

Pinterest Ads

Pinterest has recently launched its advertising campaign to allow people to spend money and promote their pins.

Because the initiative is so new, you will be asked to join the wait list before you can begin to advertise. Getting on the list is a good thing: Anything like this that's still in its infancy provides a great opportunity to strike while the iron is hot and get ahead before everyone else.

Once you join the wait list you will be asked how much you want to spend on marketing each month, but there are only two options: less than $20,000 or more than $20,000. It might seem crazy, but choose the more than $20,000 option, because Pinterest will approve your account much sooner. You don't have to spend that much but you can begin to experiment with different advertising methods to see which ones work best. Don't forget the cats.

Instagram

Instagram is owned by Facebook—it's Facebook's little hipster sister! It really is geared to young, trendy people for whom their cell phones are extra limbs, so it's no surprise that it is primarily cell phone–based—the screen in Figure 7.36 is being viewed from a cell phone. Among the 300 million active monthly users, the average user uses Instagram to showcase his beautiful life; businesses are now using Instagram to display products for these users online or in-store purchases.

Engagement is sought with multiple hashtags that are relevant to your brand and those that are being searched for a lot, so it is a very good way to raise brand awareness and to build customer loyalty.

Instagram's ad format is relatively new and you will need to use the Power Editor tool to create any sort of ad. Ads follow the same structure as Facebook or Twitter sponsored posts, in that they appear on users' Instagram feed and are marked with the sponsored tag. Carousel ads are also an option—they follow the same structure as a regular sponsored post but multiple images will roll by.

Snapchat

Snapchat is aimed at a young audience, from 13- to 18-year-olds, and there are over 100 million monthly active users, which is a huge number considered how targeted the

Figure 7.36   Instagram Post Viewed from a Cell Phone
Source: Instagram.

demographic is. If you are targeting people in this age cohort you should strongly consider this platform. No matter what your company or business does, every teenager grows up. By targeting members of the Snapchat generation early, they may become longer-term customers.

The unique aspect of Snapchat is that you can share a photo with somebody else and it disappears within 10 seconds or so. Now if this sounds as though advertising opportunities are extremely limited, the newly introduced My Story page has increased Snapchat's use and has made it far more accessible for brands. The My Story feature allows users to create a narrative 24 hours long by stitching together a vast range of disappearing photos and videos. It's a lot of work, but the Snapchat audience fully embraces it.

Advertising with Snapchat is currently only available for large-budget, single-day takeover ads, but it is worth taking a look at the Taco Bell account to get an idea of what can be done with Snapchat advertising. With over 200,000 friends on Snapchat and as pioneers in using "My Story" to advertise, the fast-food company know what it's doing and it does it very well.

Compared with the main cast members—Facebook, Twitter, and LinkedIn—social media platforms YouTube, Pinterest, Instagram and Snapchat are still supporting characters. But supporting characters often drive a story line. In the same way, deciding which platforms to utilize depends on your overall strategy and choosing a channel that is relevant to your audience.

Stage 4: Analyze

A vital aspect of running a social media campaign is to measure how it's progressing. In the same way that a sports team would never get to the top of its league without training and evaluating its game plan, a social media campaign is useless without constant analysis. You have got to flex those digital marketing muscles and to track information that will tell you what is working, what needs to be tweaked, and what should be stopped.

Analysis is stage 4 of the process, as illustrated in Figure 7.37. When you cross the finish line of this section you will:

- Know how to use the analytics features of major social media platforms to your advantage.
- Understand the importance of Google Analytics when tracking a conversion path.

What Gets Measured, Gets Done

Each social media campaign should follow these guidelines:

Set measurable goals. Choose goals that are smart, specific, measurable, and attainable.
Track your goals. Iterate them, enhance them, and improve them over time.
Use analytics tools for each platform to inform your optimization and enhancement. Have your structure in place, even before you get started, so you know how you are going to measure your outcomes from the get-go.

Figure 7.37   Focus on the Fourth Stage in the SMM Process

Let's take a look at the different measurement tools available through different social media platforms.

Facebook Insights

Facebook does not want you to sit back and enjoy the returns of Facebook advertising; like any good mentor, it wants to keep its apprentices on their toes. That is why Facebook Insights continues to expand and get more elaborate every few months. Yes, it takes work, but it's worth it in the long run because of the incredible amount of useful information you can take from it. When you click into the Insights section from your Facebook page you can see seven tabs, each of which offers different pieces of information. The tabs are called Overview, Likes, Reach, Page Views, Posts, Videos, and People.

1 Overview, which is shown in Figure 7.38, reveals how many "likes" you got in the last week, how widely your post has been distributed, and what the level of engagement has been with your page.
2 Likes shows you the total page likes, how many likes your page gained and lost each day (as shown in Figure 7.39), and also shows you where your likes are coming from (as shown in Figure 7.40).

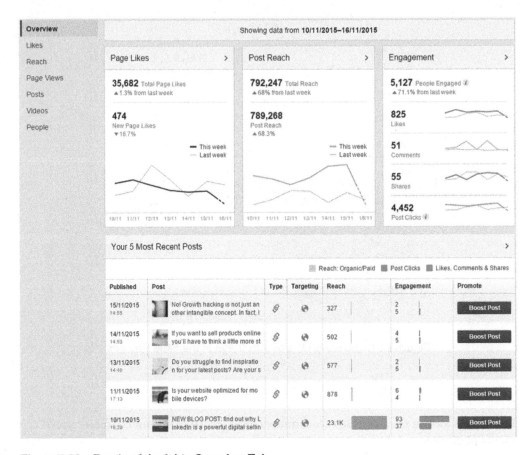

Figure 7.38   Facebook Insights Overview Tab
Source: Screenshot reproduced with permission of Facebook.

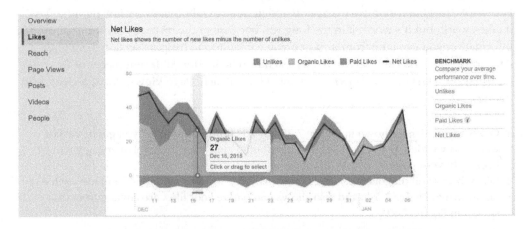

Figure 7.39   Net Likes within Facebook Insights Likes Tab

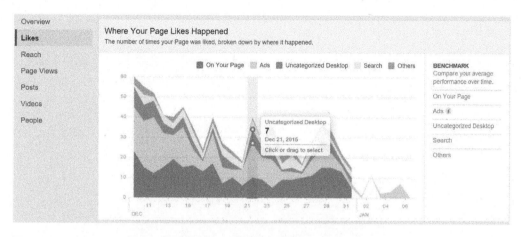

Figure 7.40   Like Attribution within Facebook Insights Likes Tab
Source: Screenshot reproduced with permission of Facebook.

Figure 7.41   Facebook Insights Reach Tab

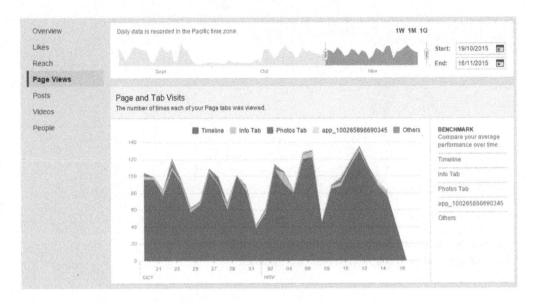

Figure 7.42   Facebook Insights Page Views Tab
Source: Screenshot reproduced with permission of Facebook.

3 Reach, as shown in Figure 7.41, shows you how many people your posts have reached organically and by exactly how much your reach will increase when you spend money. This is essential for really understanding the impact of spending money on specific ads.

4 Page Views, shown in Figure 7.42, tells you how many people have visited your page and where specifically they have visited. Is it your timeline? Your photos tab? The price list? Your info tab?

5 Posts lets you know the engagement you are getting over a number of days. Take a look at the bottom of the example in Figure 7.43. Note the time frame, which runs from midnight to midnight over a 24-hour period. This is how you will know where most of your audience is based. The figure shows much less engagement from 1:00 A.M. until about 7:00 A.M., and engagement drastically increases between 6:00 A.M. and 10:00 P.M. A subtab of the Posts tab called Post Types also gives a breakdown of every single post published on your page, including the average reach of your statuses, of your photos, and of statuses with links, as well as the level of engagement.

6 Videos allows you to see overall views based on a date range you can customize, as shown in Figure 7.44. You can also switch between view breakdowns—organic versus paid, auto-played versus clicked-to-play, and unique versus repeat—by clicking on the drop-down box at the top right-hand side of the page. As shown in Figure 7.45, you can see the number of times your page's videos were viewed for 30 seconds or more. Also, in the Top Videos section of the page you can identify your page's best performing videos based on reach, views, or average completion over a desired date range.

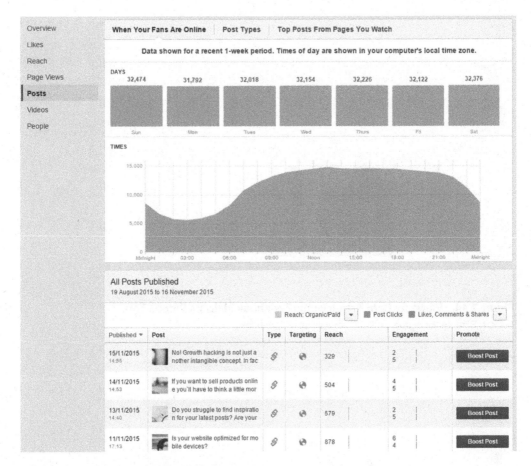

Figure 7.43   Facebook Insights Posts Tab
Source: Screenshot reproduced with permission of Facebook.

7 People delivers a breakdown of the type of people that engaged with your posts.
   In Figure 7.46, you can see that 93 percent of fans are female, 7 percent are male, and
   42 percent of all fans are between the ages of 25 and 34. This kind of information is critical
   for deciding what type of posts to publish and whom to target.

Yes, there is a huge mine of information to be uncovered with your virtual hammer and
chisel, but just as you cannot enter a mine without a hard hat and flashlight, you must
know what you are looking for before you go into Insights. Be prepared with the
specific outcomes that you want from it, such as audience information and ideas on how
to improve your posts and income.

Facebook Insights can measure numerous important factors including how your page is
performing, if it is gaining fans and "likes," if your posts are reaching the right people, if

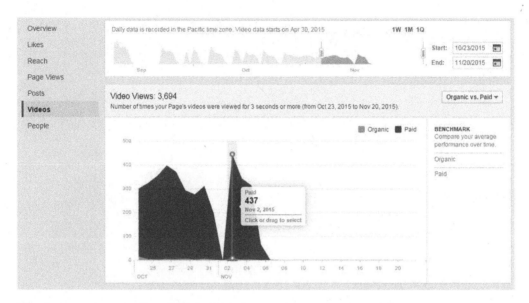

Figure 7.44   Views by Date Range within Facebook Insights Videos Tab
Source: Screenshot reproduced with permission of Facebook.

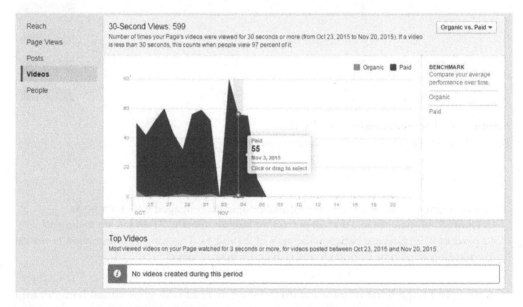

Figure 7.45   30-second View Report within Facebook Insights Video Tab
Source: Screenshot reproduced with permission of Facebook.

they are engaging with your page, and the type of content your audience prefers. If you have a Facebook page you simply must use the Insights tool. Ignore it at your peril! You may end up posting the wrong kind of content at the wrong time to the wrong audience. Could you handle the shame?

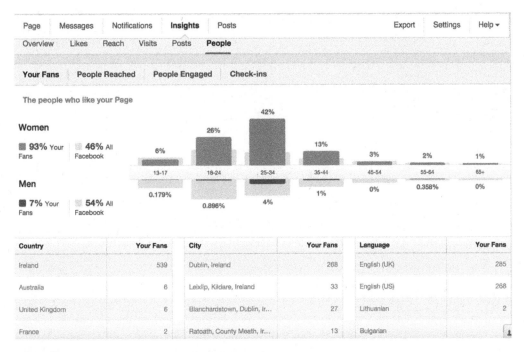

Figure 7.46   Facebook Insights People Tab
Source: Screenshot reproduced with permission of Facebook.

LinkedIn Analytics

While it may not be as comprehensive as Facebook Insights, LinkedIn Analytics offers valuable information on a number of different aspects of your campaign. Take a look at Figure 7.47 for an example of a company's analytics page; it gives a detailed overview of how every post is performing, the number of impressions, clicks, and interactions, as well as the percentage of engagement.

If that level of insight has not satisfied your appetite for data, you can look even deeper into specific posts to see the reach (unique impressions) and engagement (clicks, "likes," comments, shares, followers acquired, and engagement percentage), as shown in Figure 7.48.

As with Facebook, you can also see your audience demographics on LinkedIn, with the added bonus of being able to choose the type of demographic you are measuring. You can do this by clicking the drop-down menu on the right, which is set to Seniority in Figure 7.49. Here you can see what the level of seniority of the jobs held by your audience members is—in this example 34.2 percent are senior level, 24.9 percent entry level, 18.8 percent managers, 6.8 percent directors, and 5.5 percent owners. Other options from this audience demographic drop-down menu include company, industry type, company size, function, and employee type. A wealth of information right at your fingertips—use it!

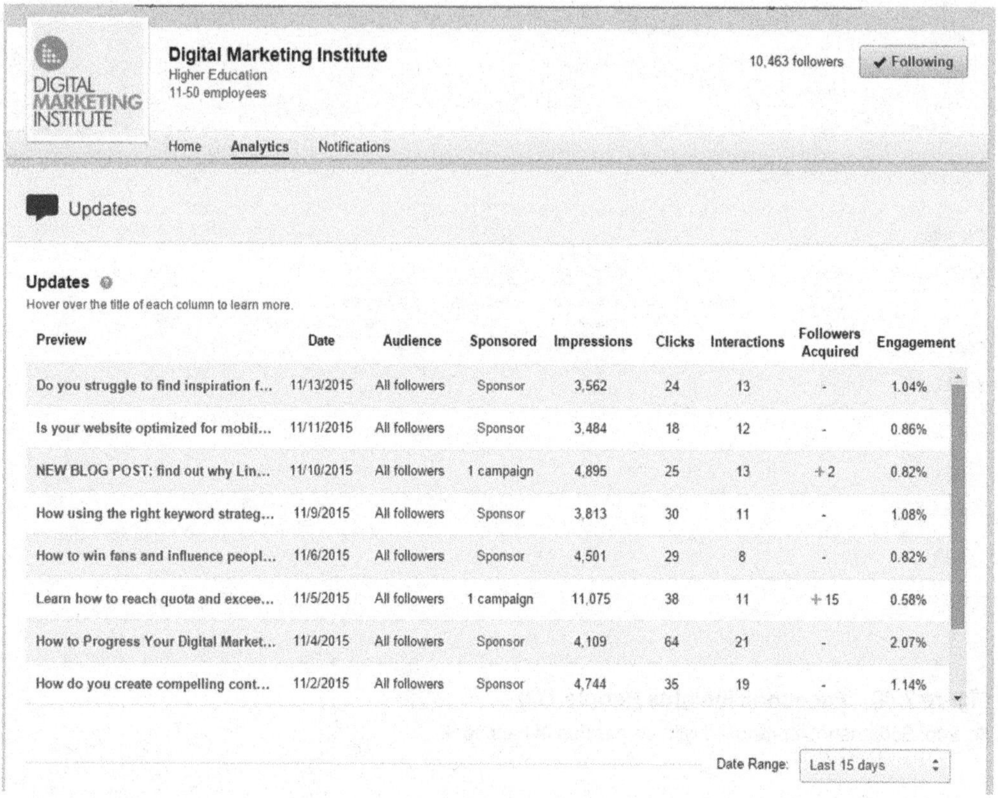

Updates
Hover over the title of each column to learn more.

Preview	Date	Audience	Sponsored	Impressions	Clicks	Interactions	Followers Acquired	Engagement
Do you struggle to find inspiration f...	11/13/2015	All followers	Sponsor	3,562	24	13	-	1.04%
Is your website optimized for mobil...	11/11/2015	All followers	Sponsor	3,484	18	12	-	0.86%
NEW BLOG POST: find out why Lin...	11/10/2015	All followers	1 campaign	4,895	25	13	+2	0.82%
How using the right keyword strateg...	11/9/2015	All followers	Sponsor	3,813	30	11	-	1.08%
How to win fans and influence peopl...	11/6/2015	All followers	Sponsor	4,501	29	8	-	0.82%
Learn how to reach quota and excee...	11/5/2015	All followers	1 campaign	11,075	38	11	+15	0.58%
How to Progress Your Digital Market...	11/4/2015	All followers	Sponsor	4,109	64	21	-	2.07%
How do you create compelling cont...	11/2/2015	All followers	Sponsor	4,744	35	19	-	1.14%

Date Range: Last 15 days

Figure 7.47 LinkedIn Analytics Overview Page
Source: LinkedIn.

You can also track your followers through LinkedIn Analytics. You can find out how many followers your company page has, if there is a trend, if your numbers are growing (as in Figure 7.50), or if they have leveled off. You should look at your followers' demographics to make sure that they are representative of your target audience. If not, your methods will need tweaking to reach the people you want to target.

Not only that, you can measure how well you are performing against your competitors. If you provide details about your primary competitors, LinkedIn will compare your company with them in terms of the number of followers each company has, as shown in Figure 7.51.

The information you can gather from LinkedIn Analytics is crucial to the success of your LinkedIn page. With it, you can monitor, test, tweak, and perfect.

Twitter Analytics

The Activity Dashboard is where all Twitter monitoring happens. As you can see in Figure 7.52, it's where you track the number of tweets, impressions, profile visits,

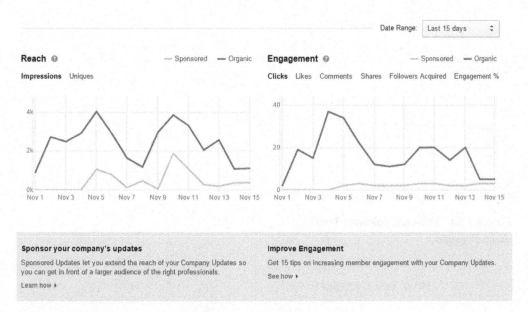

Figure 7.48　Analytics Report for Specific Post within LinkedIn
Source: LinkedIn.

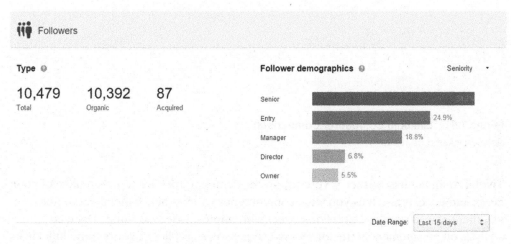

Figure 7.49　LinkedIn Demographic Drop-Down Menu
Source: LinkedIn.

mentions, and followers that link back to your account. You can track impressions daily and see how they move up or down depending on the type of tweet you sent and whether you spent money on it or not. Use this tool to look at whether your number of followers is increasing, decreasing, or staying static, and figure out why.

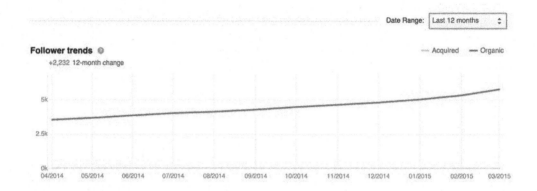

Figure 7.50   LinkedIn Follower Trends
Source: LinkedIn.

How You Compare	Total Followers
CIM	The Chartered Institute of Marketing	22,197
Digital Marketing Institute	**10,479**
The Institute of Direct and Digital Marketing (IDM)	9,402
Digital Marketing	7,568
Digital Marketing	1,603

Figure 7.51   LinkedIn Competitor Comparison
Source: LinkedIn.

Twitter Analytics lets you see if your followers' demographics are representative of your target audience. It also tells you what content types your audience members prefer, whether that is a standard tweet or a tweet with photos, videos, or links. Detailed analysis on engagement in the form of tweets, retweets, replies, favorites, and link clicks are easily obtainable. You can even see both what time of day your followers are most active and the times that deliver the best impressions for your tweets.

Google+ Insights

While Google+ is the serious older brother in the social media family, it is an advantageous channel to utilize if you have a local business or a business that is physical in any form. Your ranking on Google Search and Google Maps depends on it.

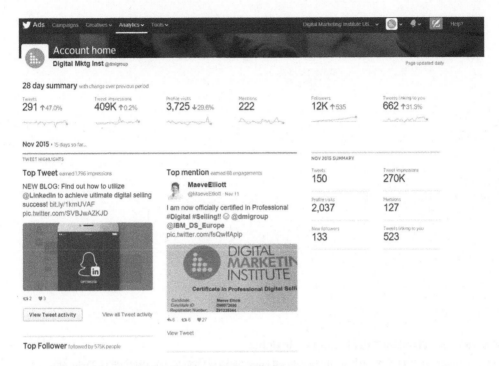

Figure 7.52   Twitter Analytics Tweet Activity Dashboard
Source: Twitter.

The function of Google+ Insights is to keep an eye on:

- *Visibility*. How many views you are getting (shown in Figure 7.53)?
- *Engagement*. How many actions of engagement have taken place over the past 30 days (shown in Figure 7.54)?
- *Audience*. How many new followers have you got and where are they coming from (shown in Figure 7.55)?

In the example shown in Figure 7.55, most followers come from the United States, and 57 percent of those are female and 43 percent male.

The types of metrics available in Google Plus are very similar to the other social media platforms. You can see how your Google+ followers are growing over time, if the demographics of your followers are representative of your target audience, how your posts are performing, and which types of posts your audience prefers. After determining that information, you can then look at how your Google+ audience members behave when they land on your website and what the conversion rate is.

YouTube Analytics

You can gain a plethora of really useful information from YouTube, thanks to its association with Google AdWords. The dashboard gives you tabs for data overview as

Figure 7.53   Visibility Tab of Google+ Insights
Source: Google and the Google logo are registered trademarks of Google Inc.; used with permission.

well as reports on real time, earnings, estimated earnings, ad performance, demographics, playback locations, traffic sources, devices, audience retention, engagement reports, subscribers, likes, dislikes and favorites. The list is exhaustive and can appear overwhelming at first. But once you are familiar with how it works, you can pluck a wealth of information left, right, and center! To navigate YouTube Analytics, work your way down the menu on the left and go through each section one by one.

Just by glancing at the demographics section, as shown in Figure 7.56, you can see your followers' gender, location, age group, and number of views. Unless you know exactly what to look for, you can become lost in YouTube Analytics, so plan ahead before you start trawling through it.

Google Analytics

Social media platform analytics are nothing in comparison to Google Analytics, the queen of all things data. It allows you to measure traffic sources, and from that, figure out the top conversion path. The bottom line is, you have to know where your visitors are coming from to get more leads and generate more income for your business.

Let's take a look at Facebook, LinkedIn, and Twitter on Google Analytics to get a better idea of how you can track a conversion path.

Figure 7.54　Engagement Tab of Google+ Insights
Source: Google and the Google logo are registered trademarks of Google Inc.; used with permission.

Take note of the specific visits from Facebook and the number of people who then converted into a specific action from Figure 7.57. This is hugely beneficial information, as when you know how to use Analytics you can give those people a conversion value. For example, if you give each lead generated a value of $10, and 94 of these gave their email addresses, the total conversion value is $940. If you could take out 173 conversions, based on the value assigned, that gives them a $940 conversion value.

Looking at Figure 7.58 and the same 173 conversions on LinkedIn, you will see that the total conversion was approximately 50 percent on top of that, amounting to $1,535.

While Facebook and LinkedIn were clearly successful, Figure 7.59 shows that Twitter only has 40 conversions with a total conversion value of $50.

Once you check what the total spend was, Google Analytics can tell you what the specific goal flow is. From this, you can see where the source of the traffic is, how many of those people went on to the Contact Us page, and how many of those people went further again and took a specific action.

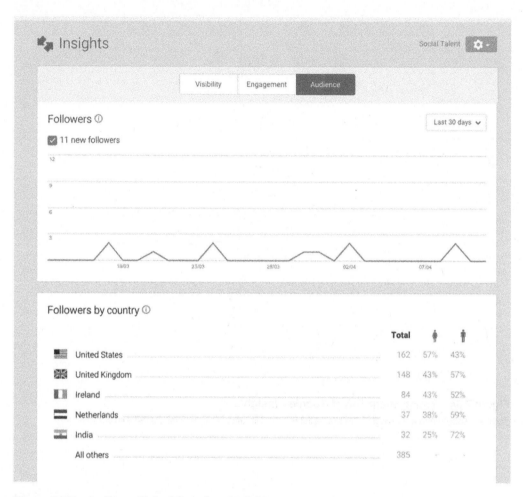

Figure 7.55 Audience Tab of Google + Insights
Source: Google and the Google logo are registered trademarks of Google Inc.; used with permission.

Social Media KPIs

Using the chart in Figure 7.60 is a good way of tracking overall performance and the KPI for each objective. Before you start along your social media adventures, you should know what KPIs to keep track of. Successful SMM is an iterative process that involves tracking and optimizing all aspects of your activities.

Neglecting to monitor your social media journey is like going for a walk while it's snowing and expecting to follow your footsteps back. No good will come of that! So, as you are setting up your overall strategy and planning your advertising campaign, make sure to set up a measurement system. The process of iteration allows you to maximize the effectiveness and ROI of your activities over time, helping you to ultimately achieve your business goals.

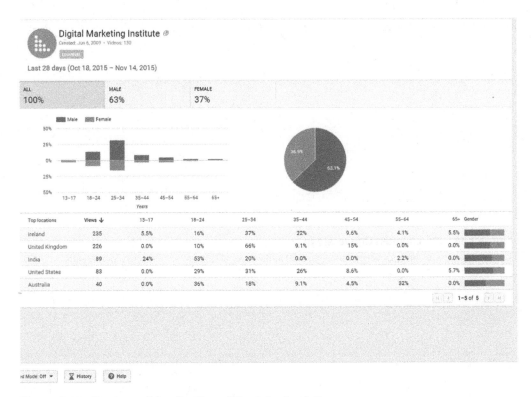

Figure 7.56   Demographics Section of Youtube Analytics
Source: Google and the Google logo are registered trademarks of Google Inc.; used with permission.

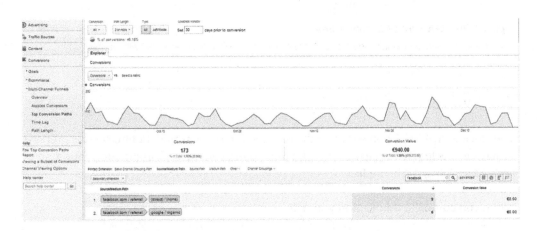

Figure 7.57   GA Facebook Conversions
Source: Google and the Google logo are registered trademarks of Google Inc.; used with permission.

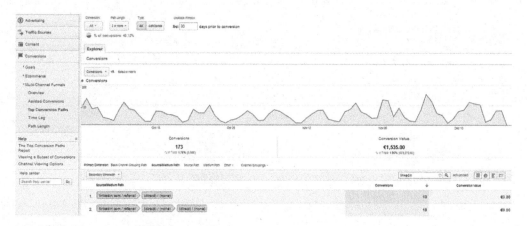

Figure 7.58   GA LinkedIn Conversions

Source: Google and the Google logo are registered trademarks of Google Inc.; used with permission.

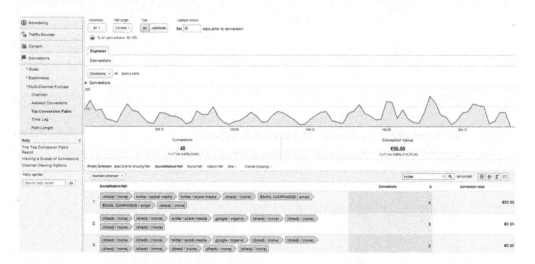

Figure 7.59   GA Twitter Conversions

Source: Google and the Google logo are registered trademarks of Google Inc.; used with permission.

Laws and Guidelines

The clock is striking 12 on social media part 2's iterative journey, but before we prepare to start the cycle all over again, let's take time to learn some important information on laws concerning social media.

When you complete this section you will:

- Be aware that certain laws apply to all social networks.
- Understand the only way to have complete control of the data about your consumers is via a forum other than social media.

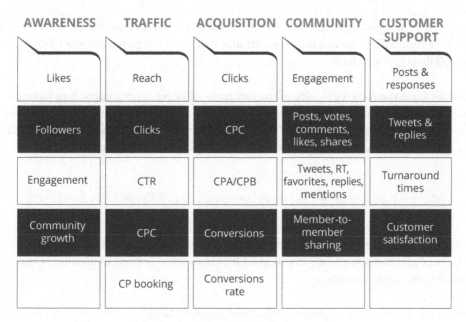

AWARENESS	TRAFFIC	ACQUISITION	COMMUNITY	CUSTOMER SUPPORT
Likes	Reach	Clicks	Engagement	Posts & responses
Followers	Clicks	CPC	Posts, votes, comments, likes, shares	Tweets & replies
Engagement	CTR	CPA/CPB	Tweets, RT, favorites, replies, mentions	Turnaround times
Community growth	CPC	Conversions	Member-to-member sharing	Customer satisfaction
	CP booking	Conversions rate		

Figure 7.60   GA Twitter Conversions

Data Protection and Privacy

Social media is an international game, so along with being up to speed on the laws in your own country you must also be aware of laws worldwide. There is no need to visit your local law library—there are various websites to help you with this, such as www .dlapiperdataprotection.com.

Do some research on data protection laws so that you know the rules that cover collecting people's data. For instance, you can only use personal data in certain ways, and you must dispose of it after a certain number of years. It is very important to remember that you can only use this kind of information for the purposes for which you collected it.

Copyright Issues

Copyright becomes more relevant when you are using websites like Pinterest and Instagram. If you are just randomly sharing people's photographs or images, be aware of what you can do and what you can't do when it comes to copyrighted images.

Organizational Policy Documents

Despite being able to freely gather information, you do not own any of these social media pages. They are the property of the company that owns the social network, such as Facebook and Twitter. Have a back-up strategy in place so that you can own as much data about your consumers as you can. Get as many people as possible off social media and into a forum that you can manage and that you have 100 percent ownership of, like an email directory database.

Social media is the New York City of the Internet—it never, ever sleeps. You have the power to keep up with the best of them by using all of the features and tools available to each platform. But be mindful that if you do not obey the guidelines that are put forth for a reason, you run the risk of your social media plan being stopped in its tracks.

So, What Have You Learned in This Chapter?

Go forth, social butterfly, and delight the masses with your engaging content across the plethora of platforms available to you. And if you are ever in need of another social media revamp, just remember:

- It's a team effort—assign members with different strengths to your SMM team and consider up-skilling if necessary.
- Listen to your customers and prove it by being reactive.
- Schedule your content—don't overwhelm your audience!
- Focus on quality rather than quantity when it comes to your social media interactions.
- Social platforms are constantly evolving—keep up-to-date and ahead of the game!

Go to www.artofdmi.com to access the case study on SMM as additional support material for this chapter.

 **Exercises**

Exercise 1

You are a new 24-hour gym opening in Manhattan and your main target market is working professionals (ages 25 to 40) who either live in the area or are visiting for business. Corporate packages are a new venture for the gym.

Create a content schedule for your Facebook page for the next seven days. Consider the type of posts that would be interesting and engaging to your potential customers.

Note: There must be a split overall into 70 percent your own content, 20 percent shared content, and 10 percent or less selling.

Exercise 2

Log into your business page on Facebook and go to https://www.facebook.com/ads/ audience_insights. Create an audience based on your gym's target market and examine the data. What does the data tell you about your audience in regards to:

- Gender split
- Age profile
- Relationship status
- Job titles
- Interests

Exercise 3

Under Manage Ads in LinkedIn, click on Create a New Campaign and create an ad that will draw people to your website. Name your campaign, choose your ad text, and upload an image. Now set up a second variant so you can split test different wording, images, or both and preview your ad. Then choose a target market for your gym based on the criteria above. (Remember you also want to target corporate clients in the area.) Choose your budget.

Exercise 4

As of tomorrow, you will be waiving your gym join-up fee for the entire month. Go to Twitter Ads and create a new followers campaign. Customize the start and end dates and compose a new tweet for your ad—remember to include the benefits and a CTA.

- Select your targeted audience.
- Add targeted followers.
- Add by interest.
- Choose your budget.

Exercise 5

If you don't already have an Instagram account, download the app and set one up. Then visit http://iconosquare.com and click Sign In with Instagram.

Click on Analytics and export your analysis report for the month.

Record the following:

- Number of "likes"
- Your most liked images for the month
- Your engagement scores
- Follower growth
- Your 10 most engaged followers

Use the information to shape your Instagram activity and compare it with your next monthly report.

 **Action Plan: SMM**

Digital Marketing Planning Scheme for SMM

Objectives

Reach, engagement, advocacy, conversion

Action Items

- Content creating (blog posts, ebooks, white papers, infographics, GIFs, video)
- Social posting (created content, curated content, images, video, links, offers)
- Engaging (CTAs, comments, questions, polls, surveys)
- Promoting (promoted social posts, ads, competitions, product promotions, events)
- Community building (conversation, customer service, comments, suggestions)

Measurement Tools and KPIs

Social media insights and analytics: Shares, comments, clicks, goals, social referral traffic to website, site content traffic, conversions

Spend

Media	Content	People	Systems
x	X	x	x

Chapter 8
Mobile Marketing

An Introduction

People have grown pretty fond of their phones. Their little devices of metal, plastic, and glass are like phantom limbs and they panic if they (gasp!) forget it, even for a few hours. This addiction means that consumers have become used to having their mobile devices with them constantly. So what opportunity does this pose for marketers? Right you are. A big one.

This chapter will focus on the mobile marketing industry, and how you, the digital marketer, can get up close and personal with your customers.

> The Mobile Marketing Association's formal definition of mobile marketing: "A set of practices that enables organizations to communicate with and engage with their audiences in an interactive and relevant manner through and with any mobile device or network."
>
> Informal definition of mobile marketing: Making your move through mobile!

Process

Effective mobile marketing is a cycle of discovery. Since it is a relatively new channel, there is no real rule book to follow—so you will need to experiment with and augment your strategy as you go along. However, as seen in Figure 8.1, a process does exist for effective mobile marketing.

This chapter will address the four main stages of mobile marketing's iterative process:

1 *Opportunity.* Chapter 8 begins by discussing how mobile use has taken off and why this presents such a great opportunity for digital marketers. You will come to understand the

Figure 8.1   Four-Step Mobile Marketing Process

sheer size and scale of the mobile marketing universe and why an ever-increasing amount of attention is being paid to it. Once you have seen what makes mobile such a big deal, you will discover a few challenges that it may throw your way.

2 *Optimize.* This stage will explain the ups and downs of mobile sites and apps. It will include considerations for devising your mobile strategy and show you how to create a mobile-optimized website. You will learn about app development too—the types of apps that you can create for various platforms, how you go about creating an app, and the benefits of building an app versus a mobile site.

3 *Advertise.* Mobile advertising has exploded faster than a pack of Mentos in a Diet Coke. In this stage, you will learn the many new ways in which you can reach customers on their precious devices.

4 *Analyze.* As with all advertising campaigns, you should use analytics to track the success of yours before optimizing them for top results. The final stage will cover how to do so from a mobile marketing perspective, because one of the great things about mobile marketing is that it is immensely measurable.

Key Terms and Concepts

This chapter will help you develop the skills you need to harness new technologies and access an increasingly mobile audience. You can be in with the cools kids, well equipped to launch your own mobile marketing campaign. Specifically, you will learn to:

- Appreciate the opportunities and challenges of mobile marketing when building your mobile strategy.
- Understand the various ways in which you can optimize your content for mobile, be it through the creation of mobile sites or apps.
- Utilize a range of technologies from Bluetooth to QR codes to enhance the mobile UX (user experience).
- Create effective mobile advertising campaigns that are in line with your objectives and budget.

- Recognize the importance of analytics in the realm of mobile marketing.
- Keep up with the mobile marketing curve by being aware of emerging trends and of the laws you need to follow.

Now that you have gotten a taste of what will be covered in this chapter, let's jump to the main course—starting with an overview of the mobile marketing industry and the opportunities that it allows digital marketers.

Stage 1: Opportunity

Mobile marketing is centered on the fact that mobile now overshadows the desktop world. As highlighted in Figure 8.2, the first step in the mobile marketing process is all about understanding the massive opportunities in this area. Tracing the move to mobile will help you to:

- Understand the opportunities that this change has meant for digital marketers.
- Realize the key characteristics and benefits of mobile.
- Be aware of mobile marketing's challenges.

Figure 8.2   Focus on the First Step in the Mobile Marketing Process

A Mobile Industry

From the first Motorola right through to the advent of the iPhone, the mobile phone has had a number of facelifts. Originally it could do little other than send and receive calls. Then SMS appeared. Then games. Then built-in cameras. And so on, until gradually consumers had personal organizers, entertainment, and education in one device. Mobile phones continue to change today, and since having the newest version of a mobile phone is a status symbol, consumers are willing to pay big money for the latest device.

Back in 2014, mobile Internet usage trumped desktop Internet usage for the first time. There was an explosion in the mobile market, which continues to increase today—for instance, there are more Android activations every day than there are babies being born! The past four or five years in particular have seen the greatest increase in the use of mobile phones and data. People are now sharing every aspect of their daily lives on social media. And they are using phones more for creating, storing, and sharing data than they are for making phone calls—the reason mobile phones were invented in the first place.

Figure 8.3 shows how this mobile boom seems likely to continue:

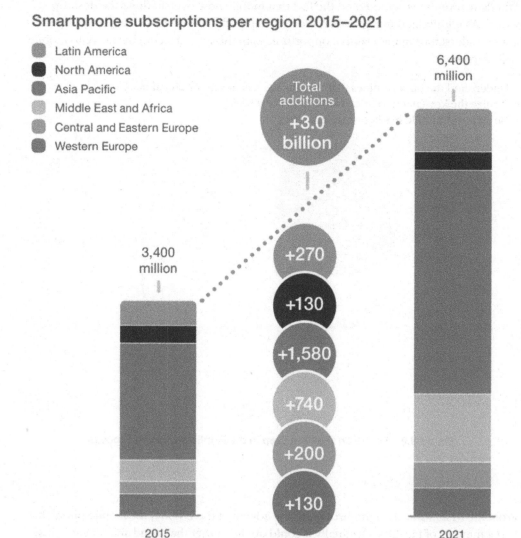

Figure 8.3   Smartphone Subscriptions Per Region 2015-2021
Source: Ericsson.

Nowadays, people prefer to experience events through their screens rather than witnessing them with their own eyes. You will probably be familiar with the same thing happening at a concert, or any mass event—everyone has their phones out and are paying attention to the screens in front of them, when in fact they should put them away and absorb what is happening. Still, people are driven to record these events, to save them, and to show them to friends. This is now possible with increased data speeds, storage capacity, and connectivity. In short, mobile encourages people to capture, store, and share the real world digitally.

Opportunities

As a digital marketer, if you want to reach the widest audience the smartphone is your new best friend—because it helps you to reach a mass audience in an incredibly easy way.

For example, Citigroup have found that while TV took 13 years to reach an audience of 50 million users, an entity like Facebook took only 3.5 years . . . and Angry Birds took just 35 days!

The sheer size of the mobile audience and the speed with which you can reach it is incredible. You instantly have a marketplace and an ecosystem that is global, with devices in the hands of everybody that you want to reach, and even a distribution mechanism that facilitates reaching them.

The key benefits of mobile include:

- *Personal connection*. Gone are the days of so-called brochure websites that contained merely a brand's logo, contact details, and location. With mobile, you can become a social media butterfly and create engaging ads that beg to be noticed—whatever you choose, you can connect with users on their personal devices to form deeper relationships.
- *Access/Immediacy*. People's phones are always with them, and unlike newspapers they do not throw them away. Generally, their phones are always on, too—so when you send a notification, it will be noticed. How quickly will it be seen? Well, 37 percent of 18- to 24-year-olds will see it within an hour, and 55 percent of those aged 25 to 40 years will see it within three hours. Well, we wouldn't want to miss anything!

On average, people check their phones 150 times a day, which roughly works out (depending on their sleep patterns) to every 6.5 minutes. They interact with their phones more than with any other technology, which means your message will be seen pretty quickly once sent.

- *Distribution*. You have seen how fast an app such as the one for *Angry Birds* can reach a global audience. That is largely due to app stores such as the iOS App Store and Google Play, which let you reach millions of consumers instantly.

- *Seamless UX.* Thanks to advances in digital wallets and built-in payment mechanisms, users can browse, select, and purchase with a few touches. And if you can provide them with a seamless, interactive experience, how could they not fall for your charms?
- *Cross-Platform capabilities.* You can use mobile to activate static media, such as print ads—more on that in the section on proximity marketing.

Challenges

Although mobile marketing comes with a host of opportunities, it does have its challenges too. For instance, smartphones have tilted the balance of power from the company to the consumer. In the past when consumers had bad experiences in restaurants they raised the matter with management there and then. Or they might post a strongly worded letter at a later date. Now they can instantly complain to the world via Facebook or Twitter.

Consumers have a digital voice that they can let loose at any time. So what does that mean for brands? Well, they need to respond immediately—which is why many have social media teams dedicated to tracking what consumers are saying via mobile.

Also, the personal nature of mobile has forced brands to rethink their delivery of content. They need to ditch their static websites in favor of a more immersive experience that is optimized for mobile, with interactive features such as click-to-call buttons.

Mobile marketing is still somewhat unchartered territory, through which you will need to gingerly find your way—and the upcoming sections will help you get off to the best start. Next up, learn how to optimize your mobile site.

Stage 2: Optimize

Now that you have explored stage 1 of the iterative process—becoming familiar with the opportunities and challenges of mobile marketing—let's look at the ways in which you can optimize your content for a mobile audience.

In stage 2, which is highlighted in Figure 8.4, you will discover all the factors to consider when creating a mobile-optimized site so that you will:

- Understand the differences between adaptive and responsive sites.
- Learn the fundamentals of an effective mobile site.
- Appreciate the benefits and challenges of mobile sites, apps, and web apps.
- Be confident in planning your own mobile-optimized site.

Figure 8.4   Focus on the Second Stage in the Mobile Marketing Process

Mobile-Optimized Websites

Basically this is an existing site that uses technologies such as JavaScript to optimize content for mobile devices.

Since people are browsing more on their mobiles than on desktops, you need to engage with them on smaller screens. Showing the desktop version of your site will not cut it. Why? Because users do not have superhuman eyesight. If your content is too small, they will get frustrated with all the pinching and zooming involved, which could make them run straight into the welcoming, mobile-optimized arms of your competitors. After all, 57 percent of people will not recommend a business with a poorly designed mobile website, while 40 percent have turned to a competitor site after a bad mobile experience, according to Compuware's 2011 report "What users want from mobile."

So how can you make these users happy? Start by knowing your audience and whether they are:

- *Desktop users*. Their screens will be bigger and they will be able to read text from farther away.
- *Tablet users*. They are probably dual screening, that is, watching TV as they browse on their tablets.
- *Mobile users*. They are on the go and want to complete tasks quickly.

Because when it comes to mobile marketing, context is key.

Changes in Mobile Marketing

Ten years ago, it was easy peasy. Monitors were a certain size and had a certain resolution—and you just had to make sure that your important content fit onto that screen. Now content is seen from a variety of devices, such as smartphones, tablets, and laptops—even TVs and other appliances now have fully featured web browsers.

At first companies tried to cope with this device overload by creating different versions of their websites—the basic one for desktop and the mobile version. With two sets of content to manage on two different websites, this gave content managers everywhere a total brain ache. Also, the mobile user was seeing a substandard version of the site, which had the bare essentials and a link to the desktop version, but was usually left to rot without ever being updated.

Sounds pretty grim, right? It was. Luckily, times have changed and the new standard practice is to have a single destination for all content. Whether users browse from mobile devices or their desktops they reach the same place, but they see content in a different way depending on the device they are using.

This is made possible by using adaptive or responsive mobile sites. For *adaptive* sites, different versions of a site are served to different devices based on common screen sizes and resolutions. The server recognizes whether, for instance, the user is browsing from a desktop with Chrome or from an iPhone with Safari and presents the relevant version of the website. In other words, the version of the site changes based on the width of the browsing device; certain pieces of content are hidden if necessary.

Figure 8.5 shows two versions of the TripAdvisor site. Firstly it shows the mobile-adaptive site as viewed from a desktop—with a big web banner image and a search box that takes up the full width of the page. But the site on a mobile is very different.

TripAdvisor used metrics and analytics to see how people interacted with its site and recognized that mobile users behave differently from desktop users. In this instance, the mobile user has been dropped into a foreign city and may want to find the nearest hotel or restaurant. And because that user's phone has GPS, TripAdvisor can send back search results based on his location without the user having to bother with typing addresses. Pretty slick, right?

Adaptive sites such as this one normally have a link labeled something like Visit the Desktop Site, for those who want a more detailed browsing experience and to do their own research, as opposed to completing quick tasks. The content differs between desktop and mobile versions.

But in a *responsive* approach exactly the same content is used all the time—it is just ordered differently depending on the browsing device. And this approach is the one that 80 to 90 percent of businesses should be using.

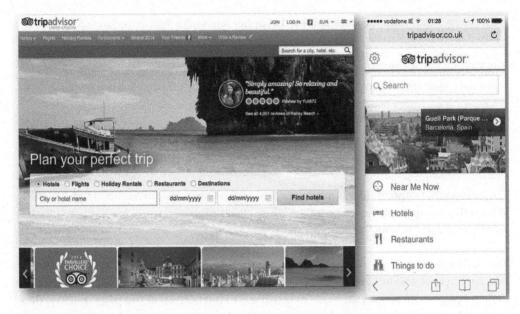

Figure 8.5   Mobile Adaptive Website Viewed from Desktop and Mobile
Source: TripAdvisor.

Characteristics of an Effective Mobile Site

When creating a mobile strategy for your own website, you should:

- *Prioritize content over navigation.* Say goodbye to bouncing back and forth between pages. Now browsing is easier with one-page scrollable websites that have become fashionable for mobile and desktop alike. In the desktop version, users can click on navigation links to jump to the areas that interest them most, rather than being directed to an entirely new page and waiting for the content of that page to download.
- *Create large tap targets.* People's thumbs are simply too big to be thumping on hyperlinked text—especially if there are a few links within a paragraph of text. Make sure that the target is big enough, with enough space around it, so as not to send users to the wrong place.
- *Remove unnecessary content.* Because of little annoyances, such as data speeds and screen real estate, remove superfluous information from your site. Be ruthless!
- *Provide for quick tasks.* Following on from the point above, remember that users only want the information they need, not an essay about your hip company culture. Make it easy for them to do what they want—if you are a hotel, for example, show them your number and location.
- *Consider download speed and power usage.* This is becoming less of a concern with powerful 4G networks, but it is still important. Websites should load quickly onto users' mobile devices so that they are not tempted to visit your competitors instead. Large images, multiple animations, and videos that play automatically run down batteries—which could deter users from hanging around or from coming back.
- *Know your limits.* It is not possible to store cookies that trace a user's browsing behavior on mobile devices as you can with desktops. So it is hard to determine how many times a

user visits a site, what she last searched for, or her login information and to tailor content based on that information.

- *Understand interactions (touch versus click).* With more searches happening on mobile devices, the click is becoming redundant. Users do not have the luxury of a mouse. They just have their thumbs and their fingers. Which is why touch design is so important.

Touch Design: The Fundamentals

When Apple produced the first iPhone, they measured people's fingertips to find the most common size of touchpoint that they could use—it was found to be 44 × 44 pixels.

This means that controls like buttons, menus, and navigational items need to be placed at least this far apart. If these controls are any closer together, users are likely to tap the wrong area and become frustrated.

Touch design has led to other methods of interacting with mobile, too. Users can point and tap or press and hold to reveal things, they can slide to move through a gallery or to the next page in an article, they can swipe to get to the bottom of the page quickly, they can pinch and stretch to expand details, and they can twist and turn elements on a page. So where possible, you should take advantage of these standard touch gestures on your mobile site.

Phone Integration: The Fundamentals

Mobile sites allow the integration of content with mobile features and functions, including:

- *GPS.* You can inform the server that you are interacting within a given location, thereby letting users know that they are five minutes away from your business.
- *Keyboard choices.* Filling in forms can be frustrating even in the desktop world, and it can get more annoying still with the small keyboard of a mobile. Try offering different keyboard choices for the user: If you want a phone number, show the number pad in the same field as the form rather than making users change keyboards themselves.
- *SMS.* Once you have users' numbers, you can send an SMS or ask them to sign up for an SMS service.
- *Click-to-call/Auto-detect numbers.* Android and iPhone devices will detect numbers on any web page and make them clickable. So users do not need to frantically search for a pen and paper—they can simply push the button that says Call Now to get through.
- *AutoCorrect.* Avoid the mistakes that AutoCorrect can bring (especially when a user is filling in personal details) by disabling this feature on any keyboard on your mobile site.
- *Visit Desktop option.* Remember, responsive websites have exactly the same content for mobile and desktop versions of a site but adaptive ones do not. So if using an adaptive site, give the user the option to visit your desktop site.

Figure 8.6 shows an example of a desktop website; beside it is the more actionable mobile site. The number provided on the mobile site is clickable and the company can leverage the GPS of users' phones to know where they are before directing them to the closest center.

Figure 8.6   Desktop Website versus Mobile Website
Source: Snap.ie.

Advantages of Mobile Sites

The advantages of having a mobile-optimized website versus an app (its advantages will be covered in more detail in the next section) are:

- *Immediacy.* Mobile sites are instantly available. Users type search terms into Google, click on a result, and are directed to a website immediately. In contrast, users have to search for an app in an app store, download it (and maybe enter a password first), wait for it to download, and then go back to their home screens to open it. It is not the shortest nor sweetest of processes.
- *Compatibility.* It makes no difference whether you are sending a link out to people with iPhones, Androids, BlackBerrys, or Windows Phones: Your mobile-optimized site will work across all devices and on desktops too.
- *Easily upgraded.* Mobile sites can be updated instantly. If you make a change to your mobile site, the next person who visits your site will see that change. Any updates to apps must be bundled together and uploaded to app stores. You might need to wait for a review of the updated app, which could take weeks. Then the user needs to replace the existing app with the upgraded version in order for any changes to appear.
- *Easily found.* You can simply include the web address for your mobile site on all of your brochures and materials and people will understand that is where they need to go, from any device. Addresses can also be easily shared between users via social media. This means that mobile sites generally have a broader reach than apps.
- *Longer life cycle.* Mobile sites cannot be deleted, whereas apps can be dissed and dismissed quite easily.
- *Cost/time-effective.* Mobile sites are generally easier and cheaper to create than apps, which are very specialized. This is because mobile sites are built with languages such as HTML,

JavaScript, and CSS that are already used in the desktop world. Not to mention the fact that there are more web designers out there than there are app developers.
- *Support and sustainability.* There are a range of content management systems or free platforms, such as WordPress, that you can use for your website. Once the core structure of your site is built, it is pretty easy to manage it yourself in terms of changing ad images or updating details. However, the same cannot be said for apps, since any updates need to be reviewed by the app stores.

Advantages of Apps

Mobile sites are not perfect. Here are a few advantages that apps have over them:

- *Uninterrupted Internet access not required.* This is a major consideration if, for example, you are building a tourism app to be used by travelers who want to avoid data-roaming charges. Travelers would be charged to browse a mobile site but not to access your app, once they have downloaded it.
- *Better phone integration.* Generally apps can leverage a phone's features (such as its GPS and camera) better than a mobile site can.
- *Platform-specific.* Apps are usually built for a specific purpose, whereas mobile sites will function the same across platforms. A site will use a recognizable interface and the same navigation across any device. Which can be good or bad, depending on what you want.

It boils down to this—mobile sites are built for a wide range of uses. Businesses usually use them for providing information in one-way contexts. Whereas businesses in the digital space generally end up using apps, because at some point they are limited by what the mobile site can do.

Apps versus Web Apps

Before you go deciding whether you would prefer a mobile-optimized site or an app, allow us to introduce the humble web app—which is like a halfway house between the two formats.

A web app uses the same core HTML functions as a mobile site and all the activity takes place within a mobile device's browser (e.g., Safari). But you can do clever things to a web app with some nifty code—for instance, users can save your site to their home screens with a bookmark. The site will then be represented by an icon that will allow users to launch the site, without the address bar at the top and the navigation bar at the bottom. It becomes a native app that happens to live on the web (and does not require approval from an app store to exist).

Bear in mind, web apps do come with certain challenges:

- *Fragmentation.* Different browsers across different devices will treat HTML5 in different ways, which can lead to inconsistencies and a disrupted user experience.
- *Online only.* Since web apps live online, they rely on connectivity.

- *Less integration*. HTML5 is still largely a desktop language despite its many enhancements, so a web app will be less integrated with a phone's functionality and features than a native app would be.
- *Visibility/distribution*. This is a major disadvantage. Users understand when a business says, "Download our app." They know where they need to go and what they should do. But it is harder to say, "Visit our mobile site. Hit the button at the bottom of your browser, which will allow you to save our site as a bookmark on your home screen so you can find it easily in the future." Bit of a mouthful, right? Also, it is easy to discover the most popular apps via charts in app stores; there is no equivalent for the top mobile sites that people browse.
- *Revenue options*. You can put a price on your native app and sell it in app stores. People will pay for it and download it—and even though Apple or Google will keep a piece of that revenue, as the developer of the app or the company that owns it, you get paid when you get noticed. So you can say goodbye to that extra pocket money if you choose a web app.

Getting Started

Luckily, in the HTML world and in the mobile-sites space there is a lot of help available. Web standards are well organized, and the HTML, CSS, and JavaScript used to build mobile sites and web apps have been around for a long time—so you can take your pick of the experts.

If you are planning a new website, consider starting out with an open and free content management system, such as WordPress. You can access an entire ecosystem of people who have built specialty themes—so if you own a bakery, you can search for *bakery themes* and install the themes you like. You can then download them as a package and customize the sites with text and images to suit your business. Usually custom sites come at a fee, but they are relatively cheap—and many are mobile-responsive too.

Developing your site from scratch? Follow the site development process in Figure 8.7 and it will be a piece of cake:

1 *Justify* why you are changing your site in the first place and why it needs to be mobile responsive or adaptive.

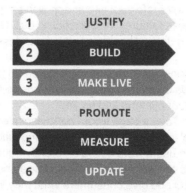

Figure 8.7   The Site Development Process

2 *Build* it with the aid of experienced developers. See whom your competitors are using and find out what those developers can do for you. If it means holding auditions, so be it.

3 *Go live* with your site—then test, test, test. Make sure it can be accessed from all the main browsers: Chrome, Safari, Internet Explorer, and Firefox.

4 *Promote* your website. This is no time to be shy—let people know that you have had a makeover. Tell them in the footer of your emails, in any printed material, and during any PR opportunities.

5 *Measure* results using Google Analytics, which you can integrate with your website. This is a really important one, as you can learn a lot about how users get to your site and what they do once they arrive.

6 *Update* your site based on what you have learned in Step 5. You can see where the hot content of your website is; maybe you want to create more like it. If part of your site is a virtual tumbleweed, change it.

It is so important to utilize analytics in your mobile marketing. Start by clicking the Audience tab in Google Analytics and selecting the devices section. Here you will see which devices people are using for browsing, what percentage of users are coming from phones, and even the operating systems they are using. You can then use this data to prioritize mobile UX over your desktop site.

Five Take-away Tips

Bear these tips in mind before you take the leap into mobile:

1 *Design from the consumer's perspective.* You need to understand what users want to do when they visit your site—are they simply doing research, or are they looking to buy or want to contact you? Cut through the clutter and make it easy for them to take action, wherever they are and whatever they are doing.

2 *Target the most popular devices.* This is much easier if you pay close attention to your analytics. For example, by focusing on providing an exceptional UX on iOS devices, you will still cater to over 90 percent of your visitors.

3 *Enhance the experience.* It is really important to use mobile-specific HTML for a better UX. Make sure to integrate your site or app with as many mobile-device features as possible. These features include click to call, GPS, and automatic detection of numbers and dates. Provide a link to your desktop site when applicable too.

4 *Put users' needs first.* Consider what they want to see up front. Once you have that figured out, you can focus on making your site responsive or adaptive, planning your SEO strategy, drafting your content, and so on.

5 *Think like the consumer.* Take a page from TripAdvisor's experience. It was only after it understood users' interactions with its site using different devices that it could appreciate that its mobile users were acting differently from its desktop users; at that point it adapted the site's content accordingly. So forget the rambling introductory paragraph from your CEO and give consumers what they want.

Now that you know many of the considerations involved in creating mobile sites, let's take a trip to the app world and explore the times when an app is necessary to woo mobile users.

App Development

By now you will appreciate the ways in which you can reach customers on mobile devices—through the creation of responsive or adaptive sites and the development of apps.

Let's continue with stage 2 of the iterative process (see Figure 8.4) and describe how to develop apps by:

• Understanding the app marketplace and the platforms available.
• Recognizing the fundamentals of an effective app.
• Learning the steps to take when developing an app.

An 'Appy Marketplace

Unless you have been living on Mars for the past few years, you will know what an app is—as the Oxford Dictionary describes it; 'a self-contained program or piece of software designed to fulfill a particular purpose'. Apps are bundled up and sent to app stores, such as Google Play and the iOS App Store, from which users can download them to their mobile devices. Pretty much everything that lives on your phone is an app, including the feature that makes phone calls and sends messages, the camera, and the GPS.

People use apps in nearly every aspect of their lives—eating, drinking, sleeping, working, relaxing, traveling, shopping, and even dating. So it should come as no surprise that app development has become a major part of mobile marketing.

The size of today's mobile app market is staggering. For instance, Statista has reported that there are over 1.5 million apps on the iOS App Store (with 100 billion downloads and counting). When the iOS store was launched in 2008, there were only 28 apps available—pretty big growth spurt, right?

A handful of these apps belong to Apple, but mainly they have been created by third parties, bundled together, and entered into the App Store ecosystem. These owners and developers put a price on their apps and earn money from them (the App Store takes around a 30 percent commission but the rest belongs to the owners or developers). And there can be big bucks in it too—for instance, Apple has given developers over $25 billion and *Angry Birds* earns more than $1 million a day in revenue!

The other big player in the app market is Google Play; like the iOS App Store, it has a huge number of apps (1.8 million according to Statista) and downloads (over 50 billion). These are the two platforms from which you will most likely launch your apps. They both involve different considerations and costs; Apple charges a yearly fee and Google a one-off payment. They also have different submission guidelines, developer agreements, and registration processes that you should chew over (not literally) before launch. For the iOS App Store, Apple reviews every app that gets submitted, and the process can take weeks. Google Play has no such approval process and your apps will be available for users to download within a few hours of submission.

Once patience has dictated what platform you want to use, you then have to decide what kind of app you will develop—web or hybrid. The section on mobile-optimized websites mentioned that the web app is like a halfway house between the mobile site and the native app. A hybrid app is like a halfway house between the native app and the web app! Basically, a hybrid app uses standard HTML5 technologies but is wrapped in the shell of an app to persuade the app stores that it is a native app. And since Apple does not like to be confused, it will most likely reject apps like this. It is easier to get away with hybrid apps on Google Play, which has fewer restrictions.

For those who have less cash to flash, a hybrid app can be a happy medium between a mobile site and an app. The good news is that hybrid apps are built with web technology (so there are lots of developers who can create them and package them for app stores), and most casual users will not even know the difference! Ah, blissful ignorance. . . .

There is nothing wrong with testing the water like this—creating a mobile-responsive site, adding some key hooks to make it more like a web app, wrapping it to make it a hybrid app, and putting it out into the marketplace for a while to understand how people are using it. If you find limitations that you think a native app can address, that will be your green light for native app development.

App Development: The Fundamentals

So what makes apps so great, anyway? Good question!

- *Needs fulfillment.* Apps have a clear utility value. They are built around a specific need and they satisfy that need like ice cream on a summer's day.
- *Integration.* Apps can integrate with a device's functionality better than a mobile site can. For instance, they can use features like the camera, GPS, and speaker to provide a great UX.
- *Simplicity.* Generally apps are well designed and easy to use. Some have a couple of introductory screens to explain how they work, but the user can normally rely on intuition alone.
- *Interactivity.* Apps can process information very quickly and have a fast response time. So today's impatient, on-the-go user can be logged in automatically (without having to re-enter details) and access data such as top scores, saved bookings, and loyalty points.
- *Accessibility.* Above all, apps do not rely on an Internet connection to work—so users can play *Angry Birds* on an airplane or read ebooks from the comfort of their outhouses.
- *Security.* For anything that uses secure information, such as login encryptions or e-commerce, native apps offer much stronger features than web apps, hybrid apps, or even mobile sites.

Getting Started

As with creating a mobile site, the most important consideration in developing an app is to understand the members of your audience. What do they want? What do they expect your app to do? How can it enhance the functionality of their phones? Will it make them prettier? And so on.

Apps have the power to completely revolutionize an industry—for instance, the taxi industry. Companies like Hailo and Uber recognized an old-fashioned problem and came up with a very simple and modern solution. The apps are incredibly intuitive and easy to use—they also benefit both the user (the person wishing to book the taxi) and the provider (the taxi driver).

Another key example of an industry game changer is Airbnb. Set up by a couple of guys to make extra cash from renting out their free space, this app has transformed the travel-sharing economy. Users everywhere can become temporary landlords and earn money while on holidays of their own. Like Hailo and Uber, the Airbnb app leverages GPS functionality and allows users to book and pay easily. The opportunities in the app world are endless and potentially very lucrative—so you too can be an industry game changer!

Having introduced the steps for developing a mobile site in the section on mobile-optimized websites, let's return to the site development process (see Figure 8.7) and apply these steps to developing an app.

1 *Justify*. Start by asking yourself why this app is needed—and you should have a better reason than: "Umm . . . because my competitors have one?" Your app should fulfill a specific purpose that will make users want to interact with it. A lot of people have great ideas for an app, but even though the idea is important, it is not enough. There must be a market, a context, and a need to be satisfied. Is it a social app? A gaming app? A utility? Remember, the best apps out there are not trying to offer a lot of things to please everyone—rather, they do one thing and do it very well.

   Once you know what your app can do, you can decide whether it will be sold or free of charge (and if you can earn revenue through advertising instead). This will inform what platforms to use—if you are in it for the money, launch on the App Store (since that is where the most sales lie).

2 *Build*. Next, you need to build the app with the help of a developer. How much will this cost? Well, that really depends on the functionality of the app. Does it have processing features? Will people need to log in? Does it have a payment function? Remember, you get what you pay for—cutting corners now may mean a shoddy UX later.

   It is easy to find and audition developers. All you need to do is find an app that you like on the app stores, see who developed it, access a list of other apps that the developer created and approach them if you like what you see. You should explain to them what makes your app better than sliced bread (or even an app that slices bread) and what technologies it requires. The developer will most likely be familiar with what you want already because let's face it—they have probably done it or similar before.

3 *Go live.* Make sure that you understand the app submission process and the time frame that can be involved in getting it approved by the App Store. It could prove risky submitting an app one week before your launch deadline, desperately hoping that it passes the Apple review process in time! Instead, try submitting an earlier version of the app to get those important boxes ticked.

4 *Promote.* Even after coming up with the idea, designing or developing the app, and submitting it, there is still a lot of work to be done. There are just so many competing apps available—and this is where promotion comes in. How can you get the word out there that your app exists? And how can you convince people to download it?

Think of relevant promotional activities to raise interest before your launch. Use app store badges on your website and all of your marketing materials. Consider creating a landing page to gather email addresses from people who want the app on the first day of release. Preparing like this will help your app to rise in the charts very quickly.

5 *Measure.* There is no point in losing your voice screaming about your app if you forget to follow up on your activity. App stores will tell you how many people downloaded the app, but if you build in metrics (such as Google Mobile Analytics or Flurry) you can get detailed activity reports—on how many times the app was opened, how long the average user spent on the app, the key pages he visited, how he interacted with it, and so on. It may be one of the only times in your life when you start to love tests!

6 *Update.* Taking these measurements and analytics into account, you can consider updates for future versions of your app. Generally you will have to update your app every year anyway, as both Google and Apple change their operating systems around September or October and you may need to talk with your developers to make sure that your app is still working.

Apple's iOS upgrades can result in massive changes to the look and feel of the operating system. This means that older iOS versions can appear old fashioned. So remember, launching an app is not a one-time thing. You need to continually update and optimize as part of the iterative mobile marketing process.

Speaking of which, you have now completed stages 1 and 2 of the mobile marketing process. Congratulations! Now let's move on to stage 3: Advertise.

Stage 3: Advertise

Having an awesome mobile-optimized site or app means nothing if no one knows you exist.

Stage 3 of mobile marketing's iterative process, highlighted in Figure 8.8, focuses on advertising so you will:

- Understand how mobile advertising can help you to achieve your goals.
- Discover the various mobile ad formats available and the places in which your ads can appear.
- Learn steps and tips for launching your own campaign.

Figure 8.8   Focus on the Third Stage in the Mobile Marketing Process

About Mobile Advertising

Right now the mobile-advertising industry is dominated by global brands and the big boys in fast-moving consumer goods (FMCGs). They use mobile advertising as just one part of their media mix—they also advertise across radio, TV, and print. And although mobile spend has grown a lot over the past few years, it is tiny compared to how much these brands spend on other media. Considering how many people are on mobile around the world, the amount spent on mobile advertising really should be higher.

So why the reluctance to fork out? Well, unlike traditional media, everything is measurable with mobile advertising. And this can be somewhat of a curse. Because at the granular level that mobile allows, the results may seem small compared to the often-inflated projections of other media. Plus you can see exactly how much it costs to serve an ad to a user. In contrast, if you place a newspaper ad on page 4, you just divide the circulation of the newspaper by the cost of the ad to work out the cost per view.

However, that cost per view may not be entirely accurate, because to be honest, not everybody will notice that newspaper ad. The reader might start from the back and never even get to page 4. So your beautifully crafted ad may not even be seen.

There are definite advantages to using mobile over traditional formats if you are willing to invest. Mobile advertising can help you to achieve:

- *Business goals*, such as lead generation and driving sales.
- *Product goals*, such as providing information about a new product or increasing downloads/upgrades if you have a digital product.

- *Communication goals*, such as engaging a new audience, showing off your personality, and getting people to interact with your brand. For instance, big brands are now reaching out to a younger market, members of which pay less attention to traditional media and spend most of their time on mobile devices.
- *Marketing goals*, such as branding, awareness, and engagement.

Mobile Ad Formats

Hate to break it to you, but size does matter—at least, it does when it comes to choosing mobile ad formats! The standard mobile banner ad format is only 300 × 50 pixels or 320 × 50 pixels. Even with iPads, you still have a very a small space in which to get your message across. See Figure 8.9 for the most common mobile ad formats.

If you do manage to engage the user's attention with an eye-catching ad (through your messaging, design, or the inclusion of a competition), you can take over her browsing experience in a way that is not possible with desktop ads. If the user clicks on your expandable mobile ad, as shown in Figure 8.10, it will take over the entire space of that user's phone.

Whatever the format, your mobile ad should drive users to take some form of action: for instance, a simple hotel banner that expands when clicked to show functional buttons with clear CTAs. The user can then book a room, earn rewards, or click to call within a UX as smooth as Morgan Freeman's voice.

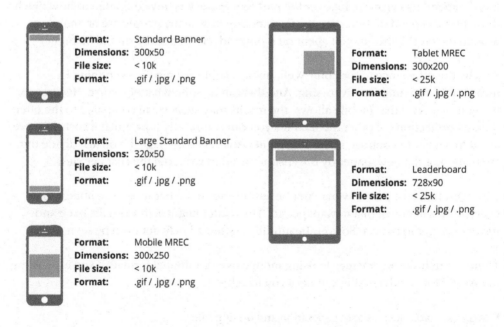

Figure 8.9   Most Common Mobile Ad Formats

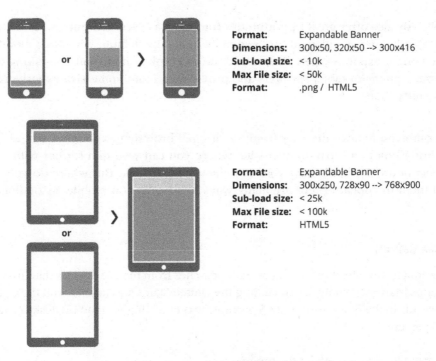

Format: Expandable Banner
Dimensions: 300x50, 320x50 --> 300x416
Sub-load size: < 10k
Max File size: < 50k
Format: .png / HTML5

Format: Expandable Banner
Dimensions: 300x250, 728x90 --> 768x900
Sub-load size: < 25k
Max File size: < 100k
Format: HTML5

Figure 8.10   Expandable Mobile Banner Ads

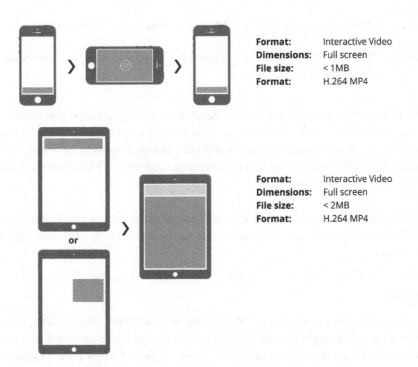

Format: Interactive Video
Dimensions: Full screen
File size: < 1MB
Format: H.264 MP4

Format: Interactive Video
Dimensions: Full screen
File size: < 2MB
Format: H.264 MP4

Figure 8.11   Interactive Mobile Video Ads

Mobile ads also offer great opportunities for video, as seen in Figure 8.11. With desktop advertising, video ads are generally muted by default, whereas a mobile video banner expands when clicked and the video plays immediately—taking over the user's phone or tablet speakers and providing a more immersive experience. Pretty nifty, huh?

You can even remove the user from his original browsing experience entirely and bring him to a separate microsite, where you can woo him further with product news. So that is how your mobile ads could look. But where do you want them to appear? There are many ways to advertise on mobile, as outlined next.

Mobile Search

According to Google, there are more daily searches from mobile devices than from desktops in over 10 countries (including the United States and Japan). And the CTR on mobile ads in the first position (27.3 percent) was much higher than on desktop ads (19.3 percent).

You could be sitting pretty at the top by:

- Making sure that you have a mobile-optimized response, be it an adaptive or responsive mobile site.
- Letting users download your app (if you have one) directly from your mobile ad onto their phones.
- Including a click-to-call button—allowing users to contact you in a more immediate way than they could on a desktop.

Truth be told, getting your mobile ads to stand out is tricky, because you are dealing with a much smaller screen. On desktops, search results might show three or four ads at the top of the page and down the right-hand side. But with mobile, only one or two ads can precede organic search results. It is likely that your ad will be below the fold, making it even harder to see.

However, with some creative thinking—such as using the phone's functionality to get users to interact with your ad—mobile search can be a great way of connecting with your audience.

In-App Ads

These ads are contained in downloaded apps and are what allow many developers to monetize the free apps that they produce. They are more targeted than mobile search, because advertisers can decide in which types of apps they would like their ads to star.

With in-app advertising, your content is directed at people who are already predisposed to your brand or product—take, for example, the cinema listings page of an entertainment app, which might include a banner for a specific film. Users can click the ad to watch a trailer, which might then drive them to buy tickets for that film instead of the other options listed. The ad is perfectly placed inside a relevant app—so you can see how in-app ads use less of a scattershot approach than mobile search or even mobile ads on sites.

However, in-app ads are not always targeted in the cleverest way. For instance, if an ad for lastminute.com suddenly appears in *Angry Birds*, it would not be relevant to the app's users (mainly children and teenagers). So be careful when selecting the apps in which you want your ads to appear—because the most popular ones may not be the best fit.

Mobile Sites

As you know by now, the standard mobile banner ad format is really small. This means that creating a brand impression or getting a message across is pretty tricky. Mobile ads rarely jump out and they are easy for the user to ignore. That is perhaps why mobile advertising is more accessible for established brands—they have a bigger budget to spend on these ads and on other formats, too.

But by making your ads interactive, such as including video or action-driven buttons, you have a better chance of engaging users on mobile sites.

Branded Apps

The teacher's pet of mobile advertising is the *branded app*, whereby the app itself is just one large piece of marketing for the brand. If you get it right, it provides a much more immersive experience for the user. It should be entertaining, funny, educational, or informative—in short, it should be an app that users will want to download and keep on their home screens.

Generally, branded apps are sponsored by a particular brand. For instance, they could be created on the back of a sporting or music event. You have probably seen *powered by* or *brought to you* in an ad's strapline—the same approach is used for branded apps.

Branded apps can help you engage customers for longer. They can also make your brand look great—now you will be seen as hip, young, and trendy rather than dated and over the hill.

For example, the Carling iPint was one of the first branded apps, released back in 2009. It used the phone's accelerometer and some clever fluid mechanics to pour a virtual pint before allowing users to "drink it" by tipping their phones. The app went viral and its success fed into Carling's overall campaign.

The other type of successful app is a *branded game*. An example of this is the Heineken app that lets rugby fans practice their virtual catching and kicking skills on the go. The branding may be secondary to the user, who is just enjoying the game, but it will sink in over time as a positive reflection of Heineken.

Mobile Networks

There are literally hundreds of networks on which you can advertise; the one you choose will be determined by your budget. Apple's iAd platform, for instance, requires a minimum budget of a mere $1 million! Other considerations include:

- *Local versus international reach*. Advertising within a specific area will usually be much cheaper.
- *Cross-media coordination*. Some advertising networks will offer desktop as well as mobile solutions—they might do radio, print, and outdoor too.
- *Service level*. When you use a self-service mobile advertising network, such as Google's AdMob, you can upload your own assets and graphics, set your budget, and pick where you want your ads to appear. Or you can take a load off and let an agency take care of everything instead.
- *Reach and scope*. Decide whether you want the whole world or just your granny to see your ads.

WiFi

One neglected digital area is ad-funded WiFi. Users have all these devices that they take everywhere and they are constantly looking for connectivity—be it in coffee shops, hotels, or trains. Usually, the login page will look for a user name and a password; sometimes there is no login page at all.

This is a missed opportunity, particularly if you are a small business like a coffee shop. If you have WiFi available for customers, use the login page as a branding opportunity—get people to sign up for your loyalty plan, tell them about special offers or discounts, inform them about upcoming events, and so on. This is an easy way to drive trade and can be much more cost effective than other mobile advertising strategies.

Getting Started

Just as with building mobile sites or apps, creating a mobile advertising strategy is made easier by using the site development process introduced earlier (see Figure 8.7):

1 *Justify*. Why are you choosing mobile advertising? What value will it bring? Determine what your potential customers will get out of it and also what goals it can achieve for your business.
2 *Build*. Next, build your campaign—with the help of an agency if you have the budget. It will put together all of the assets and everything you need.
3 *Go live*. When you are ready to roll out your campaign, send it to as many places as possible. The more the merrier and all that . . .
4 *(Cross) promote*. If possible, drive the campaign from different media—that will help you to see which channel is the most successful.
5 *Measure*. Test the effectiveness of your mobile ad campaigns using data and analytics.

6 *Update.* Once you have an idea of what works and what should take a hike, you can update your campaign accordingly.

A note on the above. All too often businesses—particularly smaller companies—initially try mobile advertising with a limited budget and scope. Then if it does not achieve instant stardom, they give up. But it is really important to try this type of advertising time and time again, going back to your old friend split testing to figure out what format works best. Give yourself a bit of leeway in terms of time and budget to find what suits your business.

Mobile Advertising: Key Tips

Consider the destination of your campaign. Where will you send people? Are you asking them to download an app or are you directing them to your mobile site? And what do you want them to do as a result of your ad—click and make a phone call, watch a video, or visit a specific landing page? There are many ways to connect with users, so try to get this clear in your head early on.

Consider the response mechanism. Rather than allowing users to just click your ad, take advantage of their phones' functionality. Your ad can expand and allow the user to call from it, to watch a video straight away, to download an app, to send a prepopulated tweet, or to "like" you on Facebook. There are many more opportunities for people to interact with your mobile ad than simply clicking.

A/B test your ad types. This is pretty easy to do in the digital space and generally for mobile ads, too. Try different ad types to see what suits you as a company and the audience that you want to reach. You will be familiar with traditional banner ads already; other types include:

- *App walls.* Where your ad appears among many other ads for different apps (useful for developers).
- *Discovery ads.* When your ad is embedded in the middle of other content.
- *Interstitial ads.* When your ad appears to users before they can get to the article or other content they want to absorb in a website.

Retargeting. Chapter 4 introduced the concept of retargeting: To recap, it is when your ad follows a user around the Internet based on their previous interactions with your brand or product. Those users are more inclined to click on your ad because they have already expressed an interest in what you offer.

Although this strategy has been widely adopted in the desktop environment, it has yet to be done well in mobile. However, progress has been made, as in the case of smart app banners. When the user visits a certain website, a banner drops down to announce that there is an app available with the same content as the website. It includes a CTA, such as *download* or *view*, and if the user already has the app installed, it knows this and simply says *open*. Not too shabby.

Test for success. In addition to A/B testing your ad types, test the creatives used within them. See what wording and images resonate with customers and remember to follow through! After each trip to your analytics reports, you should update and relaunch your ads accordingly. Because when it comes to mobile advertising, one size definitely does not fit all. And since mobile is often a big brands' game, you need to do whatever you can to maximize the impact of your mobile ads and squeeze more out of your budget.

Coming up is another way in which you can advertise via mobile—proximity marketing.

Proximity Marketing

Having covered key ways to reach users on their mobiles, let's continue with stage 3 (see Figure 8.8) and a new area that technology has brought to mobile advertising.

Learn how proximity marketing can help you get closer to customers by:

- Understanding what proximity marketing is and how it works.
- Discovering how you can utilize technology to reach customers near you.
- Knowing the best practices for leveraging this technology.

About Proximity Marketing

Proximity marketing involves sending the right content to the right place at the right time. It is a lot more valuable than the shotgun approach of mobile banner ads and is generally cheaper, simpler, and more manageable. With proximity marketing, you can target content to wireless devices based on their locations, for instance:

- *A cellular phone in a particular cell.* When users travel abroad and roam away from their home network, they get a notification from the local operator that informs them of relevant costs. And you have the opportunity to send them a welcome message of your own!
- *A Bluetooth or WiFi device within range of a transmitter.* This goes back to the days before data plans were available, when the only way to send free and accessible content to mobile users was through Bluetooth. A shopping center, for example, knew when people had walked in with their Bluetooth devices switched on and could ask them to opt in to receive messages. This was a bit of a haphazard approach at the time; however, the use of beacons has brought it to the forefront again.
- *An NFC-enabled phone.* This revolves around the user being within very close proximity (less than a foot) of certain media. NFC, or near field communication, can read content from a little chip physically placed somewhere (such as in a bus shelter). You can put a chip on your product or advertising material and use it to cleverly launch localized content—such as sending a notification to the user's phone that your store is only a few feet away. Again, this is more targeted than general mobile advertising because it is based on the user being near something.

Advances in Proximity Marketing

Bluetooth proximity marketing was seen as a dying technology until Apple gave it a new lease on life in 2013. They brought forward a technology called iBeacon, which is simply a variation of Bluetooth low-energy technology. Around 140 companies worldwide are using iBeacon now and more big brands are jumping on board too.

iBeacon provides a tailored, real-world experience that leverages what a company is already doing in its existing app. How does it work? Well, a small chip, which costs just $5 to $10 and lasts around two years, is used to broadcast a user ID to the app.

For example, if users walk into Macy's and have the Macy's app, the chip will push offers to their phones based on where they are. If that user is a man standing in front of shoes, he will see offers related to men's shoes and not women's shoes. This is a very powerful form of advertising as users are already predisposed to your brand (because they have downloaded your app and are in your store) and you are serving them the right piece of information at the right time.

However, be careful about how you use iBeacon. Technology allows you to do really cool things, but as Peter Parker's uncle wisely said: "With great power comes great responsibility." So do not stalk your potential customers or scare them away with messages at every step—after all, you do not want them turning off their Bluetooth devices, or worse, deleting your app! Instead, act as a guide that can help them through their shopping process and give them the information they need. Gently does it.

Another area in proximity marketing is QR codes—those small, square, black-and-white bar codes that can be read by your phone's camera. For advertisers, they are convenient and cost effective; in fact, they are usually free. You can just go to a website like www.qrme.com and type in the URL you would like the code to link to, and it will generate a QR code that you can download and use on promotional material. QR codes are a big deal in the Far East; however, they are used less in Europe and the United States, possibly because many brands did not use them effectively when they first came out.

If you do decide to use QR codes, bear these tips in mind . . .

Do
- Direct users to a mobile-optimized landing page.
- Include mobile coupons to engage them.
- Build a list of mobile phone users.
- Link to mobile media like apps, videos, podcasts or PDFs.

Don't
- Make the code too small or so far away that it will not scan.
- Present the code in places with no Internet, for example, subway stations.
- Send users to your homepage.

Remember, it requires a bit of effort for users to take out their phones, open the QR reader or camera app, hold it steady, focus, and wait for the browser to open and launch. It might be easier to just type in a URL. So rather than sending them to your homepage, give them content that they were not expecting. You have piqued their interest. Use that.

Psst . . . for examples of what *not* to do (or just for a giggle on a Monday morning), check out www.qrcodefails.wordpress.com.

Now that you know how to use localized mobile advertising, let's move on to the last part of stage 3 in the iterative process—SMS marketing.

SMS Marketing

There is another area of mobile advertising that is often overlooked because it has been with us for so long. However, in stage 3 (see Figure 8.8) you will learn how SMS marketing can be a key part of your mobile advertising mix.

Learn how to make SMS work in your favor by:

- Understanding the main considerations in SMS campaigns.
- Finding the right supplier to help you with your messaging.
- Taking the necessary steps in the SMS campaign process.

SMS: Highs and Lows

Although SMS marketing may be overlooked in favor of cooler, shinier technologies, it does have many advantages. For instance, it is:

- *Targeted*. You can send a message directly to phone numbers that you have gathered personally.
- *Relevant*. The people seeing your message are more likely to be interested in what you offer.
- *Timely*. You can advertise promotions or special offers at the most appropriate time, such as the week before Christmas.
- *Personalized*. This can be very effective, especially in terms of localized marketing.
- *Visible*. SMS sees a huge open rate of 99 percent.
- *Accessible*. Compared to smartphones, apps, and mobile sites, even the oldest phones can receive SMS and can be accessed by anyone.

If you decide to use SMS within your wider mobile campaign, there are a few considerations to take into account. For instance, do you have a database of phone numbers and permission from these people to be contacted? And will you need an SMS provider?

If you have a small database, you might be tempted to send messages from your own phone; however, you will not be able to see if people open your text or even see it. Using an SMS provider means you can measure your campaigns with analytics and lets your message stand out with targeted, specific keywords and your own short code or phone number. For instance, your message might read: "To receive special deals on concerts and events from Circle City Tickets, text TICKETS to 12345." The keyword in this case is *TICKETS* and the short code is *12345*. The SMS provider can pick out those people who responded to that particular number and place them into a relevant bucket—so future messages are sent to the right people at the right time.

Remember, a well-crafted SMS marketing message is concise, targeted, relevant, and context sensitive. It can have a really high impact, such as driving people through the door of your restaurant or store faster than you can say, "You've got mail!"

Unfortunately, it is not all sunshine and lollipops with SMS marketing. It does come with its own challenges, such as:

- *Strict regulations.* Because SMS has been around for so long, it is the most regulated area of mobile advertising. Messages must be relevant, targeted, and specific—and the fines can be huge if you abuse your power. Also, since mobile marketing is permission-based, you need to know how you got that mobile number in the first place. The customer must opt in to receive messages (for instance, via an online competition or a registration form) and you must keep records as proof.
- *Limited space.* Messages are normally limited to 160 characters, so it can be hard to get your message across (unless you are an expert tweeter, in which case you will have lots to spare!). A good way to combat eating into your SMS credits with multiple messages is to include a CTA that takes the user to your mobile-responsive website.
- *Opt-out requirement.* Allowing users to opt out is a necessity and you will need to use up some of your precious 160 characters by saying, "Text STOP" to a certain number. This means you have even less space in which to engage users, but it is mandatory. If you continue texting somebody who has already opted out, you could be in big trouble.
- *Anticipating response.* Even with a crystal ball, it can be very hard to see what reaction your campaign will get. For instance, if you have 20 items to give away and you send a promotional SMS to 10,000 people, you could end up annoying those 9,980 people who do not get a freebie.

To stay above board and to run a more effective campaign, using an SMS supplier is highly recommended. This will ensure that your campaign is legal and measured, with all the records to prove it. If you do engage a supplier, you need to determine the following:

- Is it a managed or self-service product?
- Can you do it all online?
- Can you change the sender ID so that your SMS does not just appear from an unknown number, but from your brand?
- Can you schedule texts based on country dialing codes? If you have a global database and want to avoid sending messages at an inappropriate time, this is vital.
- Does the SMS provider support short codes? And if so . . .
- Can you group phone numbers by category and target audience?
- What are the upfront and ongoing costs?

Getting Started

Decided to run an SMS campaign? Great. See Figure 8.12 for a few steps to set you in the right direction . . .

1 *Provider selection.* Just as with choosing a developer for your app or mobile site, finding the right provider is really important. Make sure to ask about ongoing costs in addition to the cost of setting up. Generally you will pay an upfront fee, then buy a bundle of SMS credits before any campaign.

Figure 8.12   SMS Campaign Development Process

2 *Subscriber list.* As previously mentioned, you need both to understand where your subscriber list comes from and document these sources.

3 *Landing page.* If including a CTA or URL at the end of your SMS, make sure that the landing page to which you are directing users is optimized for mobile.

4 *Message campaign.* Do not keep sending the same message time and time again, just because you happen to have a sale on. Split test and vary your campaign messaging to see what works.

5 *Review and measure.* Just as with your mobile sites, apps, and any other advertising you might do, use metrics and analytics to measure the success of your campaign. Understand what drives customers to your door and update as necessary.

For further inspiration, check out these tips for the perfect SMS message.

• Segment your audience and send appropriate messages to each customer.
• Keep your text short and sweet.
• Have a strong CTA.
• Grab their attention in the first couple of words.
• Tell your audience who you are—assign your company as your sender ID.
• Don't forget to provide an opt-out option.

That concludes stage 3 of our mobile marketing iterative process. The next section will focus on using analytics to track your campaign's success.

Stage 4: Analyze

Our model may not look at analytics until the fourth stage of the iterative process (seen in Figure 8.13), but in fact data should be part of every step of your mobile marketing campaign.

This section will remind you of the importance of analysis, so you can:

• Appreciate that metrics should be applied to a mobile marketing strategy.
• Understand what an analytics package looks like and how it can be used in your own campaign.

Figure 8.13   Focus on the Fourth Stage of the Mobile Marketing Process

Mobile Analytics

Analytics are kind of like Brussels sprouts—you know they are good for you but you cannot help being a little afraid of them. And neither is half as bad as you imagined once you get used to it!

So what does the world of analytics involve? Well, it is all about using the most relevant metrics, and measuring a campaign's effectiveness and optimizing it based on the results.

Metrics are especially invaluable in mobile marketing, because users are on personal devices. They are not sharing them as they would a PC at work or a laptop at home that the whole family can access. So whether you are using mobile sites, apps, mobile search, proximity marketing, or SMS as part of your strategy, you are communicating with a single user. You can see exactly what she is doing and how you can connect with her.

Regardless of the analytics package you go for, you can follow your campaign across different devices. For instance, in the Audience tab of Google Analytics, shown in Figure 8.14, you can see how your website performs on various devices by clicking on the Mobile category on the left and selecting Devices.

You then get a list of the devices that people are using most frequently to get to your site, as seen in Figure 8.15.

This information can feed into your mobile site strategy in terms of how you cater to users, how you accommodate what they like to do on your site, whether you build a

Figure 8.14   See How Your Website Performs on Various Devices within the Audience Tab of GA

Source: Google and the Google logo are registered trademarks of Google Inc.; used with permission.

mobile app, what platforms you target, and so on. You can also check the bounce rate for users coming from mobile devices as opposed to desktops—if it is a lot higher, maybe you need to focus more on your mobile strategy and on making your site responsive.

In short, by taking full advantage of the metrics and analytics at your disposal, you can run more informed—and more successful—mobile marketing campaigns. Simple as that.

Mobile Device Info	Acquisition			Behavior			Conversions		
	Sessions	% New Sessions	New Users	Bounce Rate	Pages / Session	Avg. Session Duration	Goal Conversion Rate	Goal Completions	Goal Value
	2,245 % of Total: 39.06% (5,747)	42.36% Avg for View: 34.31% (23.45%)	951 % of Total: 48.23% (1,972)	6.28% Avg for View: 3.85% (63.32%)	3.60 Avg for View: 5.14 (-29.92%)	00:01:29 Avg for View: 00:03:01 (-51.13%)	0.00% Avg for View: 0.00% (0.00%)	0 % of Total: 0.00% (0)	€0.00 % of Total: 0.00% (€0.00)
1. Apple iPhone	937 (41.74%)	44.40%	416 (43.74%)	11.31%	2.98	00:01:30	0.00%	0 (0.00%)	€0.00 (0.00%)
2. Apple iPad	547 (24.37%)	45.70%	250 (26.29%)	0.73%	4.59	00:01:33	0.00%	0 (0.00%)	€0.00 (0.00%)
3. Samsung GT-I9505 Galaxy S IV	115 (5.12%)	40.87%	47 (4.94%)	4.35%	2.63	00:00:40	0.00%	0 (0.00%)	€0.00 (0.00%)
4. Microsoft Windows RT Tablet	80 (3.56%)	6.25%	5 (0.53%)	0.00%	3.06	00:00:58	0.00%	0 (0.00%)	€0.00 (0.02%)
5. Samsung SM-G900F Galaxy S5	77 (3.43%)	32.47%	25 (2.63%)	2.60%	3.44	00:01:59	0.00%	0 (0.00%)	€0.00 (0.00%)
6. (not set)	59 (2.63%)	50.85%	30 (3.16%)	0.00%	4.75	00:01:26	0.00%	0 (0.00%)	€0.00 (0.00%)
7. Samsung SM-G900A Galaxy S5	33 (1.47%)	18.18%	6 (0.63%)	0.00%	2.61	00:00:11	0.00%	0 (0.00%)	€0.00 (0.00%)
8. Samsung GT-I8195 Galaxy S4 Mini	25 (1.11%)	36.00%	9 (0.95%)	8.00%	4.24	00:02:03	0.00%	0 (0.00%)	€0.00 (0.00%)
9. Motorola XT1032 Moto G	22 (0.98%)	68.18%	15 (1.58%)	0.00%	4.27	00:02:14	0.00%	0 (0.00%)	€0.00 (0.00%)
10. Samsung GT-I9195L Galaxy S4 Mini	16 (0.71%)	12.50%	2 (0.21%)	0.00%	2.82	00:00:04	0.00%	0 (0.00%)	€0.00 (0.00%)

Figure 8.15   Mobile Device Information within GA

Source: Google and the Google logo are registered trademarks of Google Inc.; used with permission.

Emerging Trends

By now you will be familiar with each stage of mobile marketing's iterative process; however, we must still finish stage 4 (see Figure 8.13). Now it's time to take a step back and look at the future of the industry so that you can:

- Be aware of current trends in the mobile marketplace.
- Find out ways in which you can capitalize on these trends.

Current Trends

Within the arena of mobile marketing, there are a few trends emerging of which you should be aware:

- *M-commerce.* Mobile commerce includes mobile wallets, NFC chips, and coupons that can be scanned. These technologies might not be widely adopted just yet, but more and more companies are competing within the m-commerce space and offering new ways for consumers to pay by mobile.
- *Geolocation.* This is really crucial, given the importance of context in mobile marketing. When you know where customers are, what they are searching for, and how they are using apps, your advertising can be more informed and targeted to their needs—for instance, with the use of iBeacon.
- *Showrooming.* This refers to users in physical stores checking online to see what a certain product might cost elsewhere. Smart brands like Apple have realized that as long as they get these users' business, it does not matter if they buy in-store or online. Apple's strategy is to use the physical store as a showroom, and the company even offers consumers devices on which they can browse. It is all about gaining the user's loyalty—so do not make the same mistake as the bookstores that tried to prevent customers from checking prices on Amazon. People now have connectivity in their pockets and they are going to use it. That is why brick-and-mortar retailers need to:
  - Offer something that makes consumers buy in the physical store. Understand that even if consumers don't buy from the physical store, they may buy from you online.
- *Wearable computing.* Slick technologies like Google Glass and Apple watches are not exactly commonplace right now, but they are certainly gaining traction. For instance, the immersive Oculus Rift has already meant huge benefits for gaming . . . what impact could such technologies have on marketing? Moreover, mobile health is a rapidly expanding area right now, given all the fitness trackers out there. These trackers can tell what people are doing, where they are, and so on—and this data could inform purchasing and marketing decisions as a result. This is one area on which you should definitely keep an eye for marketing opportunities.

By now you should have a much clearer idea of what mobile marketing is about. And now that you have seen the trends that are emerging within the industry, let's move on to the laws and guidelines to which you will need to adhere.

Laws and Guidelines

Having covered the opportunities that mobile offers digital marketers, the ways in which you can advertise, the importance of analytics, and the current trends, this chapter will conclude by addressing a few laws and guidelines.

In particular, this section will help you to:

- Understand the mobile marketing laws that apply to your country.
- Realize the fundamental areas of legislation, providing links to more information.
- Remember some key points for your mobile marketing strategy.

Laying Down the Law

In many respects, mobile is relatively new—so there are not a lot of laws or guidelines in place that relate to it. In fact, the mobile marketing industry changes so quickly that rules are often crafted as it moves along.

Still, mobile does have to adhere to certain standards such as:

- *Data protection and privacy*. These laws will differ depending on what country you are in, but www.dlapiperdataprotection.com and www.heatmap.forrestertools.com allow you to view legislation by location.
- *Copyright*. It is very easy to copy and paste digital content. Avoid temptation and ask for permission, give credit where credit is due, pay for content, or else create and copyright your own. To stay informed about updates in copyright legislation, go to www.copyright-watch.org.
- *Cookie policies*. As in the desktop world, there are laws relating to the information that you gather and retain about people's browsing habits. As mentioned in the section about effective mobile sites, there is less of an opportunity to do this on mobile devices (because you have limited access to local storage, which is usually dictated by the phone's operating system); however, even if you are only storing a little bit of information about the user, you need to make this known to the user. Because not everyone is a fan of cookies. You can find out more via www.cookielaw.org/faq.
- *Accessibility*. The nice thing about mobile is that operating systems usually cater really well to people with disabilities, in terms of accessing content. And in most instances, the operating system will take care of most of this for you with features that allow text to be spoken and images to be described, navigation assistance for the visually impaired, and so on. Learn more about accessibility issues at www.w3.org/WAI/mobile.

Thanks to the lack of laws relating to mobile, many bodies like the Mobile Marketing Association (MMA) have taken it upon themselves to enforce self-imposed guidelines. They promote best practices in the industry in the absence of laws or formal standards: Within the mobile marketing ecosystem there is a huge push towards self-regulation.

As a digital marketer, you too should operate by this code and refer to the MMA whenever you need guidance. It is all about being responsible in terms of what you do with users' data, respecting their privacy, and managing or storing content in the most sensitive way possible.

So, What Have You Learned in This Chapter?

Hopefully this chapter has shown you new ways in which you can reach customers—through the medium of mobile. Remember these key truths when devising your mobile strategy and you will be onto a winner:

- *There is only one web.* Since there is no such thing as separate desktop webs and mobile webs, everything should be responsive. Regardless of whether a user is using a desktop, a tablet, a phone, or a TV, content ends up in the same place and you should use responsive technologies to provide the best UX possible.
- *Keep in touch.* Because so many of your customers will come from mobile devices, you should make use of touch design. This lends itself to desktop too, because nowadays content is generally bigger, cleaner, and easier to use.
- *Context is key.* It has finally been understood that mobile users are absorbing information in a hurry, while they are on the go. That in turn has led to improvements in the desktop experience, with websites that use one-page scrolling, which provide concise information with a focus on clean layout and design.
- *Data is golden.* Everything is measurable and you should use your data/analytics to inform any commercial, marketing, and business decisions that you make.

Good luck, mobile marketers! May your content now shine from every screen.

 Go to www.artofdmi.com to access the case study on mobile marketing as additional support material for this chapter.

 Exercises

Exercise 1

Using Google Analytics, look at the data available for your current website and record:

- What percentage of users is coming from mobile?
- What is the mobile bounce rate versus desktop bounce rate?
- What are the most common mobile devices being used?
- Are your mobile visitors using phones or tablets?

- What time are users accessing your site?
- How long do your mobile visitors spend on your site?

Exercise 2

You have developed a new mobile app that allows users to download gluten-free recipes. You must decide on the revenue model for your app, taking the following into consideration:

- Which would work best for your customers?
- Which would yield more revenue?

Exercise 3

Set up an account on Google's AdMob Platform (www.google.com/admob). Try out the various tools that are available for banner ads and AdWords. Choose the channel that suits your business best. Set a small budget, choose channels, go live, and test the response.

Exercise 4

Create a custom QR code at http://goqr.me and make it link to a trackable page that is not your homepage. Track the number of people who use it. Put different QR codes on different media to identify media (e.g., leaflets, print ads, outdoor ads, etc.) that work best for activations.

Exercise 5

You are the manager of Groarkie's Gadgets, a local electrical store that is running a weekend clearance special. You want to send a message to customers who have previously purchased from your store. Craft an engaging SMS using the guidelines below:

- A single message with fewer than 160 characters.
- Includes an opt-out mechanism, which will eat into your character count (e.g., *text Stop to 53153*).
- Relevant and specific.
- Includes a CTA (e.g., *Sale now on* or *Save 20 percent this weekend*).
- Measurable (e.g., responses go to a URL—for online campaigns—or have a unique code—for physical campaigns—so you know what percentage of customers is getting through).

Action Plan: Mobile Marketing

Digital Marketing Planning Scheme for Mobile Marketing

Objectives

Reach, interaction, advocacy, conversion

Action Items and Frequency

- Mobile optimized website: Ongoing
- APPS: Ongoing
- SMS marketing: Per campaign
- Mobile advertising: Per campaign
- Proximity marketing: Per campaign

Measurement Tools and KPIs

- Average revenue per user (ARPU):

$$APRU = \frac{\text{Total revenue generated within a given time frame}}{\text{Total \# of active users within a given time frame}}$$

- Cost per install (CPI):

$$CPI = \frac{\text{Ad spend}}{\text{\# of new installs directly tied to ad campaign}}$$

- Cost per loyal user (CPLU):

$$CPLU = \frac{\text{Ad spend}}{\text{\# of new loyal users in response to ads}}$$

- Engagement: Session length and interval, app screens per session, conversion rates for events, interactions, opt-ins, and opt-outs
- Retention:

$$\text{Aggregate retention} = \frac{\text{\# of monthly active users}}{\text{\# of installs}}$$

$$\text{Retention for a given time period} = \frac{\text{of users retained at end of time period}}{\text{of installs at start of time period}}$$

Spend

Media	Content	People	Systems
x	x	x	X

Chapter 9
Analytics

An Introduction

Generally perceived as complex, dry, and scarily overwhelming, analytics does not have the most exciting reputation. Whilst it might give you sweaty palms, a racing heart, and keep you up all night panting breathlessly, it's for all the *wrong* reasons.

So let's look instead at what is sexy. Success. Slick marketing. Competitive advantage. Profit.

And how are these glorious things achieved? With killer insights, clues dug out of the data like rough diamonds, and wisdom polished into precise actions. Knowledge is power, after all, and analytics really brings the heat in that department! So whilst stats might not appear sexy, what can be done with them is, and this is the seductive beauty of analytics.

However, this beauty is somewhat buried. It's our job to see beyond analytics' intimidating exterior and focus on digging out the internal wisdom. Because if the inner workings of analytics can be understood, and the power of the insights gained can be optimized to meet specific needs, then a whole world of knowledge-based clarity will open up, achieving those sexy items outlined above!

> Formal definition of analytics: The process of measuring, collecting, analyzing, and reporting the behavior of visitors on a website, in order to understand and optimize web usage.
>
> Informal definition of analytics: What's the story behind the stats? (And it's a never-ending one.)

The online world shifts constantly, so analytics continually monitors and evaluates website traffic, forever asking: What is working, what isn't, why, and what are we doing about it?

It's a myth that analytics is just about data—it's actually more about reading between the lines to interpret that data. The challenge is to customize each report for specific needs, then dig out insights that help to optimize the site, understand the users, and meet business aims.

Process

In this chapter, you will explore the four key stages of the ongoing analytics process, as shown in Figure 9.1.

1 *Goals.* The process begins by setting goals for both the business and the website, then specifying how analytics will be used to help measure those goals. Analytics is about the who, what, when, how many, and why: This is the stage at which those questions are defined, the rationale behind them explored, and the answers to them discovered.
2 *Setup.* Here the groundwork is laid for answering the questions asked when setting your goals and for meeting those goals—by setting up a Google Analytics (GA) account and configuring it as needed. A solid working knowledge of GA and related tools is required for this. Once the structure and utility of GA is understood, as well as what levels of access and permissions are required, then the interface and reporting on goals can be organized.
3 *Monitor.* This stage involves top-level monitoring of audiences, traffic sources, and campaigns, as well as a critique of site performance. Having statistical context from the previous stages, the goals from stage 1 can now be refined further as preparation for diving into even deeper analysis.

Figure 9.1　Four-Stage Analytics Process

4 *Analyze*. This stage is incredibly data rich! It is both the beginning and the end of the cycle, the stage at which in-depth analysis is performed, targeted insights developed, business goals and strategy tweaked, and the reporting process started anew. This is the stage for studying to what extent KPIs and goals were met, for answering why or why not they were, and for making informed decisions to improve weak areas and to capitalize on strong ones.

Key Terms and Concepts

This chapter will teach you how to measure, monitor, and optimize your digital marketing activity using analytics. Here's what you will understand upon completion:

- Why businesses should adopt a formal analytics program.
- Which tools are available to measure and monitor online traffic.
- How to build standard, scheduled, and customized reports.
- How to set up accounts, profiles, permissions, and tracking codes.
- How to use GA to profile audiences and assess technical performance.
- How to measure engagement and conversion by tracking activities.
- The relationship between business KPIs and analytics goals.

Stage 1: Goals

Welcome to stage 1 of the analytics process, which is highlighted in Figure 9.2 and where you will learn how to set goals for both your business and website, and in turn, define how Google Analytics (GA) will be used to help measure those goals.

Figure 9.2   Focus on the First Stage in the Analytics Process

A smart digital marketing strategy provides you with the opportunity to achieve visibility in your brand and to excite potential customers. Being able to analyze your online activity, from creating content right through to serving ads, is critical to iterating its success.

However, digital professionals can sometimes find the effectiveness of their marketing difficult to measure, especially if there's an underlying uncertainty about its role within your overall digital marketing strategy.

If you want to be a successful digital marketer, you need to get existential: Before you start analyzing your online activities, ask yourself one simple question—what are you trying to find out? It's important to remember that in order to measure your success, metrics should always be aligned with your goals. You need to start by defining your objectives in using GA, some of which could include analyzing data in order to:

- Find out who your target audience is.
- Increase brand awareness and advocacy.
- Drive website traffic.
- Discover which areas of your site are causing high bounce rates.
- Increase lead generation and nurturing.
- Improve customer retention.
- Enhance upselling.
- Increase sales.

A very common reason why many digital marketing strategies fail is also an incredibly simple one—a failure to analyze the data. It might not seem like something worth spending time on, but if you give yourself the chance to really think about and identify your goals and overarching strategy you will be able to make much more informed decisions about how to use data to increase your digital marketing efforts.

Key Concepts

Before beginning, let's get familiar with some of the key concepts that will be covered in this chapter.

Dimensions and metrics. Dimensions describe data, whereas metrics measure data. For example, *users* is a dimension, and its measurement metric is the number of logged-in users. Studying both is what creates insight.

Cookies. Cookies are files exchanged between a web browser and a server that differentiate users. They track repeat views versus unique users (different visitors) without collecting personal data (no names, etc.). Cookies last 60 days, meaning one user would be counted as unique for this time period.

Data protection. All analytics services have to comply with data protection guidelines, which means not collecting personal data. Pay attention to local regulations, because not every country operates in the same way.

Key Terms

Next we introduce some key terms.

Session. A group of interactions that take place during a given time frame. For example, several different page views by the same unique user in the same window of time would be counted as one session.

Users. The number of nonduplicated users. If the user clears his cookies, he will be counted again.

Pages per session. The average number of page views that a person completed before exiting the site.

Average session duration. The average amount of time the user spent on the site. This is reported in minutes in GA, and in seconds in Google AdWords.

Percentage of new sessions. An estimate of the percentage of first-time visits.

Conversion. A completed activity that contributes to the success of the business. This could be represented by a range of different things; for example, a sale, or signing up for a newsletter.

Goal. A defined conversion, allowing measurement of the number of times that conversion was completed. There can be many different goals, and they are put in place to track performance.

Conversion rate. The rate at which users actually completed the goal or the transaction on your site.

Transaction. Different from a goal, this is a revenue metric. An e-commerce tracking function can be installed to track transactions.

Annotations. Notes (public or private) manually added to data that provide context; for example, elaborating on a spike in traffic by adding details about a related offline marketing activity.

Stage 2: Setup

To kick off our analytics module, let's examine the world's most widely used analytics tool: Google Analytics. GA has been referenced throughout this course, specifically tying in with the SEO, PPC, and social media modules, so let's dive into an examination of how it works.

This section is concerned with the second stage in the analytics process (highlighted in Figure 9.3), or setting up a GA account. Once you have finished it you will understand:

- The benefits of GA compared to other tools.
- The structure of GA and its varying access levels.
- How to set up a GA account and navigate its interface.
- Which types of reports can be pulled.

Figure 9.3 Focus on the Second Stage in the Analytics Process

GA Overview

GA operates a constant system of collection, measurement, and analysis of website data.

Technically speaking, this works in the following way:

1 When setting up GA, a code is provided that must be inserted into your website.
2 When that webpage is displayed to a user, the analytics code drops cookies.
3 Cookies (which track users) are dropped, and data is communicated back to GA.
4 This data is processed in the GA backend then presented in the interface.

Why GA?

There are other analytics tools on the market, but GA perks are difficult to beat:

• Free.
• Industry standard, used by 98 percent of brands.
• Simple to use for most e-commerce platforms and websites.
• Highly customizable for specific business/campaign needs.
• Integrates nicely with other Google products (e.g., AdWords and Webmaster).
• Extensive online support and tutorials.

Free versus Paid

There is also a paid version of GA, called Universal Analytics, which offers greater functionality and more in-depth reporting. It is used mostly by larger global brands—the free version of GA, however, is more than sufficient for most marketers.

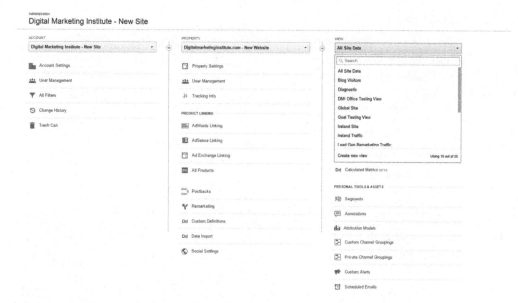

Figure 9.4   GA Three-Section Structure
Source: Google and the Google logo are registered trademarks of Google Inc.; used with permission.

GA Account Structure

To set up the account properly, it's important to first understand that GA is structured into three sections: Account, Property and View, as shown in Figure 9.4.

1 *Account* refers to the actual GA account; for example, the business or brand.
2 *Property* refers to each individual website, and businesses can add more than one.
3 *View* refers to the filter that is applied to the data. For example, a filter that excludes internal traffic can be applied.

GA Access Levels

GA provides four levels of user access, which, for administrative and security reasons, is very useful. For example, in large companies, it may be problematic to have several hundred people accessing and editing the same data! The levels of access are:

1 *Managed User.* Administrative level; can do absolutely everything.
2 *Edit.* Administrative level functions without the ability to add or delete users. This is the minimum level of access required to link GA with Google AdWords.
3 *Collaborate.* Can edit shared assets and read and analyze all reports.
4 *Read and Analyze.* Can make no changes, just observations.

GA Account Setup

Now the structure and the tiers of access are understood, let's set up an account.

1 Type in www.google.com/analytics.

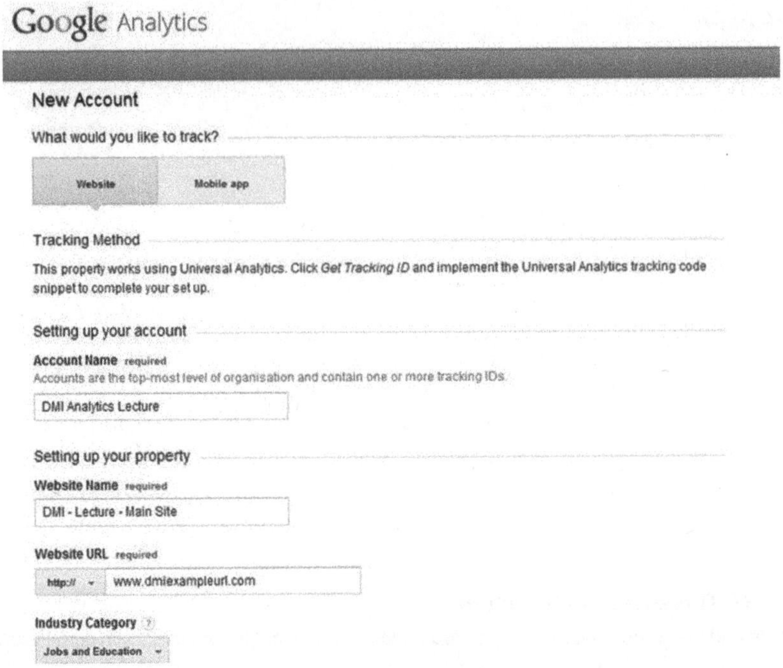

Google Analytics

New Account

What would you like to track?

| Website | Mobile app |

Tracking Method

This property works using Universal Analytics. Click *Get Tracking ID* and implement the Universal Analytics tracking code snippet to complete your set up.

Setting up your account

Account Name required
Accounts are the top-most level of organisation and contain one or more tracking IDs.

DMI Analytics Lecture

Setting up your property

Website Name required

DMI - Lecture - Main Site

Website URL required

| http:// ▾ | www.dmiexampleurl.com |

Industry Category ⓘ

Jobs and Education ▾

Figure 9.5   GA Setup

Source: Google and the Google logo are registered trademarks of Google Inc.; used with permission.

2 Click on the sign-up button to enter your details. You will need a Google account, such as Gmail or AdWords, to register.
3 Name your account in the field shown in Figure 9.5. This is you, or the brand/business you represent.
4 Add properties. Add the URLs of the sites you wish to track.
5 Set any views required; for example, one that excludes internal traffic. These filters are covered in detail later, but essentially the View function enables reports to be organized into different sets. These sets can be named for convenience and tailored for certain users.
6 Set your time zone correctly, as shown in Figure 9.6. Once set it can't be changed, and your data will be skewed if it is wrong!
7 Get your tracking code. This facilitates the tracking of the site and is shown in Figure 9.7. In some instances it may need customizing. For example, if your site accepts transactions you will need to set up a special e-commerce code.
8 Add your tracking code to your website. This should be inserted immediately before the closing header tag, at the top of the page. Remember, the lower down the code is inserted, the longer it takes to load—which could mean hits are not recorded correctly.
9 Adjust account settings. Customize the GA interface to meet your needs, using the Admin tab (see below).

GA Navigation

Having set up your account, let's now look at how to navigate around it. First, you will be presented with a page showing these tabs: Home, Reporting, Customization, and Admin.

Reporting Time Zone

| United States ▾ | (GMT-08:00) Pacific Time ▾ |

Data Sharing Settings ⑦

Data that is collected, processed, and stored in your Google Analytics account ("Google Analytics data") is secure and kept confidential. Google Analytics data is used to provide and maintain the service, to perform system critical operations, and in rare exceptions for legal reasons as described in our privacy policy.

The data sharing options give you more control over sharing your Google Analytics data. Learn more.

✓ With other Google products only RECOMMENDED
Enable enhanced ad features, and an improved experience with AdWords, AdSense and other Google products by sharing your website's Google Analytics data with other Google services, and develop better Google services by sharing non-personal data. Only Google services (no third parties) will be able to access your data. Show example

✓ Anonymously with Google and others RECOMMENDED
Enable benchmarking by sharing your website data in an anonymous form. Google will remove all identifiable information about your website, combine the data with other anonymous sites in comparable industries and report aggregate trends in the benchmarking service. Show example

✓ Technical support RECOMMENDED
Let Google technical support representatives access your Google Analytics data and account when necessary to provide service and find solutions to technical issues.

✓ Account specialists RECOMMENDED
Give Google marketing specialists and your Google sales specialists access to your Google Analytics data and account so they can find ways to improve your configuration and analysis, and share optimization tips with you. If you don't have dedicated sales specialists, give this access to authorized Google representatives.

Learn how Google Analytics safeguards your data.

Figure 9.6   Setting GA Time Zone
Source: Google and the Google logo are registered trademarks of Google Inc.; used with permission.

Home. This is the view you will be presented with upon log-in. It displays the account, with the properties and views listed beneath. If you have got multiple accounts, properties, or views, it is possible to flag specific ones to create a more customized view.

Admin. This tab configures different settings for each individual property, such as setting the default page, excluding URL query parameters, making e-commerce site selections, setting session time-out length, and setting up site search. You can also import media spends and add PPC data.

Customization. This tab is where you will find any custom reports once they have been configured.

Reporting. This is essentially the main menu, containing dashboards, shortcuts, intelligence events, and all the standard reports. The default report shown is Audience, which provides a website overview.

Under Reporting you can also set Intelligence Events. These are alerts that can be designed to go out in real time, to specific GA users, in order to flag events that are relevant to the business. For example, you may want to set an IT alert should the site stop loading.

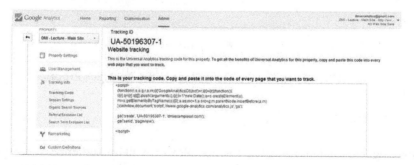

Figure 9.7   GA Tracking Code
Source: Google and the Google logo are registered trademarks of Google Inc.; used with permission.

Gaining a return from analytics requires ongoing monitoring, analysis, and enhancement, but understanding the setup, functionality, and structuring of GA is the first step in this process. Stage 3 will now apply this knowledge and explore GA at a much deeper level.

Stage 3: Monitor

Now that you understand how to set up GA, it's time to look at the different types of reports available and how these can help improve your website.

This section addresses stage 3 of the analytics process—monitoring audience data, as shown in Figure 9.8—and explains how GA can show who site users are and how they behave.

By the end of this section you will:

- Understand how analytics helps us learn about audiences.
- Recognize the user journey that analytics tools can track.
- Appreciate the wider marketing and business implications of online audience analytics.

Figure 9.8   Focus on the Third Stage in the Analytics Process

Audience Overview

When logging into the Reporting tab, the default view will be Audience, as shown in Figure 9.9. Let's explore some of the information available here, the reasons for analyzing it, and the type of insights it can produce.

Figure 9.9   Audience Overview Section of GA Reporting
Source: Google and the Google logo are registered trademarks of Google Inc.; used with permission.

Demographics

Demographics analytics is about understanding who users are so they can be better targeted. *Age and gender* are prominent filters on the GA dashboard and the data reveals how each demographic behaves. Insights can be drawn that have huge implications; for example, noticing that females convert more often than males, as in Figure 9.10, might mean an adjustment in targeting is needed.

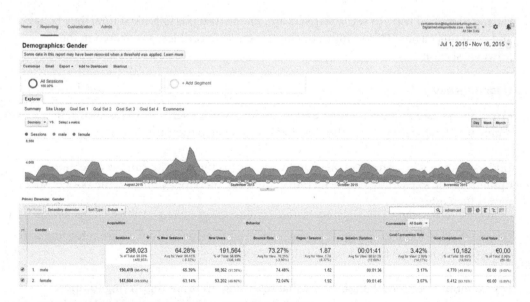

Figure 9.10   Demographics Section of GA Reporting
Source: Google and the Google logo are registered trademarks of Google Inc.; used with permission.

Country	Acquisition			Behavior			Conversions All Goals		
	Sessions	% New Sessions	New Users	Bounce Rate	Pages / Session	Avg. Session Duration	Goal Conversion Rate	Goal Completions	Goal Value
	489,937 (% of Total 100.00% (489,937))	68.65% (Avg for View: 68.61% (0.05%))	336,336 (% of Total 100.05% (336,152))	76.25% (Avg for View: 76.26% (0.00%))	1.76 (Avg for View: 1.76 (0.00%))	00:01:29 (Avg for View: 00:01:29 (0.00%))	2.99% (Avg for View: 2.99% (0.00%))	14,661 (% of Total 100.05% (14,661))	€0.00 (% of Total 0.00% (€0.00))
1. United Kingdom	95,821 (19.56%)	68.44%	65,582 (19.94%)	72.97%	1.86	00:01:27	3.57%	3,422 (23.34%)	€0.00 (0.00%)
2. Ireland	94,916 (19.36%)	59.96%	56,842 (16.90%)	77.11%	1.75	00:01:16	2.36%	2,236 (15.25%)	€0.00 (0.00%)
3. United States	57,106 (11.66%)	80.44%	45,937 (13.66%)	85.34%	1.40	00:00:46	1.25%	712 (4.86%)	€0.00 (0.00%)
4. India	33,654 (6.87%)	76.04%	25,591 (7.61%)	67.45%	1.96	00:02:16	2.92%	984 (6.71%)	€0.00 (0.00%)
5. Bahrain	26,639 (5.44%)	59.59%	15,873 (4.72%)	92.81%	1.11	00:00:30	0.49%	131 (0.89%)	€0.00 (0.00%)
6. South Africa	15,125 (3.09%)	67.70%	10,240 (3.04%)	77.41%	1.68	00:01:43	3.74%	556 (3.85%)	€0.00 (0.00%)
7. Australia	12,289 (2.51%)	71.69%	8,810 (2.62%)	78.32%	1.64	00:01:19	2.99%	368 (2.51%)	€0.00 (0.00%)
8. Belgium	10,615 (2.17%)	74.96%	7,957 (2.37%)	91.70%	1.26	00:00:26	0.71%	75 (0.51%)	€0.00 (0.00%)
9. France	8,910 (1.86%)	80.23%	7,068 (2.10%)	87.87%	1.35	00:00:41	1.38%	122 (0.83%)	€0.00 (0.00%)
10. Canada	7,684 (1.52%)	77.67%	5,968 (1.77%)	80.80%	1.56	00:01:02	1.57%	121 (0.83%)	€0.00 (0.00%)

Show rows: 10 ▼ Go to: 1 1 - 10 of 210 ◄ ►

Figure 9.11   Geo Section of GA Reporting

Source: Google and the Google logo are registered trademarks of Google Inc.; used with permission.

Geo

Location data shows which countries the site is accessed from and by how many people, as shown in Figure 9.11. It helps ensure an appropriate marketing strategy and can highlight new opportunities; for example, growing traffic from a currently untargeted country.

Language data can be very revealing; for example, learning that most of the audience are nonnative speakers of the website language would necessitate some strategy adaption!

Behavior

Having identified ways to see who users are, the next step is to look at how they behave and what this means. This requires tracking users with cookies, as covered in the previous section.

User Journey

Mapping the user journey is about understanding which users return (as shown in Figure 9.12), what they do on the site, and how engaged they are.

Understanding who converts when, and why, means the website can become more optimized, the sales funnel more lucrative, the copy more relevant, and the budget spent more efficiently.

Ultimately, it is about defining what new users want versus those who are returning and using that knowledge to guide each subtly to a sale.

For example, your report might show that returning users are registering for more information before eventually converting. In this case, it might be ideal to launch an email campaign targeting only returning users and speed up the process by selling

User Type	Acquisition: Sessions	Acquisition: % New Sessions	Acquisition: New Users	Behavior: Bounce Rate	Behavior: Pages / Session	Behavior: Avg. Session Duration	Conversions (All Goals): Goal Conversion Rate	Conversions: Goal Completions	Conversions: Goal Value
	489,940	68.65%	336,338	76.25%	1.76	00:01:29	2.99%	14,661	€0.00
1. New Visitor	336,338 (68.65%)	100.00%	336,338 (100.00%)	78.31%	1.65	00:01:08	2.11%	7,109 (48.49%)	€0.00 (0.00%)
2. Returning Visitor	153,602 (31.35%)	0.00%	0 (0.00%)	71.73%	2.00	00:02:15	4.92%	7,552 (51.51%)	€0.00 (0.00%)

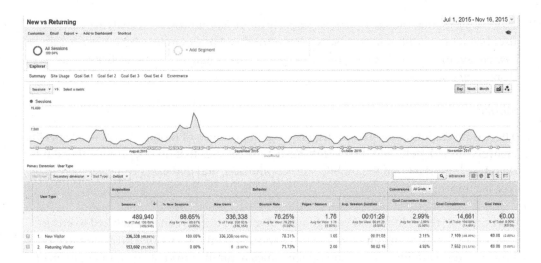

Figure 9.12 User Journey Information in GA
Source: Google and the Google logo are registered trademarks of Google Inc.; used with permission.

higher up in the sales funnel. They are already quite likely to purchase, so this would be an efficient way to capitalize on targeted leads.

Technology

Behavior also highlights technical issues. This is useful for two reasons—it improves user experience and ensures the site operates properly—both of which improve conversions!

Audiences will quickly lose interest if the site does not provide them with a beneficial user experience, so it vital that user behavior is monitored across a range of devices, to ensure that engagement is fairly consistent. See, for example, the engagement across different screen resolutions in Figure 9.13. Ultimately ensuring consistency among these resolutions will impact conversion rates.

Screen Resolution	Acquisition: Sessions	Acquisition: % New Sessions	Acquisition: New Users	Behavior: Bounce Rate	Behavior: Pages / Session	Behavior: Avg. Session Duration	Conversions (All Goals): Goal Conversion Rate	Conversions: Goal Completions	Conversions: Goal Value
	489,945	68.65%	336,342	76.25%	1.76	00:01:29	2.99%	14,662	€0.00
1. 1366x768	80,114 (16.35%)	66.73%	53,464 (15.90%)	64.23%	2.20	00:02:34	4.44%	3,556 (24.25%)	€0.00 (0.00%)
2. 768x1024	50,555 (10.32%)	62.23%	31,458 (9.35%)	86.86%	1.40	00:00:54	1.17%	592 (4.04%)	€0.00 (0.00%)
3. 360x640	43,894 (8.96%)	69.81%	30,641 (9.11%)	84.40%	1.43	00:00:54	2.32%	1,020 (6.96%)	€0.00 (0.00%)
4. 320x568	34,570 (7.06%)	73.66%	25,463 (7.57%)	86.59%	1.34	00:00:38	2.13%	737 (5.03%)	€0.00 (0.00%)
5. 1920x1080	31,347 (6.40%)	67.20%	21,066 (6.26%)	62.34%	2.36	00:02:12	4.92%	1,542 (10.52%)	€0.00 (0.00%)
6. 1280x800	28,223 (5.76%)	62.74%	17,708 (5.26%)	68.71%	2.06	00:02:04	3.67%	1,036 (7.06%)	€0.00 (0.00%)
7. 1440x900	22,751 (4.64%)	65.57%	14,918 (4.44%)	63.04%	2.30	00:02:17	4.11%	936 (6.38%)	€0.00 (0.00%)
8. 375x667	19,923 (4.07%)	71.30%	14,206 (4.22%)	83.90%	1.39	00:00:42	2.64%	525 (3.58%)	€0.00 (0.00%)
9. 1600x900	15,060 (3.07%)	65.42%	9,853 (2.93%)	63.79%	2.24	00:02:17	3.80%	573 (3.91%)	€0.00 (0.00%)
10. 1280x1024	14,500 (2.96%)	73.81%	10,702 (3.18%)	67.44%	2.14	00:01:46	3.50%	508 (3.46%)	€0.00 (0.00%)

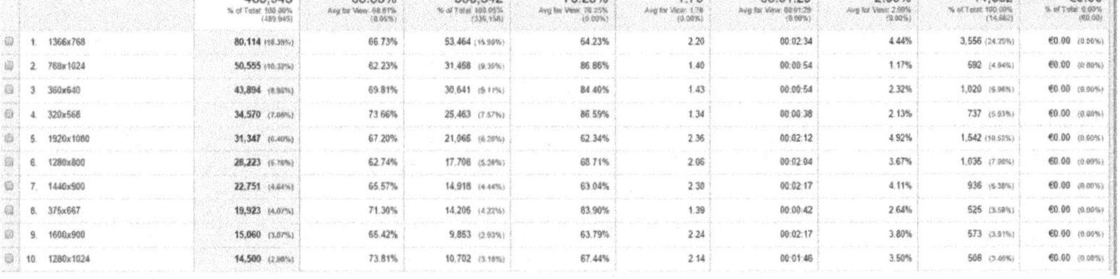

Figure 9.13 Technology Information in GA
Source: Google and the Google logo are registered trademarks of Google Inc.; used with permission.

It is important that the site operates properly on different browsers; analytics can track user behavior on different browsers to monitor this. For example, a high bounce rate or low engagement among Safari, but not Chrome, users may mean the website is not displaying correctly.

Mobile

There is no disputing the enormous, growing importance of mobile. Users want specific answers immediately, and they won't waste time on sites that do not provide them! It is therefore important that the mobile site is optimized, and that users can easily navigate to what they need.

Data (such as the volume and engagement of mobile traffic) can be analyzed to ensure this is the case. Bear in mind that the fast nature of on-the-go mobile browsing makes bounce rates naturally higher, and on-site times naturally lower, as seen in Figure 9.14. This is to be expected, but if users leave instantly or CTA conversions are pitiful, then perhaps the site needs improvement! The CTA could be stronger, for example, with a click-to-call button or reorganization of information.

Offline Implications

Online user data can powerfully inform offline marketing too. Website stats detail who audience members are and how likely they are to convert so precisely that it could lead to a real shift in wider strategy. Sometimes it can even uncover audiences the business was previously unaware of!

By understanding who users are and how they behave, a picture begins to emerge of the website changes that are required—both technical and with respect to content. The aim is to use this knowledge to make the site as targeted as possible, and as the next few sections explain, to understand and apply analytics in a way that is relevant to the business context!

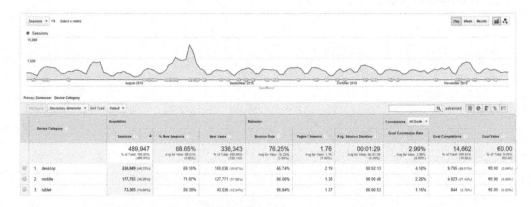

Figure 9.14   Sessions by Device Category in GA
Source: Google and the Google logo are registered trademarks of Google Inc.; used with permission.

Acquisition

Having looked at how to determine who users are and how they behave, this section now focuses on where they come from.

This section is about measuring, reporting on, and comparing the value of different website and campaign traffic sources. It provides an overview of the various channel reports GA can produce and how to go about setting these up. By the end of this section, you will understand:

- Why acquisition reporting is important and what it entails.
- The different channels that GA can report on.
- How to integrate Google AdWords and the benefits and rationale for doing so.
- How to use the Google URL Builder and set up custom tracking of online campaigns.

Acquisition Reporting

Acquisition reporting involves the measurement and evaluation of traffic sources, and there are numerous ways this can be done in GA. The abundance of data and reporting options can seem overwhelming, so remember to focus on developing and using only relevant reports. Customizing GA, Custom Channels, interpreting data, and medium and source are covered next.

Customizing GA

GA is highly customizable, and Custom Channels (used to track personalized channels as required) can be added easily under the Admin tab. Similarly, there is a comprehensive Advanced Search tool located in the top right-hand corner. This can be used to filter traffic types, among other variables, with a simple drop-down menu.

Custom Channels Overview

To begin, simply click into Acquisition and then Overview within GA to produce a top-level breakdown of the different traffic-driving channels, displayed in the basic charts seen in Figure 9.15. The aim is to understand which channels bring not just the highest volume of traffic, but crucially, the most valuable, engaged, and high-converting traffic.

Interpreting Data

Channel data such as bounce rate, total sessions, and conversions can be examined, and areas for development highlighted. An important analysis is the number of goals that each channel delivers; for example, if organic search achieves a high volume of goals, maybe paid search should expand.

Just remember to avoid assumptions—instead draw conclusions that make sense to the business in question and prioritize relevant channels!

Medium and Source

Reports can be organized and viewed by medium (the channel) and source (the specific platform), as shown in Figure 9.16. For example, you might search for the medium *organic search* and the source *Google*. Similarly, the medium might be *display* and the source the *New York Times*.

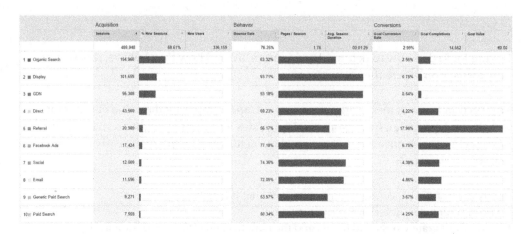

Figure 9.15   GA Custom Channels Overview
Source: Google and the Google logo are registered trademarks of Google Inc.; used with permission.

Important Traffic Channels

The following are key traffic sources that often yield very interesting data! Should you encounter a *not provided* notification, fear not! Data from users logged in to any Google account (such as YouTube, Gmail, etc.) is not passed on, and this is Google's notification that some data can't be provided.

Organic Search

Organic search can drive very high volumes of valuable traffic, as the user will already be aware of the brand and ready to engage with it. Traffic will be mostly from Google, but will also include sources such as Bing and Yahoo, despite their small share. In some contexts (such as markets where sources other than Google have a bigger share) this can be very

Source / Medium	Acquisition			Behavior		
	Sessions ↓	% New Sessions	New Users	Bounce Rate	Pages / Session	Avg. Session Duration
	1,427 % of Total: 100.00% (1,427)	77.44% Avg for View: 77.37% (0.09%)	1,105 % of Total: 100.09% (1,104)	47.93% Avg for View: 47.93% (0.00%)	2.31 Avg for View: 2.31 (0.00%)	00:01:24 Avg for View: 00:01:24 (0.00%)
1. google / organic	672 (47.09%)	79.17%	532 (48.14%)	37.20%	2.62	00:01:39
2. google / cpc	343 (24.04%)	69.39%	238 (21.54%)	43.73%	2.31	00:01:35
3. (direct) / (none)	226 (15.84%)	71.24%	161 (14.57%)	68.14%	1.83	00:01:01
4. site37.social-buttons.com / referral	37 (2.59%)	100.00%	37 (3.35%)	100.00%	1.00	00:00:00
5. social-buttons.com / referral	26 (1.82%)	100.00%	26 (2.35%)	100.00%	1.00	00:00:00
6. yahoo / organic	24 (1.68%)	75.00%	18 (1.63%)	33.33%	2.25	00:01:16
7. site21.social-buttons.com / referral	21 (1.47%)	100.00%	21 (1.90%)	100.00%	1.00	00:00:00
8. site18.social-buttons.com / referral	18 (1.26%)	100.00%	18 (1.63%)	100.00%	1.00	00:00:00
9. bing / organic	15 (1.05%)	86.67%	13 (1.18%)	33.33%	2.47	00:00:34
10. t.co / referral	6 (0.42%)	100.00%	6 (0.54%)	50.00%	3.17	00:01:21

Figure 9.16   GA Report by Source/Medium
Source: Google and the Google logo are registered trademarks of Google Inc.; used with permission.

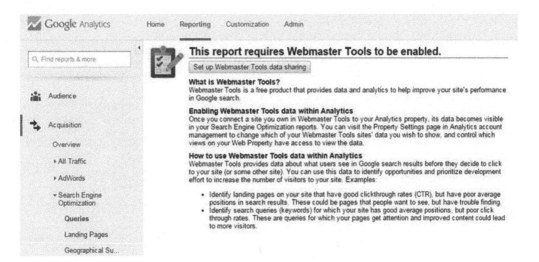

Figure 9.17   The Search Engine Optimization Section within Acquisition Leads to the Process of Linking Webmaster Tools with GA

Source: Google and the Google logo are registered trademarks of Google Inc.; used with permission.

useful data that can lead to changes in strategy; for example, if Bing traffic had a lower bounce rate associated with it.

Google Webmaster Tools

By linking Webmaster Tools with GA, a lot more data becomes available. As can be seen in Figure 9.17, the options listed under Search Engine Optimization will lead to the simple Webmaster Tools set-up process. Once the accounts are linked, it is possible to see all the organic search keywords driving traffic, the volume of traffic they drive, and how these keywords rank.

Knowing which keywords do, and do not, deliver traffic and conversions is very helpful. Keywords that perform well could inform an SEO strategy, increase organic traffic, and be used in AdWords. It is also useful to see which landing pages perform best and which could be optimized to increase rankings, achieve higher click-throughs, and ultimately get more traffic.

Referral Traffic

This means traffic that comes from another website; for example, when a user follows a link. Click on Referrals to view the sites that are referring the traffic and to compare data between different referrers.

Using the averages displayed in the top bar in Figure 9.18, it is possible to gauge the quality of that traffic; for example, to evaluate how engaged users are, how long they stay, and whether they convert. The insights gained here could direct a wider SEO strategy. If, for example, your site was drawing in a lot of traffic from a particular channel, you could capitalize on that by adding a permanent backlink.

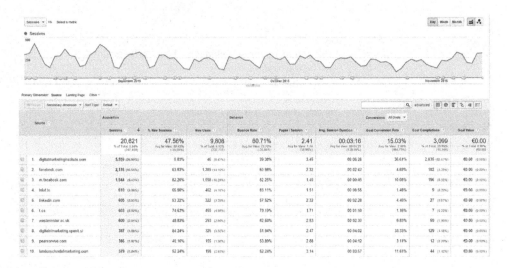

Figure 9.18   Referral Traffic Information within GA

Source: Google and the Google logo are registered trademarks of Google Inc.; used with permission.

Social

It can be tempting to think of social channels as their own entities, separate from the website. It might be said, for instance, that Facebook engages users on a page, aids brand awareness, and drives some traffic to the site—which is great. However, it would be much wiser to treat it as an extension of the sales funnel, and use it as a starting point in the conversion process! GA therefore monitors much more than social-media traffic volumes; it also reports on the quality of that traffic (as shown in Figure 9.19) and to what extent specifically goals and conversions are achieved.

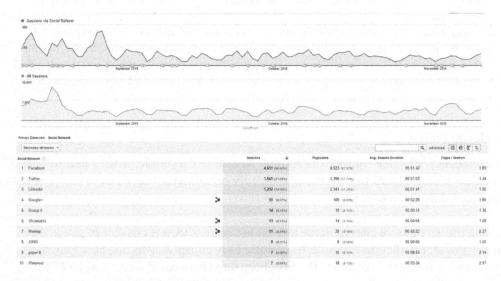

Figure 9.19   Social Referral Information within GA

Source: Google and the Google logo are registered trademarks of Google Inc.; used with permission.

Campaigns

Along with tracking channels, it is also important to report on the traffic performance of individual campaigns. Again, metrics such as bounce rate, sessions, pages per session, and average session duration are all incredibly useful in evaluating and justifying campaigns.

AdWords

The real magic of AdWords and GA is in linking them to combine their data, as shown in Figure 9.20.

Why Link AdWords and GA?

Once you you're your AdWords and GA accounts, a specific, richly detailed AdWords report is produced in GA, detailing clicks, costs, pages per session, conversion rate, and goal completions. Seeing how traffic engages helps to justify the CPC, and the most valuable campaigns can then be identified and prioritized.

Don't worry if the data displayed in GA and AdWords does not match exactly; a 20 percent discrepancy is actually normal. This is because each records things like backclicks and double clicks differently, and occasionally the GA code can be slow to load.

Figure 9.20   Process of Linking Google AdWords and GA

Source: Google and the Google logo are registered trademarks of Google Inc.; used with permission.

How to Link AdWords and Analytics

In order to link these two platforms, the same email address is required, and a minimum of Edit or Admin access is necessary in each interface. From the GA Admin tab navigate to Property, select the AdWords linking section, name the link group, and then tick the desired link view.

Day Parting

This reveals which times deliver the best value for click-throughs, engagement, and reaching particular AdWords goals. Traffic value depends entirely on the KPIs and goals in place; maybe the aim is site engagement, or perhaps it's hard conversion. Either way, progress can be reported hourly, as shown in Figure 9.21, showing when to invest or reduce effort, and when to increase or decrease bids.

Google URL Builder

The Google URL Builder tags each element within a campaign, so that analytics data can be organized very specifically and later pulled into relevant reports, as Figure 9.22 shows. The builder creates a URL for each campaign component, categorizing everything to track campaigns very precisely.

AdWords data is automatically tagged and does not need the URL Builder. It is necessary for all other campaigns, however, or traffic will simply be classified as referral traffic, and insights will lack significance. The key with the URL Builder is to use a consistent naming convention, so that elements are tagged appropriately and pulled into reports when required.

Hour	Acquisition			Behavior			Conversions All Goals		
	Sessions	% New Sessions	New Users	Bounce Rate	Pages / Session	Avg. Session Duration	Goal Conversion Rate	Goal Completions	Goal Value
	159,835 % of Total 46.01% (347,498)	68.04% Avg for View 66.43% (+0.57%)	108,756 % of Total 45.73% (237,787)	88.95% Avg for View 76.70% (15.96%)	1.28 Avg for View 1.76 (-28.22%)	00:00:33 Avg for View 00:01:25 (-60.98%)	1.09% Avg for View 2.98% (-63.40%)	1,742 % of Total 16.94% (10,344)	€0.00 % of Total 0.00% (€0.00)
1. 00	14,037 (8.78%)	79.50%	11,159 (10.26%)	93.92%	1.11	00:00:15	0.50%	70 (4.02%)	€0.00 (0.00%)
2. 01	7,684 (4.81%)	75.86%	5,829 (5.36%)	93.36%	1.15	00:00:16	0.66%	51 (2.93%)	€0.00 (0.00%)
3. 02	4,892 (3.06%)	75.02%	3,670 (3.37%)	92.52%	1.16	00:00:20	0.59%	29 (1.66%)	€0.00 (0.00%)
4. 03	4,256 (2.68%)	75.09%	3,196 (2.94%)	90.67%	1.22	00:00:29	1.08%	46 (2.64%)	€0.00 (0.00%)
5. 04	4,076 (2.55%)	73.85%	3,010 (2.77%)	90.19%	1.22	00:00:27	1.15%	47 (2.70%)	€0.00 (0.00%)
6. 05	4,318 (2.70%)	73.88%	3,190 (2.93%)	88.70%	1.27	00:00:33	1.81%	78 (4.48%)	€0.00 (0.00%)
7. 06	5,473 (3.42%)	73.09%	4,000 (3.68%)	89.80%	1.21	00:00:31	1.41%	77 (4.42%)	€0.00 (0.00%)
8. 07	8,151 (5.10%)	72.69%	5,925 (5.45%)	90.99%	1.21	00:00:28	1.19%	97 (5.57%)	€0.00 (0.00%)
9. 08	7,922 (4.96%)	67.95%	5,383 (4.95%)	89.26%	1.26	00:00:34	1.25%	99 (5.68%)	€0.00 (0.00%)
10. 09	8,329 (5.21%)	66.23%	5,516 (5.07%)	87.97%	1.31	00:00:37	1.28%	107 (6.14%)	€0.00 (0.00%)
11. 10	8,410 (5.26%)	66.80%	5,618 (5.17%)	87.22%	1.37	00:00:41	1.15%	97 (5.57%)	€0.00 (0.00%)
12. 11	8,058 (5.04%)	67.56%	5,444 (5.01%)	86.97%	1.37	00:00:37	0.97%	78 (4.48%)	€0.00 (0.00%)
13. 12	7,164 (4.48%)	64.78%	4,641 (4.27%)	85.86%	1.39	00:00:41	1.47%	105 (6.03%)	€0.00 (0.00%)
14. 13	7,048 (4.41%)	64.51%	4,547 (4.18%)	86.76%	1.38	00:00:41	1.09%	77 (4.42%)	€0.00 (0.00%)
15. 14	6,867 (4.30%)	62.94%	4,322 (3.97%)	86.76%	1.40	00:00:44	1.24%	85 (4.88%)	€0.00 (0.00%)
16. 15	6,912 (4.32%)	61.57%	4,256 (3.91%)	85.29%	1.41	00:00:49	1.29%	89 (5.11%)	€0.00 (0.00%)
17. 16	6,788 (4.25%)	62.57%	4,247 (3.91%)	85.34%	1.41	00:00:47	1.18%	80 (4.59%)	€0.00 (0.00%)
18. 17	7,327 (4.58%)	64.61%	4,734 (4.35%)	89.18%	1.27	00:00:33	1.01%	74 (4.25%)	€0.00 (0.00%)
19. 18	7,640 (4.78%)	65.18%	4,980 (4.58%)	90.37%	1.22	00:00:31	0.76%	58 (3.33%)	€0.00 (0.00%)
20. 19	6,274 (3.93%)	62.93%	3,948 (3.63%)	89.13%	1.24	00:00:34	1.07%	67 (3.85%)	€0.00 (0.00%)
21. 20	5,772 (3.61%)	62.47%	3,606 (3.32%)	88.60%	1.29	00:00:34	1.23%	71 (4.08%)	€0.00 (0.00%)

Figure 9.21   Day Parting Report within GA
Source: Google and the Google logo are registered trademarks of Google Inc.; used with permission.

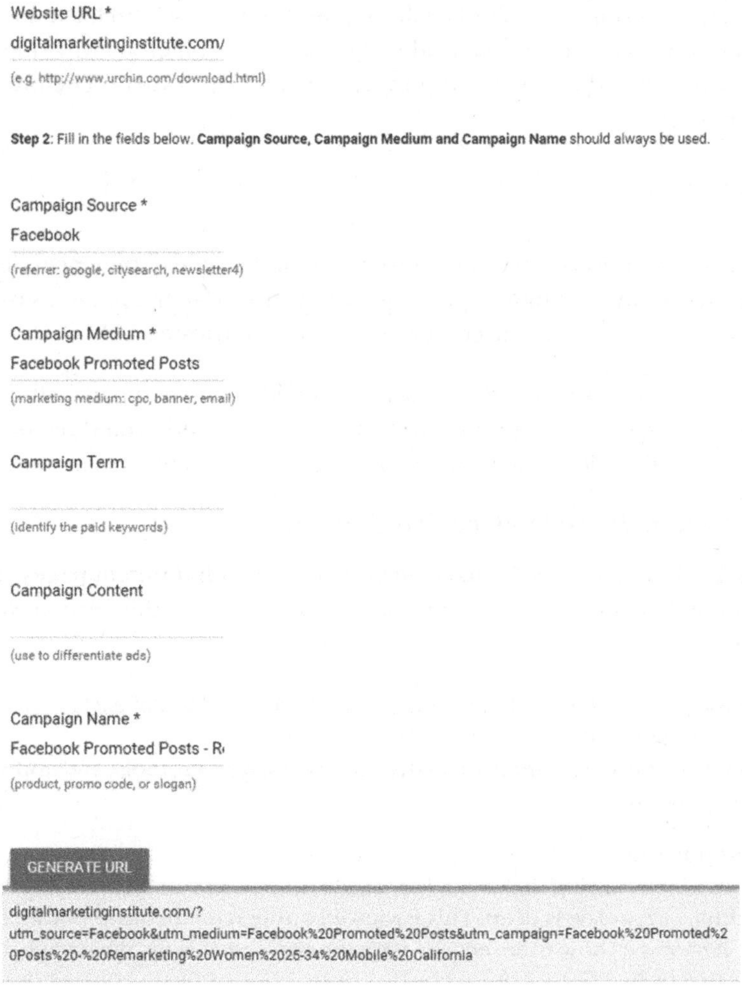

Website URL *

digitalmarketinginstitute.com/

(e.g. http://www.urchin.com/download.html)

Step 2: Fill in the fields below. **Campaign Source, Campaign Medium and Campaign Name** should always be used.

Campaign Source *

Facebook

(referrer: google, citysearch, newsletter4)

Campaign Medium *

Facebook Promoted Posts

(marketing medium: cpc, banner, email)

Campaign Term

(Identify the paid keywords)

Campaign Content

(use to differentiate ads)

Campaign Name *

Facebook Promoted Posts - R

(product, promo code, or slogan)

GENERATE URL

digitalmarketinginstitute.com/?
utm_source=Facebook&utm_medium=Facebook%20Promoted%20Posts&utm_campaign=Facebook%20Promoted%2
0Posts%20-%20Remarketing%20Women%2025-34%20Mobile%20California

Figure 9.22   Google URL Builder
Source: Google and the Google logo are registered trademarks of Google Inc.; used with permission.

As an example, when filling out URL Builder fields for the campaign, you could add the following:

- Website URL (e.g., www.external-website-campaign.com).
- Source (e.g., the *New York Times*).
- Medium (e.g., display).
- Term (e.g., optional keyword).
- Content (use a word that will differentiate among similar campaign ads).
- Campaign Name (e.g., September 2025).

Upon hitting Submit, a long URL is produced that tells GA the source, medium, name, term, and content tags—and just like that, campaign data will now be collected and organized correctly!

Depending on the business needs of each campaign, there are both basic and complex ways to track and analyze traffic. Crucially, there are also numerous ways to interpret the data, and you should ensure the reporting organization is spot-on before making wild assumptions!

Behavior

Having established various ways to monitor traffic and segment audiences, let's now examine on-site behavior. Applying what we've learned from the previous two sections, it's time to start to mapping the user journey at a more intricate level.

This section is very important and so it has been divided into two parts—the first is focused on using analytics to optimize website content by understanding the user journey; the second explores two particularly useful behavioral tools in more detail.

Using Analytics to Understand the User Journey

We will first explore how users behave on and interact with different pages, and how this behavior and interaction can be interpreted. By the end of this section, you will understand:

- The various types of behavioral reporting and the characteristics of each.
- The depth of insight that behavioral reports can provide.
- The importance of using a variety of analytical metrics, reports, tools, and approaches to really tell the full story.

Behavior Reporting
User journey. When viewing the data it is possible to see users' movement throughout the site almost three or four levels deep. This is viewed through the Behavior Flow tab shown in Figure 9.23. It shows us how users engage with the site; specifically, what page they

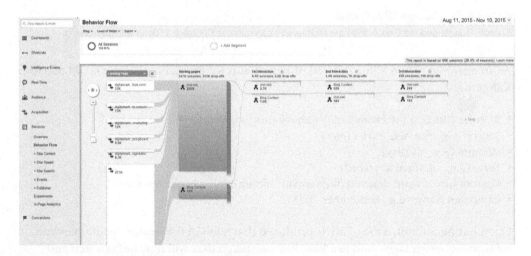

Figure 9.23   Behavior Flow Tab in GA Behavior
Source: Google and the Google logo are registered trademarks of Google Inc.; used with permission.

	Page	Pageviews	Unique Pageviews	Avg. Time on Page	Entrances	Bounce Rate
Real-Time		**172,164** % of Total: 100.00% (172,164)	**128,451** % of Total: 100.00% (128,451)	**00:01:19** Avg for View: 00:01:19 (0.00%)	**71,161** % of Total: 100.00% (71,161)	**42.43%** Avg for View: 42.43% (0.00%)
Audience	1. /	70,284 (40.82%)	57,096 (44.45%)	00:01:01	56,354 (79.19%)	40.03%
Acquisition	2. /spanish-tapas-menu/	51,500 (29.91%)	32,340 (25.18%)	00:01:56	6,305 (8.86%)	39.43%
Behavior	3. /contact-us/	12,442 (7.23%)	10,160 (7.91%)	00:01:36	3,378 (4.75%)	55.57%
Overview	4. /group-menus/	7,313 (4.25%)	3,426 (2.67%)	00:00:48	213 (0.30%)	37.56%
Behavior Flow	5. /about-spanish-restaurant/	6,660 (3.87%)	5,445 (4.24%)	00:01:01	490 (0.69%)	56.73%
▼ Site Content	6. /nights-zaragoza/	4,637 (2.69%)	3,907 (3.04%)	00:00:47	135 (0.19%)	49.62%
All Pages	7. /news/	3,033 (1.76%)	2,534 (1.97%)	00:01:21	496 (0.70%)	58.15%
Content Drilldown	8. /reviews/	2,122 (1.25%)	1,817 (1.41%)	00:00:51	92 (0.13%)	55.06%
Landing Pages	9. /christmas-parties-dublin/	1,563 (0.91%)	1,291 (1.01%)	00:01:35	302 (0.42%)	51.97%
Exit Pages	10. /menu_safe/	1,195 (0.69%)	1,081 (0.84%)	00:02:58	1,040 (1.46%)	75.00%

Figure 9.24　In-Page Analytics in GA

Source: Google and the Google logo are registered trademarks of Google Inc.; used with permission.

initially entered, where they visited next, when they dropped off, and where they went afterwards.

In-page analytics. This is essentially a heat map of the site that shows how users engage with specific pages; virtually anything can be analyzed, as shown in Figure 9.24. We recommend that you sort the top-performing pages by various metrics; you can do this simply by clicking on each of the individual headings.

Site speed. This is an important issue for SEO and also user experience—both factors that influence the goal conversion rate and SERP ranking. Users' perceptions on websites are formed very quickly, and getting a negative reaction can cost a business a lot! Just a one-second delay in page load times can result in a 7 percent reduction in conversions. For a business earning $100,000 per day, this equates to over $2.5 million in lost revenue in a year—not cool.

Site speed can be analyzed by browser, country, or even by page, as shown in Figure 9.25. By combining this with other data, such as technology reports, it is possible to really assess site performance and isolate issues.

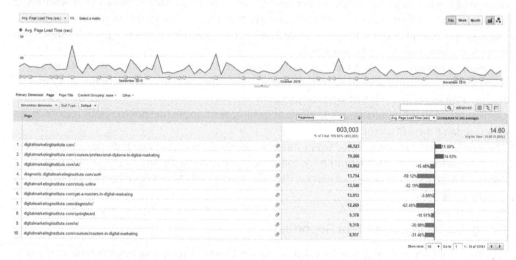

Figure 9.25　Site Speed by Page in GA

Source: Google and the Google logo are registered trademarks of Google Inc.; used with permission.

Figure 9.26   Google Page Speed Insights Tool
Source: Google and the Google logo are registered trademarks of Google Inc.; used with permission.

PageSpeed Insights tool. GA can even score individual pages from 0 to 100 and provide suggestions for improvement in a handy pop-up—as shown in Figure 9.26. You can take action on these suggestions and then monitor how successful the fixes are.
AdSense. If the site runs ads from this program, their performance can be viewed here.
Experiments. This option allows for A/B testing of different elements of the site, such as moving buttons around, trying different optimization ideas, and assessing conversions based on different settings.

Analyzing Behavior
Benchmarks. A reoccurring lesson in this chapter is that analysis must be done within the context of the business and its goals. For instance, not every website requires long sessions—some may have a short sales funnel and a speedy conversion aim. In this context, a longer engagement period could actually be an indication that something is wrong; for example, that users cannot navigate the site easily.
Combining reports. To avoid making assumptions, it is important to assess data across all relevant reports. Using several reports to analyze your data will give you a richer story and convey a more realistic idea of what is going on.
Combining metrics. Similarly, it's important to look at multiple metrics in relation to each other to paint the full picture.
The user journey. The key, once user journeys have been mapped and reports compared, is to work backwards to understand why consumers are leaving the site or not converting. If there is a high exit rate in certain places, then the next step is to use appropriate reports to try to determine why.

Using Site Search and Event Reporting

Having established why it is important to understand the user journey and the various metrics for monitoring and analyzing it, we're now going to examine two very useful behavioral reports: Site Search and Event Reporting. These are detailed tools to further understand user behavior and they will now be explored fully. By the end of this section, you will understand:

- How to pull the Site Search report and the rich benefits from doing so.
- What event tagging is, how to set it up, and why it is useful.

Site Search

Using this tool, shown in Figure 9.27, it is possible to see what users have been looking for—and more importantly, what they were unable to find. This is very actionable data, as it tells us specifically where the website is falling short—both in terms of user experience and content.

For example, the rule of thumb is that users should find content within three clicks, so the site might need reorganizing to accomplish this. Or perhaps new content could be added to fulfill a previously unknown need. These improvements should positively impact goal conversion rates, especially since users searching the site are typically more engaged.

To access site search data, simply import user queries from under the Admin tab.

Event Reporting

If you need to track engagement at a more in-depth level, such as brochure downloads or video playback, then Event Reporting, shown in Figure 9.28, is the answer! This is the ideal way to track users through very precise steps, especially those that leave the site. Event Reporting is also very goal orientated, as it allows you to assign a custom value to each event. For example, while standard reporting may show how many people visited a page containing a video, Event Reporting indicates how many people are pressing play, pause, or even turning down the volume of the video. It is possible to learn at what point they click away, and track the percentage of direct conversions the video produces. This data is great for assessing things qualitatively, to get an idea of what people think or feel about the video, and how it might be improved. An explanation of how to use Event Reporting follows.

- *Combining reports.* The real beauty of Event Reporting data comes from merging and analyzing it with standard reporting, so that you get a lot more insight into the story. For

Search Term	Total Unique Searches	Results Pageviews / Search	% Search Exits	% Search Refinements	Time after Search	Search Depth
air filter	68 (0.13%)	1.13	0.00%	42.86%	00:06:20	5.97
Snow Socks	64 (0.12%)	1.59	21.88%	22.22%	00:04:46	5.25
jack	63 (0.12%)	1.25	3.17%	21.52%	00:04:23	4.94
alternator	62 (0.12%)	1.40	9.68%	14.94%	00:03:36	3.21
brake pads	60 (0.11%)	1.50	10.00%	11.11%	00:04:44	3.20
Accessories	59 (0.11%)	1.78	16.95%	4.76%	00:06:53	7.80
exhaust	59 (0.11%)	1.25	3.39%	13.51%	00:04:57	6.97
wing mirror	58 (0.11%)	1.17	1.72%	8.82%	00:04:29	3.66
clutch	57 (0.11%)	1.19	10.53%	11.76%	00:04:09	4.26
Condenser	56 (0.11%)	1.12	10.71%	30.16%	00:04:28	3.52
Tool	55 (0.10%)	1.35	12.73%	10.81%	00:06:53	8.69
tow bar	54 (0.10%)	1.26	3.70%	22.06%	00:04:29	4.06
mirror	53 (0.10%)	1.26	5.66%	14.93%	00:04:12	3.81

Figure 9.27   Site Search Report in GA

Source: Google and the Google logo are registered trademarks of Google Inc.; used with permission.

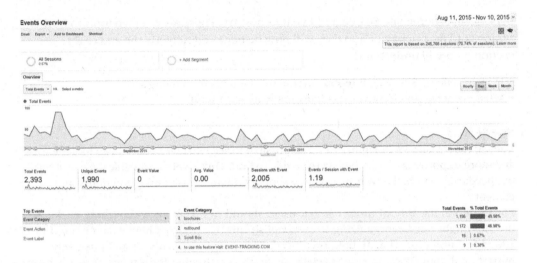

Figure 9.28   Event Reporting in GA

Source: Google and the Google logo are registered trademarks of Google Inc.; used with permission.

example, standard reporting might show that one particular page has a high bounce rate; but by tracking every single element on that page (as in Figure 9.29) the exact moment a user exited (and why) can be pinpointed and analyzed.

- *Setup.* This is done using an event-tracking generator called the GA Configuration Tool (go to www.GAconfig.com). Fill out the required fields, ensuring that the naming convention you use is consistent. It will produce a piece of code to be attached to whatever requires monitoring; for example, a Download button. Depending on your technical abilities, a developer's assistance may be needed to attach the code—now is the time to cozy up to your IT department!

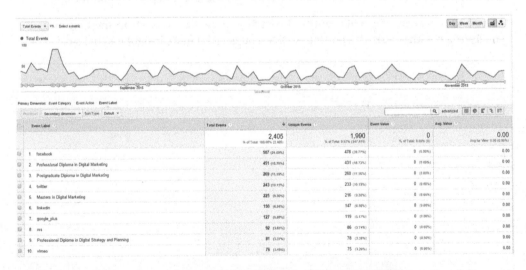

Figure 9.29   Combining Event Reporting and Standard Reporting in GA

Source: Google and the Google logo are registered trademarks of Google Inc.; used with permission.

- *Actions, labels, and categories.* There are three components to naming events in Event Reporting: actions, labels, and categories. To use a video example as an example, the tracking could be named as follows:

1 *Action:* Video playback
2 *Label:* Product video
3 *Category:* Face cream

This event can be tracked in many ways. For example, the event could be tracked with the action named *social share* instead, with the aim of seeing how many people are sharing the video instead of watching it. By comparing all this data, interesting in-depth analysis can be carried out to see how users are behaving in relation to very specific elements.

There are lots of ways to monitor and understand users, but the important thing is to use a mixture of them all, so that conclusions are informed and balanced. It is not enough to rely on one report, one tool, or one basic assumption! Instead, aim for a well-rounded approach, using several reports, data sets, and methods to tell a complete story and produce deeper insights.

Stage 4: Analyze

Having touched on conversions in the previous sections, this section now looks in some detail at what it means to use analytics in the context of specific goals. This section deals with the highlighted stage in Figure 9.30—stage 4 of the analytics process—at which marketing efforts are evaluated with regard to how they deliver on conversion KPIs.

Figure 9.30   Focus on the Fourth Stage in the Analytics Process

By the end of this section, you will understand:

- Why conversion goals are important.
- The different types of conversion reporting possible in GA.
- What the sales funnel is and how it relates to meeting certain goals.
- How to set different goals and the various characteristics of goals.

What Is a Conversion?

It's the completion of a site activity that represents success to your business—a sale, for example. Measures of success will vary wildly among different businesses and markets, so once again bear in mind that context is absolutely everything in analytics and setting goals.

To decide what your conversion goals should be, simply consider what your website is trying to achieve in order to meet your business objectives. It might be a transaction, it might be clicking on a link, or it might be registering for an email newsletter.

The Sales Funnel

This refers to the group of clearly defined steps that lead to particular conversions; analyzing them can help in measuring the conversion process. The reports show where users have entered into each step in the funnel, where they leave, and the percentage of users that go all the way through it. Creating a sales funnel is straightforward and can be added to any goal at any time—but it is best suited to events and URL destination goals. Figure 9.31 shows a sales funnel that was created for a URL destination goal.

Figure 9.31   Sales Funnel Report in GA for URL Destination Goal
Source: Google and the Google logo are registered trademarks of Google Inc.; used with permission.

Conversion Reporting

There are four sections to the Conversions report in GA: e-commerce, goals, multichannel funnels, and attribution. The first two are discussed next; the latter two will be discussed later in this chapter.

E-commerce

This section is for sales-focused sites with specific transactions.

The reports here go into quite some detail, allowing us to look at products sold, the volumes involved, and revenues generated—for example, Figure 9.32 shows product performance comparisons. The detail can also extend to the value of products in baskets per product across all users compared to the value of products actually purchased.

This type of data is perfect for justifying investment and demonstrating the value of upsell marketing! It's also useful when deciding how long a campaign should run for, because the data shows how long users take to make purchase decisions and how long they need to complete transactions.

Goals Overview

Figure 9.33 shows a multistep conversion process within the Goals section of GA. This subtab is extremely important for highlighting any weak points in the conversion journey. There are four main types of goals:

1 *URL destination goal.* This is a specific page shown in response to a positive user event; for example, a thank-you page being displayed after someone signs up for an email

Figure 9.32   Product Performance Comparison Report in GA eCommerce Section
Source: Google and the Google logo are registered trademarks of Google Inc.; used with permission.

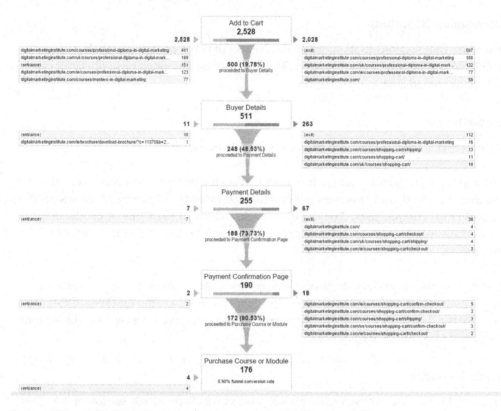

Figure 9.33   Multi-Step Conversion Process in Goals Section of GA

Source: Google and the Google logo are registered trademarks of Google Inc.; used with permission.

newsletter. In Figure 9.34 the name of such a page is set as Contact Us Form Page and the request URL has been entered. You can assign a value to the goal and easily check that it is set up correctly.

2 *Time on site.* Shown in Figure 9.35, this is very useful for content-driven goals; for example, if you wish to encourage lengthier engagement with your blog. The goal set here could be related to engagement (you desire that more time be spent on a site generally) or microconversions (how long it takes for a user to convert specifically).

3 *Pages per session.* Shown in Figure 9.36, this is similar to time on site; however, you must select a whole number for your goal, regardless what the current average is. Always aim above it, so there is a target to reach for.

4 *Event Tracking report.* Remember we covered this earlier in the section about behavior? Simply follow the on-screen prompts shown in Figure 9.37 to set it up and get a great insight into your customer's actions.

Setting Goals

Goals are visible at the View level, and up to 20 can be set for every new view that is added (although they can also be added under the Admin tab). You can opt to set either a custom or standard goal, and both can be set up very simply by following the prompts (shown in Figure 9.38).

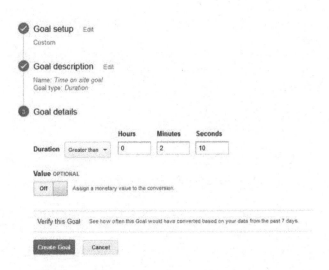

Figure 9.34   URL Destination Goal in GA
Source: Google and the Google logo are registered trademarks of Google Inc.; used with permission.

Figure 9.35   Time on Site Goal in GA
Source: Google and the Google logo are registered trademarks of Google Inc.; used with permission.

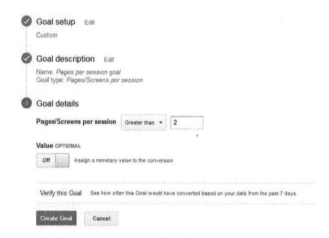

Figure 9.36   Pages Per Session Goal in GA
Source: Google and the Google logo are registered trademarks of Google Inc.; used with permission.

Remember, goal data cannot be tracked retrospectively; it can only be tracked forward from the date it is set.

Goals are a brilliant way to optimize analytics for the measurement of specific KPIs, helping the site meet relevant business aims. This function of reporting is really versatile, and its application across several reports will now be examined.

Figure 9.37   Event Goal in GA
Source: Google and the Google logo are registered trademarks of Google Inc.; used with permission.

Figure 9.38   Goal Setup in GA

Source: Google and the Google logo are registered trademarks of Google Inc.; used with permission.

Attribution

Having established the importance of goals, let's now look at assigning values to the channels that help achieve them. This section will ensure you:

- Understand the nonlinear nature of conversions.
- Understand the benefits of assigning a value to each channel.
- Recognize the different models for assigning value, and when these might be required.

Attribution reporting. The first report under the Conversions tab is multichannel funnels, which looks at the paths users take when they're journeying to conversion. Look at Figure 9.39 for examples of these paths.

Why assign values? The way users make purchasing decisions is not always straightforward, and they may arrive at conversions by many different means! As such, it's important to understand the role each channel plays, as seen in Figure 9.40, so that a given channel can be optimized properly and any expenditure justified.

Assigning values allows credit to be given to channels that helped secure a conversion, so that the influential steps in the sales funnel can be discovered. Websites can then be adapted to influence users where it resonates!

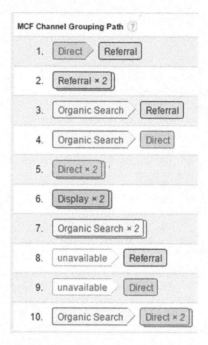

Figure 9.39   Channel Grouping Paths in GA
Source: Google and the Google logo are registered trademarks of Google Inc.; used with permission.

Attribution models. These models assign a value to each channel that played a role in the purchasing path, and they provide varying frameworks for assessing and evaluating each channel.

The model that is used to evaluate the channel's role will vary depending on the business context. For example, an e-commerce site might wish to value the search

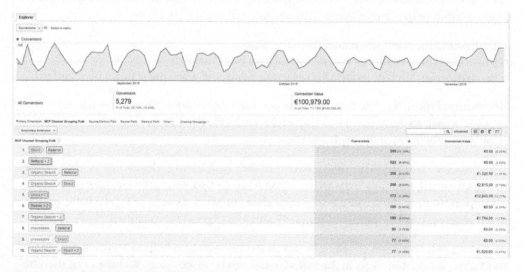

Figure 9.40   Attribution Reporting in GA
Source: Google and the Google logo are registered trademarks of Google Inc.; used with permission.

Figure 9.41 Time Decay Attribution Model in GA
Source: Google and the Google logo are registered trademarks of Google Inc.; used with permission.

activity very highly, regardless of how much traffic it drives, simply because searching is hugely influential in purchasing decisions. Models include:

- *Last click.* Favors the last channel, because it is the one that referred the converting user.
- *First click.* Champions the very first channel—the introducer—for inspiring the purchase.
- *Linear.* Assigns equal value to every channel that played a role.
- *Time decay.* Seen in Figure 9.41, this model assigns an increasing value to each channel as the user gets closer to conversion; for example, the first channel might be awarded 10 percent; the second, 20 percent; the third, 30 percent, and so on.
- *Position-based.* Assigns a value to the first and last interaction only.

Attribution values will be dictated by different contexts, KPIs, and products, now examined in more detail in the next section, which looks at customizing GA.

Customization

Having examined the standard GA reports, let's now address how to customize them so that sets of data tailored to a particular business context can be developed. This will show you how to monitor custom reports as defined by your goals in a very specific way.

Once you have read this section you will know:

- Why and when to customize reports.
- How to set up custom reports using the Views and Advanced Segments filters.
- The benefits and limitations of Views and Advanced Segments.

Why Use Customization?

Segmentation helps us to make informed decisions because it lets us make comparisons across areas that matter to the business's needs and goals. Customized reports, such as those shown in Figure 9.42, really drive this—promoting assessment of specific data with the most relevance and leading to clear and actionable insights.

Figure 9.42   List of Customized Reports in a GA Account
Source: Google and the Google logo are registered trademarks of Google Inc.; used with permission.

Views and Advanced Segments

There are three ways to produce custom sets of data using these filters:

1 *Drill down*. Drilling down is when you combine two different reports in order to compare relevant data. This is relatively self-explanatory; an example would be comparing the behavior of converting females with converting males in order to see how to improve user experience for each gender.
2 *Views*. Views provide a permanent subset of filtered data. This data is already available in standard reports, but setting up a view simply means you can access it quickly and easily in your dashboard, allowing you to concentrate on the metrics that matter.

   A new view is created through the Admin tab that sits above the property. Simply select Create a New View and fill out the filter name in the field, as shown in Figure 9.43.

   Views are commonly used to display various time zones around the world (as shown at the bottom of Figure 9.44), so be sure to select the right one, as your time zone setting can't be changed later. Another common use is to exclude internal traffic or to focus on one campaign; for example, filtering for PPC traffic only.

   Be very careful with how you filter and be sure to retain one default view that includes all the traffic—you can only apply 25 filters, and they cannot be removed! We have all experienced that stomach-churning sense of doom after realizing that important information has fallen victim to accidental deletion! Also remember that you cannot filter data retrospectively: It will be sorted only from the day you applied the view.
3 *Advanced Segments*. This is a flexible way of organizing reports, and allows segments to be added and removed as required, and data to be segmented and viewed in a range of directly applicable ways.

   The Advanced Segments filter can be applied to any standard report in the form of subsets and can also be added along the top of the screen, as shown in Figure 9.45. The GA

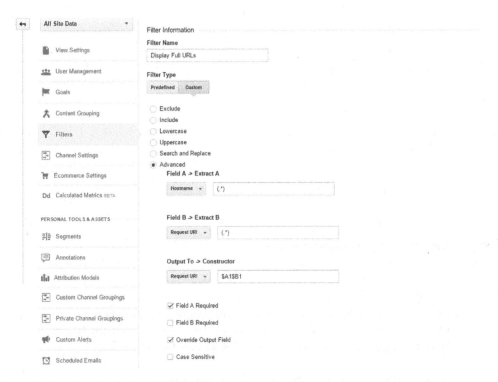

Figure 9.43   Creating a New View in GA

Source: Google and the Google logo are registered trademarks of Google Inc.; used with permission.

interface displays an overview of these segments and provides comparisons between them.

To give an example, a demographic segment could be applied to acquisition reports to compare site traffic coming from the UK, the United States, and Canada. Rich insights can

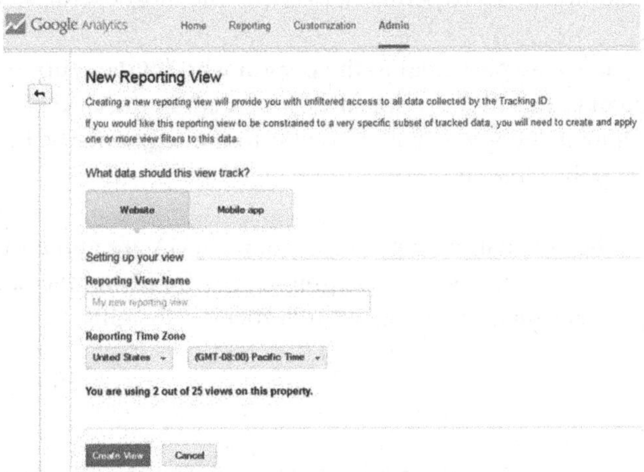

Figure 9.44   Specifying Time Zone for a New View in GA

Source: Google and the Google logo are registered trademarks of Google Inc.; used with permission.

Figure 9.45 Creating Advanced Segments

Source: Google and the Google logo are registered trademarks of Google Inc.; used with permission.

be drawn from comparing data in this way; in this example you might notice, for instance, that while traffic volumes are similar across countries, conversions in the UK are lower, which would suggest that a greater focus on UK audiences is needed.

You can set up Advanced Segments in two different ways:

1 Select an existing predefined segment.
2 Create a new unique segment.

Default segments include a wide range of variables, ranging from, for example, conditional circumstances (such as anyone who has purchased in the last 30 days) to basic or advanced demographics. Custom segments can include virtually anything and any number of conditions. Just experiment to create the most useful set of reports!

Be aware that segments are particular to the person who set them up, so no one else will be able to view them unless they are specifically shared. In the case of a company account, for which many people will need access to the segment, the best solution is to create a view and apply a filter instead.

Take advantage of the fact that the reporting options in GA are numerous and gloriously varied; the key is to get creative with the segments you build and the data you compare, all while keeping it relevant and aiming for goal-focused insights.

KPIs

Having so far laid out a solid working knowledge of analytics and an understanding of the depths of reporting available, this final section will explain how to ensure that everything is applied properly.

This is where insights are reviewed, applied to a specific context, and used to meet precise business aims. However, the actual process of setting and using key performance indicators (KPIs) is ongoing and takes something from each stage. By the end of this section, you will understand:

- Why KPIs are a vital element in any campaign.
- Why analytics is important for setting and achieving KPIs.
- Each stage of the four-step KPI iterative process: setting business goals, defining KPIs, analyzing results, and making informed decisions.

Why KPIs?

We've established that business success requires targeted goals, focused actions, and continual evaluation. KPIs, as a set of specific targets, are incredibly important in facilitating this for the following reasons:

- KPIs encourage precise monitoring of a campaign before, during, and after it runs because they provide a numerical target to aim for, a figure to continually benchmark against.
- By analyzing to what extent these numerical targets are or were met and using analytics to answer why, a series of actionable insights can be produced.
- These insights isolate what is working to achieve KPI benchmarks and therefore justify expenses and decisions. The insights gained also highlight necessary marketing and business changes and helps marketers make smarter choices to get there.

Analytics and KPIs

Trying to reach KPIs will dictate analytics reporting, because relevant insights are needed to understand what is working and why. For example, if the aim is to maximize a converting page and there is a specific KPI to meet for that, then analytics reporting would be tweaked to track this at the level of detail required, and used as a basis for informed changes.

In short, KPIs are hard numerical targets, and analytics answer how they can be reached.

The Four-Step KPI Iterative Process

Optimizing analytics to define and meet KPIs is an iterative, ongoing, four-step process:

1 Define business and website objectives.
2 Develop KPIs based on these objectives.
3 Analyze marketing activity using GA.
4 Make informed decisions.

Let's look at each of these steps in detail.

Define business and website objectives. There are three layers of detail here: business objectives, business goals, and website goals.

The first step is to define wider business objectives, such as an increase in revenue. Next, set a more detailed goal to achieve this objective, such as an increase in the volume of sales. Finally, goals are set for how the website might help facilitate this, such as an increase in conversions.

Develop KPIs from these objectives. These basic goals are then clarified into harder targets, using insights and data from analytics reporting. A specific numerical value is assigned to each objective, and KPIs are developed.

Continuing with the previous example:

> **Business objective:** Increased revenue—an extra $1,000 per month is the aim.
> **Business goal:** Increased sales volume—an extra $1,000 is 100 more sales per month.
> **Website goal:** Increased conversions—an extra 100 sales equals 100 new conversions.

The specific KPIs in this instance would be conversion CPA and conversion rate. The aim is to increase engagement and amount of time spent on site and to lower the bounce rate.

Analyze your marketing activity using GA. Having set targets, the next step is to use analytics to report on them. This stage of the process deals with how and why—understanding what is and isn't working within the context of your KPIs.

While KPIs deal with the macroconversion (the sale), analytics delves into the finer details and examines the microconversions (the steps that lead to the sale). Microconversions are tipping points along the user journey, such as watching a product video or filling out a contact form. Relevant analytics reports help decipher which microconversions lead to a macroconversion (sale), and crucially, why. This is when analytics becomes very powerful, because if marketers understand the steps that users take before they convert (and likewise, the ones they take before they don't), then the website can be optimized and successes replicated.

Make informed decisions. Using this rich knowledge, informed decisions are then made to achieve the KPIs. Action is taken based on the findings, using analytics to tweak strategy. For example, the site could remarket to users who converted previously, or it could target individuals who have performed certain microconversions. By understanding microconversions and the user journey, the site focus can be adapted at specific points along the sales funnel, promoting elements that lead to conversion and improving those that do not. Overall, relatively simple changes can be made based on this information, without altering media spend or AdWords investment.

Of course, these changes should be continually analyzed, assessing whether they help to meet KPIs or not, as part of an ongoing process of refinement.

It is important to use relevant analytics reports to help achieve KPIs—to understand what needs achieving, what is working, what is not working, and how it can be fixed!

So, What Have You Learned in This Chapter?

In this chapter we have looked at the importance of GA, how and why it should be set up, the types of reporting available, and the different methods for drawing perceptive conclusions. Remember that practice makes perfect and keep a few tips in mind for your next GA journey:

- Don't panic—fear not the mind-boggling array of reports, data sets, and customization options. Stick to what is relevant and use only the reports that mean something to the context.
- Use reports wisely! Contrast, compare, and get creative with the segments and the measurement metrics.
- Always develop insights with a view to achieving the business aims.
- Keep asking why! This is how we get the sexy payoffs such as profit, competitive advantage, and slick marketing.

Go to www.artofdmi.com to access the case study on analytics as additional support material for this chapter.

 Exercises

Exercise 1

You would like to be able to view performance in GA for *just* your PPC traffic. Create a new view from the Admin tab in GA and apply a filter to this view that includes traffic from the medium, CPC. The view will show you only CPC, otherwise known as PPC traffic. Give this view a meaningful name.

Exercise 2

You run a restaurant that takes bookings both over the phone and online. Your online booking process finishes with users landing on a booking confirmation page, which you would like to use to track the number of bookings coming through your site. The request URL of this page is bookingconfirmed.

Create a URL destination goal in your default profile for this online booking, and create a funnel for the steps preceding the goal completion as shown below:

1 Choose date and time: /choosedate.
2 Select number of people: /tablesize.
3 Enter payment options: /payment.
4 Thank you/booking confirmation: /bookingconfirmed.

Exercise 3

Due to budget constraints, your Google AdWords budget has been reduced this year. As a result you have to find ways to reduce spend without impacting performance.

Using the Google AdWords reports under Channels, find the following:

1 Poorest performing keywords.
2 Poorest performing campaigns.
3 Poorest performing time of day.

Use the total number of goal completions as the metric for performance measurement.

Exercise 4

You are the website manager for an online fashion retailer. Despite seeing the same volume of sessions coming through your site, your purchases have decreased significantly over the last quarter.

To understand why this is happening, you need to look at where users are leaving the site. Analyze the following reports:

1 Look at Top Exit Pages (under Behavior) to see where users are most often leaving the site.
2 View the Funnel Visualization report under Conversions to see where users are dropping off on the path to purchasing.

Based on this data decide what action to take and explain your decision.

Exercise 5

Your manager has asked you to report on hourly website sales performance at your weekly Friday morning sales meetings.

1 Create an hour-of-day custom report in GA.
2 Schedule it to be emailed to you on the Thursday of every week so you can prepare in advance of your meeting.

 **Action Plan: Analytics**

Digital Marketing Planning Scheme for Analytics

Objectives

Conversions, leads, sales, traffic, visibility, brand awareness

Action Items and Frequency

- Keyword research: Quarterly
- Targeting: Monthly
- Scheduling: Weekly
- Bidding and budgeting: Weekly/monthly
- Tracking and reporting: Daily/weekly

Measurement Tools and KPIs

Analytics: e-Commerce transactions, goal completions, traffic share, AdWords sessions, pageviews, new versus. returning visitors

Spend

Media	Content	People	Systems
x		x	x

Chapter 10
Strategy and Planning

An Introduction

Let's make a digital marketing cake. You have all the ingredients lined up and ready to go, now let's put them all into the strategy bowl and mix it together with your planning spoon. After some time baking in the oven, you will have a successful campaign!

A successful digital marketing campaign is one that uses the most appropriate channels to achieve the maximum impact—this chapter will guide you through the process.

You will be able to recognize the most suitable channels for a particular campaign, how to cost and resource your plan appropriately, and how to set and align business objectives with tight implementation plans and well-considered tactical solutions.

> Formal definition of strategy and planning: The process of integrating digital marketing activities with a plan, buying for it, and executing a successful digital marketing campaign.
>
> Informal definition of strategy and planning: Composing your digital marketing masterpiece.

Process

This chapter will give you full knowledge of the four stages of the strategy and planning process shown in Figure 10.1:

1 *Approach.* Before you begin to plan a digital marketing campaign, you have to step back and look at the big picture, spot gaps, and find ways to fill them. Your campaign should be an amazing couture gown—not a dress made from itchy material that the dressmaker forgot to take pins out of!

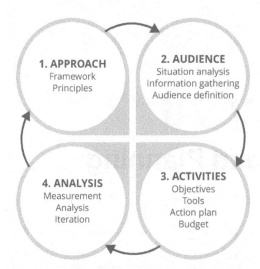

Figure 10.1   Four-Step Strategy and Planning Process

2 *Audience*. Your campaign will not be a success unless the right people see it. This section will teach you how to identify your target audience members and how to efficiently communicate your message to them.

3 *Activities*. Planning involves setting specific objectives—here's where you will learn to recognize different types of action plans and how to use them.

4 *Analysis*. Your digital marketing plan will not have a definitive beginning, middle, and end—it's an iterative process that you will need to keep a close eye on. This section will explain the tools used to analyze data so that you can monitor what is working, what is not, and how to make any necessary adjustments.

Key Terms and Concepts

The focus of this chapter is to arm you with the complete set of skills you need to create an awesome digital marketing campaign. When you reach the end of this chapter, you will be able to:

- Understand and implement the 3i principles.
- Gather essential information on the most important elements of the campaign: the market, your competitors, and your audience.
- Define and segment your target audience.
- Recognize the exact objectives for your specific business plan.
- Know which digital tools to use for every type of business plan.
- Separate your budget and identify the most useful resources to spend money on.
- Manage and monitor your campaign with the suitable digital tools for the entire iterative process.

As a digital marketer, you need to be an expert on every element of a campaign from SEO to analytics—but only a digital marketing maestro can bring them all together. That is where strategy and planning come in; so when the curtain closes on this chapter, you will be a digital marketing Mozart!

Stage 1: Approach

It's all coming together; you've mastered every digital marketing tool you need to get started on your digital marketing journey. But—and this is a big but (and I cannot lie)—you cannot jump into the deep end and expect to float along nicely in calm waters. There are sharks in the ocean—and they bite!

The most important thing to remember about the strategy and planning process is that you must always be prepared, so when it comes to planning a digital marketing campaign you should never take the plunge unprepared. Test the waters first—strategic planning is everything. This is all down to stage 1 of the process, as highlighted in Figure 10.2.

Navigate this section wisely and you will be equipped to:

- Structure the campaign around a specially tailored framework
- Identify and implement the key 3i principles
- Have a complete understanding of your capabilities.

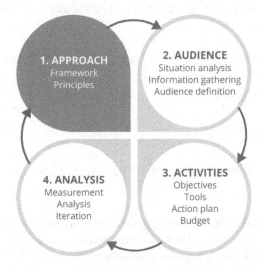

Figure 10.2   Focus on the First Stage in the Strategy and Planning Process

Structure the Plan—Before You Paint the Picture, Frame It

Imagine if Van Gogh's *Starry Night* was displayed with a frame made from dry pasta stuck onto cardboard. Yes, the painting would still be beautiful, but no one would take it seriously—and picture frames made out of cardboard tend to fall apart pretty quickly.

The first element making up stage 1 of the iterative process is figuring out a cohesive structure to your digital marketing plan so that you can quickly assess your activities and capabilities.

The biggest advantage to digital marketing over traditional marketing is that you do not have to commit to a set budget or stick to one particular channel. In traditional marketing, everything must be decided all at once, whereas your digital marketing strategy and plan is more fluid and can evolve over the course of the campaign.

There are four main factors to keep in mind at the start of your planning process:

1 *Structure.* Digital marketing gives you the power to test the waters, so start small. Use available funds wisely and carry out a small test campaign with an equally small budget: You don't have to commit to anything unless you can be sure that it works.
2 *Budget.* Again, it's best to start small and perform small tests. When you see that a particular method is working, increase the budget. Only then will you have a good idea of how much a bigger campaign will cost you over time.
3 *Calendar.* Your calendar should be totally organic, with no specific end point. This rolling calendar approach can help you track the success of each test.
4 *Personnel.* Unless you are Oz the Great and Powerful (or your budget and time constraints limit your plan to a one-person team), you cannot do everything, so this is the time to choose your team members. For those who must go it alone, select channels that can be managed based on your specific skill set and the amount of time you can dedicate to the campaign.

Whether a campaign is run entirely by one person or a team, it should be tailored to the skills of those involved, to the budget, and to what you see is actually working from the tests you run in this early stage.

The Customer Is Always . . . First

So you have a solid framework but you don't have your work of art. Don't worry—that comes in good time.

A brilliant plan is wasted if the right people don't engage with it. Despite being regarded as one of the world's best artists, Van Gogh only sold one painting. Could that be because he didn't quite know whom he was selling to?

To really make the most of what you have got, you must start with the customer and work out towards your digital strategy. Here is where the 3i principles come into play.

1 *Initiate.* Think about your customers: Figure out what they are looking for by looking at their online behavior.
2 *Iterate.* Continuously carry out small tests and try new approaches to determine what method works best for your audience.
3 *Integrate.* Use lots of different channels coherently. This may include traditional (offline) marketing methods, as mixing both online and offline methods will get you the best impact. But of course, you have to know your audience to know if using both will be necessary.

Getting to Know You

Gathering information on customers does not require anyone to lurk around corners with a notepad and pen while wearing a trench coat, trilby hat, and shades. With that said, there are ways to research customers without them knowing what's going on (as seen in Figure 10.3).

Sound ominous? It's not! Social listening is simply the act of tuning into a conversation to get a better grip on what people are most interested or uninterested in. For example, you could follow a specific page on Facebook or a particular Twitter hashtag.

For a more transparent way of gathering audience information, polls, questionnaires, and surveys are good ways of getting to know customers' likes or dislikes about a particular topic or their feelings about a product.

On a bigger scale, focus groups can be set up to gather information in a more detailed way than polls or surveys, which provide broader results.

Perhaps the easiest ways to get basic information on audiences is through the analytic features found on websites and social media platforms such as Facebook and Twitter. Most email marketing tools also have analytics packages.

Are We There Yet?

You have thought about the framework and gathered information on your audience, now it's time to clearly plan out your marketing strategy. Your plan should include all the sections listed below. Take a moment to soak in the headlines: all will be covered in greater detail in the coming sections.

Figure 10.3   Combining Traditional and Digital Research Strategies

Digital Marketing Plan: Structure

A digital marketing plan should include the following elements:

- Situation analysis
- Information gathering
- Audience definition
- Business objectives
- Digital tools
- Action plan
- Budget
- Measurement
- Iteration and management

Situation Analysis: Time to Embrace Your Inner Socrates

You don't exactly have to be a deep thinker to be a digital marketer, but you should ask these questions—and know the answers!

Take a deep breath:

- Where am I now?
- How do I measure up to competitors?
- How effective have I been so far?
- What are my main strengths and weaknesses?
- How successful have previous activities been?

Situation analysis is all about assessing the campaign in its naked form, and you have got to poke and prod it until its truth is revealed. Like the most challenging of jigsaw puzzles, your campaign will be missing some pieces, so this is the time to spot the gaps and fill them in.

Whether this means cutting the campaign into a new shape that fits or changing the look of the game completely, it's important that these gaps are filled now.

A number of factors should be considered when in this deep thinking mode:

- Your customer.
- Your specific sector in the industry.
- How your company measures up to your competitors.
- Industry trends.

Taking information from past experiences, knowing your strengths and weaknesses, seeing what worked and what did not, and deciding what channels you are going to use are all essential.

	Basic knowledge	Limited experience	Practical skills	Advanced application	Expert practitioner
Website					
SEO					
SEM					
Email					
Display					
Social Media					
Mobile					
Analytics					

Figure 10.4   Situation Analysis Chart

Think of situation analysis as the foundation of your entire campaign—you do not want to start an unstable game of digital marketing Jenga!

A great way to keep track of all of these factors is to create a framework similar to the one outlined in Figure 10.4, which will lay out your strengths and potential weaknesses.

Complete a chart like this one by ticking the boxes you think will provide the best rating of your digital marketing capabilities. The aim is to have a quick and handy snapshot of where you are, the gaps that may need to be filled, and where your strengths lie.

Assessing your activities is another critical element in analyzing your situation. Again, it is helpful to create a framework like Figure 10.5 to outline how effective your active digital marketing channels have worked previously.

	Describe your current activities	Pre-course rating	Post-course rating
Website			
SEO			
SEM			
Email			
Display			
Social Media			
Mobile			
Analytics			

Figure 10.5   Previous Activity Analysis Chart

By analyzing your situation from the start, you can discover the best route to take towards your digital marketing campaign goals.

Now that you have mastered the basic elements needed to secure the foundation of your campaign, you can move onto the next step of the iterative process: audience.

Stage 2: Audience

Wouldn't it be the craziest thing if you saw glasses or contact lenses being advertised in the waiting room of a laser eye-surgery clinic? It just wouldn't make *any* sense.

The point is, being prepared is the foundation for developing a digital marketing campaign that will not only do well, but will thrive.

Now it's time to get your feet wet and move on to stage 2 of the iterative process, as highlighted in Figure 10.6. The goal is to learn what lies behind the scenes and how to pull the strings; pay close attention as you weave through this section so you can:

• Learn the best tools to use to gather as much background information as you can.
• Master the art of creating a customer profile.
• Understand that not all audiences are equal, and know how to hit the sweet spot.

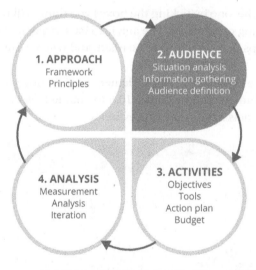

Figure 10.6   Focus on the Second Stage in the Strategy and Planning Process

Information Gathering—What's Everybody Up To?

So, you know where you stand in terms of your capabilities and activity track record, but what about everyone else? Yes, the Internet is a universe of information. Deciding where to begin may seem daunting, but the start point is obvious.

Google.

Millions of people use Google every day for all sorts of reasons, be it for general information or for research, so it actually makes a lot of sense that when planning campaigns, digital marketers should start here too.

A quick Google search gives you essential information instantly.

Let's imagine a Vitamin Water business in the Canadian market. The first thing a digital marketer will do is Google the words *vitamin water*, and voila—behold the top-ranking sites. This informs you about your competitors, which is a key step in the information-gathering process.

Once competitors have been identified, every aspect of their campaigns must be noted.

- How good they are at what they are doing?
- What are their prices?
- What are their delivery options?
- What is their range of products?
- How well do they articulate the value of their goods?

With this information gathered, you will have excellent insight into how your business compares.

Google Tools

While you should keep information on your competitors close, keep information on the marketplace closer. Google comes up with the goods in this respect too.

- *Google Analytics.* Keep tabs on who is visiting your website, where they are coming from, how they found it, and what they are specifically searching for.
- *Google alerts.* Set up alerts about specific subjects to keep a close eye on your marketplace—for example, every time a competitor is mentioned—that will come straight to your email inbox.
- *Google AdWords Keyword Planner.* See exactly how consumers search, what words they use to search, and what terms they use, as well as getting ideas for keywords that may prove useful to your campaign.
- *Google Trends.* Allowing you to search for a certain subject over time, this tool gives insight into whether a search topic is gaining in popularity or if the topic is in decline.

Building a Customer Profile

When people go online, they expect to find exactly the information they need.

If they can't find it on the first go, they will find it elsewhere.

That is the nature of the Internet, and as such, being vague is never an option. You have to engage your audience from the moment they enter that search term.

Knowing what your audience needs is vital, and once you know what they need, you can provide it! Even better—by discovering essential information and building audience profiles you can go one step further and know what your audience wants before they even know it

In order to craft an effective digital marketing plan, you have to get to know every aspect of your audience members, including but not restricted to:

- Age
- Gender
- Where they work
- Where they live   *, Demographics*
- If they have children
- Their marital status
- What their hobbies are   *Psychographics*
- What their particular preferences and needs are

Once you have reached their core, you can start to think about what your target audience's online behaviors entail.

Let's return to our example of the Vitamin Water company and think about its target audience. To profile that imaginary person—the customer persona—let's imagine Debbie Digital is a health conscious, 30-year-old, single female, living in Canada. *Ta-da!* You have the basic information about her.

Next step—let's contemplate her online activities.

- She logs into Facebook multiple times a day.
- She uses Google to do her Internet searches.
- She receives emails into her inbox at work that she checks often.
- She looks at websites online to try to find out more information about healthy living.

So what channels are the most appropriate to utilize? Yes, Debbie Digital uses Facebook, but she may not use this social media platform to research Vitamin Water. In this context, the product would be better placed in a Google search ranking—given that it is more likely she would first Google *Vitamin Water* to see where she could buy it.

This is very useful information. But we need more, *more*! Such as, where does she hang out, where does she go to look to for information, and what are her ambitions and motivations beyond the obvious information—some of the gold nuggets of intelligence seen in Figure 10.7.

Let's dig even deeper. Let's find *the real Debbie*—or at least someone who represents someone like her. Remember back in the section called Getting to Know You in this chapter, when we mentioned polls, surveys, questionnaires, and focus groups? A focus group in this case would be an excellent way to profile Debbie properly.

Figure 10.7   Debbie Digital Customer Persona

Sweet SPOT = Right Audience + Right Content + Excellent Execution

Audience Ranking

Just when you thought the core had been reached, there's more. Believe it or not, we can delve *even deeper* into our audience—for not all audiences are equally important.

It's not as harsh as it sounds—it's just a matter of getting to the nucleus of your specified audience so that you are hitting the digital marketing bull's-eye from the very beginning of your campaign.

Now that you've defined your audience, the next step is to rank them. Ranking your audience allows you to:

• Prioritize your target audience.
• Focus your activities.
• Align your budget.
• Allocate resources.

Two important factors should be considered when ranking members of your audience, as seen in Figure 10.8. They are; value to the business, and how easy or hard they are to reach:

1 *Value to the business.* How much can they buy, how often can they buy, what is the likely expenditure you can get from them in a total year, and so on.
2 *Accessibility.* Even if a person seems like a valuable member of your audience, might he be hard to get to? The bottom line is, if he is not active online, you can't reach him.

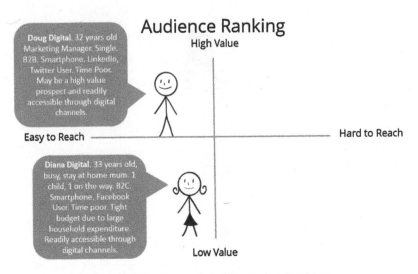

Figure 10.8   Examples of Audience Ranking

Additional considerations include:

- *What* they are interested in, what they are trying to do online, and how do you respond?
- *Why* are they online? What are they looking for; how do they get there, what devices do they use; and when, where, and why do they use those devices?
- *How* can their problems be solved?

You can't send the same message to every single audience member—it just won't work. The content you create must be carefully considered and based on the interests of each audience group.

Hitting the Sweet Spot

If Willy Wonka were a digital marketer, he would have been super successful. His business was candy and chocolate and all the treats kids can't resist. Willy's primary target audience would most definitely have been children. With this in mind, it is not surprising that the priority audience is known as the sweet-spot customer.

Sweet-spot customers are the easiest people to sell to. Not only do they really want what you have, but they also respond very well to what you have on offer, so they should make up the audience that you spend most time trying to engage, sell to, and influence online.

Unless you are lucky enough to be as rich as Willy Wonka, you must concentrate on the most important audience in the first instance. Prioritizing means that you can:

- Focus on the activities that make most sense to that particular audience.
- Align your budget up with the specific tactics that will work effectively with the audience.
- Allocate your effort with your resources.

From here, you are on the road to successfully engaging with your target audience.

Multiscreening

Have you ever looked around on a family-film night to see your sister watching a video on her mobile phone and your mother searching for holiday destinations on her tablet, all while your brother uses the TV screen to play video games? Can't we just sit down, relax, and read a good book? No! User device habits have now shifted from a single focus to a relatively new, all-consuming habit known as multiscreening.

This is the act of viewing content on numerous devices, such as your cell phone and TV, with one device triggering specific behavior on the other (for example, searching for a new pair of shoes on your cell phone but then moving to your laptop to pay for it).

We are no longer mono-channel beings: Instead we jump from channel to channel, receiving messages and soaking in information. As a digital marketer, you have got to get a good feeling of how people are moving among devices and why they are using those devices.

We know that Debbie Digital uses Twitter but how does she use it? Is she on her desktop? Her smartphone? Her tablet? If she is using her smartphone, is she using it while she watches TV?

Using Social Media in the Business Environment

In terms of B2B, Eurostat has some great insights into people's use of social media in the business environment, as can be seen in Figure 10.9. The top reason for using social media is to develop a brand image and market their product, but it is also a very useful tool for obtaining customer feedback and opinions. Trying out different ideas and observing how people respond is a good way to get to know the target audience.

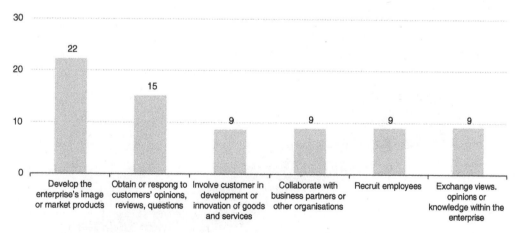

Figure 10.9   Percentage of Enterprises Using Social Media by Purpose of Use
Source: Eurostat. EU-28, 2013.

The size of a business also determines what social media platform it uses—differently sized businesses use various social media channels for different reasons. If you are planning on engaging with an audience in a B2B environment, it's important to understand your audience deeply in this respect.

Here Comes Google!

We know that website analytics provides extensive information on customers and that information can be broadened to get a deep understanding of your target audience. When you can see exactly what people type into Google Search and how they got to you, you can begin to develop a plan to satisfy your audiences' need. For instance, if someone searches for *Vitamin Water flavors*, you can attract her and increase her interest in your site by offering a range of different flavors.

Digging deeper into search terms gives lots of food for thought. Check out Figure 10.10 to see all that can be discovered.

The 5P framework, which is shown in Figure 10.11, is a great base to work from: it lets you break down useful information to better understand your target audiences' motivations and needs in order to eventually market back to them.

Understanding and defining your audience is always critical in digital marketing. Put yourself in Debbie Digital's shoes: If you can't find exactly the right information as a consumer, you will simply go elsewhere. The digital world is the consumers' oyster—make your product your target audience's pearl.

Now that you have learned the most effective way to gather information to create a profile based on your target audience, you can begin to form an efficient, compelling, and successful plan.

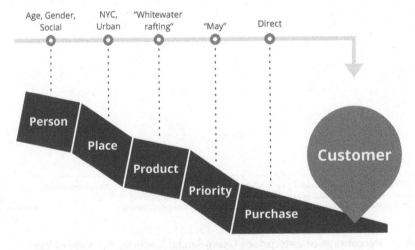

Figure 10.10   5P Framework

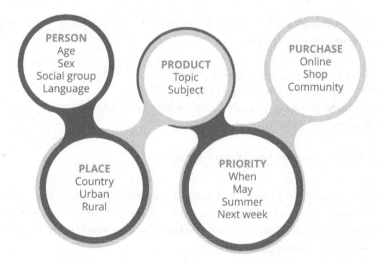

Figure 10.11   Further Insights into the 5P Framework

Stage 3: Activities

By now you know your sweet-spot customers so well that you could talk to them for an entire long-haul flight on a budget airline. You could challenge your competitor to a game of golf and not break a sweat. You can recite your strengths and weaknesses like a bright kindergarten student recites her ABCs.

The moment has come—you are ready to plan and implement stage 3, which is highlighted in Figure 10.12.

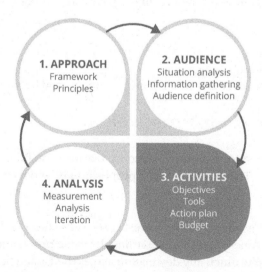

Figure 10.12   Focus on the Third Stage in the Strategy and Planning Process

This section encompasses stage 3 of the iterative process—planning—and by the end of it you will be confident enough to:

- Determine your competitive advantage and utilize your value proposition.
- Take a SMART approach to your entire plan.
- Segment your budget and successfully decide where best to spend resources.
- Recognize and run different types of action plans.

Gaining the Competitive Edge

Rocky didn't get to be the number-one champion fighter by chance. The only way to outdo your competitors is to be better than them. At the planning stage you must observe competitors' tactics—this is essential because you need to see if, and more importantly, how, you can outdo them.

- If they rank highly in search engine results, how can you get around them?
- Is there something your product can do and theirs can't?
- Can you use that difference to your advantage?

You need to consider what will give you a competitive advantage. The best grade school teachers always say this, and it's true: It's *good* to be different!

By returning to our Vitamin Water example, you now know that customers are looking for different flavors. If your competitors fail to deliver on that front, this would be a good way for you to outdo them and gain a competitive advantage. By concentrating on a particular area in which your competitors fall down, *you* have the opportunity to rank higher in search.

Engagement with your audience before any of your competitors can do it is the goal, so you must:

- Define your audience.
- Thoroughly research your competitors.
- Discover what you can offer that your competitors can't—and be the best at it.

Defining Your Value Proposition

Being the go-to business for a product or service because you fill a niche is a highly valuable asset to have. That is what a value proposition is, and it can be defined in many ways.

One way is to be the business with the lowest costs. Let's take a real-life example: Southwest Airlines is America's low-cost darling. Its value proposition is that it offers the cheapest flights to pretty much any destination across the United States. Its hook is that it has lower fares than every one of its competitors.

Southwest Airlines clearly has an impeccable value proposition. It is outdoing its competitors, and because it's resolving customer pain (expensive airfare), they are doing something different—and doing it well.

Another example of a value proposition is an innovative product—having something that will solve a real problem that everybody needs a solution to.

And yet another way to offer a value proposition is through your distribution network. Let's observe another real-life example. Coca-Cola is without a doubt hugely successful. It can't be denied that the brand has been marketed extremely well, but in reality what really differentiates Coke from its competitors is its colossal distribution network.

Go anywhere in the world—New York City, a small town in Ireland, or the South American metropolis of São Paulo—and what will you find? A Coke machine.

Coca-Cola's distribution network is so vast and complete that it gives the company an extremely large advantage.

When you have something that customers want and need, something that your competitors can't deliver as well as you can, the next important thing to do is to communicate that fact effectively. Not just on your website, but in every single aspect of your marketing plan. Our online attention spans are very short, and as such, your message has to be sharp and immediate—while being clear about what you offer and what makes you better.

Setting Objectives

At the end of it all, a digital marketing plan is designed to expand your business, so you have got to have business objectives. Setting objectives as part of your digital marketing plan provides:

- Structure
- Defined targets
- Accountability for ROI
- A basis for measurement and analysis

You can employ many specific tactics to help your business grow. Search position is important for building brand awareness, as is digital advertising. These channels allow you to be seen by a new audience, and they can help extend your reach.

Let's assume the Vitamin Water business is on page two of SERPs. Obviously, to build brand awareness the business has got to appear on page one, preferably in the top three search results. If, for example, your business objective is to increase sales, setting targets is a great idea. Assuming you already possess a solid database, your target could be to email priority customers a newsletter once a month. And to be even more effective, send out a different version of that email to different segments of your target audience.

Don't be vague about any aspect of your business objectives: Put numbers against them. Define the percentage increase in sales you want, for example, and the period of time in which you want to achieve that goal.

Being Smart

There's nothing more demotivating than setting targets that are unattainable. It's worse than training for a marathon and discovering that you have miscalculated the distance and *there's a long way to go.*

Let's use the mnemonic introduced in Chapter 6 to remind you how to set objectives—be SMART, as shown in Figure 10.13.

The key to setting targets that work is to be realistic. By doing some research and looking at any historic information you have, you can set a target to aim towards. Pick a specific, measurable target—such as sales growth in the previous year—and then set a target to improve upon that.

If this is your first campaign, look to something like Google Keyword Planner and decide what share of the market you can reasonably hope for. Whether you are improving on past activities or planning a brand new campaign, be specific and base your targets on something that can realistically be achieved.

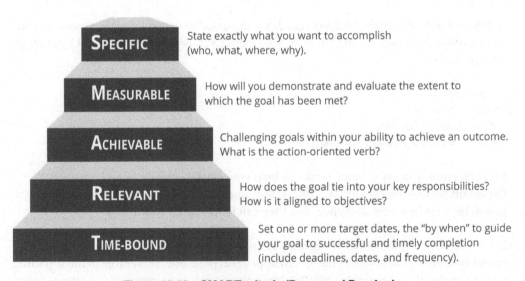

Figure 10.13   SMART criteria (Doran and Drucker)

Knowing Your Focus

There are different types of objectives, and when you plan your campaign you have to decide which one you need to home in on. What exactly do you want to achieve with your digital marketing campaign? Key objectives include:

- *Business objectives* focus on generating a certain number of sales or level of revenue over a year.
- *Audience objectives* focus on adding new audiences or making an existing one more aware of your product.
- *Product objectives* focus on launching test products or new products.
- *Brand objectives* focus on building brand awareness, so people know who you are.
- *Marketing objectives* focus on building awareness of your brand in different markets.

Channel Suitability

Your choice of channels will be based on understanding a particular audience. You should select the channels using the DMI 3i framework, which will help you determine how effective each is likely to be in engaging your target audience.

B2C Customer Profile	B2B Customer Profile
Debbie Digital	Doug Digital
33 years old	27 years old
Stay-at-home mom	Marketing Manager
Married, one child, one on the way	Single, no children
Smartphone, Facebook use	Smartphone, LinkedIn, Twitter user
Time poor	Time poor
Tight budget due to large household expenditure	May be a high-value prospect
Readily accessible through digital channels	Readily accessible through digital channels

Look at the table above. What we understand about Debbie Digital's online habits determines the channels you will use and the kind of information she will be provided with once you engage with her.

Doug Digital will be completely different from Debbie—different age group, different online habits, a bigger budget—so you will engage with him in a different way.

Budget

As with digital marketing objectives, there are many different types of costs—and you need to be able to distinguish among all of these different varieties so that you can allocate your budget and decide what kind of resources you need to spend money on. Take a look at the variety of cost types listed below:

Media spend. Third-party costs, such as AdWords or display advertising.
Digital media. The text, visuals, and graphics that will make up the content for your website and social media channels. You will have to decide whether your budget allows you to use

your own time and skill or whether you'll have to outsource the content creation. If you plan on creating the content yourself, you will have to count your time as a cost.

People costs. The amount you will have to spend on internal and/or external staff.

Systems. For example, the cost of upgrading to a professional version of a hosting service such as LinkedIn's SlideShare, or the cost of hosting a site in a foreign market.

As mentioned at the very beginning of this chapter, the beautiful thing about digital marketing is that in the online world, testing is an option.

Before investing a huge chunk of your budget towards something like PPC advertising, run a little test to learn how much the channel may cost for the duration of a complete campaign. Use this test as the barometer, and then set your budget based on the test; if you continue with that channel, you can calculate how much of your budget you will need to set aside for it.

Ad Budget Estimation

Each advertising channel has budget-estimation tools. These tools will allow you to estimate budget based on the mechanism for payment:

PPC. Google AdWords, Facebook advertising, some banner advertising.
CPM. Digital display, LinkedIn.
Cost per engagement. Twitter advertising.

Content

Content is the pretty bow on your digital marketing campaign gift box. Not only does it tie everything together, it should look good too. That's why you have to be strategic when building it into your action plan. The content you publish on your website or through social media must engage your audience immediately *and* over time.

It's easier to explain when put into context, so let's look at an example. Say your product is a vineyard hotel in California that you wish to rent out for weddings. Wine + wedding = a winning formula, right?

The first thing to do, of course, is to research keywords to see what people look for. The types of results that are likely to be found will be what the searcher wants in terms of location, hotel type, and number of rooms. So at the very beginning of your campaign, you must decide what content will work best for the target audience.

Plan it so that the content will run over a specified time period, and ensure you decide upon the type of content that will be created, who will write it, and when. Detailed planning is essential for ensuring a coherent, constant stream of content on your website to satisfy the needs of your customer and increase your search ranking.

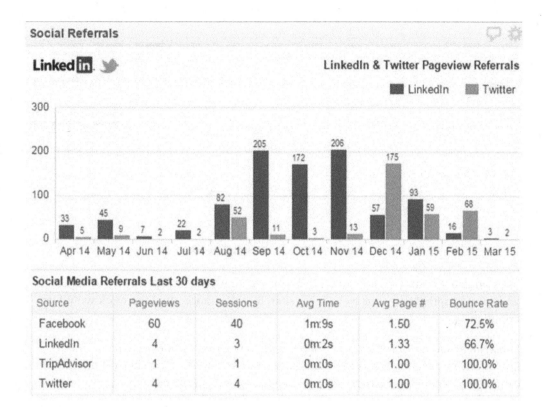

Social Media Referrals Last 30 days

Source	Pageviews	Sessions	Avg Time	Avg Page #	Bounce Rate
Facebook	60	40	1m:9s	1.50	72.5%
LinkedIn	4	3	0m:2s	1.33	66.7%
TripAdvisor	1	1	0m:0s	1.00	100.0%
Twitter	4	4	0m:0s	1.00	100.0%

Figure 10.14   Google Social Referrals Tool
Source: Google and the Google logo are registered trademarks of Google Inc.; used with permission.

Tools

It is possible to produce KPIs to illustrate and visualize lots of different information from different sources by using Google's Social Referrals tool, which covers everything in one place, as seen in Figure 10.14. This not only saves time but it gives you a clear idea of what platform may be working better and what you may need to work on.

There is also a feature that can build dashboards with key information about your website based on your activity in GA.

Calendars

It is highly useful to create a calendar that enables you to map out your campaign on a week-to-week or monthly basis.

Look at how the test period for a product launch is mapped out in Figure 10.15. Obviously, you will be monitoring progress throughout the month, but decisions on how to proceed should only be made after the campaign has been given time to gain some traction.

Digital Marketing Media Plan - May 2016									
Medium	Type	% Spend	Impressions	Clicks/Views	CTR	CPC	CPM	Cost	
Facebook Content Promotion	Acquisition	15.00%	2,647,059	2,328	0.09%	€0.58	€0.51	€1,350.00	
Facebook Lead Gen	Retargeting	10.00%	45,685	228	0.50%	€3.95	€19.70	€900.00	
Facebook Video	Retargeting	5.00%	136,364	32,143	23.57%	€0.01	€3.30	€450.00	
Twitter Content Promotion	Retargeting	5.00%	149,007	238	0.16%	€1.89	€3.02	€450.00	
Twitter Lead Gen	Retargeting	5.00%	53,957	563	1.04%	€0.80	€8.34	€450.00	
LinkedIn Content Promotion	Acquisition	5.00%	22,167	107	0.48%	€4.20	€20.30	€450.00	
LinkedIn Ads	Acquisition	5.00%	283,019	94	0.03%	€4.80	€1.59	€450.00	
Google Paid Search	Acquisition	10.00%	5,625	257	4.57%	€3.50	€160.00	€900.00	
Google Display	Acquisition	10.00%	681,818	2,571	0.38%	€0.35	€1.32	€900.00	
Google Display	Retargeting	15.00%	519,231	2,813	0.54%	€0.48	€2.60	€1,350.00	
YouTube Pre-Rolls	Retargeting	5.00%	478,723	818	0.17%	€0.55	€0.94	€450.00	
Gmail Sponsored Promotions	Acquisition	5.00%	18,908	726	5.84%	€0.62	€23.80	€450.00	
Gmail Sponsored Promotions	Retargeting	5.00%	18,908	849	4.49%	€0.53	€23.80	€450.00	
Totals		100.00%	5,060,470	43,734	0.86%	€0.21	€1.78	€9,000.00	

Audience Targets	Retargeting	Geo	Excluded
Sales People	1. All Site Visitors	Ireland	16 locations
Sales Managers	2. Course Page	UK	
Small Business Owners	3. Blog Visitors	Australia	
Start-Ups	4. Past Purchasers	United States	
Inside Sales Reps	5. Email Lists	Canada	
Outside Sales Reps	6. Campaign Page		
	7. Watched a YouTube		

Campaign Active [X]

Campaign Heavy Burst ■

Figure 10.15   Campaign Calendar

The end date for this particular plan is the end of May, but some plans never stop: If your plan is optimizing your website for search, for instance, then the work would be ongoing.

Subsequent actions or follow-ups will depend on whether or not you have a strict timeline or budget that needs to be reviewed, and how well a channel worked for the campaign. It could be expanded or improved on—or it could be dropped.

Many channels can be seen on the calendar in Figure 10.15 including YouTube, Facebook, Twitter and LinkedIn. The audience to target via LinkedIn in this particular campaign will be marketing and digital professionals.

The message that will come from LinkedIn is that you are offering free resources such as brochures and content that from your point of view will amplify your message. Obviously your objective is product purchase, but your KPI could be that you want a certain number of resources to be downloaded directly as a result of the campaign.

Planning takes time and effort, but all that work is worth it when you achieve your goals. However, your digital marketing campaign does not end when those goals are met; it is an iterative process that needs constant monitoring. Now that you have learned the steps to take in planning your campaign, you can move on to the last stage of the iterative process: analysis.

Stage 4: Analysis

Your digital marketing campaign is like a committed relationship—you have to keep on working on it.

You should *always* be keeping an eye on what is working for you and capitalizing on what's successful.

So just like the time your partner's ugly, misshapen shirt mysteriously went missing, you should get rid of the ideas that you tested but just didn't work. And nobody needs to know about it.

Analysis is an ongoing element of your digital marketing campaign that allows you to keep track of and maximize your online activities, while learning what your audience wants from what it does.

We have reached the final hurdle of the strategy and planning process—stage 4—which you can see highlighted in Figure 10.16! So sit up straight, pay close attention, and get ready to be able to:

• Recognize the benefits of monitoring and analysis.
• Know the importance of calculating ROI.
• Understand the importance of keeping the iterative process in motion.

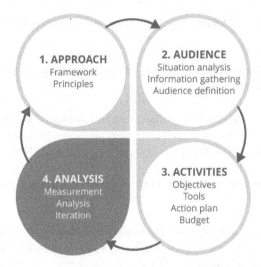

Figure 10.16   Focus on the Fourth Stage in the Strategy and Planning Process

Keep the Wheel Spinning

Strategy and planning is, of course, an iterative process, but the tools you use for each channel drive the wheel.

As a recap, check out the different tools that can be adopted to track specific objectives:

• *Search optimization*. GA and AdWords Keyword Planner.
• *Search marketing*. AdWords and GA.
• *Social media marketing*. Listening tools, insights, and analytics.
• *Mobile marketing*. Mobile analytics.
• *Email marketing*. ESP reporting and analytics.
• *Digital display*. Publisher reporting and analytics.

Focus on Google Analytics

GA is like a guardian angel when it comes to analyzing your campaign. Used frequently, it is the most useful tool for:

- Keeping track of where your audience members come from.
- How often they come.
- How they move through the site.
- How engaged they are.
- How long they spend on any particular page.
- What the most popular topics are.

When you check in on analytics regularly, a constant influx of beneficial information will flow your way.

Return on Investment

There are many ways to calculate ROI. Let's return to the trusty example of Vitamin Water.

The objective of the Vitamin Water company is to increase the percentage of search results pointing to their website.

The company estimates that 25,000 unique searches are made per month through Google for a particular, relevant search term: *lemon flavor Vitamin Water*. So its aim now is to attract 10 percent of those searches to its website—2,500 visitors.

Out of those, the aim is to convert 2 percent of those visitors—50 inquiries—so that they become leads.

If 50 percent of those inquiries qualify as good-quality leads, 25 inquiries become sales—a conversion rate of one in four. So in this case, four new customers come at a cost of $8,000. Got all that? Good!

The Wheel That Never Stops Turning

Strategy and planning is a never-ending circle—see Figure 10.17! You plan things, you publish, you track, you tweak, and you start all over again.

Figure 10.17   The Iterative Process

Maximize what works and ditch what does not. Most importantly, learn from what your analytics reveal and your mastery of understanding audiences will be unyielding!

Before concluding, let's take an example: Facebook.

Examine your most popular posts and take close note of who is engaging with those posts—remember that they may not "like" the post or share it. Track what kinds of posts get the most comments, as opposed to the posts that people like but do not interact with. Then, you can tweak the way you post. Publish, learn, track, tweak . . . and ultimately maximize what works.

So, What Have You Learned in This Chapter?

From figuring out his place in the market and understanding her audience to implementing the best tools for carrying out a specific plan—a digital marketing maestro has got every facet of the strategy and planning process covered. But just in case, here are a few notes to keep you in tune:

- Keep your friends close, but your enemies closer—research your competitors thoroughly.
- Understand that not all customers are created equal and concentrate on your sweet-spot customers.
- Calculate ROI regularly to highlight the areas that are working and the areas that need improvement.
- Evaluate your own capabilities and plan accordingly.

Think of this process as a majestic Ferris wheel—it pauses from time to time, but only so more customers can get on. It continues to turn round and round, delighting those who have boarded. Now that you have learned all there is to know about strategy and planning, you can devise your own entertaining and compelling digital marketing ride, improving on it after each iteration!

Go to www.artofdmi.com to access the case study on strategy and planning as additional support material for this chapter.

Conclusion

At the first-ever lecture given by the DMI in Dublin, Ireland in January 2009, a single phrase was displayed in large text. It was an attempt to explain the transformation that digital has wrought in our lives. That phrase was "Start with the customer and work backwards."

This has been the fundamental change that has directly impacted both people and businesses during the digital revolution. And the implication of this change is just as important now as it was when this revolution began. This change has resulted in the need for a new breed of professionals—people who recognize the power of the individual and who understand and appreciate how digital works and how to work with it to implement marketing strategies centered on the customer.

The objective of this book has been to enlighten you about the core concepts of digital marketing, to provide inspiration, and to provoke you to take those concepts and alchemize them into practical application. You should feel empowered by the practical skills gained through the exercises, action plans, and additional resources; and you should feel ready to apply these skills to produce measureable results.

In recent years we have seen a steady decline in consumers' trust in companies, which has been driven by a lack of contact, an inability to "talk to someone," and an emphasis on process over people. There is a gap in the market—and you are now equipped to fill it. You have the knowledge and skills to bridge the gap between customer and company. Customers desperately want to be listened to, and we can do it efficiently, comprehensively, and precisely through the digital channels you have encountered in the last 10 chapters. As a digital marketing virtuoso, you can talk to your customers via their cell phones, excite their imagination with digital display masterpieces, delve into their psyches through SEO research, and intrigue them with email marketing that speaks to their own particular interests.

The road to a customer's heart has never been so smooth. But as we know, hearts change. This fluctuation is integral to human nature and we must embrace this fact and use it to our advantage—by analyzing the market and constantly adapting to the dynamic nature of the customer. Change is at the core of digital marketing, and undoubtedly one of the most challenging things about digital marketing is the rate at which tools and platforms adapt. However, with every change comes even more possibility, and while digital can be one of the most challenging industries to work in, it is also one of the most exciting. We must embrace this reality and seize every opportunity to be industry leaders, innovators—and active and informed consumers ourselves.

Of course the new world of digital marketing and the empowered consumer can be intimidating. But like many things in life, it's all about perspective. Every day we witness consumers on social media eviscerate a company for shoddy products—but if we use this communication to our advantage by being responsive through social media or even by predicting consumer attitudes through market reality insights, we can be the answer to the detached corporations that consumers know and hate.

People constantly ask, "What will the next big thing in digital be?" There are so many possibilities—it could be an app, a technology, a platform, or a service. But the one thing we know for sure is that it will be characterized by an increase in consumer clout. Because that's what's important to us. We have it now. And we are not going to give it up.

Acknowledgments

None of this would have been possible without the following people. Eternal gratitude to:

Anthony Quigley, my cofounder of the DMI and partner in crime for the past eight years, for his enduring energy and enthusiasm for our "little project."

Ken Fitzpatrick, CEO of the DMI, for bringing our ideas to fruition, making it all real, and bringing the much-needed adult supervision.

The Product team at the Digital Marketing Institute, who have created the most widely taught digital marketing certification programs, doing so with skill, talent, and dedication. This book would not exist without them. Kudos and thanks go to the Product team (past and present, in-house and external.) Managed by Paul Groarke, they include: Conor Tyrrell, Sophie Smith, Niamh Healy, Deirdre Wyer, Claire Monahan, and Garry Cleere.

The whole gang at the Digital Marketing Institute who bring their talent and energy to bear on our activities, on a daily basis.

The constellation of digital marketing practitioners who have informed, taught, and validated the DMI programs over the years. This book is an expression of all of their expert knowledge and hard won experience.

The many thousands of students who have taken Digital Marketing Institute courses through the years and are a constant source of challenge, inspiration, and encouragement. You keep us on the straight and narrow.

—Ian Dodson

Glossary

ad A marketing communications message conveyed to the consumer.

ad click A click on an ad impression served in the period being measured.

ad impression arrival A user arriving at a site who has been exposed to an ad served on behalf of that site.

ad impression An instance of a consumer being exposed to an online ad.

ad network A system that aggregates ad inventory from publishers and operators to efficiently match the inventory with advertiser demand. Examples include Google Search Network (which includes Google Search and other search sites) and Google Display Network (which includes a collection of websites termed display partners that have partnered with Google, as well as YouTube and specific Google properties that display Google AdWords ads). Ads can appear beside or above search results for keywords that an advertiser chooses. See also network.

ad space The area within a mobile app or mobile website dedicated to displaying ads.

ad unique user A unique device (e.g., a computer, PDA, or mobile phone) that has made a request for an ad impression served in the period being measured.

ad unit An advertising vehicle (e.g., a mobile banner) that includes creative assets inside a mobile ad space.

advertiser An organization that wants to get its message to the right audience, efficiently and effectively.

alt text A description of a graphic in a website.

analytics The technology and measurement systems used to understand what is working in a digital marketing campaign and what is not based on data collected during the campaign.

analytics tool A software and web application that can help indicate whether activity being undertaken by a business is having an impact on its goals. See also insights tool.

app monetization Making money from a mobile app through advertising, app download promotion, or other methods.

app An abbreviation for application. An app is typically a small, specialized program that is downloaded onto a mobile device. Apps can be downloaded from an app store, which is a centralized repository of mobile applications. App stores include Apple's App Store, Android Marketplace, Blackberry World, and Google's Play Store.

average position The position at which an ad appears on a search results page (the page that a search engine returns with results relevant to search terms entered by a user).

average visit duration The average duration of a session.

banner ad A mobile ad unit that employs simple creative assets and hyperlinks.

blog A website with regular entries of commentary, descriptions of events, and other embedded multimedia content such as graphics, videos, and presentations.

bounce rate The percentage of single-page visits (i.e., visits in which a user left a site from the entry page).

campaign and ad groups Advertising on social media platforms is generally organized into campaigns and ad groups. A business will typically start with one campaign, which has its own budget and targeting preferences, and then add more campaigns as it expands its advertising.

canvas application An application that is not loaded up in the context of, or visually connected with, a Facebook business page. Instead, the application is consumed elsewhere on Facebook (e.g., in an app directory).

channel For the purposes of this book, a channel (or platform) is a term used to describe an individual social network. For example, Facebook is a platform or channel on which businesses can connect with fans via a business page. See also platform.

click To select something by clicking on it. For example, a customer may see a business's ad and click on it to learn more or to do business with that company.

CTR An abbreviation for click-through rate. CTR is the number of clicks a business's ad receives divided by the number of times its ad is shown (impressions).

click-to-call A service within an ad that enables a mobile user to initiate a mobile phone call by clicking within a mobile ad.

completed download A file (typically audio or video) transfer, especially from the Internet to a user's device, in which the percentage of the file transferred is greater than 95 percent. The user downloads the file for use offline.

conversion Activities carried out by a user that fulfills the intended purpose of the webpage; for example, downloads, filling in forms, purchases, contacts, and newsletter subscriptions.

conversion tracking A form of tracking that gives advertisers insight into how consumers are interacting with their brands throughout the marketing funnel. Advertisers do this by defining traceable events on mobile websites or within apps to assess consumer engagement or the impact of direct-response campaigns.

cookie A text file placed on a web user's hard drive by a website to remember data about the website's user.

CPC An abbreviation for cost per click. Under a CPC pricing arrangement, advertisers pay only when a user clicks on their ads.

CPM An abbreviation for cost per mille or cost per thousand. Under a CPM pricing arrangement, advertisers pay for every 1,000 impressions of their ads.

CPA mobile campaign A cost-per-acquisition campaign. A CPA mobile campaign involves an advertising model under which the advertiser pays for each specified action linked to the advertisement; in a CPA campaign, the specified action is typically registration for an online application.

CPD mobile campaign A cost-per-download campaign. A CPD mobile campaign involves an advertising model under which the advertiser pays for each specified action linked to the advertisement; in a CPD campaign, the specified action is typically the downloading of an application or other file.

digital display advertising A form of digital marketing that uses display ads appearing on webpages as a means of communicating relevant commercial messages to a specific audience based on the profile of its members.

direct marketing A channel-agnostic form of advertising that allows businesses and nonprofit organizations to communicate directly with customers via advertising techniques such as mobile messaging, email, interactive consumer websites, online display ads, fliers, catalog distribution, promotional letters, and outdoor advertising.

email marketing A form of permission-based direct marketing, which uses electronic mail as a means of communicating relevant commercial messages to a specific audience based on the profile of its members.

entry page The first page viewed by a website visitor.

exit page The last page viewed by a website visitor.

filter A rule that limits or shapes the results that are returned from an analytics database when an information query is submitted to it.

Flash impressions The total number of requests made for pages that include Flash-based content by users of that site in the period being measured.

followers Nonmutual connections to which data and updates are ascribed.

forum A website that allows the exchange of ideas and other information among users; usually it is monitored by a moderator.

friends Users social networks who are mutually connected and who typically exchange data and updates.

funnels The pathway visitors follow on a website towards a conversion point.

geofencing A technology that allows an advertiser to select a geographic point using latitude and longitude information and thereby create a virtual fence around a given radius of that point. For example, an advertiser could select a geographic point representing the location of a bank branch in order to deliver a specific ad to anyone who comes within a 200-meter radius. Ads delivered through geofencing typically yield higher conversions and better ROI for advertisers.

geographical IP analysis A way of establishing the percentage of users by country for a given metric, such as unique users.

hashtag A clickable keyword that sums up the content of a tweet or status update. A hashtag is a dominant feature of both Twitter and Instagram.

HTML An abbreviation for hypertext markup language, which is the set of commands used by web browsers to interpret and display page content to users.

HTML5 An emerging standard markup language for presenting and structuring information on the web, including the mobile web. Most modern mobile and desktop browsers support HTML5.

impression An ad being displayed on its associated platform.

in-app ad An ad that appears in a mobile app. Formats include standard banners, video, and rich-media ads.

inbound link Inbound links from related pages are the source of trust and page rank. Also called in-link and incoming link.

indexed page A page on a site that has been indexed.

insights tool A software and web application that can help indicate whether activity being undertaken by a business is having an impact on its goals. See also analytics tool.

instant message A message sent between two connections in real time through a social media network or email platform. Facebook, Google +, Skype, and WhatsApp all support instant messaging.

interstitial ad A mobile ad unit that appears between two views on a mobile website or mobile app. The word interstitial derives from interstice, which means a small space between things, especially when part of a series of uniform spaces and parts (think of a picket fence, which has interstitial spaces between slats).

inventory Available advertising space on all mobile channels, including video, in-app, SMS, audio, and mobile web.

keyword A search term or phrase. The keywords that advertisers choose are those that cause an ad to appear when entered by users. See also key phrase.

keyword density The percentage of words on a webpage that are keywords.

keyword research The process an advertiser uses to determine which keywords are appropriate for targeting.

keyword spam Inappropriately high keyword density. Also called keyword stuffing.

key phrase A search phrase. The keywords that advertisers choose are those that cause an ad to appear when entered by users. See also keyword.

landing page The page that users land on when they click on a link in a search engine result page.

link building The process of actively cultivating incoming links to a site.

link popularity A measure of the popularity of a site based upon the number and quality of sites that link to it.

listening The act of monitoring keywords, topics, individuals, and groups for the purpose of either engagement or research.

location-based advertising A mobile ad unit being delivered to mobile users based on specific geographic coordinates (e.g., latitude/longitude, DMA, etc.).

metatag A statement in the HTML that makes up a webpage that provides important information about the page's content. The information provided is used by search engines to index a site.

mobile ad server A scalable, high-performance system made up of hardware and software that reliably delivers mobile ad units across all mobile channels.

mobile marketing Marketing using mobile devices in order to disseminate promotional or advertising messages to targeted customers through ubiquitous wireless networks.

MRAID ad An acronym for mobile rich media ad interface definitions, which is a specification written by the Interactive Advertising Bureau (IAB).

natural search results Search engine results that are not sponsored or paid for.

NFC An abbreviation for near field communication, a set of standards for smartphones and other mobile devices that allows them to communicate over short distances (typically less than 4 centimeters, or 1.75 inches).

network A system that aggregates ad inventory from publishers and operators to efficiently match the inventory with advertiser demand. Examples include Google Search Network (which includes Google Search and other search sites) and Google Display Network (which includes a collection of websites termed display partners that have partnered with Google, as well as YouTube and specific Google properties that display Google AdWords ads). Ads can appear beside or above search results for keywords that an advertiser chooses. See also ad network.

nofollow A command found in either the head section of a webpage or within individual link code that instructs robots either not to follow any links on the page or not to follow a specific link.

page application An application that is loaded as part of a Facebook business page to provide more functionality to the page. Page applications include competitions, inquiry forms, storefronts, embedded websites, and more. Page applications sit underneath the cover photo.

page impression A request for a page of a site's content made by a user of that site; advertisers are charged per period being measured.

page views The total number of pages viewed. Repeated views of a single page are counted.

pages per visit The average number of pages viewed during a visit to a site. Repeated views of a single page are counted.

paid search Search engine results that are sponsored or paid for in some way.

percentage of new visits The percentage of visits to a site that came from people who had never visited a site before.

permission-based marketing Marketing efforts in which recipients of the marketing have opted in or given their permission to the marketer to send them information.

plan of action A clear road map for carrying out all the tactics necessary for your email strategy. It specifies the staff, time frame, and budget or other resources that are required for each tactic. The plan coordinates these elements in chronological order where necessary.

platform For the purposes of this book, a platform (or channel) is a term used to describe an individual social network. For example, Facebook is a platform or channel on which businesses can connect with fans via a business page. See also channel.

quality score A measure of relevance applied to an ad, keyword, or webpage.

real-time bidding Technology that allows advertisers to bid on each ad impression as it is served. Serving is based on behavioral targeting via cookies. Advertisers buy an audience, not a placement. Ad placements are auctioned to the marketplace and the highest bidder's ad is shown.

reciprocal link A link allowing two sites to link to each other.

remarketing A system that allows an advertiser to continue to show ads to people who have visited a mobile website.

remnant inventory Advertising space that a publisher or operator is unable to sell directly through its sales force. It is typically sold at a discounted price through an intermediary.

rich media A broad range of interactive and engaging ad formats, including expandable banners and embedded audio and video.

robots.txt A file in the root directory of a website used to restrict and control the behavior of search engine spiders.

scheduling The act of prescheduling your activity on a social media channel. Actions on Facebook, Twitter, and LinkedIn can be scheduled in advance in order to save time.

search engine marketing Advertising on a search engine in order to drive traffic to a website. Advertisers pay only when a user clicks on its ad.

Segmentation Distinguishing among different groups of subscribers based on what is known (e.g., demographics, age, or gender) or what can be learned about them (e.g., interests and preferences).

SEO An abbreviation for search engine optimization, or the process of improving the visibility of a website or a webpage in a search engine's natural, or unpaid (organic), search results.

site map A page or structured group of pages on a website that link to every page accessible to users.

smartphone A mobile phone built on a mobile computing platform that has more advanced computing and connectivity capabilities than a feature phone. Advanced capabilities or elements can include portable media players, low-end compact digital cameras, pocket video camera, and GPS navigation units.

SMS An abbreviation for short message service. The term is generally used to describe text messages sent to a mobile device. The original SMS specification limited messages to 160 characters in length. If multimedia elements are associated with an SMS message, it's referred to as an MMS.

social bookmark A form of social media in which users' bookmarks are aggregated for public access.

social media A catchall term used to describe the tools and technologies that facilitate social interaction over the Internet.

social media marketing The process of gaining traffic or attention through engagement on social media sites.

social network A web-based platform that allows users to construct a personal or professional profile from which they can share news and data and connect and communicate with other users.

spider A specialized bot (web robot) used by search engines to find and add web pages to their indexes. Also know as web crawler.

strategy The general approach businesses take to achieve objectives (for example, increasing widget sales through sales calls, a direct mail campaign, and sales incentives).

tactics The specific actions, decisions, and resources required to implement predefined strategies.

targeting The act of channeling marketing efforts and resources to specific market segments defined by demographic, contextual, and behavioral traits that have the highest payoff potential.

text link A plain HTML link that does not include graphic or special code such as Flash or Java script.

tweet A message sent from Twitter, a microblogging service that enables users to send and read text-based messages of up to 140 characters.

unique user A unique device (e.g., a computer or mobile phone) making requests for site content in the period being measured.

unique user duration The average length of all visits (of more than one page impression) per unique user made in the period being measured.

unique visitors The number of unduplicated (counted only once) visitors to a website over the course of a specified time period.

URL An abbreviation for uniform resource locator; also know as a web address.

video interstitial An interstitial mobile ad unit that displays a video between views within a mobile app or between pages within a mobile website.

visit The total number of times that a user (a device) has engaged in a single burst of activity with less than 30 minutes between requests for content. A new visit occurs when the gap between requests for content is at least 30 minutes.

Additional Resources

Go to www.artofdmi.com for select case studies and insightful DMI blog posts as additional support material for each chapter. To access the cases you will need to enter a password, which is the first word in the second paragraph of Chapter 7.

About the Digital Marketing Institute

The Digital Marketing Institute is the global standard in digital marketing education certification. To date over 10,000 people in five continents have graduated with a DMI qualification—making it the most widely taught digital marketing qualification in the world. We have trained more graduates to a single digital marketing standard than any other certification body. The Digital Marketing Institute works with global digital experts and leaders to define the skills and qualifications required by today's digital marketing professionals, certifying graduates at diploma, postgraduate, and masters levels.

Eighty percent of our postgraduate students now work in digital. That might have something to do with the fact that our courses are taught by leading, expert practitioners currently working in the digital marketing field. Your learning will be shaped by their practical experiences and case studies, so you'll benefit from real industry advice and tips about best practices.

Gain Up-to-Date Industry Knowledge

Our specialist product team works closely with leading industry subject matter experts to craft, review, and update your course material on a continual basis. Their job is to ensure you gain the up-to-date knowledge needed to thrive in a rapidly growing and ever-changing industry. That's why they work hard to keep your syllabus content fresh, structured, and brand new.

Benefit from Flexible Study Options

Your course content is available anytime, from anywhere in the world. Whether you are studying at home or on a tablet on your way to work, you can enjoy 24-hour access to prerecorded lectures, notes, practical exercises, webinars, and a supportive class network. Never fear missing a class again.

Enjoy an Industry-Validated Syllabus

It's our mission to ensure that you learn the most up-to-date, valuable, and sought-after industry skills. That's why we bring together the world's leading digital brands and agencies to review and approve your syllabus content. We work with companies such as Facebook, Twitter, and Google to define a syllabus that will enhance or kick start your digital career.

Earn an Internationally Recognized Accreditation

Upon completion you'll receive an academically accredited and globally recognized qualification. Course content is set against the examination, meaning every student, wherever you are, is certified to the same standard.

About the Author

Ian Dodson is Co-founder and Director of the Digital Marketing Institute. The Institute has defined a set of qualifications for the digital marketing industry that are now the most widely taught global certifications, available in over 70 countries worldwide.

Ian chairs the Digital Standards Authority, which consists of representatives from major digital companies and agencies, who contribute to and validate the DMI framework of qualifications. These qualifications act as an educational and professional pathway for students, educators, and employers.

Passionate about student-centric outcomes and an advocate of education and digital literacy, Ian believes digital technologies are enabling tools for raising economic and social standards globally.

Index